Collaboration
A Multidisciplinary Approach
to Educating Students
With Disabilities

Collaboration

A Multidisciplinary Approach to Educating Students With Disabilities

Edited by Cynthia G. Simpson, Ph.D.,
& Jeffrey P. Bakken, Ph.D.

PRUFROCK PRESS INC.
WACO, TEXAS

Library of Congress Cataloging-in-Publication Data

Collaboration : a multidisciplinary approach to educating students with disabilities / edited by Cynthia G. Simpson & Jeffrey P. Bakken.
  p. cm.
Includes bibliographical references.
ISBN 978-1-59363-716-3 (pbk.)
1. Learning disabled children--Education--United States. 2. Special education--United States. 3. Children with disabilities--Education--United States. 4. Inclusive education--United States. 5. Lesson planning--United States. I. Simpson, Cynthia G. II. Bakken, Jeffrey P. III. Title.

LC4705.C645 2011
371.90973--dc22

2011003722

Edited by Lacy Compton

Layout Design by Raquel Trevino

ISBN-13: 978-1-59363-716-3

Prufrock Press Inc.
P.O. Box 8813
Waco, TX 76714-8813
Phone: (800) 998-2208
Fax: (800) 240-0333
http://www.prufrock.com

Contents

Foreword

The need for a book for teachers that addresses the importance and effectiveness of collaboration for successful inclusion of students with special needs is apparent and critical to help them understand the process of how instruction is multidisciplinary. Given that most professionals who work in the education field specialize in their own unique discipline, yet are required to work with many other professionals regarding the instruction of students with disabilities, a resource is needed that outlines and explains the importance of collaboration and how individuals can work together to help students with disabilities achieve success in the general education classroom. Collaboration is a process, and it is important for all individuals who are involved in educating a student with a disability to understand what everyone brings to the conversation. *Collaboration: A Multidisciplinary Approach to Educating Students With Disabilities* focuses on all aspects of collaboration and working with others effectively to promote the most positive learning environment possible for students with disabilities. We believe it is essential for all professionals who are involved with a student with a disability to understand the specific knowledge and expertise each professional brings to the table. In addition, it is also important to understand the importance of working together. Understanding these key aspects will help all participants in this process achieve success and be more efficient and effective.

Collaboration: A Multidisciplinary Approach to Educating Students With Disabilities discusses critical components of collaboration and the specific expertise of professionals and how they function regarding students with disabilities in inclusive classrooms. This book is comprised of six main sections that include Collaboration and Consultation: The First Steps; Effective Communication in Collaboration and Consultation; Working Collaboratively With Families; School Services: Working Together; High School Years and Beyond; and Bringing It Together: The Full Circle. The first three sections focus on key aspects of collaboration and consultation, effective communication, and working with families. The next two sections focus on chapters written about key professionals, the knowledge and expertise they bring to the conversation about students with disabilities, and what these professionals have to offer and how they can help. The last section explains how all of these components fit together. Each section describes a very important part of the process required to be effective when working with a student with a disability in an inclusive environment as well as offers case studies, charts, diagrams, and resources to help teachers be more efficient and effective.

Upon completion of a comprehensive literature search, we found very few resources available to assist teachers in understanding the importance of collaboration and information and viewpoints from professionals who work in the education field. This book is an innovative way to provide specific content knowledge about collaboration. It covers all of the essential components that need to be considered and is unique in that it not only is very informative, but also provides teachers with case studies and solutions to these case studies to guide real-life practice.

The text is written in a style that readers can comprehend and understand and is supported with many examples. In addition, the information on specific professionals is written by these professionals—the writers of these chapters are working in the fields they are writing about. We hope all teachers can use this resource to better understand collaboration, the impact collaborators can make, and how to effectively communicate and work with one another to help students with disabilities. In preparing this book, we wanted to explain and provide a detailed and comprehensive analysis of all of the different components a teacher must consider when working with a student with a disability in an inclusion setting. On the whole, this book will be an added resource to teachers as they try to educate students with disabilities to their fullest potential. We have found that this book is an excellent required or supplementary text for teacher preparation programs as well as for teachers already in the field.

This book would not be possible without the support of family, friends, and colleagues. We thank all of the authors for sharing their information and explaining their jobs and how they perform them effectively.

Cynthia G. Simpson and Jeffrey P. Bakken

Section 1

Collaboration and Consultation: The First Steps

This section addresses collaboration and consultation. A foundation of collaboration and consultation is provided to the reader so that he or she may better understand the importance of working together to achieve a common goal (improving the education of a student with a disability). Collaboration and consultation are defined, as well as the importance of these key factors, along with the benefits and challenges posed when in a collaborative relationship. This section will provide a brief historical overview of the collaboration process, discuss the steps in building a collaborative team, and provide strategies for establishing an effective collaborative team.

Chapter 1

Collaboration and Consultation: The First Steps

Stacey Jones Bock, Nichelle Michalak, and Shana Brownlee

INTRODUCTION

Historically, the teaching structure of schools was divided between special and general education programs. In this antiquated structure, students were grouped by ability levels, language, or special needs and separated into these areas for educational purposes (Spraker, 2003). These groupings effectively led to separate schools housed within one building, and teachers and students within this structure were separated by walls, curricula, and educational philosophies. In recent years, however, several movements have converged and school reform is at the forefront.

The inclusion movement, in conjunction with federal mandates, has begun to tear down the once isolating structures in education. The No Child Left Behind (NCLB, 2001) legislation mandated that all students, including those with disabilities, make adequate yearly progress on state academic standards—academic standards based upon the general education curriculum. In light of NCLB accountability mandates, inclusive education has taken on a significant level of importance (Harvey, Yssel, Bauserman, & Merbler, 2010). Similarly, the Individuals with Disabilities Education Improvement Act (IDEA, 2004) emphasized high expectations for students with disabilities and ensured their right to have access to the general education curriculum in the general education classroom. Both laws acknowledge that educational personnel must collaborate with one another in order to meet the unique and diverse learning needs of today's children and youth in the inclusive classroom (Leatherman, 2009). Furthermore, the convergence of these two mandates precipitated a national conversation regarding what it means to teach all students within the general education environment (Pugach & Blanton, 2009).

These conversations led to a national school reform movement called Response to Intervention (RtI). With RtI, school teams provide instruction and intervention based on the students' assessed needs; students are not viewed as falling into either general or special education. The RtI team monitors progress frequently by using performance data to determine if any changes in instruction or goals are needed (Elliott, 2008). Elliott (2008) found that in order for RtI to be implemented effectively the team requires leadership, collaborative planning, and implementation by professionals across the education system. School teams that previously used IQ-achievement discrepancy to identify children with learning disabilities can use the alternative method of RtI (Fuchs & Fuchs, 2006). RtI has facilitated collaboration between general and special education, has lowered the amount of children referred for special education services, and has opened many opportunities for dialogue among professionals.

WHAT IS COLLABORATION AND CONSULTATION?

Collaboration is a school philosophy and teacher practice that manifests itself in many different forms under many different names (Leatherman, 2009). It has been applied to school-based service configurations such as multidisciplinary teams, teaming, and co-teaching, and to school-based professional development practices including staff development and curriculum planning (Villa, Thousand, Nevin, & Malgeri, 1996). There are a couple of broad collaboration definitions that are widely accepted by the education community. Nevin, Paolucci-Whitcomb, and Idol (1994) defined collaboration as an interactive process that enables people with diverse expertise to generate creative solutions to mutually defined problems. Cook and Friend's (1993) definition of collaboration notes it is a style of direct interaction between at least two equal parties voluntarily engaging in shared decision making as they work toward a common goal. Both definitions are broad and encompass many important aspects that are not necessarily written into the definition. Cook and Friend identified seven characteristics to further clarify their definition. Those characteristics include interchanges that are voluntary, based on parity, share a common goal, include shared decision making, are accountable with resources, and have emerging trust and respect. At the core of the two definitions lie at least two people with mutual respect and interest working together to solve problems and achieve common goals.

Oftentimes, collaborative efforts involve an aspect of consultation. In most work environments, consultation is an expert-driven model in which someone with extensive knowledge in a certain content area is paired with a teacher or other professional. In the past, schools have relied on the expert-driven model however, today's reformed educational structure calls for ongoing collaboration. Teachers who have a consultative coaching relationship—that is, who share aspects of teaching, have effective means of communication, plan together, and pool their experiences—practice and implement new skills and strategies and apply them more appropriately (Joyce & Showers, 2002).

A consultative coach models the qualities of a skilled facilitator. Coaches have both content and instructional expertise and promote and support high-quality instruction through direct, school-based work with other teachers and professionals. Coaches model lessons, observe classroom instruction, and coach teachers one-on-one or in small groups. The coach role combines the skills of active listening and strong facilitation to help create an environment that impacts teaching and learning. Consultative coaches are a part of the collaborative team and are present at team meetings for collaborative learning, brainstorming, and problem solving.

HISTORICAL PERSPECTIVE OF COLLABORATION IN EDUCATION

Since the passage of P.L. 94-142, the Education for All Handicapped Children Act of 1975, special educators have collaborated with related service providers to meet the unique needs of children with disabilities in the public school setting. Special educators adopted the teaming and collaboration model as a means to access resources and create effective learning environments (Skrtic, Sailor, & Gee, 1996). This collaboration occurred within the public school setting but was not a part of the general education structure.

In the 1980s, the Regular Education Initiative (REI) called for the merging of regular (general) education and special education in order to share the responsibility of educating and caring for children with diverse needs (Fuchs & Fuchs, 1994). This initiative, a cornerstone of the inclusion movement, came from the special education structure and was not formally prioritized or adopted by the general education community.

General education also had a strong collaboration movement in the 1980s that resulted in the reorganization of middle schools to meet the needs of adolescents who required more support to facilitate their learning and growth. This movement grew out of a desire to de-bureaucratize middle schools and create places where students felt a sense of relevancy and belonging (Cook & Friend, 1993). This collaborative movement focused solely on general education students in the general education setting.

Throughout the next 20 years, general and special educators practiced collaboration among themselves, both creating and refining their own collaborative structures within their silos. During this time, some professionals argued that collaboration was an option (Friend & Cook, 1992). Today, however, the driving philosophy behind school reform is that collaboration is not an option but an expectation.

BENEFITS OF COLLABORATION

BENEFITS TO STUDENTS

Students, professionals, and parents benefit when schools adopt the philosophy and practices of a collaborative educational environment. Students with and without disabilities agree that when general and special education teachers collaborate to provide instruction there is a positive effect on grades, deeper understanding of material, a rise in self-esteem, and an increase in the amount of teacher help they receive (Gerber & Popp, 1999). Similarly, Spraker (2003) reported that there was a positive correlation between teacher collaboration and grade point averages of students in the collaborative educational environment. The results were derived from studies investigating the impact of collaboration on both general and special education students. General education teachers teach students using their area of expertise and specific content, and special educators apply learning strategies and make modifications for all learners in the environment, not just those with Individualized Education Programs (IEPs). Thus, when both teachers collaborate to teach students, the students receive the benefit of instruction and intervention planned by two teachers (Cook & Friend, 1993). It is not surprising that grades would be positively influenced.

One of the biggest benefits of collaboration for individuals with disabilities is that the stigma of "disability" is reduced (Cook & Friend, 1993). When the wall between the two systems is eliminated, many of the barriers existing between the students are also eliminated. Children with disabilities no longer stand out in the crowd as they enter and exit the general education classroom. In fact, they become members of the classroom—not just visitors.

Lastly, when collaboration is valued and practiced in schools, teacher referrals decrease as do the number of students eligible for special education services (Cook & Friend, 1993). The focus of the collaborative team is to support the child, and there is a sense of ownership shared by everyone. There is no longer a need to remove a child from one system and place him or her into another. Children remain in a unified system and even though the intensity of support may increase, their environment will not change.

Benefits to Teachers and Other Professionals

Researchers have found that collaborative teaming improves the overall school climate for teachers and increases their feelings of efficacy (Spraker, 2003). The concept itself promotes socialization with and learning from other professionals. This process helps to diminish the sense of isolation teachers may feel when they are secluded within their classroom for the better part of a day. When teachers are connected in the education community, higher rates of teacher retention and job satisfaction have been reported (Cook & Friend, 1993).

Most importantly, because the barrier between general and special education is removed, communication is increased and everyone's roles and responsibilities are valued (Cook & Friend, 1993). This removes the doubt and frustration on both sides. For instance, the general educator no longer feels that he or she does all of the planning while the special education teacher floats around the room. The opposite would also be a good example.

Barriers to Effective Collaboration

With the benefits to collaboration come barriers that exist until the school as a whole recognizes them and plans to address them. The primary barrier to teacher collaboration cited in the literature would be time (Conderman & Johnston-Rodriguez, 2009; Cook & Friend, 1993; Worrell, 2008). At the very least, collaboration should occur face-to-face on a weekly basis. This type of schedule can be difficult to uphold given scheduling conflicts and the nature of the traditional school structure.

Inadequate teacher preparation is also cited as a barrier. Most preservice teachers are not taught collaborative skills and ethics in their college or university training (Villa et al., 1996). At the most, general education majors are exposed to one course on the characteristics associated with different disabilities. This does not provide the preservice teachers with the skills necessary for collaborative success. Even though they may feel like they are good collaborators, ongoing professional collaboration requires sophisticated skills in the areas of communication and conflict resolution. Other important skills include how to run efficient meetings, how to listen, and how to manage resistance (Cook & Friend, 1993).

BUILDING A COLLABORATIVE TEAM

Building a collaborative team does not happen overnight. Characteristics of successful collaborative teams have been identified. Villa et al. (1996) identified nine elements of collaboration. They asserted that members agree that every stakeholder possess a unique and needed expertise, engage in frequent face-to-face contact, distribute leadership roles and hold other members accountable, understand the importance of reciprocity, emphasize task completion and relationship building, and agree to consciously practice and increase their social interaction opportunities.

Gerber and Popp (1999) emphasized the importance that administrators and education staff develop a districtwide and schoolwide policy that makes a commitment to inclusive practices and collaboration. This policy must be communicated with all stakeholders, including parents of children with and without disabilities. In effect, collaboration should be a code of ethics and an integral part of the culture of the school (Cook & Friend, 1993). Education of all children should be the defining element in the district's and school's mission statements. Special attention should be paid to ensuring that teachers and other personnel have ownership in the ethic and culture of collaboration. In order for that to occur, teachers need to be a part of the initial decision-making process.

For effective collaboration to occur, administrators should provide their staff with adequate time for planning activities and evaluating progress toward goals (Gerber & Popp, 1999; Leatherman, 2009). At minimum weekly, but optimally, daily planning meetings are vital in order for all collaborative teams to run efficiently and effectively.

Several researchers discussed the importance of providing professional development opportunities (Cook & Friend, 1993; Gerber & Popp, 1999). Training should focus on effective communication skills, running efficient meetings, and conflict resolution strategies. According to Spraker (2003), teachers are more likely to collaborate if they receive support and ongoing training about the collaborative process. Ensuring that general and special education teachers have an opportunity to participate in collaboration training together (Villa et al., 1996) will only serve to encourage relationships between the team members.

Effective collaborative teams have team members with identified roles and responsibilities (Cook & Friend, 1993). This incorporates a feeling of shared contribution by all team members. People should not feel like visitors or unequal partners (Leatherman, 2009). In addition, team procedures are respected and adhered to in order to promote efficacy and accountability. Setting clear team goals is another characteristic of collaborative teams (Cook & Friend, 1993). Goals should be understood and supported by each member of the team (Worrell, 2008). Lastly, the collaborative process has to have administrative support (Leatherman, 2009). Villa et al. (1996) also pointed out the importance that administration has the courage to deal with the resistance to change and new processes they will encounter, as collaboration becomes a part of their school culture.

First Steps for Developing a Collaborative Team

De-jargon the Jargon

Everyone must know each other's terminology. This should be approached in a nonthreatening manner where members of the team do not have to self-identify a lack of knowledge about a term. There are a couple of ways this can be addressed. One way is to charge members of the team with identifying common terminology and acronyms within their disciplines that may not be easily understood by other team members. Write the terms on a note card with a definition and an example. Plan on covering one terminology card from each discipline area at each meeting. Leave time to ask and answer questions about the terms. Another way is to use a free online puzzle maker and input the terms. There are many options to choose from, including word searches and crossword puzzles. Hand out the puzzle at one of the initial team meetings and have members work in groups to complete them. Allow time to ask and answer questions regarding the terminology.

Set the Relationship up for Success

At times, collaborative relationships can experience strain. Members may not agree on decisions, roles or responsibilities may change, and workloads may fluctuate. These can become significant issues if a collaborative relationship is not nurtured, established, or maintained. A few ideas for establishing and maintaining relationships include: (a) plan a time to meet outside of the school environment to talk about goals, teaching styles, and life in general; (b) intentionally compliment team members or bring a positive comment to the table each time the team meets (it is vitally important to the team's health to take time to celebrate the successes); and (c) be flexible and choose your battles (not every team member will agree on all decisions that are made). Give it the "Is it going to impact our team in 30 days?" test. If it is going to negatively impact the collaborative process of the team, then you need to choose it as a battle. If it will not have a negative impact, then you need to move on.

Train the Team

Develop a training schedule for the collaborative team. Training should be considered an ongoing process. Teams need training in many areas, including using effective communication skills, developing best practices, using teaching strategies, differentiating instruction, and understanding the legal mandates of educating all children in the general education setting. Trainings should be offered so collaborative teams can attend them together. There are a variety of training options available from attending a conference to watching a video series or enrolling in an online course.

Obtain a Time Commitment Agreement With Administrators

Collaborative teaming takes time out of an already fully scheduled school day. Teams must meet weekly in order to be fully effective. When districts and schools commit to the culture of collaboration, they must also commit to the time involved in developing and maintaining the relationships. Administrators need to be a part of the team so they understand the dynamics and importance of adequate planning time. Additionally, when provided with the time, team members must use it efficiently. If administrators are unable to regularly attend meetings, then it is the team's responsibility to share the outcomes of the meetings and ask for resources and feedback when needed.

Develop Guidelines and Procedures

Collaborative teams operate more efficiently when there are guidelines and set procedures outlining the collaborative process. Teams need to develop their own guidelines and procedures. Some examples of common procedures include (a) start and end meetings at the scheduled time, (b) all members agree to follow their assigned responsibilities, (c) each member will hold other members accountable for tasks and responsibilities, and (d) agenda items are dispersed to all team members with adequate time to review prior to the meeting.

Document Team Meetings

Documentation of team meetings provides a record of discussions and action items while working on collaborative team goals. Create a team form or use a predeveloped form that meets your needs such as the Team Collaboration Report (see Figure 1.1). If you are creating your own form, consider the following areas for inclusion: (a) a sign-in for team members present, not present, and others; (b) role assignment including the meeting facilitator, time keeper, and recorder; (c) agenda items with an area to denote time limit for agenda item discussion; (d) an agenda item action plan with the discussion notes, person responsible for completing the task, and a deadline; (e) an information sharing plan; (f) a positive comments area; and (g) an area to build the agenda for the next meeting.

Conclusion

The general and special education systems have collaborated within their own structures for years. The inclusion movement in conjunction with federal mandates and Response to Intervention has made collaboration between the two systems and other related service providers a necessity. Students, professionals, and parents benefit when schools adopt the philosophy and practices of a collaborative educational environment. Successful collaborative environments result in a unified educational system. Elliott (2008) described this reformed system not as "special ed" or "general ed" but rather as "every ed" (p. 10).

References

Conderman, G., & Johnston-Rodriguez, S. (2009). Beginning teachers' views of their collaborative roles. *Preventing School Failure, 53,* 235–244.

Cook, L., & Friend, M. (1993). Educational leadership for teacher collaboration. In B. S. Billingsley, D. Peterson, D. Bodkins, & M. B. Hendricks (Eds.), *Program leadership for serving students with disabilities* (pp. 421–444). Blacksburg: Virginia Polytechnic Institute and State University.

Education for All Handicapped Children Act of 1975, Pub. Law 94-142 (November 29, 1975).

Elliott, J. (2008). Response to intervention: What and why? *School Administrator, 65,* 10–18.

Friend, M., & Cook, L. (1992). *Interactions: Collaboration skills for school professionals.* White Plains, NY: Longman.

Fuchs, D., & Fuchs, L. S. (1994). Inclusive schools movement and the radicalization of special education reform. *Exceptional Children, 60,* 294–309.

Fuchs, D., & Fuchs, L. S. (2006). Introduction to Response to Intervention: What, why, and how valid is it? *Reading Research Quarterly, 41,* 93–99.

Gerber, P. J., & Popp, P. A. (1999). Consumer perspectives on the collaborative teaching model. *Remedial and Special Education, 20,* 288–296.

Harvey, M. W., Yssel, N., Bauserman, A. D., & Merbler, J. B. (2010). Preservice teacher preparation for inclusion: An exploration of higher education teacher-training institutions. *Remedial and Special Education, 31,* 24–33.

Individuals with Disabilities Education Improvement Act, Pub. Law 108-446 (December 3, 2004).

Joyce, B., & Showers, B. (2002). *Student achievement through staff development* (3rd ed.). Alexandria, VA: Association for Supervision and Curriculum Development.

Leatherman, J. (2009). Teachers' voices concerning collaborative teams within an inclusive elementary school. *Teaching Education, 20,* 189–202.

Nevin, A., Paolucci-Whitcomb, P., & Idol, L. (1994). *Collaborative consultation* (2nd ed.). Austin, TX: PRO-ED.

No Child Left Behind Act, 20 U.S.C. §6301 (2001).

Pugach, M. C., & Blanton, L. P. (2009). A framework for conducting research on collaborative teacher education. *Teaching and Teacher Education, 25,* 575–582.

Skrtic, T. M., Sailor, W., & Gee, K. (1996). Voice, collaboration, and inclusion: Democratic themes in educational and social reform initiatives. *Remedial and Special Education, 17,* 142–157.

Spraker, J. (2003). *Teacher teaming in relation to student performance: Findings from the literature.* Portland, OR: Northwest Regional Educational Laboratory.

Villa, R. A., Thousand, J. S., Nevin, A. I., & Malgeri, C. (1996). Instilling collaboration for inclusive schooling as a way of doing business in public schools. *Remedial and Special Education, 17,* 169–181.

Worrell, J. L. (2008). How secondary schools can avoid the seven deadly sins of inclusion. *American Secondary Education, 36,* 43–56.

Team Collaboration Report

Team	Date

A. Team Members

Please provide your name and title.

Team Members Present	Team Members Not Present	Others Identified to Enroll
_____	_____	_____
_____	_____	_____
_____	_____	_____
_____	_____	_____
_____	_____	_____
_____	_____	_____

B. Roles

	This Meeting	Next Meeting
Facilitator	_____	_____
Time Keeper	_____	_____
Recorder	_____	_____
Other	_____	_____

C. Agenda

Item	Time Limit
1. _____	_____
2. _____	_____
3. _____	_____
4. _____	_____

Figure 1.1. Team collaboration report.

D. Action Plan

Agenda Item		
Discussion Notes		
Action Plan/Task	Person Responsible	Deadline

Agenda Item		
Discussion Notes		
Action Plan/Task	Person Responsible	Deadline

Agenda Item		
Discussion Notes		
Action Plan/Task	Person Responsible	Deadline

Figure 1.1. Team collaboration report, continued

E. Information Sharing

The way in which we will communicate outcomes to absent team members and others who have been identified to enroll is:

G. Positive Comments

H. Agenda Building for Next Meeting

Item

1. _____

2. _____

3. _____

4. _____

Figure 1.1. Team collaboration report, continued

Section 2

Effective Communication in Collaboration and Consultation

This section addresses effective communication in the collaboration and consultation process. It begins by discussing the importance of effective communication. Next, types of communication are described and explained along with information on how a person goes about recognizing differences in communication styles and what works best for each type of style. This section will also focus on how to properly define roles and how to effectively build and develop relationships/teams. Lastly, strategies for effective communication will be explained and described. After finishing this section, the reader should have a better understanding of the importance of effective communication, developing relationships, and how to communicate effectively.

Chapter 2

Effective Communication in Collaboration and Consultation

Barbara M. Fulk

INTRODUCTION

Collaboration is a way of doing business as well as a style of working with others. It is not uncommon for individuals to work together without being collaborative about that work. However, when professionals truly collaborate they engage in the shared task willingly, demonstrating with their positive demeanors that they value interpersonal interactions and believing that their combined efforts toward a mutual goal will result in more successful outcomes than would any individual effort. The mantra of a good collaborator is "two heads are better than one" as opposed to "I'd rather do it myself!" In a true collaboration, participants also have parity, described as equal responsibility to make shared decisions with shared accountability for outcomes (Friend & Cook, 2007). Each team member should have a relevant and meaningful role to fulfill.

All relationships, both personal and professional, are highly dependent on effective communications. This book focuses on collaboration between parents, teachers, and related services personnel from across the disciplines involved with students with special needs. In order for these multidisciplinary interactions to be beneficial, that is, to seamlessly serve students with disabilities and their families, effective communications are essential.

Think about a communication exchange from your own experience that resulted in either a glaring miscommunication or any other less-than-successful interaction between participants. What went wrong? Common problems include confusion due to a lack of clarity, inattentive listening, and/or different or competing goals, among others. Read the following scenario and analyze the problem that occurred.

> A novice special education teacher (Miss B.) approached a fourth-grade teacher with 20 years experience (Mrs. R.) to arrange a mutually convenient time to schedule a student with learning disabilities (LD) for targeted reading intervention. "Good morning, Mrs. R., I'm here to schedule Kris for her additional reading instruction. Because your students have their group reading instruction after lunch, I thought a morning time would be best. Would either 9:00 or 10:30 work for you on Mondays, Wednesdays, and Fridays?" Mrs. R replied, "Kris can't leave my class at 9:00 since we do our math work then. I don't want Kris to fall behind in math, too! Ten-thirty doesn't work because we have social studies, which is very important in fourth grade. Really, the only time that Kris can miss my class is the last period of the day, so let's say from 3:00 until 3:30. Now, I have a fourth-grade team meeting to attend, so I'm on my way."

What went wrong in that communication exchange? A first issue was that Mrs. R. dominated the conversation by dictating her preferred time. She failed to ask whether or not that time slot was agreeable for Miss B. In contrast, Miss B. was too passive in her communication style. Perhaps she was intimidated by Mrs. R.'s aggressive communication style and/or by her many years' experience. Miss B. did not affirm the importance of the targeted reading intervention as part of Kris' IEP, nor did she express any concerns about the time that Mrs. R selected. In addition to those communication mistakes, it seems that Mrs. R. and Miss B. had competing goals; each thought that their work with Kris was of primary importance with little regard for the other's contribution. A final problem was that time constraints abruptly ended the meeting, which precluded any discussion of the issues.

This chapter defines collaboration as well as teams and presents an overview of various types of communications. It also describes strategies for building relationships and teams, recognizing differences in communication styles, defining roles, planning meetings, and solving problems. The final sections describe strategies for difficult interactions and cross-cultural communications.

Rationale

What constitutes effective communication and why is it so important? Effective communications facilitate understanding between team members, thus enabling participants to achieve their mutual goals of better serving individuals with disabilities. The building blocks of communication include active listening, appropriate body language, and clear verbalizations. Each of these will be described below in greater detail.

Active Listening

Listening may seem as though it should be a simple task. However, for many of us, attentive listening is difficult, inhibited by loss of concentration, daydreaming, time constraints, or by mental rehearsal of our next response. At times we hear one part of the message, which elicits a strong emotion, which then inhibits listening to the rest of the speaker's message. Active listening requires engagement when focusing on the spoken words and their meanings, while concurrently observing the speaker's body language. Effective listeners also encourage the speaker to continue with appropriate eye contact as well as use of minimal encouragement such as a head nods, "uh-huh," or "I see" kind of responses. Good listeners wait until the speaker finishes talking before responding, rather than interrupting. It may also be helpful for the listener to note a word or phrase for major points to talk about or to question in the subsequent discussion.

Appropriate Body Language

If you think about communications from your own experience you can likely recall examples of unspoken yet obvious messages that body language can convey. For example, a rigid posture with arms and legs crossed may indicate tension or an unspoken message of disagreement. Anger may be reflected with furrowed brows, a flushed face, clenched fists, or hands on hips. In contrast, a more natural posture with uncrossed, relaxed arms and legs indicate openness to the speaker's message as does an upright posture with a slight lean forward toward the speaker.

Clear Verbal Communication

The speaker's role is also more difficult than it appears at first glance. Parents are often told to "mean what you say and say what you mean" as a preamble to disciplining their children; this is also the golden rule of effective verbalizations. Speakers must first know what they are trying to express and second, state what they want as clearly and directly as possible. Pauses may be used to emphasize particular points. The speaker may summarize the key points or ask the receiver of the message to summarize the main points to assure both parties that they have reached an understanding.

To further enhance multidisciplinary collaboration, speakers should deliver the message in a nonthreatening manner avoiding jargon or terminology specific to their field or acronyms for those terms. It is important to remember that the message recipient may be unfamiliar with specific terms. Parents and paraprofessionals, in particular, may be on opposite ends of the spectrum with regard to education. In my first year of teaching, for example, one of my student's parents had the equivalent of a fourth- or fifth-grade education whereas a second set of parents consisted of an attorney and a university professor. In the same vein, paraprofessionals may be high school graduates or certified master teachers.

Special education is known for its many acronyms, such as IEP, LD, BD, ODD, and ADHD. Therefore, it is good communication practice to explain the terms that are used as well as to provide a print copy of definitions (translated to parents' native language, if needed). Providing a blank sheet of paper with a pen or pencil for note taking is also a thoughtful gesture to make parents and guardians feel more like a part of the team. It can be overwhelming to parents to have huge multidisciplinary teams gathered around a conference table when they enter the meeting room, conveying an "us against all of them" impression.

Questioning is also important for effective communications. Open-ended questions such as "How is Erica doing in your class?" may be good conversation openers, whereas more specific questions are needed to focus on specific topics such as "How did Erica do on her last science test?" Questions asked one at a time are more conducive to two-way communication than are multiple questions fired in a series. Multiple questions may seem more like interrogation than interest, in addition to leaving the message receiver befuddled and confused about which question he or she should answer. It is helpful to come to the meeting with key questions in mind or written down to expedite the meeting.

TEAM BUILDING

Teams are described by Friend and Cook (2007) as two or more individuals who come together to work in a cohesive and interdependent way to achieve an agreed-upon common goal. Direct communication, coordination, and clear procedures are other elements essential to teaming. Trust and relationship building are the foundation for the team to function successfully.

Consequently, it is generally worth the extra time invested for team building, particularly when participants will be working together over any extended time period (e.g., more than a few weeks). The purpose of team building is to let participants get acquainted, build rapport and trust, and to establish more comfortable working relationships. Introducing participants and their roles is a simple but effective starting point. This may begin with small groups of two members who chat together briefly, then introduce one another to the entire group. Other partner or team activities such as puzzle or problem-solving scenarios are widely available. One such scenario asks participants to collaborate to balance 20 two-inch nails on the head of a single nail affixed to a wooden block (approximately 4 inches by 6 inches). Rules state that none of the 20 nails can touch the wooden block and that additional materials may not be used. In this exercise, a few participants can function as observers/recorders of communication, focusing on phrases that were particularly helpful in moving the team toward a successful outcome. The correct solution employs laying two of the nails (heads on opposite ends) to build a spine with the remaining nails facing out, alternating from side to side. Once the structure is constructed on a flat surface, the final step is to carefully lift and balance the structure from the nail that is centered on the block.

Many other ice-breaking activities can be created quickly from participants' biographical information. A list of descriptors (e.g., speaks three languages, has an identical twin) can be created on a page, each followed by a blank. Participants can be instructed to mingle to see how many items they can complete in a specified time period, using each individual's name only once. More extensive team-building exercises for the workplace can be located with a quick Internet search.

ROLE CLARIFICATION

Team membership should be flexible, changeable, and complimentary to represent the gamut of services needed for each individual case, bringing a wide range of expertise and experience to the table. Team members should be added and subtracted as issues resolve or additional needs arise. As new teams are established, it is helpful for team members to explain their roles as well as their responsibilities toward the team effort, particularly when family members are included on the team. Members can also assume the roles of timekeeper and recorder, with the leader/facilitator role rotated among various team members rather than being fixed.

Types of Communication

Three types of communication that are commonly used include non-verbal, verbal, and written messages. Each type can be beneficial to teams when selected purposefully and used appropriately.

Nonverbal Communication

Nonverbal communication including body language was mentioned above as being related to active listening. Clearly, we use body language to express and interpret various emotions such as anger, boredom, nervousness, confidence, excitement, or frustration. Taken together, facial expressions, gestures, and posture constitute our nonverbal communications, which have been said by some to count for nearly 90% of the message, with the verbalization contributing only less than 10%. Mehrabian (as cited in Friend and Cook, 2007) emphasized the impact of a spoken message as consisting of the following: 55% facial expression and 38% vocal (e.g., rhythm, volume, and pitch), with only 7% attributed to the verbal components. Think about each of the emotions listed in the second sentence in this paragraph and the body language samples that you have noticed. What facial expressions, gestures, and posture might you see in someone who was feeling nervous? Rapid eye blinking, fingers twisting through hair, knocking knees, and quivering voices are some common indicators. Clearly, team members who become observers of nonverbal behaviors and body language will be better communicators than those who overlook these important indicators.

Verbal Communication

Verbal communications are easily delivered and the most frequently used mode of communications among team members. Team members can make statements to share information, ask questions, state opinions, and problem solve. These may occur in quick exchanges as folks pass in hallways, on walks to the parking lot, or prior to the start of a school day. Of all types of verbal communications, problem solving is the most complex strategy, so it will be described in more detail later.

Written Communication

One advantage of written communication is that it provides a permanent record that can be gathered, saved, and passed along as the need arises. Examples of written communication include items such as meeting agendas, notes sent between team members and parents, lesson activity logs, or formal assessment reports. Clearly, the formal assessment report will be more time- and labor-intensive than the first three examples, which can be used expeditiously. All types of written communication should be checked for accuracy to prevent turning the advantage into a disadvantage, thus creating a permanent record of misinformation.

In communications with parents, consider readability and the use of jargon. Often-used information (e.g., checklists of accommodations, modifications, behaviors) between professionals can be formulated as checklists that also increase time-efficiency.

COMMUNICATION STYLES

Students of communication can easily distinguish between these three distinct communication styles: passive, assertive, and aggressive. Descriptions of each style are presented below.

PASSIVE STYLES

Individuals with passive communication styles routinely place others' rights and opinions before their own, which conveys uncertainty about their own self-esteem. Body language indicators of the passive style include a stooped or slouched posture. Passive persons may speak very softly and apologize frequently, even for circumstances beyond their control. They may avoid formulating or expressing their own opinions to be easily led into agreement by more dominant team members. Passive styles may result in negative consequences such as being undervalued as team members, which may further damage the individuals' feelings of self-worth. The unassuming mannerisms of passive personalities may mask these individuals' contributions to the team effort.

ASSERTIVE STYLES

Individuals with assertive communication styles generally express their own opinions in ways that also demonstrate respect for the rights and opinions of others. This conveys a "we both matter" attitude. Body language indicators of the assertive style include a confident, relaxed posture and fluid movements. Assertive persons generally speak firmly and use "I statements" that express their wants and needs calmly and without blame or reproach (see Table 2.1 for samples). Assertive communicators are generally respected and valued as team members and are frequently chosen for leadership roles.

Table 2.1

"You Statements" Revised to "I Statements"

"You" Message	"I" Message
You always come late to our meetings.	I am asking everyone to arrive on time for our meetings.
Your talking is distracting the group.	I need everyone's attention here. Let's refocus our attention to this topic now.

Aggressive Styles

Individuals with aggressive communication styles tend to try to dominate interpersonal interactions by bullying others. They convey that they value their own rights more than the rights of others. Aggressive individuals display an attitude of superiority over others with a "my way or the highway" demeanor. They generally speak far more than they listen, often using loud voices. In addition, they violate others' personal space while using dramatic gestures such as finger pointing. Negative consequences of aggressive communications include avoidance and anger by other team members. See Table 2.2 for a brief matching quiz of statements representing these three communication styles.

Planning Meetings

When planning meetings, the first rule is as follows: The larger the group, the shorter the scheduled meeting time. This being said, it is essential to schedule adequate time to fulfill the objectives of the meeting. Parent meetings, particularly IEP meetings, should be scheduled to allow sufficient time for thoughtful sharing, reflecting, and IEP development.

A printed agenda is conducive to an efficient and productive meeting. Preparations should consider space and equipment needs as well as a welcoming environment and comfortable seating for all participants. Have you ever attended a meeting seated on a kindergarten chair or on a chair smaller than the others in the grouping? If so, you can understand the importance of scheduling an appropriate meeting location. Be sure that all participants can see one another, avoiding barriers such as desks between members. If technology is to be utilized, it is helpful to pretest all equipment and files well ahead of the scheduled meeting time. This allows time to troubleshoot any equipment snafus, resulting in more productive and efficient meetings.

Table 2.2

Phrases Reflecting Three Communication Styles

Match each phrase to the communication style it best reflects.

A. Passive	1. "Wait! Listen to me. I have a perfect plan to resolve all of our issues."
B. Assertive	2. "I'm not sure. You have had much more experience with this than I have."
C. Aggressive	3. "I think we can find a solution that we both agree with."

Note. Answers are A=2, B=3, C=1.

PROBLEM SOLVING

Well-functioning multidisciplinary teams are particularly well-suited for problem solving regarding student issues because each team member contributes his or her unique expertise and experience. The general steps to problem solving include: (a) clarifying the problem, (b) actively brainstorming solutions, (c) selecting and implementing a solution, and (d) evaluating the results. If the results are effective, all is well. If not, the team can reconvene to utilize any or all of the previous steps again. During the brainstorming phase, any and all suggestions are acceptable, including impossible and humorous ideas. It is during the selection/implementation phase that each suggestion is discussed in greater detail or dismissed.

Dettmer, Thurston, and Dyck (1993) proposed a 10-step consultation process that focuses on problem solving as well as provides detailed information regarding implementation (see Figure 2.1). The CLASP problem-solving model (Voltz, Elliott, & Harris, 1995) is notable for its built-in mnemonic to guide users through the intervention steps. Figure 2.2 contains the steps of the CLASP model. Fleming and Monda-Amaya (2001) emphasized the importance of consensus building (as well as harmonizing) and encouraging during the problem-solving process. These models are particularly useful with multidisciplinary teams because they provide systematic approaches for sharing information as well as strategies from an extensive range of perspectives and disciplines. As professionals and families work together effectively with positive energy, synergy develops with more creative solutions to address the student's issues.

The 10-Step Consultation Model

1. **Plan:** Focus on key issues and possible actions. Prepare materials and meeting space.
2. **Initiate the consultation:** Establish rapport and the common interest.
3. **Collect information:** Solicit all data. Take notes. Summarize available data. Decide if more data are needed.
4. **Identify the problem:** Encourage listening and sharing. Identify issues while avoiding jargon. Steer focus to pertinent issues. Check for agreement.
5. **Generate options and alternatives:** Engage in collaborative problem solving, discussing a range of possible solutions. Select the most workable solution for the child's environment.
6. **Formulate the plan:** Decide who is responsible and how they will implement the solution. Agree on an evaluation plan and a date to review progress.
7. **Evaluate progress and process:** Meet to share all data to determine effectiveness of the plan and the collaboration.
8. **Follow up on the plan:** Reassess periodically and make changes as needed. Close the case if goals are met.
9. **Interact informally with the consultee when possible:** Continue to support and share information with the consultee.
10. **Repeat consultation as appropriate.**

Figure 2.1. The 10-step consultation model (Dettmer et al., 1993).

DIFFICULT INTERACTIONS

Conflicts and difficult interactions are likely to emerge even among well-established multidisciplinary teams. Team members, both professionals and parents, can feel strongly about an issue and have very different ideas about the optimal resolution. A passive communicator, who often is a peacemaker, may try to avoid conflict at all costs; however, conflict is beneficial to uncover hidden resistance, thus opening key issues for discussion. Issues, rather than personalities, should be the team focus. If a meeting becomes too impassioned, one strategy is to temporarily park the issue in a "parking garage," conclude the meeting, and agree to reconvene at a later time. Ideally, this gives the emotional parties time to calm down until they are able to discuss the issue more rationally.

A second prerequisite to solve a difficult interaction is to negotiate with a win-win mentality. The optimal result of negotiation is that all parties are satisfied with the final outcome. Each party must clarify its position and goals, offer alternatives, and consider offers/trades. In addition, each party must also listen respectfully to the others' perspective until participants finally agree on a solution acceptable to all parties. It is essential to focus on areas of agreement. Always speak respectfully and calmly when discussing

---

1. Clarify the problem.
2. Look for influencing factors.
3. Actively brainstorm solutions.
4. Select a solution to implement.
5. Prepare to implement and evaluate.

Figure 2.2. The CLASP model (Voltz et al., 1995).

---

your view and your reasoning. Listening to a divergent opinion is essential as is checking, clarifying, and paraphrasing. Helpful phrases are, "Help me to understand . . . " and "If I understand you correctly, you believe that . . ."

Other errors to avoid are making promises you can't keep and dismissing the other parties' comments. In some cases, when compromising is unsuccessful, the parties can "agree to disagree" about that particular issue. When a family and the school have an escalating disagreement, a mediator can be used to resolve differences.

Cross-cultural Considerations

Cross-cultural communication adds another important variable for team effectiveness. Therefore, it is essential that team members are sensitive to cross-cultural perspectives, beliefs, communication patterns, and interactions (Jairrels, 1999). For example, different cultures may have unique family structures as well as differing beliefs about the nature and cause of disabilities, childrearing, the family-school relationship, and the purpose of schools. Team members must be aware of their own perspectives and beliefs in order to avoid common pitfalls related to cross-cultural interactions such as stereotyping or assuming that all members of a particular group have identical values and beliefs.

Various cultures have their own rules regarding turn taking as well as other verbal and nonverbal rules of conversation. For example, eye contact, personal space, touch, proximity, and the use of gestures have different meanings in different cultures (Salend, 2005). Paraprofessionals and community members may be valuable resources for interpreting behaviors and interactions in a social and cultural context. Interpreters who speak the same dialect also are required when educators and families speak different languages. However, Salend (2005) strongly advised against using children or other students as interpreters, which can have adverse effects on both the child and the family.

This chapter has provided an overview of the building blocks to effective communication that is prerequisite to building successful multidisciplinary teams. Several problem-solving models were presented, including additional guidelines for implementation. Effective teams are often highly successful in discovering more positive outcomes for students with disabilities and their families. In addition, parents, teachers, and other related service providers often find team collaboration to be both personally and professionally rewarding.

REFERENCES

Dettmer, P., Thurston, L. P., & Dyck, N. (1993). *Consultation, collaboration and teamwork*. Needham Heights, MA: Allyn & Bacon.

Fleming, J. L., & Monda-Amaya, L. E. (2001). Process variables critical for team effectiveness. *Remedial and Special Education, 22,* 158–171.

Friend, M., & Cook, L. (2007). *Interactions: Collaboration skills for school professionals* (5th ed.). White Plains, NY: Longman.

Jairrels, V. (1999). Cultural diversity: Implications for collaboration. *Intervention in School and Clinic, 34,* 236–238.

Salend, S. J. (2005). *Creating inclusive classrooms: Effective and reflective practices* (5th ed.). Upper Saddle River, NJ: Merrill.

Voltz, D. L., Elliott, R. N., & Harris, W. B. (1995). Promising practices in facilitating collaboration between resource room teachers and general education teachers. *Learning Disabilities Research & Practice, 10,* 129–136.

Section 3

Working Collaboratively With Families

This section will focus on how to work collaboratively with families. It will discuss legal mandates to be aware of and consider for family involvement, the role of the family in the collaboration process, and building effective and positive relationships. In addition, strategies for successfully including the family will be discussed and explained. This section will also address the role of the student in the decision-making process, recognizing specific family structures and cultural aspects and overcoming challenges posed regarding these issues. After reading this section, the reader should have a better understanding of the importance of working collaboratively with families and how to effectively develop a collaborative relationship with families of children with special needs.

Chapter 3

Working Collaboratively With Families

Diana Nabors

CASE STUDY: JENNA

Jenna is a new student enrolling in school. She and her family have just moved from another state where she was in second grade. Jenna's mother enrolls her and mentions that at her previous school she had some special classes for a portion of the day but that the majority of her school day she was in the general education second-grade class. Jenna's school records and the paperwork describing the classes she was in last year are in one of the boxes that they haven't unpacked yet. Her mom stated that she will bring these to the school in the next few weeks, but she does have the necessary documents for enrolling her into school with her now.

You are Jenna's new teacher. What do you know? What do you want to know? Where will you gain the information to best provide for Jenna's education? What and who are *your* resources? This chapter will help you, as the classroom teacher, understand the need to collaborate with the family in order to provide the best experiences for all of the children in your classroom.

LEARNING ABOUT THE FAMILY

Families struggle to provide the best environment for their children. This includes a safe, nurturing, and stimulating environment. In the early years of life, the child's socialization and learning is primarily guided and structured under the parents' supervision. Parents carefully choose who, where, and how the child participates and learns. Parents are concerned with who influences the development of their child as well as the specific experiences the child has (Barbour, Barbour, & Scully, 2010). As the child grows and begins to engage with others outside the home environment, teachers, community leaders, physicians, therapists, ministers, social workers, and others begin to play a greater role in the upbringing of the child. Although schools assume more of the academic responsibilities, parents continue to be the *first and most important* teachers for their children (Olsen & Fuller, 2008). Parents of children with disabilities are no different from parents with typically developing children. As a classroom teacher, you may have children with special needs in your classroom. It is important that teachers recognize that parents of children with special needs have a strong desire for their children to have the best opportunity to develop, socialize, learn, and enjoy life (Barbour et al., 2010).

Children learn what they experience. The child's initial learning is based on the family traditions, experiences, and knowledge of how to live successfully in their world. Through the family bonds of interaction, children learn appropriate and valued family behavior. This includes the language and vocabulary used, the way language and interactions with others occur, the family's beliefs of how to behave in various situations, and the family's concepts of appropriate and inappropriate behavior (Olsen & Fuller, 2008). Formal instruction is typically not provided to address all of these different aspects. Most of these values and behaviors are learned through parental guidance, discipline, and observation of how others in the family interact in various life situations. This initial learning becomes the foundation for the behavior the child will exhibit as he interacts with others in his environment.

Teachers should seek to understand the family, the family bonds, and the family culture and traditions in order to understand the child. Family interactions and experiences greatly impact the development of a child. The importance of these interactions is magnified in a family that has a child with special needs. The family functioning is also impacted by the individual needs of the child (Barbour et al., 2010). Because parents serve as the primary means of support, guidance, and nurturance of children, schools have a responsibility to support families in their caregiving responsibilities (Dettmer, Thurston, Knackendoffel, & Dyck, 2009). This holds especially true with children who have identified special needs. Schools and, more specifically, teachers can support the family through education, referrals, and connections with various agencies including educational, health, and social welfare supports. Teachers who connect and collaborate with the parents will provide a foundation for a quality relationship with the child and family.

In an inclusive classroom environment, teachers will quickly recognize that each family is unique, as is each child. Families all have their own successful experiences and their areas of difficulty. Each family has its own unique history, traditions, manners of expression, and values. These unique family qualities provide the wonderfully diverse thinking and opportunities that we all access at differing levels (Dettmer et al., 2009). This diversity allows each child to grow in experiences and knowledge. Teachers who embrace the differences in the children and families as an additional set of experiences can help them feel valued and become a catalyst for sharing these differences with others (Coots, 2007). The teacher's view is vitally important to the success of the interactions with the child and family. The teacher who views the differences as new knowledge rather than a different viewpoint is supporting the family and the child (Dettmer et al., 2009).

Each child, with or without special needs, comes to school with unique challenges. If teachers think of these challenges as a *backpack of experiences* they will begin to understand the child and family more fully. For example, some children have medical needs and must make lengthy trips to get to their appointments. Some children are cared for by relatives or others during the times that parents are working or involved in other activities.

As teachers begin to learn about the children in their classroom, they need to reflect on their own beliefs and past experiences. Teachers should embrace their own uniqueness, traditions, expectations, and ways of doing things with knowledge that others have different experiences. Quality teachers respect the different experiences and needs that children have with appreciation for these experiences rather than judging them (Dettmer et al., 2009). There is no "right or wrong" experience. It is the teacher's obligation to understand the child and the family while focusing on the family traits as an opportunity to build classroom experiences and support the family. This may include providing additional experiences and supports that highlight the growth and development of the child and family (Olsen & Fuller, 2008). These experiences and services will be designed so that they are specific to the needs of each individual family.

Parents have a lot of knowledge that the teachers need in order to be fully effective in teaching the children in their classroom. Parents know their child. They know what their child likes and dislikes, the child's strengths, and his areas of challenge. They know how the child may react to certain situations, and they have expectations and dreams for their child's future. The teacher who has insight into the parents' knowledge can plan and interact with the child more fully (Barbour et al., 2010). The challenge is to find out the "back story" of each child in a classroom and design appropriate experiences for him or her—while still meeting school, state, and national standards.

PARENT INVOLVEMENT

Many books and articles state the necessity of creating true partnerships between teachers and parents. When parents are involved in the school experience, the child will achieve more regardless of her socioeconomic status, parents' educational level, or ethnic or racial background. The positive collaboration between teachers and parents results in positive child outcomes including higher grades, test scores, and attendance (Henderson & Berla, 1994). Children who have involved parents complete their homework at a higher rate and have a more positive attitude about school (Henderson & Berla, 1994). Teachers tend to unknowingly spend more time working to modify curriculum and accommodate for a child with special needs if the parent is involved.

Parents also benefit as they become more involved with the education of their child. Involved parents have the knowledge of what goes on in the classroom and have increased discussion and interaction with their child about the school day. Additionally, parents become more confident in their parenting abilities and decision-making skills. Parents who know the unwritten rules of how schools function can make more informed decisions when it comes to the child's academic planning and the needs for assistance to achieve academic and life goals.

Parents can easily be involved in the child's education in a variety of ways. Unfortunately, many parents do not know how to get involved. Involving parents as a true partner is not an easy thing to achieve but it can be done with purposeful planning. It is generally considered that teachers, who have been specifically trained and certified, are responsible for the schooling of the child. Many parents may be uneasy with a partnership in which they are included in academic decision making. They may even be uneasy about their parenting knowledge. Teachers can link parents to child development information and support the parents in their parenting roles. The teacher must inform parents of how they are involved in their child's academic growth and provide ways for parents to become more involved. Epstein and colleagues (1997) listed six types of parent involvement. These will be discussed next.

Type 1: Basic Responsibilities of Families

Providing the child with food, shelter, clothing, and a healthy and safe environment in which the child grows is fundamental—"Parenting 101." These essential needs of child development are easily passed off as "everyone does—or should do—this." To the parent who is daily providing these basic necessities for her child this is her *job*. But does she *know* that she is doing it correctly? How does the parent *know* that he is making good decisions when it comes to his child? Parents rarely get recognized for this 24/7 job that they have. Teachers who realize that children need to have these basic needs met in order to develop and learn also recognize that they can increase the likelihood of the child's basic needs being met if the parents feel that they are doing what is best for the child. Teachers have been educated in what children need so that they develop to their fullest potential. Parents are learning from others who may or may not know about nutrition, rest, ideal environments, and other components of quality childrearing. Parents are parenting as they know best.

Teachers who provide information to parents on quality of life components add to the parents' knowledge base. This means that teachers of young children are *also* teachers of parents. Teachers who thank parents for the daily care and nurturance of the child reassure the parents that what they do for and with their child is vitally important for the child's growth. Meeting the child's basic needs helps get the child ready for the school day. The child who is well rested, clothed, and fed is ready for the day's experiences. This forgotten type of parent involvement is essential to the development of the child both in and out of the classroom. Teachers must share with the parents the knowledge that what they do each day to get the child ready for school does make a positive impact on the child's school learning. If the child isn't at school, he can't learn. The parent who got him to school *is* involved in the academic support of the child.

Type 2: Communication

Ongoing communication with parents is essential. There are a variety of ways teachers and parents communicate. One form of communication is through notes, newsletters, and bulletins initiated by either the parent or teacher with little or no response from the recipient. Two-way communications allow both teacher and parent to share ideas about the child and the child's day and make plans for the child's experiences. Two-way communication can include face-to-face conferences and meetings, phone calls, or journaling. The important element of this two-way communication is that both the parent and teacher are exchanging information about the child. Many parents and teachers think of parent conferences as a time for the teacher to tell the parent about the school program, the child's accomplishments, and the child's needs, but much more is involved. Teachers must listen to the parent and ask questions to engage the parent in a collaboration of ideas as they plan for the child's educational program. During this two-way communication, a relationship is built between the teacher and parent. This relationship will help to form a valuable and effective transition between home and school for the child. The parent knows the child better than anyone else, and she can provide needed information to assist the teacher in making the learning experiences relevant to the child.

Type 3: Volunteering

Parent volunteering may be the most well-known way of parent involvement. This consists of parents assisting the teacher with field trips or parties, reading to the class, helping with a school project or festival, or preparing classroom materials. Parents volunteer their time and talents to the classroom when and how they feel most comfortable. Parents who volunteer are gaining much more than the experience of the single volunteer event. Parents are able to observe their child and other children. This is a fresh look at what their child is accomplishing in relation to the other children in the classroom. This can be an eye-opening experience for many parents. Some parents realize that their child exhibits different behaviors in the school setting that they do not see in the home or community setting. It is important to talk with the parent prior to and during the volunteering experience to help the parent place the observations into an appropriate context.

Meeting with the parent before the volunteer event and providing the parent with information on the volunteer activity and possible additional observations will help the parent observe his child with a more knowledgeable lens. Each child in the classroom brings strengths and challenges to the classroom. The volunteering experience can also be beneficial for the child. The child has additional recognition from his peers and other staff while his parent is involved in the activity. Lastly, the volunteering experience is very beneficial to the teacher. Parent volunteers help to reduce the teacher-student ratio so more students are getting individualized attention. The parent volunteer creates an extra pair of hands to assist with an event or lesson. The volunteering experience will be most valuable for all parties if the teacher plans and prepares for the volunteer being in the classroom. Along with the planning, the teacher must communicate the scope, purpose, and limitations of the experience with the parent so that everyone will understand the expectations. This will help the event or lesson run more smoothly.

Type 4: Learning at Home

Parents often ask what they can do at home to support their child's learning. Providing parents opportunities and information to assist their child at home with activities can reinforce, support, and strengthen learning that has been introduced at school. This can include games, homework, and parent-child activities that are parallel with the school learning. Teachers should plan for these at-home learning experiences by providing detailed instructions to the parent on how to help, how much to assist the child, and how to lead the child in an activity through questions or turn-taking skills. Providing activities that use common household items can make the at-home learning experience beneficial to both child and parent.

Activities for at-home learning can be scheduled occasionally or on a regular basis. An example of something that could be done at home would be a 20-minute math game or related activity. This can be assigned to increase a specific math skill. Each week the teacher can send home information on the specific skill and directions for participating in the game or activity so that the child has reinforced practice on that skill. Occasional larger projects should be assigned with enough lead time for the parent to plan time into the family schedule so the project can be completed in smaller segments. Providing the parent with instructions, goals, and anticipated time requirements will make this an enjoyable and beneficial activity for both the parent and the child.

Type 5: Decision Making

Parents must have information on the school issues, school decisions, and school policies so that they can make quality choices for their children. Parents can be involved in many aspects of school decision making. The first and most obvious decision of the parents is the choice they have made in the selection of the school their child attends. Parents ultimately do choose the school. It may be chosen based on location, financial means, or the curriculum or support opportunities the school will provide to the child.

Additionally, parents choose how and at what level they advocate for the school and school-related issues. Parent decision making involves a process in which parents and teachers jointly share ideas and views concerning the school goals and policies. Through discussion and information sharing, quality decisions can be made that affect change in school programs that benefit the child. Parents can also get involved with parent-teacher organizations that allow for parents to have a chance to share opinions. Parents are natural advocates for their child and for the experiences that their child and others have and must realize the impact they can make.

Type 6: Collaborating With the Community

Teachers and schools work in a community. Each community consists of homeowners, families, and businesses, and all of these constituents benefit when the school provides quality programming. Word of mouth, as well as written publicity pieces that are distributed within the community, can highlight the quality programs and activities of the school. Community members are a valuable resource to the school and should be involved as members on school committees. These outside community members have a broader view of community issues and this additional knowledge can help to enhance or create school activities. Schools and teachers should become aware of the resources within the community. Teachers who collaborate with parents about opportunities in the community will become more informed about the community, the resources, and the ways in which they can become involved with the families of the children they teach (Fiedler, Simpson, & Clark, 2007).

Communicating With the Family

Communication with the family is one of the most critical components for creating and constructing quality collaboration with the family. Knowledge is power. This knowledge will assist the parents in making informed decisions about the child's services, education, and opportunities. Families have different ways that they are most comfortable communicating. These communications can range from oral communication to written communication. This includes face-to-face discussions, telephone conversations, paper notes or bulletins, or electronic media. Teachers must create a variety of ways in which they communicate with parents. The use of notes, newsletters, voicemail, e-mail, and school websites allow parents to become informed of school happenings. Providing school information in a variety of modes will help parents gain the needed information at the time that they need it and in the format that is most accessible to them.

Teachers should also have a routine for sending out updates and information. It is important to create a routine schedule so that the parents are accustomed to looking for new information on certain dates. Setting a weekly or monthly update schedule will assist the teacher and parent in transferring important information from the school to the home and from the home back to the school. Creating a way for parents to reply or return information that is on this standard timeline is also good practice.

Not all families are available to meet with the teacher during school hours due to work or other commitments. Flexible conference hours or scheduled phone conferences after school hours can help the parent and teacher to continue a collaborative communication. When teachers do schedule face-to-face or phone conferences, respect for the parents' time should be considered. Parents have many roles that they undertake. They juggle meals, children's schedules, doctor visits, therapy sessions, work schedules, and childcare time requirements. Each conference should begin on time, allow ample time for both teacher and parents to discuss and listen to each other (i.e., 30-minute minimum), and end at the stated time. If the conference does seem to need additional time that was not in the initial agreed-upon time schedule, it is best to reconvene at another mutually agreed time so that neither the parents nor teacher is rushed into a decision or does not have the time to share information.

BUILDING EFFECTIVE POSITIVE RELATIONSHIPS

Parents of children with special needs are learning to navigate a variety of new systems and services in search of the best opportunities for their children. These systems may include the school community, the medical field, childcare, and social services. Each of these services has an impact on the educational setting and development of the child. The negotiation between the various services, as well as the access to the services, often baffles parents. The classroom teacher has repeated encounters with the various services and can be a valuable resource for the parent. Teachers need to help parents understand the importance of all of these services and how they can work together to help their child (Fiedler et al., 2007).

As a certified teaching professional, you will be viewed by many parents as the person who has connections to these services and the knowledge of how these services fit best for their child. It is not your duty to diagnose the specific services needed but rather to provide that link for the parents to talk with special service providers and design a program for the child. If the services are provided through the school, then a collaborative meeting such as an Individualized Education Program (IEP) meeting or an Admission, Review, and Dismissal (ARD) meeting will allow for discussion and sharing of information. If the services are provided outside of the school program, then the teacher may provide the information to the parent in conferences. There is a complex relationship between family resources, values, and needs as families interact with the various services. This includes school schedules and services as well as the individual costs and benefits for each child and family.

LEGAL AND LEGISLATIVE MANDATES

Communicating with parents is not just a good idea—it also has evolved as a best practice. Various legal and legislative mandates over the last 30 years have highlighted the responsibility of teachers and parents to focus on collaboration in order to provide the best opportunities for children with disabilities. In 1975, PL-94-142, the Education for All Handicapped Children Act set the stage for students to be included in the general education classroom or the least restrictive environment (LRE). This has set up the need for teacher and parent collaboration. Before this collaboration, teachers needed information about the children in their classroom who learned differently so that they could make quality decisions for each child. Parents also wanted assurance that the services being designed for their child would best meet his needs. Parent involvement was essential in improving all services for children with special needs.

Over time the scope of the legislative mandate requiring all educators to work as partners with parents, schools, and the community helped to design the amendments now known as the 1986 legislation, Education for All Handicapped Children Act Amendments (PL 99-457). This legislation *expanded* the scope of programs to add services for children younger than the typical school age and included children birth to age 5. Again, the schools were embarking on uncharted territory. The collaboration with parents and other community services allowed for a continued flow of information to be used to provide the best education for each child. With the new mandates to provide programs for all children, schools and teachers refocused how they looked at the curriculum and services they provided. Schools and teachers were responsible for quality programs in which *all* children were learning to the best of their ability. This required teachers to collaborate with parents, other school personnel, and the community to provide the best program decisions for each student's success.

Teachers are responsible for including parents as active participants in the child's programming while identifying the standards for individual student success. Collaboration meetings or ARD/IEP meetings need to include the school administration, teachers, parents, and other necessary personnel. These meetings are held to share information and design programs for each child. Each person in the ARD/IEP meeting provides information and resources to enhance the child's success. Included in ARD/IEP meetings are: (a) the *school administrator*, who shares information about the budget available to provide the needed services; (b) the *diagnostician or school psychologist*, who has information on how the child compares to others on standard measures (assessments) as well as resources and determinations of qualifications for additional services; (c) the *general education teacher*, who has the grade-level content information and the knowledge of the child's day-to-day interaction within the general education classroom; (d) the *special education teacher*, who has the knowledge of needed modifications and adaptations for student success; (e) the *specialized educational support personnel*, who have information on the child's needs for additional services, which may include speech therapy, occupational therapy, physical therapy, assistive devices, medical assistance, and other services and how these services can best be provided for student success; and most importantly (f) the *parent*, who knows the child better than anyone else.

These initial legislative mandates were reviewed and refined with the Individuals with Disabilities Education Improvement Act (IDEA) of 2004 and the No Child Left Behind Act of 2001 (NCLB; PL 107-110). Through these legislative acts, parents are guaranteed the right of greater participation in their child's education. This includes active involvement in decision making for the child's placement and programming and collaboration with others.

Within the ARD/IEP meeting, each child's IEP must be developed by the team of advocates for the child, which includes parents, teachers, service providers, and administrators. However, even when the law does not require specific collaborations, compliance with legal mandates is a responsibility shared by all educators, with collaboration a key in successful implementation.

Parent participation has been one of the key principles of the Individuals with Disabilities Education Improvement Act (IDEA) since it was first authorized in 1975 as the Education for All Handicapped Children Act (EAHCA) and has continued through the most recent reauthorization in 2004. Parents of children with special needs have decision-making roles about their children's education mandated by law in part based upon historical lack of involvement in such decisions provided by school personnel and the resultant lack of effective education for these children (Turnbull, 1993). Beyond these legal mandates, best practice standards would suggest that services will be most effective when parents and professionals work in collaboration (Coots, 2007).

The parents' desire for their child's success is constant. It does not span a single academic year—it spans a lifetime. Collaborating with the parents and gaining information from the most knowledgeable persons about the child is a must. Child success depends on the collaboration of many people. The most important is collaboration with the parents—the child's first teachers.

SOLUTION TO THE CASE STUDY

Jenna's first day with you will be the beginning of the communication with the family. As Jenna enters your classroom, you make a point of talking with her mother briefly and setting up a time for the two of you to meet in person or on the phone in the next few days. You help Jenna become oriented to the classroom and observe her interactions with others, then determine if she tends to be shy or more outgoing—does she initiate interactions with others? How does she respond to the interactions of the other class members? This information will assist you as you talk with her mother. Share your observations and the strengths that you have observed in Jenna's classroom behavior. Ask the mother about Jenna's previous school, her friends, and any activities in which she participated prior to her move. Ask the parent about her plans and desires for Jenna this year both in and out of school. You can provide information to the mom about her new community. As you casually talk about Jenna and her mother's desires for Jenna, you will learn much about the family. You will find out what is important to the parent and the family, the concerns that they have, and the supports that they have for Jenna.

WHAT DO YOU KNOW?

From your conversation with the parent and the observations of the first few days, you will know much about the child, the child's needs, the parents, the supports, and the needs of the family.

WHAT DO YOU WANT TO KNOW?

Continued conversation will help you, the classroom teacher, learn about the family values and traditions as well as the academic strengths, supports, and needs of the child.

WHERE WILL YOU GAIN THE INFORMATION TO BEST PROVIDE FOR JENNA'S EDUCATION?

Continued conversation with the family in a true dialogue fashion of providing information and listening to the views of the family will give the classroom teacher needed information to adjust the classroom environment, curriculum, or presentation modes to best meet the needs of the child.

WHAT AND WHO ARE YOUR RESOURCES?

Teachers have the in-school resources of general education teachers, special education teachers, specialized therapists and assistants, and administration, and the out-of-school resources of physician, therapists, community agencies, and most importantly, the parents. The parents' connection to the child's school, through the teacher, will increase the success of the child. Everyone will be working together and everyone will communicate about the child's needs and successes.

REFERENCES

Barbour, C., Barbour, N. H., & Scully, P. A. (2010). *Families, schools, and communities: Building partnerships for educating children* (5th ed.). Upper Saddle River, NJ: Pearson.

Coots, J. J. (2007). Building bridges with families: Honoring the mandates of IDEIA. *Issues in Teacher Education, 16*(2), 33–40.

Dettmer, P., Thurston, L. P., Knackendoffel, J., & Dyck, N. J. (2009). *Collaboration, consultation, and teamwork: For students with special needs* (6th ed.). Upper Saddle River, NJ: Pearson.

Education for All Handicapped Children Act of 1975, Pub. Law 94-142 (November 29, 1975).

Epstein, J. L., Sanders, M. G., Simon, B. S., Salinas, K. C., Jansorn, N. R., & Van Voorhis, F. L. (1997). *School, family, and community partnerships: Your handbook for action* (2nd ed.). Thousand Oaks, CA: Corwin Press.

Fiedler, C. R., Simpson, R. L., & Clark, D. M. (2007). *Parents and families of children with disabilities: Effective school-based support services.* Upper Saddle River, NJ: Pearson.

Henderson, A., & Berla, N. (1994). *A new generation of evidence: The family is critical to student achievement.* Columbia, MD: National Committee for Citizens in Education.

Individuals with Disabilities Education Improvement Act, Pub. Law 108-446 (December 3, 2004).

No Child Left Behind Act, 20 U.S.C. §6301 (2001).

Olsen, G., & Fuller, M. L. (2008). *Home-school relations* (3rd ed.). Upper Saddle River, NJ: Pearson.

Turnbull, H. R. (1993). *Free appropriate public education: The law and children with disabilities* (4th ed.). Denver, CO: Love.

Section 4

School Services: Working Together

This section addresses the role that each professional in the elementary and middle school setting takes and the knowledge and expertise he or she brings to the conversation. Each chapter begins with a case study that has a problem. The next sections address the general roles and responsibilities of the professionals, how and what they communicate to teachers and parents, direct services they provide to students, direct services they provide to teachers, charts and/or checklists of information needed from the teacher, and a solution to the case study. After reading all of the chapters in this section, the reader will have a better understanding of the different professionals he may work with, how to better collaborate with them, and what to expect regarding information they will provide.

Chapter 4

General Educator

Jennifer Gibson

CASE STUDY: BENJAMIN

Benjamin is a 9-year-old, third-grade boy. He is the second of five children in his family. His mother and father both have advanced degrees and are nurturing, involved parents.

As Benjamin entered third grade, the second-grade teacher told Mrs. Elder, his classroom teacher, that Benjamin had some idiosyncrasies. After the first few days of school, Mrs. Elder realized that Benjamin was probably gifted. His vocabulary, voracious reading habits, his immense scientific knowledge, and his creative thinking skills were far above that of a typical third grader. The teacher immediately began keeping artifacts, anecdotal records, and other items that she thought would aid in his identification by the district's gifted identification committee.

Benjamin liked to answer questions for the class in a long, detailed way. His ideas were usually very unusual, and the teacher felt they were often used as a way to get his classmates' (and her) attention. Benjamin was socially awkward. He had one good friend that he'd known since kindergarten, but he did not make efforts to get along with his other peers. He nearly always chose to work alone if that was an option. He was even impatient with his kindergarten buddy and did not look forward to working with him weekly.

However, as verbose and articulate as Benjamin was, his written work did not match up. His writing was not only labored, but it was sparse compared to his verbal output. Additionally, Benjamin's letter formation and spelling were labored and very poor. Not only was his writing lacking most grammatical and spelling conventions, but also it was oftentimes illegible. Benjamin avoided writing tasks, and when forced to complete one, it was a very time-consuming process for him.

Soon Mrs. Elder began putting accommodations into place for Benjamin in order to support his written output. Oftentimes he was allowed to dictate his responses to another adult or he was allowed to use a portable keyboard to do written work. The use of graphic organizers was modeled for him and his classmates, and he was encouraged and supported in his use of them to prepare for writing tasks.

When the teacher and his parents met for conferences in October, these items were discussed with regard to Benjamin and his success in third grade. He was doing well with the necessary supports in place, so it was decided that things would just continue in a similar manner for a while and both parties would talk about it again during the second semester.

GENERAL ROLES AND RESPONSIBILITIES

It is the responsibility of the general educator to present the grade-level's core curriculum for all students in the classroom. This means that the classroom teacher very often prepares material for a large array of learners. She must differentiate her lessons not only to meet the different learning styles in the classroom but also for varying academic levels. This differentiation can be done by presenting material visually, auditorily, and kinesthetically; providing a variety of texts at different reading levels; giving supports to students who need it; asking questions at varying levels; and allowing students choices in how and what they learn.

Besides planning lessons for all subjects, the general educator is typically the primary contact with the parents and/or guardians in the student's home. This teacher sends home newsletters or notes and sets up necessary conferences with the parents or guardians. This home-school connection is key to helping the child feel that all are working for his benefit. The open communication and shared vision of the parents and the teachers help to keep the child and his progress as the focus.

It is also the responsibility of the teacher to be aware of the individual needs of his or her students. This could vary from knowing that a child needs to be allowed to use the bathroom more often than others to co-planning and co-teaching with a learning specialist. The general educator is responsible for knowing the goals on children's Individualized Education Programs (IEPs) and being sure that any accommodations or modifications from this IEP are implemented in the classroom.

The teacher becomes more aware of his or her students' individual needs by regular progress monitoring and using the data to guide decisions for instruction. These data help to determine a child's strengths and weaknesses. The child's response to interventions allows the teacher to know that her methods of reteaching are reaching the student. When the child does not respond to the interventions, it is the teacher's responsibility to find other ways of presenting the information to the student or to seek additional assessment information. The data from this constant progress monitoring also aid both the teacher and student to better measure growth throughout the year.

COMMUNICATION WITH TEACHERS AND PARENTS

The general educator should meet and talk regularly with any other teachers that her students might have. She should co-plan when possible so that the teachers can best meet the student's needs in a least restrictive environment (LRE). If a child meets with more than one learning specialist per week, the classroom teacher should be in continual contact with each teacher to be sure that the student's needs are being met. The teachers work together to look at upcoming lessons and assignments and determine what might need to be changed to help the child find success. The teachers should put the child in the center of their conference discussion as they work to provide a nourishing learning environment for him.

In addition to communicating with colleagues, the teacher is responsible for communication with her students' homes. This communication can come in many forms and should be used for both positive comments and concerns that she might have. Similarly, it is necessary for the parents to share what is or is not working in the home. In this way, both home and school can provide the student with common approaches to meet his needs. With all students, it is important that the teacher and home celebrate the things that the child does well; these achievements can be the building blocks for future success.

The teacher is responsible for communication with all of her students' families, but she needs to be cognizant that some students and their families will need more direct contact. It is also the responsibility of the general educator to work to understand what method of communication is most effective with each child. Some homes may be more easily reached by phone than by e-mail, and some may respond better to a written note than to a phone call. Children, too, may respond better to different communications.

The teacher should know if praising the child aloud will bother him or if he would respond better to a handwritten note. Some students may require a daily communication log with parents. This is a great method of communication to consider for students and parents who need more consistent feedback.

When formal conferences occur, it is the role of the general educator to invite any support staff who work with each child and might have some stakes in the conference discussion. It is not always possible for other teachers to make it to these conferences, so it is the role of the classroom teacher to relay any concerns that others might be having with the child.

Direct Services Provided to Students

The general educator is often the main provider of services to a student with a disability in her classroom. The teacher takes the information provided by the special educator and uses it to plan and implement her lesson. If special accommodations or modifications to the lesson need to occur, the teacher is the one who implements them. Examples of this would be using manipulatives, reading or rewording directions for a student, providing a checklist of steps for a project, or providing a different assignment for the student. The teacher should consult with the special educator before putting such accommodations in place. It is extremely important, too, that the teacher work to provide all students with lessons in which they learn best, thus not making any child feeling left out or different because of accommodations put in place for him.

If a student has a personal teaching assistant, the general educator is responsible for discussing with her what is expected from the lesson and what types of support the child may need. This is better done if discussed prior to the beginning of the lesson.

Direct Services Provided to Teachers

The general educator provides the special educators and the child's support staff with data gathered during classroom learning. These data could be quantitative or qualitative, but they should measure a definite goal for the child. The teachers then work together, using the data to determine further instruction for the child.

It is also important that, if the teacher and special educators do not have time to co-plan, the general educator provide the special educator with lesson plans and upcoming classwork that the child will be expected to do. This sharing should be done early enough that the special educator has time to make changes or suggestions that might help the child do better in the classroom.

Charts and/or Checklists of Information Needed From the Teacher

Any classroom data that the teacher might have should be shared with the team. These data should be clear and understandable to the parents as well as to the other teachers. They should be relevant to the needs of the child.

Checklists or special charts for the child's use are often provided by special educators, but are supported by the general educator. It is important that she understand the use of these checklists or charts so that she can best help the child to use them properly. These checklists could be as simple as a visual schedule to help the child get his day started to a more detailed behavior plan with daily goals. All efforts should be made by the general educator to reinforce the use of these tools consistently and properly to make them as effective as possible.

It is also the general educator's responsibility to discuss with the student's case manager or special educator if she feels there is an accommodation that she cannot implement with integrity. Although the classroom teacher is accountable to the child, she must also be honest with herself and her colleagues when there are supports, procedures, or accommodations that she is not comfortable implementing.

Solution to the Case Study

Benjamin's mother and Mrs. Elder met again in February to review his needs. Both agreed on seeking out his gifted identification. The teacher felt strongly that her artifacts and anecdotal records would help with this identification. However, Benjamin's mother was still very concerned with his ever-worsening handwriting and spelling. The teacher and his mother decided to go ahead and take him forward to the building's teacher assistance team with the hopes that he would receive some occupational therapy evaluations. Mrs. Elder pointed out that he could not receive occupational therapy without an IEP, but they decided to proceed anyway.

The teacher assistance team recommended that Benjamin receive an occupational therapy screening and a brief intelligence screening. Benjamin was not pleased with the time he was missing in the classroom for these assessments, and he did not always act cooperatively for the teachers. However, both were able to get good information from their meetings with him.

When the team met again to discuss Benjamin's screening results, it was noted by the school psychologist that his IQ was 142 and that while he struggled socially with her, he did share with her some of his unusual thinking and large vocabulary. The occupational therapist also was able to get to know Benjamin's personality and to witness his struggles with handwriting, spelling, and writing organization. She suggested to the team that Benjamin be identified with dysgraphia, and that he receive services to support his difficulty with writing. The team agreed, and an IEP was written to allow Benjamin additional classroom supports for writing difficulties.

Less than a month later, after an interview by a member of the gifted identification team and a review of the artifacts presented by the teacher, Benjamin was also identified as a gifted learner. This meant that he would receive additional pull-out time for extension activities. In the end, Benjamin left third grade identified as a twice-exceptional learner.

Chapter 5

Special Education Teacher

Nicole M. Uphold

Case Study: Zachary

Zachary is a seventh-grade student at Jackson Middle School, and he is currently served in special education because of a learning disability in reading. He has difficulty comprehending written materials, although he has no difficulties with comprehending oral information and he is in all general education classes. Recently, Zachary had his IEP meeting. At the meeting were Zachary; Mrs. Carper, Zachary's mom; Ms. Smith, his special education teacher; Mrs. Rochelle, his English teacher; Mr. Lawson, the school's assistant principal; Mr. Chan, the agriculture teacher; and Mr. Blake, the school psychologist. Mrs. Carper discussed Zachary's failing grade in English. She does not feel that Zachary is receiving the support that he needs to be successful. Ms. Smith reported that Zachary should have books on tape and his tests read aloud. Mrs. Rochelle stated that she reads all tests aloud for Zachary and he does very well on them. However, several of the novels they are reading in class did not come on books on tape in time, and he struggled to keep up. Zachary's mom reported that she was trying to read the books aloud to him at home but has other children who need homework assistance too. Mrs. Rochelle reported that Zachary also needs assistance completing worksheets because the amount of reading involved. Mr. Chan reported that he does not read the tests aloud because he does not have the time.

INTRODUCTION

The special education teacher will be the primary point of contact for information about the student. The special education teacher wears many hats, including case manager, collaborator, instructor, supporter, and communicator. As case manager for the student, the special education teacher is responsible for all special education paperwork and making sure the child is receiving his or her accommodations. The special education teacher coordinates services for the student, including speech therapy, physical therapy, occupational therapy, special transportation, assistive technology, and services provided by outside agencies (e.g., vocational assessment, job coaching, counseling). The special education teacher may not be providing instruction to the student as the student may be in all general education courses or in another special education teacher's class. The special education teacher supports the student both academically and socially. Finally, the special education teacher communicates with parents and students to express progress and concerns.

GENERAL ROLES AND RESPONSIBILITIES

The special education teacher has two primary roles and responsibilities. The first is to serve as case manager for the student. This involves directing the Individualized Education Program process, assisting in IEP goal development, conducting assessments, managing evaluations, tracking student progress, and communicating with students, parents, and other IEP team members. The second role is as an instructor. The special education teacher will either instruct students in his own classroom or co-teach with a general education teacher.

CASE MANAGER

As the case manager, the special education teacher will schedule the IEP meeting, invite the participants, and conduct the meeting. The special education teacher is responsible for leading the IEP team in the development of the student's IEP. This includes determining the student's present level of performance, developing goals and objectives, selecting accommodations and/or modifications, and deciding placement (i.e., where the student will receive instruction). All members of the IEP team should contribute to the development of the IEP, and the special educator will make sure each person has a chance to discuss the strengths and needs of the student at the meeting.

The special education teacher also manages the student's evaluation and reevaluations. Evaluations are conducted every 3 years to determine if the student remains eligible to receive special education services. As part of this process, the special education teacher communicates with all members of the IEP team to determine if additional testing is needed. If the testing is needed, the teacher remains in contact with the appropriate IEP team members to track evaluation completion. See Table 5.1 for a sample communication form.

Once the IEP is developed, the special education teacher is responsible for making sure it is carried out. This means that the student is receiving instruction in the correct placement and the accommodations and/or modifications listed in the IEP are being implemented. In addition, the special education teacher keeps in contact with the student and his or her family regarding progress on IEP goals.

INSTRUCTOR

In addition to serving as the IEP case manager, special education teachers instruct students. This instruction can take place in a self-contained classroom setting with students needing intensive instruction, a resource classroom where students are learning grade-level content in a small group, or a co-teaching classroom where the special education teacher assists the regular education teacher with instruction. Because the focus of this book is inclusion, only the co-teaching responsibilities of special education teachers will be discussed later in this chapter.

COMMUNICATION WITH TEACHERS AND PARENTS

TEACHERS

The special education teacher should stay in frequent contact with any regular education teachers providing instruction to a student on his or her caseload. The special education teacher wants to track the progress of the student in the class. If the student is having any difficulties, the special education teacher can provide assistance to the regular education teacher and/or the student. The special education teacher can help differentiate instruction, provide tutoring to the student, or call an IEP meeting to change accommodations/modifications. In addition, if the regular education teacher is providing instruction to the student, the special education teacher will need to find out about IEP goal progress from the regular education teacher.

Table 5.1
Sample Communication Form Between Special
Education Teachers and IEP Team Members

To: IEP Team Members
From: Special Education Teacher
Date: April 1
Re: John's reevaluation due April 26 (Meeting scheduled for April 27)

Evaluator	Evaluation Required?	Evaluation Complete?	Date Evaluation Completed or to Be Completed	Brief Results
Diagnostician	Y N	Y N		
School Psychologist	Y N	Y N		
Speech Therapist	Y N	Y N		
Occupational Therapist	Y N	Y N		
Physical Therapist	Y N	Y N		
Assistive Technology Specialist	Y N	Y N		
Adaptive Physical Education Teacher	Y N	Y N		

Because the special education teacher will be teaching his or her own classes and might have different planning times than the regular education teachers, the special education teacher will probably need to use written communication with the regular education teacher. The special education teacher can send a form to the regular education teacher asking specific questions about the student's progress. This information will be used to decide on IEP goal progress. It is important that the regular education teacher discusses any concerns he or she may have about the student.

In reality, many special education teachers have a difficult time staying in contact with regular education teachers (Scruggs, Mastropieri, & McDuffie, 2007). In addition to his or her teaching duties, the special education teacher is busy developing IEPs, attending IEP meetings, and communicating with students, parents, and other service providers. General education teachers stay busy planning for their classes and deciding how to instruct all of their students. Both teachers rarely have common planning time. Oftentimes, the only reason these two teachers would communicate is if a student was performing poorly in the general education teacher's class. However, it is important for educational planning that the special education teacher has a good idea of the student's needs *and* strengths in her classes. The special education teacher can make better educational decisions if she knows what is working for the student and what additional supports the student might need to be successful. Constant communication between the general and special education teachers is essential.

The regular education teacher needs to understand his role in planning for the educational success of a student. A student in an inclusion setting is receiving most, if not all, of her education from the regular education teacher. Therefore, the only people with information related to the student's academic progress are regular education teachers. The general education teacher needs to work with the special education teacher to plan goals and accommodations so the student is successful in the regular education class.

There are many strategies that special education teachers can implement to stay in contact with regular education teachers. One strategy is to develop a form that can be sent to a regular education teacher for written feedback. This form needs to be easily and quickly completed. Another strategy is to have set meetings times with regular education teachers to discuss students' progress. Having a communication guide will make the meeting run smoothly and quickly (see Table 5.2 for example). These meetings can be weekly or monthly, depending on the information that needs to be shared.

Table 5.2

Sample Communication Form for Meeting Between Regular
Education Teacher and Special Education Teacher

Student name:			
Goals	Progress		Comments
1. Student will . . .	None Adequate Met		
2. Student will . . .	None Adequate Met		

Student name:			
Goals	Progress		Comments
1. Student will . . .	None Adequate Met		

General Information			
Are students prepared for class?	Y	N	
Do students complete all assignments?	Y	N	
Are students passing class?	Y	N	
Are student using accommodations?	Y	N	

Recent success/achievements:

Any concerns:

Table 5.3
Sample IEP Progress Report

IEP Goal:	Progress:			Comments:
Student will come prepared for class.	None	(Adequate)	Met	Student has been bringing notebook and pen to class. Student has completed 80% of homework assignments. Student needs to complete all homework assignments so it does not negatively affect grade.
Student will comprehend a variety of print material.	None	(Adequate)	Met	Student is doing a great job at previewing before reading a passage. Student is working on highlighting important information. Continue to read with student at home.

PARENTS

The special education teacher also needs to stay in contact with parents. The special education teacher must provide reports on the student's progress toward his IEP goals. The frequency of progress is determined at the IEP meeting, but IEP progress is usually communicated at the same time as progress reports for classes. The IEP progress reports are usually formal documents associated with the IEP; however, some teachers customize the report (see Table 5.3 for an example). With IEP progress reports, the special education teacher wants to tell the parent if the student is making no progress or adequate progress toward meeting goals, or if the student has met the goal. In addition, the teacher wants to let the parents know the areas that the student needs to continue working on to meet the goal. For many teachers and parents, this is the only communication the parent receives about their child's IEP progress.

Additionally, the special education teacher wants the parents to discuss any concerns they have about the student. Parents can often give insight to an academic need. Frequent communication with parents is key; however, it is often difficult. Parents and teachers might work the same hours and cannot communicate by telephone during the day. Parents often do not trust the school personnel because of previous difficulties. Any parent/teacher communication issues need to be overcome to benefit the student. Special education teachers should contact parents at the start of every school year to gather input from them and make sure the first contact with the parents is a positive one.

Daily checklists of the student's day are beneficial for younger students so parents can get an understanding of what the student did at school and any issues that arise can be quickly relayed to home (see Figure 5.1). A weekly newsletter can be used to let parents know the content being taught in the classroom and upcoming events (see Figure 5.2). Monthly progress reports can be individualized for each student and give the parent an overview of the skills the child has learned (see Figure 5.3).

DIRECT SERVICES PROVIDED TO STUDENTS

A special education teacher provides support and instruction to students with disabilities. Support comes in the form of frequent contact to find out how the student is doing in school and to discuss any concerns or issues the student has. A good special education teacher meets regularly with the student to discuss progress, concerns, and successes. The special education teacher wants to determine what part of the IEP might need to be changed (see Table 5.3). The teacher also wants to determine if the student is having difficulty in any of his classes, problems with peer relationships, or any other concerns, both in school and at home. The checklist in Table 5.4 would need to be modified to match the grade and reading level of the student. For example, with a younger student, the teacher might use pictures to ask about classes.

A special education teacher also instructs students. A special education teacher might also serve a student who is included in the general education class in a co-teaching situation. The special education teacher works with the regular education teacher to differentiate instruction and provide accommodations.

DIRECT SERVICES PROVIDED TO TEACHERS

Many students with disabilities are served in the regular education classroom. This means that their academic and IEP goal instruction is conducted in the general curriculum with the regular education teacher. With

Tommy's Daily Progress

Stayed in seat?

Brought materials?

Turned in homework?

Quiet in class?

Homework for tonight:

Comments:

Figure 5.1. Sample daily checklist.

Figure 5.2. Sample newsletter.

Progress Report—Monthly

Student Name_____ Jane D. _____ Date _____ Jan. 26, 2010 _____

M = Mastery   MP = Minimal Progress
SP = Satisfactory Progress   NP = No Progress

Goal	Date			
	10/09	1/10	3/10	6/10
Student will organize belongings.	NP	SP		
Student will improve listening comprehension skills by responding appropriately to oral questions in conversation, directions, and text read aloud in class.	MP	MP		
Student will answer who, what, when, and where questions related to print material she has read.	SP	SP		

Jane is making progress toward her IEP goals. She has made excellent progress in her organization skills. She is always prepared for class and has her books, notebook, and writing utensil with her. She still has difficulty turning in homework assignments. Jane works hard when she knows she will receive a reward for completing assignments. She needs to continue to put forth effort when working on her goals. She needs to use coping strategies to stay on-task when listening.

Parent's Signature _____

Figure 5.3. Monthly progress report.

the push toward accountability of all students, more and more special education students are being educated in the regular education classroom (U. S. Department of Education, 2006). However, regular education teachers rarely receive training on how to effectively educate students with learning disabilities. In response, schools have moved to a co-teaching model in which a general education teacher is paired with a special education teacher and together they instruct all students in their class. There are five co-teaching models: one teaching/one helping, parallel teaching, station teaching, alternative teaching, and team teaching (Salend, 2008). Before co-teaching, both general and special education teachers should meet to define their roles and responsibilities related to instruction, classroom management, and other classroom policies so both teachers can be as efficient and effective as possible.

One Teaching/One Helping

The one teaching/one helping co-teaching model involves one teacher instructing the whole class, while the other teacher monitors or assists students. This is the most common model of co-teaching (Scruggs et al., 2007). The content specialist will instruct the whole class, while the second teacher monitors student performance. The second teacher can assist any student who needs extra assistance learning the content. When using this model, it is important to include the second teacher in planning instruction. The content specialist is usually the regular education teacher, and the second teacher is the special education teacher. Although the regular education teacher is the most knowledgeable about the content, the special education teacher can assist with differentiating instruction.

Parallel Teaching

The second co-teaching model is parallel teaching. The class is split into two heterogeneous groups and both the regular education teacher and special education teacher teach the same content to both groups. The advantage to this approach is that students can learn, practice, or review material in a small-group format and teachers are better able to determine which students need further instruction. However, this approach requires two teachers who are able to deliver instruction.

Station Teaching

With station teaching, the class is broken into small groups that move to different stations for instruction or activities. The teachers can teach new information, review content, or practice material. For example, if the teachers decide they would like their students to practice recognizing and saying short vowel sounds, then they set up three stations. At the first station, the general education teacher works with students to state short vowel sounds in isolation. At the second station, the special education teacher works with students to state the short vowel sounds in words. The final station would be independent seatwork where the students find words with short vowel sounds in magazines and cut them out. The students would be broken into small groups and rotate through each station.

Alternative Teaching

Alternative teaching is when one teacher instructs a small group of students while the other teacher instructs the whole class. Students who need extra assistance learning or practicing a particular piece of information can receive this help without leaving the classroom. The teachers can differenti-

Table 5.4
Sample Checklist to Communicate With Student

Are you receiving your accommodations?	Y N
Are you benefitting from your accommodations?	Y N
Are you having difficulty in any of your classes? If yes, which ones? Please explain.	Y N
Are you having difficulty with peers? If yes, please explain.	
Other problems/concerns?	
Recent achievements?	
Anything else?	

ate instruction to meet the needs of students in small groups. For example, the teachers might decide to teach multiplication. The majority of students will work with the regular education teacher practicing their skills with a worksheet. However, a small number of students will not be able to complete their worksheets without the assistance of a calculator so the special education teacher works with these students in a small group.

TEAM TEACHING

The final co-teaching model is team teaching. Both teachers plan and deliver instruction together to the whole class. The teachers trade off during the lesson, as one teaches and one circulates around the room, observing student behavior and assisting students. This is the most time-consuming of the co-teaching models, as it requires continuous co-planning and teachers that can "feed off" of one another during instruction. The teachers need to have a solid relationship with each other.

Teachers involved in a co-teaching classroom need to have regular meetings to plan instruction. The regular and special education teachers need to have common planning to design instruction and decide on an effective delivery method. In addition, their roles and responsibilities should be discussed and clearly delineated. See http://ritter.tea.state.tx.us/special. ed/reading/pdf/coteach.pdf for a sample co-teaching lesson planning form and more information on co-teaching. Depending on the co-teaching team, the special education teacher's role and responsibilities will vary, sometimes even daily. It is important to remember that special education should not be used only as a "helper" in the classroom, but also in an instructional role.

The special education teacher can also help differentiate instruction for students. Differentiating instruction allows teachers to provide instruction that meets the needs of individual students. Differentiated instruction involves both changing what you teach and how you to teach it (Salend, 2008). For example, an English class might read *The Call of the Wild*. The majority of the students read the book independently; discuss the plot, main ideas, and characters; and are tested using essay comprehension questions. For a small number of students, using an adapted book with repeated storylines and pictures might differentiate the instruction. The students are also tested on their comprehension, but are given multiple-choice questions instead of essay questions. The special education teacher receives training in how to assist content specialists with changing instruction to meet the diverse needs of students. The regular education teacher should use the special education teacher as a resource to meet the needs of all students in his classes.

SOLUTION TO THE CASE STUDY

After the discussion at the IEP meeting, the team members came up with some solutions. Mr. Lawson reported that the school is moving to having co-teachers in all math and English classes. Mrs. Rochelle stated that would be great because she could use the extra person to help teach. Mrs. Rochelle stated that she could break the class into groups have them move around the room to different stations and receive more specialized instruction. Ms. Smith would also be able to read the tests aloud to Zachary and assist him while he completes worksheets. In addition, Mrs. Rochelle stated she could have the students work with partners more frequently because someone else would be able to assist with monitoring groups. The team agreed that Zachary needs to continue to have tests read aloud and receive books on tape. In addition, the team agreed that he could have a peer read him the directions on worksheets. Ms. Smith also told Mr. Chan that she is available to read tests aloud, and Zachary should be sent to her when he has to take a test.

REFERENCES

Salend, A. J. (2008). *Creating inclusive classrooms: Effective and reflective practices.* Upper Saddle River, NJ: Pearson.

Scruggs, T. E., Mastropieri, M. A., & McDuffie, K. A. (2007). Co-teaching in inclusive classrooms: A meta-synthesis of qualitative research. *Exceptional Children, 73*, 392–416.

U.S. Department of Education. (2006). *28th annual report to Congress on the implementation of the Individuals with Disabilities Education Act, 2006.* Retrieved from http://www2.ed.gov/about/reports/annual/osep/2006/parts-b-c/28th-vol-2.pdf

Chapter 6

Paraeducators

Tammy L. Stephens and Christine Woodbury

CASE STUDY: MS. GARDNER AND MR. PETHICK

Ms. Gardner, a first-year special education teacher is energetic and eager to begin her first teaching assignment within a fifth-grade special education placement. Her major responsibilities include teaching several resource classes, the implementation of inclusion for several students on her caseload, and supervising her first-year paraeducator, Mr. Pethick. During the few days prior to the start of the school year, Ms. Gardner attends mandatory faculty development meetings and busily prepares for the upcoming school year by reviewing student records, planning lessons, and reviewing schedules for the first week of classes. She keeps Mr. Pethick busy organizing the classroom, decorating bulletin boards, making copies of worksheets, and attending faculty meetings. The week of planning quickly passes and before Ms. Gardner realizes, the first day of classes is upon her.

On the first day of classes, Ms. Gardner eagerly welcomes her students at the classroom door with a smile as Mr. Pethick organizes student folders in the back of the room. However, Ms. Gardner's energy and excitement quickly diminishes as the day progresses. Throughout the day, several issues occur that cause frustration for Ms. Gardner and Mr. Pethick. For example, on several occasions Ms. Gardner and Mr. Pethick find themselves "falling over one another," confused about which adult will assist students in need. Furthermore, Ms. Gardner spends most of her day providing instructions to Mr. Pethick, taking away from instructional time. During a student outburst, Mr. Pethick steps in and administers a punishment rather than following the classroom management steps laid out by Ms. Gardner. Lastly, during lunch break Ms. Gardner overhears Mr. Pethick talking openly to other staff members about several students in their special education class. By the end of the day, Ms. Gardner and Mr. Pethick are exhausted and extremely frustrated . . .

INTRODUCTION

In order to ensure adequate instructional programming for students with disabilities, it is imperative that educators, paraeducators, related service personnel, and parents work together collaboratively. Historically, the paraeducator has worked alongside teachers and played a key role in providing support services. Over the past few decades, the role and presence of the paraeducator in schools has evolved into providing increased services to students with disabilities (Lamont & Hill, 1991) while carrying out Individualized Education Programs (IEPs).

The position of paraeducator is not new to the field of education. Instead, paraeducators have worked within education and human services since the 1900s. However, their value to education was not formally recognized until the mid-1950s (Wallace, 2003). According to Pickett, Likins, and Wallace (2002), paraeducators, sometimes referred to as "paraprofessionals" or "teacher's assistants," are defined as school employees who work under the supervision of teachers and/or other certified personnel to conduct a variety of roles. Such roles and responsibilities range from administrative tasks to assisting teachers in the delivery of instructional and other support services. Paraeducators have been compared to their counterparts in law (paralegals) and medicine (paramedics). The prefix "para" means "alongside of," as in working alongside an educator (Wallace, 2003).

In most public education systems, the use of paraeducators has escalated (Tews & Lupart, 2008). Pickett and Gerlach (1997) identified several events and trends that have contributed to the increase in the numbers and roles of paraeducators. Such events included: the continual shortage of special education teachers (Office of Special Education Programs in Rehabilitation Services [OSERS], 1993), increased inclusive practices (Hofmeister, 1993), a growing need for related services (Fenichel & Eggbeer, 1990), and increased diversity of student populations (Haselkorn & Fiedeler, 1996). As the number of paraeducators has increased over the years, their roles have expanded.

General Role and Responsibilities

The paraeducator is an important member of an educational team and works closely with students, teachers, service providers, and parents to provide support and ensure student success (Tews & Lupart, 2008). Specifically, the paraeducator plays a vital role in supporting the implementation of IEPs. The roles and responsibilities of paraeducators vary depending on the population of students they serve and the instructional settings to which they are assigned (Giangreco, Edelman, Broer, & Doyle, 2001).

A lack of consensus regarding the roles of the paraeducator has resulted in responsibilities varying across regions of the United States and from district to district (Wallace, 2003). The Study of Personnel Needs in Special Education (SPeNSE Fact Sheet, 2001) found that there were differences in regions and districts with regard to the types of services provided by paraeducators. Additionally, results of the study indicated that the majority of special education paraeducators nationwide spent at least 10% of their time on each of the following activities (SPeNSE Fact Sheet, 2001):

- providing instructional support in small groups,
- providing one-on-one instruction,
- modifying materials,
- implementing behavior management plans,
- collecting student data, and
- providing personal care assistance.

Although the role of a paraeducator has evolved from mostly administrative to more instructional in nature (Lamont & Hill, 1991), paraeducators continue to serve dual responsibilities in both noninstructional and instructional roles.

Noninstructional Roles

Paraeducators serve the teachers, students, and the schools in which they are assigned through a variety of noninstructional roles. In addition to the traditional clerical roles (e.g., making copies and organizing paperwork), paraeducators are often involved in duties that assist teachers in the preparation of lesson delivery (e.g., modification of assignments and organization of lesson materials). Other noninstructional duties include the supervision of students in various educational settings (e.g., bus, cafeteria, playground, transitions), meetings with teachers and related service personnel, housekeeping tasks within the classroom, running errands for teachers, personal care assistance for students, completion of daily progress sheets for school-to-home communication, maintaining student confidentiality, and attending professional training.

INSTRUCTIONAL ROLES

As the field of special education has evolved over the years, so have the instructional roles of the paraeducator. Traditionally, students with disabilities received special education services within self-contained classrooms. Consequently, paraeducators have traditionally provided one-on-one and small-group instructional support within a self-contained classroom. However, educational reform efforts (e.g., inclusion) have and continue to promote new and expanded roles for the paraeducator.

The increased inclusion of students with disabilities within the general education classroom has allowed paraeducators to expand their services outside of the special education classroom. As students with disabilities are being educated within their least restrictive environment (LRE), paraeducators are assisting these students within inclusive settings (Tews & Lupart, 2008). Instructional duties paraeducators are performing within inclusive settings include: assisting general education teachers with the implementation of student accommodations and modifications, observations, small-group instruction (under the direct supervision of teachers), individual student assistance, collection of assessment data, implementation of behavior management plans, documentation of daily/weekly student academic and behavioral performance, and the facilitation of peer interactions.

COMMUNICATION WITH
TEACHERS, STUDENTS, AND OTHER
EDUCATIONAL PERSONNEL

Effective communication is the cornerstone of education (Friend & Cook, 2007). Without effective communication, paraeducators would not understand teacher expectations; students would not understand lecture material, directions, or other thoughts; and parents would not understand student progress. Communication has been defined as the ability to share information with people and to understand what information and feelings others convey (Project PARA, 2010). Furthermore, in addition to verbal and written communication, various forms of communication exist that include vocalizations (pitch and tones), gestures, facial expressions, and signs.

Open and effective communication skills are vital among all individuals responsible for the delivery of services to students with disabilities. This is especially true for paraeducators. Because they work closely with supervising teachers, students, administrators, and other educational personnel, it is imperative that paraeducators exhibit adequate communication skills. Teachers and paraeducators must have an open line of communication, for it is through such interactions that information about job expectations, student learning, and daily occurrences are relayed.

As paraeducators interact daily with numerous individuals, their ability to contribute to the special education program is dependent upon their communication skills. Specifically, according to Project PARA (2010), communication is essential for:

- understanding roles and assignments,
- planning and carrying out learning activities,
- coordinating approaches with students,
- providing information to teachers on student progress and behaviors, and
- building a positive relationship with students, teachers, and other staff.

EFFECTIVE COMMUNICATION WITH TEACHERS, STUDENTS, AND PARENTS

As teachers and paraeducators work together to promote the academic and socioemotional well-being of all students (Carnahan, Williamson, Clarke, & Sorensen, 2009), it is imperative that effective communication skills are demonstrated. Effective communication begins with the establishment of rapport. Paraeducators should work to establish good rapport and regular communication with the supervising teachers and students with whom they work (Project PARA, 2010). The paraeducator and supervising teacher should meet early and regularly to discuss job responsibilities and classroom procedures. Additionally, rapport can be established by dealing openly with attitudes pertaining to student learning, student expectations, educational procedures, and duties. Table 6.1 provides a list of suggested practices that will encourage positive communication practices between the paraeducator and teachers.

To ensure paraeducators and teachers get along with one another and meet the needs of their students, they must work together as a team in creating an effective learning environment. Frequent, daily meetings should occur to discuss the lesson plans and activities and to discuss any concerns they might have. Meetings should be structured to ensure productive use of time. Table 6.2 provides suggested procedures for planning structured meetings. Additionally, Figure 6.1 provides a sample agenda. Such predetermined meeting times allow the paraeducator and teacher to establish and

Table 6.1

Procedures for Establishing Effective Communication

Procedure	Description
Use explicit and concrete language.	▪ Teachers should provide paraeducators with detailed descriptions of all relevant information.
Provide examples and nonexamples.	▪ When possible, teachers should draw examples and nonexamples from actual occurrences in the classroom.
Model information.	▪ Paraeducators learn from watching teachers, such as how to use a quiet voice to provide feedback to individual students or how to use proximity and nonverbal cues to manage student behaviors.
Check for understanding.	▪ Ask paraeducators to paraphrase what they learned, teach the strategy back to the teacher, or describe what they observed the teacher doing with the student.

Note. From Carnahan et al. (2009).

maintain open channels of communication. A list of suggested practices that will encourage positive teaming practices between the paraeducator and teachers are presented in Table 6.3.

The development of a shared philosophy between the supervising teacher and paraeducator is helpful in establishing positive and consistent classroom management (Carnahan et al., 2009). Charney (2002) found that through a shared philosophy, teams could agree on articulate, consistent, and predictable ways of working in the classroom. A "shared philosophy" has been defined as "a statement of what is aspired to, rather than necessarily what currently is" (Giangreco et al., 1999, p. 2). A summary of the team's values, goals, and desires for the school year should be included within the shared philosophy. Specifically, commitments to specific actions such as positive verbal and nonverbal supports should be included.

Open communication between paraeducators and students is essential to ensure adequate and effective instructional practices. It is important when talking to students that paraeducators engage in certain behaviors that facilitate openness and acceptance (Project PARA, 2010). Students tend to be more receptive to listening and communicating when the paraeducator has established a positive relationship with the students (e.g., respect, courtesy, friendship). Students should be encouraged by the paraeducator; the use of control should not be used. Table 6.4 provides a list of helpful hints to encourage positive interaction between the paraeducator and the student.

Although paraeducators communicate directly with general education teachers and students, direct communication is seldom made between paraeducators and parents. Typically, direct interactions and communi-

Table 6.2

Procedures for Conducting Productive Meetings

Schedule meetings for 30–45 minutes once a week (if this amount of time is not available, discuss one point at start or end of each school day).
Limit the number of agenda items to afford time for in-depth discussions around important topics.
Post a call for agenda items in a private central location prior to scheduled meeting.
Create an agenda prior to meeting.
Maintain a highly organized and productive meeting to facilitate team collaboration.
Clarify the roles and responsibilities of team members.
Discuss important but less time-sensitive topics.

Note. From Carnahan et al. (2009).

cations between the school and family members regarding the academics and behavior of a student are conducted through the student's teacher. Correspondence between family members and paraeducators are typically conducted informally (e.g., through daily behavior charts, journal entries, and assignment sheets).

Beginning the school year with clearly stated expectations, effective and open communication, and a shared philosophy sets a positive tone for the rest of the school year (Carnahan et al., 2009). Additionally, the establishment of effective communication practices ensures that all individuals are on the same page (Friend & Cook, 2007). This, in turn, will alleviate inconsistencies and miscommunication.

DIRECT SERVICES PROVIDED TO TEACHERS

An analysis of earlier research pertaining to the utilization of paraeducators within the field of education indicated a more administrative role. Fifty years ago, the role of the paraeducator was to assist the teacher or related service personnel with clerical duties (Boomer, 1982). In today's classrooms, paraeducators continue to assist teachers with clerical tasks (e.g., paperwork, copies) but they also play a more active role within the special education and general education classrooms. Specifically, research indicates that paraeducators also serve teachers by providing instructional support to students, collecting and managing student data, and conducting classroom management techniques (Wallace, 2003).

Sample Meeting Agenda

- Introduction of members
- Develop shared philosophy
  o Discuss beliefs, expectations, yearly goals for class

- Review job responsibilities
  o Teacher
  o Paraeducator

- Establish class schedule
- Review student Individualized Education Programs (IEPs)
  o Review goals and objectives
  o Review modifications and accommodations
  o Review schedule of services

- Wrap-up
  o Ensure participants understand results/tasks

Figure 6.1. Sample meeting agenda.

The following is a synopsis of various roles and responsibilities of paraeducators previously suggested throughout the chapter as well as additional types of specific services they may provide to teachers (Carnahan et al., 2009; Project PARA, 2010; SPeNSE Fact Sheet, 2001).

NONINSTRUCTIONAL SUPPORT TO TEACHERS

- Check daily assignment logs:
  □ Check parent signatures on daily logs.
  □ Ensure assignments are written correctly.
  □ Check for parent notations.

- Record keeping:
  □ Take daily attendance.
  □ Do daily lunch count.
  □ Post student grades in grade book.
  □ Collect paperwork (e.g., field trip slips, picture money).

INSTRUCTIONAL-RELATED SUPPORT TO TEACHERS

- Collection of student data:
  □ Administer curriculum-based measurement (CBM).
  □ Monitor progress.

Table 6.3
Enhancing Positive Team Procedures Between Teachers and Paraeducators

Effective Practices	Description of Effective Practices
Establish rapport.	The teacher and paraeducator should get to know one another's likes, dislikes, pet peeves, expectations, belief systems, backgrounds, and so on. Interactions between individuals should be respectful.
Develop shared philosophy.	Establish a summary of the team's values, goals, and desires for the school year. Include commitments to specific actions such as positive verbal and nonverbal supports.
Review job description and expectations.	All job responsibilities should be thoroughly reviewed between the supervising teacher and paraeducator early and often. All expectations should be identified and reviewed often. A schedule should be created and reviewed often.
Discuss student expectations.	The teacher and paraeducator should meet early in the semester to review student disabilities. Student academic and behavioral goals should be organized and easily accessible by the teacher and paraeducator. Student goals and objectives should be thoroughly reviewed and discussed to ensure understanding. Student schedules of services should be discussed. Student accommodations and modifications should be reviewed often and monitored to ensure implementation.
Schedule meetings often.	A predetermined meeting should be scheduled daily between the teacher and paraeducator. Meetings should be productive and targeted (follow agenda). Maintain positivity during meetings (always begin meetings with something positive).
Maintain respectful communication.	The supervising teacher and paraeducator should maintain open communication. Conflicts should be discussed immediately to ensure quick resolution.

Note. From Carnahan et al. (2009).

Table 6.4
Strategies to Enhance Positive Communication
Between Paraeducators and Students

Characteristics	Description of Characteristics
Rapport	Establish rapport with student by exhibiting respect, courtesy, and friendship.
Posture	Posture should mirror that of the student. Shoulders should be squared with student. Slight lean forward toward student.
Eye contact	Establish and maintain eye contact with student to show interest.
Distance	Distance between paraeducator and student should be around 3-4 feet (e.g., standing too close to student may make student uncomfortable; standing too far away my relay message of disinterest).
Facial expression	Match facial expression with that of student.
Distracting behaviors	Refrain from engaging in distracting behaviors (e.g., playing with hands, staring out window, working on computer) when interacting with student. Engage in active listening practices (e.g., nod, repeat portions of student's response to ensure understanding).
Voice quality	Voice tone should match that of student. Speak in a calm manner. If frustration, anger, or boredom occur, stop.
Accepting language	Use student name when interacting with student. Be positive when speaking with student; do not put him or her down. Use encouraging language. Refrain from using controlling language. Avoid discussing student issues in front of other students.
Initiating and directing student responses	Use questions to involve the student in monitoring and understanding. Refrain from asking closed questions and ask open-ended questions to encourage student elaboration.

Note. From Project PARA (2010).

- ☐ Observe and document behavior.
- ☐ Measure IEP goals.
- ☐ Grade student papers.

- Preparation of instructional materials:
  - ☐ Reproduce/type instructional material.
  - ☐ Assist in embedding student IEP goals and objectives in lessons.
  - ☐ Develop practice lesson sheets.
  - ☐ Discuss/plan lesson reviews.
  - ☐ Organize student work samples.

- Meet with teachers:
  - ☐ Assist in planning of instructional activities.
  - ☐ Collaborate with special education teachers regarding student needs.
  - ☐ Update special education teachers on students' progress within inclusive settings.
  - ☐ Relay messages/updates between general and special education teachers.

- Attend meetings/in-services:
  - ☐ Attend faculty meetings.
  - ☐ Attend district-level professional development.

- Behavioral management activities:
  - ☐ Supervise students during transition activities.
  - ☐ Perform lunch, recess, bus, and detention duty.
  - ☐ Enforce behavior management systems.

DIRECT SERVICES PROVIDED TO STUDENTS

Paraeducators work closely with students through the implementation of various responsibilities. According to Giangreco, Broer, and Edelman (2002), paraeducators have been widely used to expand services provided within special education programs. Increased inclusive practices have inadvertently led to increased and expanded roles of the paraeducator. According to Werts, Zigmond, and Leeper (2001), there has been an escalation in the use of paraeducators within the public school systems, with a major focus on assisting students with disabilities within inclusive settings. The following is a synopsis of various roles and responsibilities of paraeducators previously suggested throughout the chapter as well as specific types of services they may provide to the students (Carnahan et al., 2009; Project PARA, 2010; SPeNSE Fact Sheet, 2001).

NONINSTRUCTIONAL SUPPORT TO STUDENTS

- Assist in the selection of programs to meet learner's needs:
  - Research computer software programs.
  - Provide feedback on effectiveness of current programs.

- Assess learner's performance:
  - Check for understanding.
  - Administer CBM.
  - Conduct oral questioning of material covered during lessons.

- Liaison between home and school:
  - Provide instructional support to students and their parents (e.g., provide a short note on homework assignment giving additional explanation).
  - Ensure important reminders are written in assignment agendas (e.g., project timelines and/or upcoming events).

- Behavior management:
  - Implement behavior management plans (e.g., PBS, point system, token economies).
  - Provide feedback and positive reinforcement to students regarding behaviors.
  - Provide appropriate assistance with academic and behavioral tasks without having the student become overreliant on the services (e.g., learned helplessness).
  - Provide redirection as needed.
  - Enforce behavior management strategies.
  - Assist in training general education teachers on behavior management procedures.
  - Update daily behavior logs.
  - Promote self-advocacy.
  - Encourage age-appropriate behaviors.

- Student supervision:
  - Supervise children on the playground.

- ☐ Monitor hallways and study halls.
- ☐ Monitor student arrival at and departure from school.

- ■ Providing personal care assistance to students:
  - ☐ Assist with feeding students.
  - ☐ Assist with dressing activities.
  - ☐ Assist with toileting activities.

- ■ Student observations:
  - ☐ Observe and document frequency of target behaviors.
  - ☐ Observe and document peer interactions.
  - ☐ Observe and document on-task behaviors.
  - ☐ Check for student understanding of materials.

INSTRUCTIONAL SUPPORT TO STUDENTS

- ■ Modify material for specialized needs:
  - ☐ Reduce the number of items on worksheets.
  - ☐ Enlarge materials.
  - ☐ Administer test and worksheet items orally.

- ■ Delivery of instruction:
  - ☐ Provide one-on-one, small-group, and large-group instruction.
  - ☐ Assist in the integration of IEP goals and objectives within the curriculum.
  - ☐ Conduct storytelling and read alouds.
  - ☐ Teach students how to problem solve academic tasks.
  - ☐ Reteach necessary skills.
  - ☐ Utilize various methods of instruction based on individual needs.
  - ☐ Promote generalization and maintenance of skills.

- ■ Facilitate peer interactions:
  - ☐ Assist in making and supporting appropriate friendship choices with fading of assistance as appropriate to ensure student autonomy.
  - ☐ Develop age-appropriate peer networks.
  - ☐ Teach students how to react appropriately in bullying and difficult social situations.

SOLUTION TO THE CASE STUDY

Ms. Gardner and Mr. Pethick immediately schedule a time to meet after school to discuss the day. Prior to the start of the meeting, Ms. Gardner and Mr. Pethick collaboratively create an agenda to guide the meeting; they list items of concern that they wish to discuss. Agenda items include: the establishment of a shared philosophy, a review of teacher and paraeducator responsibilities and expectations, a discussion regarding daily schedules, a discussion of effective communication techniques, a review of students' needs, and a discussion of classroom management techniques.

Through open discussion and active listening, the meeting between Ms. Gardner and Mr. Pethick was very effective. Specifically, they were able to establish a philosophy that included shared beliefs and goals for the class. Both individuals agreed to maintain high student expectations and positive interactions with each other and their students. They also reviewed and agreed upon teacher and paraeducator responsibilities. Together they created daily schedules and ensured they each understood their roles. A review of each student's IEP provided helpful information regarding their students' strengths and weaknesses. Ms. Gardner reminded Mr. Pethick of confidentiality issues related to students receiving special education services. Furthermore, they discussed and agreed upon classroom management techniques to ensure consistency. Finally, they scheduled a 45-minute collaboration meeting weekly and a 15-minute debriefing meeting at the end of each school day to discuss issues of the day. Needless to say . . . the second day of class ran much more smoothly!

REFERENCES

Boomer, L. (1982). The paraprofessional: A valued resource for special children and their teacher. *TEACHING Exceptional Children, 14,* 104–113.

Carnahan, C., Williamson, P., Clarke, L., & Sorensen, R. (2009). A systematic approach for supporting paraeducators in educational settings: A guide for teachers. *TEACHING Exceptional Children, 41*(5), 34–43.

Charney, R. (2002). *Teaching children to care: Management in the responsive classroom.* Greenfield, MA: Northeast Foundation for Children.

Fenichel, E., & Eggbeer, L. (1990). *Preparing practitioners to work with infants, toddlers and their families: Issue and recommendations for educators and trainers.* Arlington, VA: National Center for Clinical Infant Toddler Programs, Zero to Three.

Friend, M., & Cook, L. (2007). *Interactions: Collaboration skills for school professionals* (5th ed.). Upper Saddle River, NJ: Pearson.

Giangreco, M., Broer, S., & Edelman, S. (2002). "That was then, this is now!" Paraprofessional supports for students with disabilities in general education classrooms. *Exceptionality, 10*(1), 47–64.

Giangreco, M., CichoskiKelly, E., Backus, L., Edelman, S., Broer, S., CichoskiKelly, C., & Spinnery, P. (1999). Developing a shared understanding: Paraeducators support for students with disabilities in general education. *TASH Newsletter, 25*(1), 21–23.

Giangreco, M., Edelman, S., Broer, S., & Doyle, M. (2001). Paraprofessional support of students with disabilities: Literature from the past decade. *Exceptional Children, 68*(1), 45–63.

Haselkorn, D., & Fiedeler, E. (1996). *Breaking the class ceiling: Paraprofessional pathways to teaching.* Belmont, MA: Recruiting New Teachers.

Hofmeister, A. (1993). Paraprofessionals in special education: Alternatives to customs. *Utah Special Educators, 14*(3), 1.

Lamont, L., & Hill, J. (1991). Roles and responsibilities of paraprofessionals in the regular elementary classroom. *British Journal of Special Education, 15*, 1–21.

Office of Special Education Programs in Rehabilitation Services. (1993). *15th annual report to Congress on the implementation of the Individuals with Disabilities Education Act.* Washington, DC: U.S. Department of Education.

Pickett, A., & Gerlach, K. (1997). *Supervising paraeducators effectively in the classroom.* Austin, TX: Pro-Ed.

Pickett, A., Likins, M., & Wallace, T. (2002). *A state of the art report on paraeducators in education and related services.* Logan, UT: National Resource Center for Paraprofessionals in Education and Related Services.

Project PARA. (2010). *Paraeducator self study program.* Retrieved from http://para.unl.edu/ec

SPeNSE Fact Sheet. (2001). *The role of paraprofessionals in special education.* Retrieved from http://spense.education.ufl.edu/parasFinal.pdf

Tews, L., & Lupart, J. (2008). Students with disabilities' perspective of the role and impact of paraprofessionals in inclusive education settings. *Journal of Policy and Practice in Intellectual Disabilities, 5*(1), 39–46.

Wallace, T. (2003). *Paraprofessionals.* Retrieved from http://ufdc.ufl.edu/UF00090882/00001/1j

Werts, M., Zigmond, N., & Leeper, D. (2001). Paraprofessional proximity and academic engagement: Students with disabilities in primary aged classrooms. *Education and Training in Mental Retardation and Developmental Disabilities, 36*, 424–440.

Chapter 7

School Psychologist

Carrie Kreissl, Jacob V. Linnell, and Gary L. Cates

CASE STUDY: MRS. GOSSMAN

Arriving at the school about 7:30 a.m., Mrs. Gossman settles in at her desk. She has about half an hour to answer e-mails and phone messages related to a variety of issues and tasks spanning her district, assigned schools, and individual students on her caseload. After the communication time Mrs. Gossman examines her daily schedule to discover:

    8:00–9:00: Individualized Education Program (IEP) meeting

    9:30–11:00: Schoolwide reading screenings

    11:00–11:30: Supervision time with a student studying to be a school psychologist

    11:30–12:00: Leading an intervention group

    12:00–1:00: Working lunch with a school psychologist from another building to discuss an ongoing district initiative

    1:00–2:00: A problem-solving team meeting to discuss the evaluation of Tier II intervention services

    2:00–3:00: Finishing up a presentation on effective functional behavior assessment for the following half-day teacher in-service training she will lead

Mrs. Gossman certainly enjoys the responsibility of working on a variety of tasks on any given day. Working as a jack of many trades she does find some situations particularly challenging. Currently, she is dealing with a situation within her building related to a student receiving special education services for a specific learning disability in math. Specifically, a fifth-grade student on her caseload named Ryan has been receiving services for mathematics since the third grade. Today's 8:00 meeting will be held to determine if the student is still eligible for these services and what kinds of educational programming the student may require to be successful in the area of mathematics.

THE SCHOOL PSYCHOLOGIST'S LANDSCAPE

A school psychologist is a well-rounded professional who works collaboratively with a variety of qualified individuals and coordinated teams to ensure that the needs of all students are being met. In order to ensure that students' needs are being met, the school psychologist must function in a variety of roles while navigating through a field of laws. From a general perspective, the school psychologist must work within the framework of the No Child Left Behind Act (NCLB), the Individuals with Disabilities Education Improvement Act (IDEA), and, in many states, Response to Intervention (RTI), to assist in the insurance that (a) scientifically based intervention is being provided to all students, (b) progress monitoring of student performance is being conducted for all students, (c) the effectiveness of interventions is being evaluated, and (d) appropriate data-based decisions are being made and adhered to with regard to moving students along a continuum of service delivery (Mellard & Johnson, 2008; Prasse, 2008). To accomplish this, the school psychologist follows a systematic framework for problem solving. The following is a description of the roles and functions Mrs. Gossman will serve at the 8 a.m. meeting and the activities she has completed to prepare for this meeting.

GENERAL ROLES AND RESPONSIBILITIES OF THE SCHOOL PSYCHOLOGIST

In general, most school psychologists are trained in assessment (e.g., behavioral observation, cognitive, achievement), intervention (e.g., counseling, behavioral programming), consultation with teachers, and program evaluation (Harvey & Struzziero, 2008). Although the roles and responsibilities of a school psychologist can vary greatly according to the district (or districts) in which one is employed, the training that a school psychologist receives provides the tools and skill sets required to be successful in each of the selected roles from the district level to the individual student level.

DISTRICT-LEVEL ROLES

At a district level, a school psychologist may provide a range of services to a variety of schools. One role that a school psychologist can take is that of a data manager. With the increasing emphasis of federal legislation on accountability and implementation of RTI, school psychologists have access to important data that can be analyzed and used to predict student performance (Cates, Blum, & Swerdlik, 2011). Another role that a school psychologist can take is that of a collaborative educator. More specifically, school psychologists are able to present information in the form of district in-services and direct trainings on specific concerns within the district or in education in general.

BUILDING-LEVEL ROLES

At the building level, a school psychologist can provide a range of services that specifically relate to serving students, parents, and faculty. School psychologists are active members in problem-solving teams that target crisis intervention planning, multidisciplinary teams for special education, and the implementation of schoolwide initiatives and programs (e.g., Positive Behavioral Intervention and Support [PBIS]; Brock, Nickerson, Reeves, & Jimerson, 2008). Furthermore, school psychologists can also be active members with regard to data management and training other building personnel on initiatives and programs.

At a specific grade level, the school psychologist can provide a range of services that are tailored to a group of students. At this level, school psychologists engage in consultation with teachers about student concerns at the class level, manage data for specific students within a class, provide small-group interventions, conduct treatment integrity for small-group interventions and teacher interventions, and provide appropriate feedback to other professionals (Cates et al., 2011).

INDIVIDUAL STUDENT-LEVEL ROLES

At the individual student level, school psychologists often have direct interactions with both the students and their parents. School psychologists engage in consultation with parents and direct services with specific students to ensure that students are making adequate progress and that their needs are being met (Esler, Godber, & Christenson, 2008). School psychologists are also in the unique position to advocate for families according to state and federal law.

COMMUNICATION WITH TEACHERS AND PARENTS

One primary role for school psychologists is to ensure that teachers and parents share a common understanding. The school psychologist is likely to focus on a home-school collaboration approach (Esler et al., 2008). This approach is critical for several reasons including avoiding misunderstandings, leaving out valuable data provided by parents, and increasing generalization of skills across multiple settings. Minke and Anderson (2008) suggested that the key component in avoiding misunderstandings and other negative interactions while also gaining the most from parent involvement is through the development of a collaborative relationship between the family and the school. Research has shown that students, teachers, and parents benefit significantly in numerous ways when the students' parents are effectively engaged in their children's schooling (Henderson & Mapp, 2002).

Prior to the IEP meeting, the school psychologist may spend time with the students' parents, teachers, and other school professionals who interact with the students on a daily basis. The purpose of these interactions is to gain input from all of the IEP team members and explain the next steps in the process. Some of the basic communication skills the school psychologist has in her "tool belt" include attending to nonverbal communication, listening to understand and reflect, modeling the collaborative role, searching for strengths and positive qualities, reframing, delivering negative information, receiving negative information, and blocking blame (Minke & Anderson, 2008). The school psychologist utilizes these skills when communicating with the team members and assists in the process of developing a collaborative relationship between parents and teachers.

GENERAL PARENT AND TEACHER COMMUNICATION

Specific data that are gathered come from more systematic and structured interviews with teachers and parents. These interviews help determine whether the current struggles are based on a skill or performance deficit, specific situations when the problem is most and least likely to occur, and other contextual factors that could be contributing to the problem (Cates et al., 2011). The data are used to validate or refute hypotheses, and the hypothesis that is observable, measurable, and has the most support is identified. To accomplish this, Mrs. Gossman, the school psychologist in our case study, prepares specific questions for her structured interviews with the student's teachers and his parents. In these interviews, she focuses on establishing an operational definition of the problem, determining the specific areas of concern with mathematics, and deciding whether this is a performance or skill deficit (VanDerHeyden & Witt, 2008). The school psychologist keeps both parties updated with the current ideas and plans to ensure that everyone is working toward the same goal.

Based on an analysis of the data gathered from these interviews, the school psychologist will bring empirically supported intervention ideas to the teacher and parents and they will provide insights on the practicality of the interventions and potential obstacles in return. Once the final touches are made to the intervention, Mrs. Gossman will inform the student's parents how the intervention will look in the classroom and exactly what the procedure will be. Additionally, the student's teachers are informed how the intervention will impact the student at home (if at all). The school psychologist will also work with the student's teachers and parents on how the interventions will be monitored, establish obtainable goals, and develop a plan for checking on the integrity of implementation of the intervention (Hixson, Christ, & Bradley-Johnson, 2008). The school psychologist is in charge of creating progress monitoring data sheets for the student's teacher to use in school as well as sheets for the student's parents to use when he completes his math homework.

Mrs. Gossman, the student's teacher, and his parents will collaborate to determine if their plan was effective at a subsequent meeting. At this point, the school psychologist will gather information on treatment integrity (i.e., the extent to which the intervention was implemented as agreed upon) of the school-based interventions and self-reported integrity from the student's parents (Roach & Elliott, 2008). Additionally, the school psychologist will have collected the progress monitoring data sheets from both parties and will have entered the data into a computer program that allows her to graph data. She will therefore have detailed graphs ready for the meeting to facilitate the discussion of whether or not the intervention has been effective. During this meeting, Mrs. Gossman will work collaboratively with both parties to determine whether to continue the intervention, adjust the intervention, reduce the intensity, or drop the intervention completely (Cates et al., 2011).

Specific Teacher Communication

When a teacher becomes concerned with a student's academic or behavioral functioning, the school psychologist is often the first person formally contacted. To learn more, the school psychologist will gather additional information from the teacher on what strategies were attempted and the extent to which the strategies were successful. The school psychologist will ask the student's teacher about the current curriculum and how it is delivered. Specifically, she will ask questions about the teacher's instruction including the amount of instructional time for the subject, the arrangement of instruction, how feedback is provided, and so forth. Additionally, the school psychologist will contact any other personnel who have worked with the student at previous grade levels to determine if the current referral is a new issue or one that has been progressing over time.

In addition to communicating with teachers to determine the nature of the problem, the school psychologist will meet with the student's current teacher at the end of each week during the intervention period to update her on the student's progress with the interventions being implemented at home, ask about his progress in school, and try to address any concerns the teacher may have.

Specific Parent Communication

The school psychologist will also have ongoing communication with the student's parents. This communication will allow the student's parents to know that the school is concerned with their child's current placement and is continuing to ensure that appropriate services are being provided (Esler et al., 2008). In addition, the school psychologist will ask the student's parents to share their perspectives on his academic and/or behavioral functioning at home, inquire about any strategies that have been used, and ask about the effectiveness of these strategies. Furthermore, the school psychologist will offer up available times for the student's parents and his teacher to meet prior to any larger team meeting. The school psychologist's main goals with these interactions are to gather data from multiple settings and sources and to open the lines of communication between home and school, regardless of who made the referral (Esler et al., 2008).

In addition to opening communication with parents and gaining valuable information, the school psychologist agrees to contact the student's parents every 2 weeks to provide an update of their child's progress in school. During these phone calls the school psychologist will address any concerns the parents may have about the intervention.

Direct Services to Students

General Direct Services to Students

One of the most critical and important roles of a school psychologist lies in her direct interaction with students. School psychologists interact with students on a variety of levels and in a variety of settings. Within a RTI process, school psychologists provide services to students at a Tier 1 level. Tier 1 level services include addressing the needs of all students either schoolwide or classwide (Cates et al., 2011). This can resemble the implementation of a schoolwide system intervention, such as schoolwide universal screenings in reading, or a classwide intervention, such as a reteaching of classroom material because all students are demonstrating difficulty with a particular task (Ikeda, Neessen, & Witt, 2008). School psychologists also provide direct services to students at Tier 2. Tier 2 services include conducting more in-depth assessment and conducting small-group interventions (Cates et al., 2011). School psychologists may also provide services at the Tier 3 level. Tier 3 level services include intensified individualized evaluation and intervention services to students who are unresponsive to Tier 1 and 2 interventions (Cates et al., 2011).

Specific Direct Student Services

Interview. At the beginning of the process, Mrs. Gossman conducted an unstructured interview with the student to obtain information about him (Christ, 2008). Mrs. Gossman asked the student questions about things that he likes and does not like in school and at home to get an idea of what reinforcers/rewards may be appropriate if selected as part of the intervention plan. She also talked to him about strategies and interventions found to be helpful in the past and what he thinks his problems in mathematics are. Furthermore, Mrs. Gossman inquired about how the student thinks he learns best and which instructional methods appear to help him more in class (Christ, 2008).

Record review. To help focus her questions more systematically and have them tailored to the student, Mrs. Gossman also completed a thorough review of educational records, health records, prior tests, and reports (Christ, 2008). In addition, the review included an examination of permanent products (e.g., work samples) and records of prior strategies and their effects (Christ, 2008). A record review helps provide the school psychologist a history of the student's educational career and will help inform future decisions. After conducting the student interview and a record review, along with additional information gathered from teachers and parents, Mrs.

Gossman began to formulate and operationally define the student's problem in mathematics.

Testing. After the record review and interview, Mrs. Gossman completed specific assessments that targeted the student's problem in mathematics. Such assessments that are typically completed by school psychologists are standardized achievement tests (i.e., tests that examine many areas such as reading, writing, and math), standardized domain-specific tests (i.e., tests that examine one specific academic area), curriculum-based assessments (i.e., finding out where a student is relative to peers or a standard), curriculum-based evaluations (i.e., finding out where a student's strengths and weaknesses are relative to a curriculum), and rating scales (Cates et al., 2011; Christ, 2008).

Observations. In addition to conducting assessments, Mrs. Gossman conducted classroom observations in the student's mathematics class to get an understanding of the percentage of time the student is on-task and academically engaged in instruction. She obtained a peer comparison observation to make generalizations about the student's behavior relative to his same-grade peers. Mrs. Gossman also conducted observations of the student in different classroom environments to determine where the student's behaviors are more likely and least likely to occur. This was necessary to ensure that the student's problems are specific to mathematics or to see if they generalize to other settings.

Informed assent. After conducting the interview, record review, and classroom observations, and working out the details of the intervention logistics with the teacher and parent, Mrs. Gossman discussed the process of implementing the intervention with the student and explained to him what was expected and who he would be working with. Because the student was an otherwise bright student, Mrs. Gossman asked for input on the intervention to help increase his motivation to do well. In addition, Mrs. Gossman completed grade-level progress monitoring probes in mathematics at least twice a month. Graphing the student's progress on the progress monitoring probes provided descriptive data such as his average rate of improvement relative to peers and whether or not he was closing the gap relative to his peers.

DIRECT SERVICES TO TEACHERS

In most scenarios, the classroom teacher is responsible for implementing the agreed-upon intervention. The rationale is that the student's teacher works with the student on a daily basis and is therefore in the best position to consistently implement the agreed-upon strategy. The school psychologist is often responsible for providing fidelity checks of the intervention implementation (Roach & Elliott, 2008). The fidelity checklist is usually a sheet created by the school psychologist that outlines the specific protocol for the intervention and whether each step was followed in the observation of implementation. The school psychologist often has the responsibility to progress monitor the teacher's level of treatment integrity across multiple implementation periods (Roach & Elliott, 2008). The school psychologist utilizes this data during feedback sessions with the teacher. Finally, two other important components of this stage are the regular check-ins, where the school psychologist would provide support through positive reinforcement, and troubleshooting intervention trouble spots when necessary.

Materials Used by the School Psychologist in Making Data-Based Decisions

The school psychologist commonly uses data to make decisions. As outlined above, the most essential of these materials include: structured interviews, classroom observations, progress monitoring graphs, and fidelity checklists. Figure 7.1 displays a framework for understanding a generic path a school psychologist may travel to arrive at an IEP meeting.

Notice there are three shades to the boxes. These shades represent preintervention activities (light gray), during intervention activities (dark gray), and postintervention activities (black). Each of the above points of the school psychologist's path involves systematic data collection. We will now discuss a few methods of data collection at each point.

Tools for Preintervention Activities

One commonly utilized protocol of obtaining data at the preintervention stage is through the acronym RIOT (Christ, 2008). This multimethod, multidomain, and multisource matrix is helpful when assessing the academic environment and factors that may contribute to a student's learning difficulties (Christ, 2008).

The R in RIOT stands for review, and it is necessary to review multiple aspects, such as the student's cumulative record, the student's current and past grades to determine if a pattern is present, and examples of the student's permanent products (i.e., work samples; Christ, 2008).

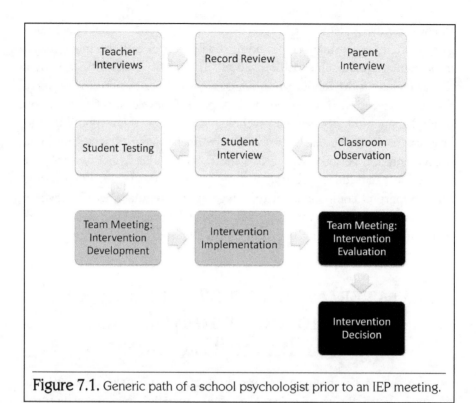

Figure 7.1. Generic path of a school psychologist prior to an IEP meeting.

The I in RIOT stands for interview and it is important for the school psychologist to conduct interviews with the teacher, the student, and the parent (Christ, 2008). Table 7.1 displays 12 questions that the authors deem crucial during teacher and parent interviews. Although this case only involves an academic concern, it is not uncommon for both academics and behavior to be a concern. We therefore provide six questions for each.

In addition to these questions, the authors find it helpful to use an instructional matrix to understand academic concerns. Figure 7.2 displays an instructional matrix that is completed for the specific area of academic concern during the teacher interview.

The O in RIOT stands for observations, which are used to help corroborate what was delineated in interviews. When conducting observations, school psychologists should collect systematic data across multiple days, times, and settings (Christ, 2008). Although a school psychologist may have his own personal methods for collecting data systematically, the teacher may sometimes be required to collect behavioral observation data. This is particularly true when (a) the behavior is not very frequent, but is intense (e.g., tantrums), (b) the school psychologist would like to get a more systematic description of the events that precede and follow the behavior, and/or (c)

Table 7.1
Crucial Questions Asked by the School Psychologist

Questions About Academics	Questions About Behavior
How are instructional assignments presented?	What does the behavior look like?
What is expected?	How often does it occur?
Where is the student currently?	What happens immediately before the behavior?
How are opportunities for practice presented?	What happens immediately after the behavior?
How is feedback provided?	What have you tried so far?
What has or has not worked?	What would you rather see?

when the psychologist is trying to determine when the most appropriate time is to visit the classroom to ensure he will be able to observe the target behavior. Figure 7.3 displays an Antecedent-Behavior-Consequence (ABC) log. Although this was not needed in the case of the student in our case study, it is a very common tool and the authors provide it here for consideration.

The T in RIOT stands for test, and testing can consist of formal and informal measures. There are essentially three levels of assessment a school psychologist may conduct. These three levels correspond to tiers in a Response to Intervention model (Cates et al., 2011) and are screening (e.g., brief skill probes), broad diagnostic testing (e.g., standardized domain-specific assessment), and individualized evaluation (e.g., curriculum-based evaluation).

Tools for During Intervention Activities

During intervention it is important that the school psychologist document two things. First, it is essential to document that the interventions are being implemented in the manner in which they were agreed upon (Roach & Elliott, 2008). This measurement of intervention integrity can be accomplished in a number of ways. Figure 7.4 is a generic intervention integrity checklist that can be adapted for a variety of interventions at a variety of levels of service for a variety of students.

In addition to evaluating treatment integrity, it is important to also document treatment effectiveness. This is usually conducted through the use of graphs depicting progress monitoring data. Figure 7.5 displays an example of progress monitoring data on a graph.

Instructional Matrix

Teacher: _____   Grade: _____

Subject: _____   Date: _____

Skill	Instructional Strategy	Materials	Arrangement	Time	Motivational Strategy	Assessment Method

Figure 7.2. Instructional matrix.

Antecedent-Behavior-Consequence Log

Student:_____   Dates: _____

Teacher: _____   Grade:_____

Date/Time	Antecedent (Where, who, and what was going on?)	Behavior (What did the student do instead?)	Consequence (What did the student get out of the behavior?)

Figure 7.3. Sample antecedent-behavior-consequence log.

TOOLS FOR POSTINTERVENTION ACTIVITIES

The data on postintervention activities can be the easiest to collect. Essentially, the postintervention activities include the final progress monitoring graph and any posttest evaluation data that may accompany the progress monitoring data.

SOLUTION TO THE CASE STUDY

It is apparent that the school psychologist, Mrs. Gossman, engaged in numerous activities related to the student's case prior to the IEP meeting. These activities included a teacher interview, parent interview, student interview, classroom observation, academic testing, teacher consultation, fidelity checks, progress monitoring, and continuous communication with both the teacher and parents. It is important to note that all of these activities required the collection and analysis of data in order to make decisions. It is not surprising that this same data-based decision-making approach will be utilized during the IEP meeting. At this point

Intervention Integrity Checklist

Student: _____   Dates: _____

Teacher: _____   Grade: _____

Integrity Observer: _____   Number of Observations: _____

Steps in the intervention	Completed	Not Completed
1.		
2.		
3.		
4.		
5.		
6.		
7.		

Place an "X" in either the "Completed" or "Not Completed" field for each step. You should have one "X" for each observation of each step.

Figure 7.4. Example of an intervention integrity checklist.

Mrs. Gossman has reviewed all of the progress monitoring data that were collected during the implementation of the intervention and all corresponding data that were generated by the selected intervention. Through a careful review of all data, Mrs. Gossman and others will decide if the student is making adequate progress. If the student is making adequate progress, the intervention can be reduced in intensity. However, if he does not demonstrate progress, the intervention may continue to be implemented or a different intervention may be implemented.

Once the team makes the decision, it is also helpful for Mrs. Gossman and the student to discuss his current progress. At this time, Mrs. Gossman will show the student graphed data and provide feedback about his performance, stressing both his strengths and areas that need continued work. The student can ask Mrs. Gossman any questions he has about his progress and be part of the decision-mak-

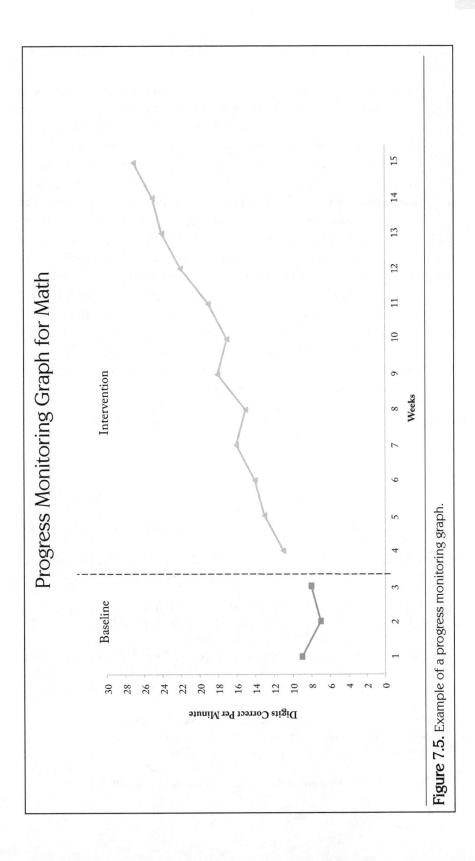

Figure 7.5. Example of a progress monitoring graph.

ing process with regard to what to will best help him next as he continues his academic career.

At 8 a.m., Mrs. Gossman enters the conference room with both parents and a parent advocate of the student. Also present at the meeting are the classroom teacher, a special education teacher, the principal, and the school social worker. Mrs. Gossman begins the meeting by suggesting that everyone introduce him- or herself. She then provides an outline for the meeting that will require about 30 minutes. The activities include a review of the reason for referral (i.e., mathematics performance with initial level of performance specified), review of the intervention that was administered (e.g., start period, frequency, duration, arrangement, logistics), review of the goals set at the initial start period (based on peer rate of improvement), a description of the treatment fidelity data, and a description of the progress monitoring data. At this point, Mrs. Gossman will open discussion to all team members about the intervention and the student's progress. After everyone has had an opportunity to provide input, a team decision is made. Based on the decision, the process described above may continue in the general education setting or special education services will be provided. In either case, Mrs. Gossman will continue engaging in similar collaborative activities with the student, his teacher, his parents, and perhaps other support professionals.

References

Brock, S. E., Nickerson, A. B., Reeves, M. A., & Jimerson, S. R. (2008). Best practices for school psychologists as members of crisis teams: The PREPaRE Model. In A. Thomas & J. Grimes (Eds.), *Best practices in school psychology* (Vol. 4; pp. 1487–1504). Bethesda, MD: National Association of School Psychologists.

Cates, G. L., Blum, C. H., & Swerdlik, M. E. (2011). *Effective RTI training and practices: Helping school and district teams improve academic performance and social behavior.* Champaign, IL: Research Press.

Christ, T. J. (2008). Best practices in problem analysis. In A. Thomas & J. Grimes (Eds.), *Best practices in school psychology* (Vol. 2; pp. 159–176). Bethesda, MD: National Association of School Psychologists.

Esler, A. N., Godber, Y., & Christenson, S. L. (2008). Best practices in supporting school-family partnerships. In A. Thomas & J. Grimes (Eds.), *Best practices in school psychology* (Vol. 3; pp. 917–936). Bethesda, MD: National Association of School Psychologists.

Harvey, V. S., & Struzziero, J. A. (2008). *Professional development and supervision of school psychologists* (2nd ed.). Thousand Oaks, CA: Corwin Press.

Henderson, A. T., & Mapp, K. L. (2002). *A new wave of evidence: The impact of school, family, and community connections on student achievement.* Austin, TX: National Center for Family & Community Connections with Schools.

Hixson, M., Christ, T. J., & Bradley-Johnson, S. (2008). Best practices in the analysis of progress-monitoring data and decision making. In A. Thomas & J. Grimes (Eds.), *Best practices in school psychology* (Vol. 6; pp. 2133–2146). Bethesda, MD: National Association of School Psychologists.

Ikeda, M. J., Neessen, E., & Witt, J. C. (2008). Best practices in universal screening. In A. Thomas & J. Grimes (Eds.), *Best practices in school psychology* (Vol. 2; pp. 103–114). Bethesda, MD: National Association of School Psychologists.

Mellard, D. F., & Johnson, E. (2008). *RTI: A practitioner's guide to implementing Response to Intervention*. Thousand Oaks, CA: Corwin Press.

Minke, K. M., & Anderson, K. J. (2008). Best practices in facilitating family-school meetings. In A. Thomas & J. Grimes (Eds.), *Best practices in school psychology* (Vol. 3; pp. 969–981). Bethesda, MD: National Association of School Psychologists.

Prasse, D. P. (2008). Best practices in school psychology and the law. In A. Thomas & J. Grimes (Eds.), *Best practices in school psychology* (Vol. 6; pp. 1903–1920). Bethesda, MD: National Association of School Psychologists.

Roach, A. T., & Elliott, S. N. (2008). Best practices in facilitating and evaluating intervention integrity. In A. Thomas & J. Grimes (Eds.), *Best practices in school psychology* (Vol. 2; pp. 195–208). Bethesda, MD: National Association of School Psychologists.

VanDerHeyden, A. M., & Witt, J. C. (2008). Best practices in can't do/won't do assessment. In A. Thomas & J. Grimes (Eds.), *Best practices in school psychology* (Vol. 2; pp. 131–139). Bethesda, MD: National Association of School Psychologists.

Chapter 8

Speech-Language Pathologist

Rita Bailey

Case Study: Joshua

Joshua Daniels is a 10-year-old boy who attends middle school in a large Midwestern town. Joshua is the second oldest of four boys and he has a language-based learning disability, which presents a difficulty with understanding and/or processing both written and spoken language. Joshua has particular difficulty learning new vocabulary as it is taught across the fifth-grade curriculum, but this difficulty is most apparent in the areas of science and mathematics. He also struggles with understanding and following directions that he hears or reads. Joshua's expressive language is filled with filler words, such as "um," "thing," or "stuff" because of his difficulties with finding words. He also has trouble recalling details of a classroom lecture.

In addition to his language-learning disability, Joshua also struggles with social anxiety disorder, which is an anxiety disorder that causes him to have an excessive and unreasonable fear of social situations. For this reason, he chooses to do everything he can to stay unnoticed in the classroom. He is well-behaved and quiet and he insists on wearing gray, nondescript T-shirts and plain blue jeans to school every day. His parents report that he often stresses about school events, such as a school holiday program, for weeks ahead of time. He has thrown tantrums at home and even has hidden from his family on the day of an event in an attempt to avoid situations that he fears most; however, these extreme responses have decreased as he has gotten older. Currently, Joshua typically tends to endure social situations when he must, but avoids them whenever possible, and he is extremely fearful of having attention called to him. Because of this disorder, Joshua masks his level of under-standing while at school and will not ask peers or adults for help when he does not understand. He does not raise his hand or look at his teachers when they ask questions, so he will not be called on to respond. His general education teacher reports that she has no indication that he is lost or confused until she grades his work.

INTRODUCTION

Speech-language pathology services for students with communication disorders in the public schools involve a variety of intervention and service delivery options. Decisions regarding intervention and service delivery are determined by multiple factors. According to the American Speech-Language-Hearing Association's (ASHA, 2000) guidelines for the roles and responsibilities of school-based speech-language pathologists (SLPs), the following principles must guide SLPs as they determine treatment plans for school-based services:

a. "Disability is a natural part of the human experience and in no way diminishes the right of individuals to participate in or contribute to society. Improving educational results for children with disabilities is an essential element of our national policy of ensuring equality of opportunity, full participation, independent living, and economic self-sufficiency for individuals with disabilities." (U.S. Congress, 1997 [Sec. 601(c)]).

b. Society's trends and challenges affect the role of SLPs.

c. Educational success leads to productive citizens.

d. Language is the foundation for learning within all academic subjects.

e. School-based SLPs help students maximize their communication skills to support learning.

f. The school-based SLP's goal is to remediate, ameliorate, or alleviate student communication problems within the educational environment.

g. A student-centered focus drives team decision-making.

h. Comprehensive assessment and thorough evaluation provide information for appropriate eligibility, intervention, and dismissal decisions.

i. Intervention focuses on the student's abilities, rather than disabilities.

j. Intervention plans are consistent with current research and practice.

k. Address the need for the specific service provider and the relation to the "team" of members involved in instruction of a child receiving this service. (p. 2)

By following these guidelines, SLPs can determine appropriate services and service delivery methods for students with communication and/or swallowing impairments.

SLPs and Services for Students With Language-Based Learning Disabilities

SLPs promote student success through interventions that target language-based learning disabilities with a focus on helping students develop language skills that will support them in the classroom. For example, SLPs may preteach key curricular vocabulary and assess students' understanding and functional use of the vocabulary prior to the introduction of a lesson or unit of study. They may work on students' ability to generalize newly learned information across the curriculum. They often work with team members to review and modify curricula according to students' specific communication needs and skills. They work directly with students or collaboratively through others to teach specific language and/or target cognitive skills that are determined to be deficient.

Clinical evidence has found that children with language disorders benefit from treatment provided by SLPs. In fact, more than 200 published investigations have indicated a high degree of effectiveness of a variety of language interventions for an overwhelming majority of children with language disorders or delays (Law, Boyle, Harris, Harkness, & Nye, 1998). Historically, the majority of SLP services were provided outside of general education classrooms. The American Speech-Language-Hearing Association introduced a model for collaborative service delivery for students with language-learning disorders in the public schools in 1991. At that time, the report indicated that the most common service delivery method involved SLPs who were working independently as they pulled students out of their general education classrooms for individual or small-group treatment sessions (ASHA, 1991). Currently, however, SLPs provide a wide range of communication services across a continuum of service delivery mechanisms within the public schools.

General Roles and Responsibilities of Speech-Language Pathologists

SLPs assess, diagnose, treat, and help to alleviate delays in development and prevent disorders related to speech, language, cognitive-communication, voice, swallowing, and fluency. In school settings, they provide individualized instruction and training for students who are not able to produce speech sounds clearly or at all. They work with students who have fluency problems, such as stuttering. They also provide interventions for students with voice problems, such as abnormal vocal pitch or quality. When students experience cognitive-communicative impairments, such as decreased attention, memory, and problem-solving abilities, SLPs provide therapy services to minimize the effects of these problems and/or to improve skills in these areas. SLPs also provide therapy services for students with difficulties understanding and producing language and students who use augmentative and/or alternative forms of communication (AAC). Students with swallowing impairments, known as dysphagia, may also receive speech therapy services from school-based SLPs (Bailey, Stoner, Angell, & Fetzer, 2008).

SLPs develop individualized therapy plans, which are tailored to each student's needs. For individuals with little or no oral speech capability, SLPs may determine appropriate AAC systems, including both low- and high-tech AAC devices, such as programmable voice output communication aids or devices, and/or sign language, and teach students their use. They help students learn to articulate sounds correctly, and teach them to decrease vocal misuse and abuse while improving their vocal qualities. They work to increase students' oral or written language skills so that they are able to understand, learn, and communicate more effectively. When students are determined to have auditory processing difficulties, SLPs help them improve their processing skills and/or learn to compensate for these deficits within classroom settings. They may work with classroom personnel to modify the classroom environment in order to maximize students' ability to learn. They also teach students with dysphagia how to improve swallowing function or use compensatory strategies to swallow without choking or inhaling foods or liquids. SLPs help individuals develop, or recover, reliable communication and swallowing skills so that students with communication and swallowing disabilities can fulfill their educational, vocational, and social roles (Bureau of Labor Statistics, 2009).

SLPs keep detailed data about initial evaluation results, individual student progress, and discharge criteria. This helps with identification of problems, monitors progress, and justifies the cost of treatment when applying for state and federal funding or, when it is appropriate, to bill Medicaid for school-based SLP services. They work closely with other professionals and school staff members by providing information that will assist them in helping students' generalize communication or swallowing skills to other settings. They also work to tie students' communication goals directly to functional gains in learning within their general education curriculum. Through use of collaborative service delivery models, they provide education and counseling for school staff members, students, and students' families concerning communication disorders and how to manage these complex issues in multiple settings. They also work with family members to recognize and change behavior patterns that may limit students' gains in areas of communication and treatment and teach communication-enhancing techniques to use at home.

COMMUNICATION WITH TEACHERS AND PARENTS

All Individualized Education Program (IEP) team members should be informed and provide input to the decision-making process in order to provide the most effective delivery of communication and/or swallowing services. The absence of establishing a consensus during the decision-making process has exacerbating effects, including gaps and overlaps in services, contradicting recommendations, and services that do not match student needs (Giangreco, 1990; Knackendoffel, 2007). It is assumed that duplication and fragmentation of services can be eliminated when the performances of diverse, specialized professionals are orchestrated (Lawson & Sailor, 2000). Strategies for improving communication within teams may include team meetings, e-mail exchanges, written notes, and verbal consultation. SLPs often need to set aside time in their daily schedules for formal or informal collaborations with team members.

SLPs and other support personnel must be willing and prepared to collaborate with others in order to maximize their efficiency and effectiveness. Effective communication between team members may provide opportunities for individuals to ask questions and to gain understanding on issues about which they are unsure. This will foster improved services for students with disabilities. Collaboration among all team members is essential when providing services for students with complex and diverse communication needs. In the past decade, there has been a clear move to foster greater collaboration among special educators to decrease segregation of staff and students (McLaughlin & Verstegen, 1998).

Collaboration as a concept is well-accepted; however, effective collaboration is sometimes difficult to effectively manage in real situations. School-based collaborative relationships are difficult to develop and even more challenging to uphold because of many factors, such as limited resources, competing priorities, and lack of professional development (Walther-Thomas, Korinek, & McLaughlin, 1999). An understanding of team dynamics and team styles, along with collaboration among team members, is needed in educational environments in order to effectively meet children's needs. Service integration and development of school connections, in addition to collaboration, are also important factors to consider when implementing team activities in schools (Bailey, Stoner, Parette, & Angell, 2006; Lawson & Sailor, 2000).

COMMUNICATION WITH PARENTS

Clear, open communication between school personnel and parents/guardians is important and usually key to fostering an effective school environment for individuals working with students with disabilities. It may be necessary to schedule extra team meetings in order to keep all individuals aware of students' changing needs and programs. Direct, face-to-face communication is often a preferred method for problem solving or even exchanging information about a student. When this isn't possible, a variety of communication options are available. New or emerging technologies may make interactive communication easier than ever before. For example, online Wikispaces may be created as a way to share general information or resources that might help other team members. A school's assistive technology team might create an online Wikispace where members post information, resources, or exchange comments. Team members can post items such as video clips depicting examples of video modeling, social stories, or scripting strategies for students using high-tech AAC devices. This may enhance communication among team members and serve to encourage collaboration and use of available resources. Other teams may prefer to use e-mail or even social networking sites to share general information. Obviously, confidential student information should be shared in more secure ways.

Some school staff members choose to communicate with parents and guardians by phone or written communication logs or exchanges. A daily communication log is one way to exchange information when students have complex communication needs (CCN) and are minimally verbal. In some environments, it may be preferable to record messages about the events of a student's school day, as recorded from her perspective, on an AAC device for parents and guardians. Parents and guardians might appreciate being able to interact with school personnel in the same way. Families of students who are verbal may not require communication from school personnel as often as those whose children are not able to share the events of their day. It is important that school personnel individualize the type and amount of communication so that it matches the needs of families of students with disabilities.

DIRECT SERVICES PROVIDED TO STUDENTS BY SLPs

SLPs often work directly with students on helping them to correct speech sound errors. This often requires a quiet environment, so this type of speech service is often provided in pull-out settings with individuals or in small groups. Students with disorders of fluency may receive education and counseling about these disorders. They may learn strategies for becoming more fluent first in smaller environments, and then work on generalizing these skills in larger group settings.

For students with language delays or disorders, SLPs determine areas of language need and develop individualized intervention plans to help them learn and successfully use language skills. For some students, this means additional support for understanding and expressing new or less familiar vocabulary. For others, it may mean instruction on language structures, such as use of appropriate syntax/grammatical structures. Still other students may have difficulties with pragmatic language, which refers to understanding and mastery of skills that enable appropriate use of language. For example, students with pragmatic language deficits may have problems understanding social language use, which may manifest as problems making and keeping friends. They may not be able to interpret others' tone of voice, facial expressions, sarcasm, use of idioms, or social communication expectations. Students with pragmatic language disorders often require direct, explicit instruction in deficient skills. Intensive speech and language intervention has been documented to produce generalizable gains in pragmatic language and communication skills in students with pragmatic language impairments (Adams & Lloyd, 2007). SLPs may also work with students without disabilities to teach peer-tutoring strategies that may benefit students with pragmatic language deficits. Supervised peer tutoring has also been used as a successful strategy to teach social language skills to students with pragmatic language disorders (Xu, Gelfer, Sileo, Filler, & Perkins, 2008).

Reading and writing are written language skills that are used to give and receive information. According to ASHA (2007), these areas are also within the scope of practice for SLPs. Spoken and written language are closely tied together. Spoken language provides a foundation for development of reading and writing. In fact, a focus on written language often can improve spoken language (Apel, 2009). For young children, SLPs provide phonological and phonemic awareness interventions. They may also be involved in teaching print awareness, letter-sound correspondences, early decoding skills, and early writing practice. While targeting reading and/or writing skills, SLPs' consistent focus is on securing the language underpinnings that support development of students' reading and writing skills. For older children with reading problems or delays, SLPs may provide direct services to improve students' reading comprehension, fluency, and rate. For students who struggle with writing, SLPs may provide direct services to improve writing competence and organizational abilities, including skills such as planning, organizing, drafting, reflecting, revising, and editing written text.

Students who are minimally verbal or who are judged to have complex communication needs may require direct services that provide instruction and support for use of augmentative/alternative modes of communication. This may include services that range from development and use of picture schedules and visual strategies (Hodgdon, 1995) to instruction, programming, use, and integration of low- and high-tech AAC devices and systems. They may work directly with students at different times during the school day to encourage use of AAC across classes and school settings.

Students with voice disorders often receive direct SLP services that involve education, instruction, and practice in voice modification. They may need to learn identification and reduction of vocal activities that are abusive or damaging to their voice. They often receive instruction and practice in use of strategies for improving vocal characteristics and qualities. Use of these strategies will need to generalize from small to larger settings within and outside of the school.

Students with cognitive-communicative impairments may require direct support in learning memory strategies or in practice in use of memory aids. They may need to work on strategies to improve their attention and focus. They often require direct support in executive functioning activities, such as reasoning, and problem-solving practice involving situations that occur in students' daily lives.

SLPs may also provide direct interventions for students with dysphagia. They may work with students to improve oral-motor movements and facilitate improved sensory reactions to oral-sensory stimuli through oral-motor exercises, oral-stimulation activities, and therapeutic feeding strategies. Some students with dysphagia may benefit from use of individually determined swallowing maneuvers or positioning strategies. SLPs may also work directly on improving students' mealtime behaviors through use of specific strategies such as antecedent manipulation or positive reinforcement methods (Bailey & Angell, 2008).

DIRECT SERVICES PROVIDED TO TEACHERS

From a speech pathology perspective, collaborative service delivery is designed to assess and treat communication impairments within natural settings and to enhance the learning experiences of children with and without disabilities (ASHA, 1991). Collaborative services may or may not replace direct services to students; they may extend or supplement students' speech pathology services. SLPs often work to provide general education teachers with specific information about individual students' communication difficulties and their instruction and learning needs. Because generalization of skills to naturalized environments is so important, SLPs may work directly with teachers to determine methods to integrate students' communication goals into their classwork. SLPs are often available for individual consultation with teachers about individualized or general curriculum modification and adaptation to promote an optimal environment for enhancing students' communication skills.

INFORMATION SLPs NEED FROM TEACHERS

In order to optimally manage students' communication impairments to help them access and succeed within the general education curriculum, SLPs need information about the scope and sequence of the curriculum. It is important to learn about individual students' areas of academic strength and difficulty. It is helpful for SLPs to be informed about weekly progress as well as problems. The following reporting tools may be helpful in promoting communication between teachers and SLPs:

- *Weekly Communication Form*: This simple form will provide SLPs with information about a teacher's perception of a student's current progress within the general education curriculum, and their perceptions about a student's areas of strength and need that may be related to their communication delay or disorder. This should help SLPs with planning communication interventions that support students' success within the general education curriculum. See Appendix A for a sample form.

- *Ecological Inventory/Classroom Communication*: An ecological inventory occurs when a team member identifies and describes in detail specific activities that occur during a classroom activity or activities. Next, the team member observes the target student and his peers during that activity, noting communication behaviors that are being displayed by the target student and those that are being displayed by his peers. From this list, activities can be identified where an increase in the quality of the student's communication abilities would be desired (i.e., the team member identifies a discrepancy in type, amount, or quality of communication between the target student and that produced by his peers). Finally, the SLP and IEP team design and implement therapeutic or instructional programs or determine adaptations, use of AAC systems, or other communication interventions that will increase the target student's ability to communicate at a level similar to his peers with greater independence and effectiveness. See Appendix B for a sample form.

- *Observation of Mealtime and Request for Interdisciplinary Consultation Form for Students With Possible Feeding and/or Swallowing Disorders (Dysphagia)*: This form was created for individuals who feed students with disabilities or supervise them during meal or snack times. By filling out this form and documenting observations, the SLP and/or other appropriate professionals will have background information and a preliminary understanding of concerns related to a student's swallowing and eating issues. This information will help school-based dysphagia team members plan for evaluations. See Appendix C for a sample form.

SOLUTION TO THE CASE STUDY

Joshua's parents reported that they were able to provide the additional support and attention needed at home to help him keep up with his peers until about the fourth grade. At this time, the level and amount of schoolwork became overwhelming to Joshua, and he began to do poorly across the curriculum, but especially on math and science seatwork and homework. His once-pleasant behavior at home began to deteriorate, and he exhibited aggression toward his brothers, as well as hiding from, hitting, yelling, and kicking his parents when it was time for him to complete homework. He often hid his assignments from his parents. He began to call himself "stupid" and "dumb" and make statements such as "I can't do that." His parents made several calls and visits to the teacher, which resulted in a referral and testing for special education and related services at the end of his fourth-grade year. Results of his case study determined that he had a language-learning disorder and also presented with characteristics of social anxiety disorder. Speech-language pathology services were scheduled to start at the beginning of Joshua's fifth-grade year, and an inclusive service delivery model was selected for use with Joshua and another student in the same class with a language-learning disability.

Joshua's IEP included a combination of pull-out and inclusive speech-language pathology services within the general education classroom and direct pull-out services provided by a school social worker. He received 60 minutes per week of language therapy provided by an ASHA certified speech-language pathologist and 40 minutes per week of direct social work support, which was delivered outside of the classroom. Joshua's social worker provided cognitive-behavior therapy on an individualized basis. This intervention helped to guide his thoughts into a more rational direction while helping him stop avoiding situations that caused him anxiety. This therapy included use of systematic desensitization procedures. This involved Joshua imagining a frightening social situation and working through various response scenarios in a safe and relaxed therapy environment. His social work program also involved real-life exposure (with the support of his social worker) to situations that Joshua feared. In addition, his social work program involved counseling to improve Joshua's self-esteem and social skills and instruction and practice in relaxation techniques, such as use of deep breathing when anxious. His parents were involved in providing the therapist with weekly written notes that highlighted Joshua's progress and any notable anxiety that he had displayed at home. His social worker also wrote a weekly progress note that was sent home. Joshua's teachers were informed to avoid certain situations that caused him anxiety, but when the social worker felt that he was able to manage certain situations in the classroom, she informed the teacher. This way, Joshua was able to take small steps toward his social work goals in a more controlled environment. The teachers were asked to collect data on Joshua's responses to certain classroom situations, and to inform the social worker about any perceived progress or problems as they occurred.

Joshua's language-learning disability included a pragmatic component, in that he had great difficulty reading social situations and understanding social language routines and expectations. This was a factor that increased his social anxiety. The SLP worked on pragmatic language skills, including communication partner expectations for conversational turn-taking, and communication breakdown, repair, and maintenance skills. She also focused on use of inferencing skills in conversational contexts. Next, practice using video clips of social communication situations was used to help Joshua improve understanding of facial expressions and body language. Finally, the SLP invited two of Joshua's more accepting peers into the therapy setting so that he could practice social conversations in a structured way, within a more comfortable environment. Joshua made rapid progress in this small-group setting, so small goals were set for spontaneous interactions with peers in his classroom. The SLP provided support as needed within the classroom to help him generalize these goals.

Joshua's speech pathology goals also included improved understanding of curricular vocabulary. This was targeted by preteaching key vocabulary from math and science units prior to class instruction on those units. Joshua and another student with a similar language-learning disability worked in the classroom during station or seatwork time with the SLP. The SLP also targeted Joshua's word-finding difficulties by creating semantic maps using written and pictorial cues of key concepts contained within his curriculum. She also worked with him on use of reading comprehension strategies such as prediction, finding the main idea, summarizing written passages, and paragraph retelling. Each week, the SLP met with the teacher to plan instruction and/or assignment modifications as needed.

Joshua was successful with these services, so additional resource time with a special educator was not needed. His grades ranged from A's to C's at the midterm, and he was judged to be performing at a level that was consistent with his abilities. Instead of providing direct services, the special educator monitored his progress and needs by consulting with the teacher, the SLP, and the social worker. The special educator attended at least one of the weekly meetings between the teacher and SLP per month. Joshua's parents reported that his behavior at home had greatly improved, and that he was experiencing fewer bouts of anxiety. When he did become anxious, he maintained his composure more frequently and verbalized his feelings more often. In the spring, he tried out for and made the track team, which was the first time he had ever willingly joined a team where he might be a focus of the attention of others. This was seen as evidence of great improvement in his self-confidence and use of coping strategies.

References

Adams, C., & Lloyd, J. (2007). The effect of speech and language therapy intervention on children with pragmatic impairments in mainstream school. *British Journal of Special Education, 34,* 226–233.

American Speech-Language-Hearing Association. (1991). *A model for collaborative service delivery for students with language-learning disorders in the public schools.* Retrieved from http://www.asha.org/docs/html/RP1991-00123.html

American Speech-Language-Hearing Association. (2000). *Roles and responsibilities of speech-language pathologists in schools* [Professional Issues Statement]. Retrieved from http://www.asha.org/docs/html/PI2010-00317.html

American Speech-Language-Hearing Association. (2007). *Scope of practice in speech-language pathology.* Retrieved from http://www.asha.org/docs/html/SP2007-00283.html

Apel, K. (2009). The acquisition of mental orthographic representations for reading and spelling development. *Communication Disorders Quarterly, 31*, 42–52.

Bailey, R. L., & Angell, M. E. (2008). ABCs of dysphagia management in schools. *ASHA Leader, 13*, 8–11.

Bailey, R. L., Stoner, J. B., Angell, M. E., & Fetzer, A. (2008). School-based speech language pathologists' perspectives on feeding/swallowing management in the schools. *Language, Speech, and Hearing Services in Schools, 39*, 441–450.

Bailey, R. L., Stoner, J. B., Parette, H. P., & Angell, M. E. (2006). AAC team perceptions: Augmentative and alternative communication device use. *Education and Training in Developmental Disabilities, 41*, 139–154.

Bureau of Labor Statistics. (2009). *Occupational outlook handbook, 2010–11 edition, Speech-language pathologists.* Retrieved from http://www.bls.gov/oco/ocos099. htm

Giangreco, M. F. (1990). Making related service decisions for students with severe disabilities: Roles, criteria, and authority. *Journal of the Association for Persons With Severe Handicaps, 15*, 22–31.

Hodgdon, L. A. (1995). *Visual strategies for improving communication: Practical supports for school and home.* Troy, MI: Quirk Roberts.

Knackendoffel, E. A. (2007). Collaborative teaming in the secondary school. *Focus on Exceptional Children, 40*(4), 1–20.

Law, J., Boyle, J., Harris, F., Harkness, A., & Nye, C. (1998). *Screening for speech and language delay: A systematic review of the literature* (Vol. 2). Southampton, UK: The National Coordinating Centre for Health Technology Assessment.

Lawson, H. A., & Sailor, W. (2000). Integrating services, collaborating, and developing connections with schools. *Focus on Exceptional Children, 33*, 1–22.

McLaughlin, M. J., & Verstegen, D. A. (1998). Increasing regulatory flexibility of special education programs: Problems and promising strategies. *Exceptional Children, 64*, 371–384.

U.S. Congress. (1997). *Individuals with Disabilities Education Act Amendments of 1997.* Washington, DC: U.S. Government Printing Office.

Walther-Thomas, C., Korinek, L., & McLaughlin, V. L. (1999). Collaboration to support students' success. *Focus on Exceptional Children, 32*(3), 1–18.

Xu, Y., Gelfer, J. I., Sileo, N., Filler, J., & Perkins, P. G. (2008). Effects of peer-tutoring on young children's social interactions. *Early Child Development and Care, 178*, 617–635.

APPENDIX A
Weekly Communication Form

Please return to SLP by _____ **(date)**

Student Name: _____ Date: _____

Teacher Name: _____

Class Name: _____

Current issues or concerns that you are having about this student that may
be related to his or her communication delay/disorder: _____

_____

_____

_____

_____

_____

Current areas of strength or accomplishments: _____

_____

_____

_____

_____

_____

Current curricular challenges: _____

_____

_____

_____

_____

Appendix B
Ecological Inventory: Classroom Communication

Student Name: _____ Student Age: _____

Teacher/Staff Member Filling Out Form: _____

How often are you with this student? (Please estimate percentage of typical school day.)_____

Date of Completion: _____

Please fill out the following form as completely as possible. Please observe the student in at least three events, focusing specifically on his or her communication behaviors in comparison to his or her peers.

Activity/Event: List student's schedule in boxes below	Describe student's communication behavior during this activity/event	Describe other students' communication behavior during this activity/event
Time of day: _____ Activity: _____		
Time of day: _____ Activity: _____		
Time of day: _____ Activity: _____		
Time of day: _____ Activity: _____		

APPENDIX C

Observation of Mealtime and Request for Interdisciplinary Consultation Form for Students With Possible Feeding and/or Swallowing Disorders (Dysphagia)

Student: _____ Age: _____ DOB: _____

Person filling out the form: _____ Title: _____

Consultation date: _____ Physician: _____

Diagnosis: _____ Disability: _____

Case manager: _____ Present diet: _____

Medical history: _____

_____

_____

_____

_____

_____

Positioning during meals: _____

Informal observations by person feeding and/or supervising school meal and/or snack times:	Yes	No	Unknown	Comments
Student's current nutritional intake appears adequate.				
Student remains alert and oriented for duration of meal.				
Student requires more time to eat than peers.				
Student exhibits audible "wet" vocal sound, cough, and vocal changes with eating or drinking.				
Student has observable respiratory changes with eating.				

Informal observations by person feeding and/or supervising school meal and/or snack times:	Yes	No	Unknown	Comments
Student gagging noticed.				
Student displays specific food avoidance behaviors.				
Student displays other limiting mealtime behaviors (i.e., crying, frustration, off-task behavior).				
Staff has noticed that student has had frequent upper respiratory infections or pneumonia.				
Student has a history of a cleft palate or other craniofacial anomalies.				
Student has documented aspiration in his or her known history.				
Student has diagnosed or known neurological impairment.				
Student has a history of non-oral feeding.				
Student has known food allergies.				
Student has a feeding tube.				
Other (please list):				

General observations: _____

_____

_____

_____

_____

_____

_____

_____

What is the primary reason for this referral for a clinical swallow assessment? What are your concerns? _____

_____

_____

_____

_____

_____

_____

_____

Request for Interdisciplinary Consultation

School: _____

Name of person making referral: _____

Given the observations that you have made, please check the individuals that should be involved in this consultation:

_____ SLP: _____

_____ OT: _____

_____ PT: _____

_____ Behavior specialist: _____

_____ Other school support personnel and/or services: _____

_____

_____

Chapter 9

Early Childhood Intervention Specialist

Laura Casey, Nicole E. Boivin, and Judah B. Axe

CASE STUDY: JASON

Jason is an 18-month-old boy whose parents contacted an early intervention agency due to their concerns about Jason's significant difficulty with transitioning to eating solid foods, his recent weight loss, and his limited communication. The child history form completed by Jason's parents indicated a history of food refusal from birth and delays in acquiring motor and communication milestones such as sitting independently, crawling, and speaking single words. Susan, an early childhood intervention specialist, completed an initial screening that indicated delays in Jason's development in the areas of communication and motor skills. A comprehensive assessment revealed moderate to significant delays in the areas of motor skills, communication, cognition, and feeding. Based on the results of the assessment and interviews with Jason's parents, Susan assisted Jason's parents in developing an Individualized Family Service Plan (IFSP) that included goals for improving each of the areas of concern. The plan recommended the initiation of early intervention services to address the concerns with Jason's development. In addition, the plan recommended that Jason participate in an evaluation with the pediatric feeding team at the local children's hospital to respond to the family's most pressing priority of improving Jason's ability to eat solid foods.

Introduction

From the moment they are born, many children are burdened with developmental delays, health problems, and social-emotional issues (Dunlap, 2009). Developmental delays manifest themselves in the areas of communication, cognition, motor abilities, sensory functioning, adaptive skills, and play. Challenges seen in a child's first few years of life arise from myriad complications including genetic and chromosomal abnormalities, brain injury, drug abuse during pregnancy, premature birth, child abuse, nutrition problems, and poor healthcare. In addition to children diagnosed with particular developmental delays, such as cerebral palsy, autism, and mental retardation, many other children are at risk for developing these disabilities.

The early childhood intervention specialist (ECIS) serves to ameliorate the difficulties associated with developmental delays and prevent further complications for children with disabilities and those at risk for delays. Children from birth to age 3 are served by the ECIS in the field of early intervention (EI), and children between the ages of 3 and 5 are served in the field of early childhood special education (Heward, 2009). Because children are within their first 5 years of life, EI services take place in children's homes, daycare settings, preschools, and center-based programs.

The importance of EI is widely agreed upon and the role of ECIS can vary (Dawson & Osterling, 1997). Parents and the ECIS are the primary providers of intervention for children under 3 years old. The period of development between birth and age 5 is perhaps the most critical for children. Foundational skills such as language, play, motor development, and social interaction develop rapidly during this time, and children with developmental delays cannot afford to miss out on this crucial period of growth. Moreover, children themselves are not the only beneficiaries of EI services; parents and other family members directly benefit by gaining the information and skills needed to foster their child's development (Brooks-Gunn, Berlin, & Fuligni, 2000). The potential effects EI can have on a child cannot be overstated. They include not only the immediate effects on the child's developmental trajectory, but also outcomes seen in later years. Specifically, EI has been shown to prevent or reduce the need for special education services and improve a child's chances of positive long-term gains (Guralnick, 2005).

The Individuals with Disabilities Education Improvement Act (IDEA, 2004) is the federal law governing the services and service delivery models for EI, special education, and related services. EI services are outlined in Part C of IDEA and are designed to:

- enhance the development of infants and toddlers (birth to 3 years) with disabilities,
- reduce educational costs by minimizing the need for special education through early intervention,
- minimize the likelihood of institutionalization by maximizing independent living, and
- ensure a smooth transition to Part B services (school-age) before the child's third birthday.

Among other changes, the 2004 reauthorization of IDEA called for employment of highly qualified teachers in EI services. To that end, in conjunction with mandates to enhance the quality of EI providers from the Division of Early Childhood of the Council for Exceptional Children (Smith et al., 2002), scholars have addressed qualifications of exemplary EI providers (Peterander, 2008). As the ECIS works with both children and families, she should have advanced knowledge of child development and family psychology. The ECIS should be apt at recognizing and treating the disorders of young children. Given the delays her clients present, the ECIS should be skilled in identifying learning and therapeutic needs as well as planning and implementing therapy. Finally, as the ECIS works on a team, she is responsible for cooperating with parents and collaborating with other professionals.

GENERAL ROLES AND RESPONSIBILITIES

In addition to general competencies, the ECIS is responsible for specific tasks required to best serve the needs of her client. Given the developmental, behavioral, and holistic nature of EI services, the ECIS must have competence in family centered practice, cross-disciplinary models of service delivery, service coordination, developing the IFSP, and teaching in natural environments (Bruder & Dunst, 2005). These five competencies are described here.

FAMILY CENTERED PRACTICE

Experts believe that the long-term success of EI programs depends not on their capacity to alter child development directly but on their capacity to alter the environment in which the child lives, especially in terms of parental and familial functioning (Shonkoff & Meisels, 2000). According to the ECIS Service Framework (Department of Education and Early Childhood

Development, Victoria, 2005), encouraging the family to take an active role in the implementation of EI services involves:

- providing family members with the opportunity to take part in the planning and evaluation of the service they receive,
- taking the family's needs and expectations into account when selecting times and locations for services and supports,
- fitting services and programs into the child's life instead of fitting the child into a program, and
- being culturally and socioeconomically sensitive to families.

Children of different cultures vary in terms of communication, play, and learning (Trawick-Smith, 2003). Family centered practice requires the ECIS to collect information regarding the culture and life experiences for each individual family. In addition to a child's immediate family, his or her neighbors, community, and societal structures are considered worthy of examination. Goals must be established that are essential to the family and will maximize the use of available resources to promote lasting change. The ECIS must also be sensitive to differences in various cultures' impressions of the nature and causes of disabilities. Families of children with disabilities may be perceived as having been given a special spiritual gift or as having engaged in some immoral activity that resulted in the child's condition (Groce, 1999). Identifying the family's cultural perspective of the child's disability will be required prior to enlisting parental participation in the intervention process. Cultural factors can strongly influence parents' social, emotional, and financial ability to be involved in their child's care.

CROSSDISCIPLINARY APPROACH TO SERVICES

Given the various needs of children receiving EI services, best practices recognize the importance and necessity of a team approach to service provision (Myers & Johnson, 2007; Shonkoff & Meisels, 2000). EI team members include parents, special education teachers, service coordinators, early childhood teachers, teacher assistants, daycare providers, speech-language pathologists (SLP), occupational therapists (OT), physical therapists (PT), and behavior therapists. In a multidisciplinary model, these professionals share assessment and intervention information with each other to provide coordinated services. However a more desirable model is transdisciplinary collaboration, in which professionals share their expertise with other team members and collaborate to conduct assessments, determine appropriate goals, and implement intervention strategies (Bruder, 1994).

Another function of crossdisciplinary services is addressing the limited number of clinicians and programs available to children. According to Myers and Johnson (2007), the breadth and depth of services can vary within a state or region as children in more rural areas are often placed on waiting lists for services. For many children, more than one clinician is required to provide adequate supports and promote improved outcomes across developmental domains. As the ECIS works most regularly with the child and family, it is ideal that she have specialized training in OT, PT, SLP, or social work. Utilizing the transdisciplinary approach to service delivery prevents fragmentation of services along disciplinary lines and the duplication of services, while emphasizing the importance of the whole child's integrated development (Trawick-Smith, 2003).

Developing the Individualized Family Service Plan (IFSP)

The IFSP is the foundation of early childhood intervention. The plan is a comprehensive picture of the child's overall levels of functioning—both areas of strength and areas requiring specialized instruction—and an outline of precisely how the intervention will be conducted. Both long-term goals and short-term objectives describe the specific skills to be addressed in the intervention plan. A child's and family's goals are identified through an assessment process, typically involving observation, a caregiver report, and direct recording of a child's performance on formal and informal measures. In addition to the results derived from evaluations, parent priority carries significant weight in the development of the IFSP. Once the priority goal areas have been identified, the ECIS assists the family in writing them in an observable, measurable format that allows all parties to assess the child's progress over time.

Another critical component of the IFSP is the service delivery plan. This specifies the amount, frequency, and type of services required for the child to achieve the goals established by the team. It also stipulates the service delivery environments most closely matching the child's areas of strengths and needs. A regular schedule of progress reporting, time frame for reevaluation, and duration of services are outlined in this plan. In all cases, the IFSP is a legal document that changes with the child to remain current and responsive to the child's ongoing developmental progress and identified areas of need. It serves as a continuous assessment of the efficacy of the intervention and a measure of the child's changing profile.

Service Coordination

According to Myers and Johnson (2007), one of the chief strategies for helping families raise children with developmental delays is providing access to ongoing supports during critical periods and crises. Service coordination requires the ECIS to connect families with natural supports and community agencies. Natural supports include spouses, extended family members, neighbors, religious institutions, and friends who can help with caregiving and provide psychological and emotional support. Community agencies may assist families in locating supports such as recreational activities, parent training opportunities, respite services, and medical and dental services, as well as funding opportunities for these services. In providing service coordination for families, the ECIS should expect to work toward the following goals:

- developing a comprehensive assessment to identify the child's and family's strengths;
- creating a strength-based, outcome-focused service plan;
- educating the family in accessing community resources;
- helping the family develop self-advocacy skills; and
- assisting the family in coordinating schedules and completing application and documentation requirements.

In some cases, the child's needs may require highly specialized interventions such as those provided by medical specialists. The ECIS will be expected to coordinate referrals to the appropriate sources if this level of care is required. An example of such a referral was seen in the case study at the beginning of this chapter. Jason's significant delays in the development of age-appropriate feeding patterns precipitated the need for evaluation by professionals specializing in pediatric feeding issues. Jason's parents relied on the ECIS to (a) recognize the need for the specialized service, (b) have knowledge of available resources in their geographical area, and (c) provide them with the appropriate contact information and process for setting up an appointment.

The ECIS carries a significant responsibility as a service coordinator, as he or she must have sufficient knowledge of the many domains of child development to identify when a child and family may need to be referred for services above and beyond those provided by the IFSP.

Focus on Teaching in the Natural Environment

A final competency of the ECIS is teaching in the natural environment. The most natural environment for a child between birth and 3 years old is her home and this is where the ECIS commonly provides services. It is in the home where a child can learn to communicate to request preferred items, open and close jars and fasteners, and take turns during a play activity with a parent or sibling. In addition to working in the home, a primary responsibility of the ECIS is developing goals and support systems leading to successful integration of children into settings considered natural or typical for same-age peers (Guralnick, 2000). Learning in inclusive settings provides the best opportunity to promote early childhood development as well as strengthen the family's capacity to support the child's growth. In typical environments, children can learn appropriate social and communication skills, practice generalizing those skills, participate in the community, and experience a sense of belonging. Facilitating integration into the community and coordination among parents and professionals requires exemplary communication skills on the part of the ECIS.

COMMUNICATION WITH FAMILY MEMBERS AND TEACHERS

As stated above, the 2004 reauthorization of IDEA called for more employment of highly qualified teachers. Another important revision was the call for more parental participation. This requires the ECIS to carefully consider the manner in which she communicates with parents and the strategies she uses to ensure complete participation. In addition to communicating with family members, the ECIS must be skilled at working together with a team of other professionals.

COMMUNICATING WITH FAMILY MEMBERS

First and foremost, the ECIS must be sensitive to the uniqueness of families and the cultural backgrounds forming a family's perspectives. Withrow (2008) suggested that two cultural competencies of the ECIS are awareness of her own culture and biases and awareness of her client's culture. Withrow recommended four steps for achieving those competencies:

- developing self-awareness of one's own culture and assumptions,
- inquiring about and understanding the family's community,
- identifying the family's approach to raising a child and coping with a disability, and
- assessing the extent to which the family assimilates with the mainstream culture.

Cultural competence can be a lifelong pursuit and critical for effectively communicating with families.

For many families, EI involves multiple assessments and appointments with various specialists. Given this complexity, the ECIS is responsible for informing parents of all specialists' and team members' roles and respon-

Parent Perspectives for Program Development

1. What are your major priorities for your child's program for the next year?
2. What do you believe to be your child's strengths and weaknesses?
3. Are there concerns about your child's functioning that could/should be addressed in other settings (outside of the home)?
4. What kind of support or help, if any, does your child need during routines such as eating, dressing, toileting, napping, and so forth?
5. Are there aspects of your child's behavior that you believe need to be improved?
6. What methods have you found to be effective in rewarding or disciplining your child?
7. To what extent does your child interact with children in the neighborhood? Do you want help increasing your child's social skills?
8. How would you like to be involved in your child's program?

Please use the back of this form to share any additional information about your child and to ask any questions you may have about your child's program.

Figure 9.1. Parent perspectives for program development questionnaire.

sibilities throughout the process. Pragmatically and ethically, the ECIS is obligated to describe and explain in *nontechnical language* assessment procedures and ongoing goal development for the child, as well as the specific intervention strategies being employed. As children are evaluated, families must know about eligibility determination. The ECIS must be well-informed as eligibility criteria vary by state. Further, parents and caregivers may need information about typical child development. New parents may not fully understand the typical milestones or timeframes in which developmental skills are acquired. Typical development has implications for parents' ability to comprehend their child's skill level, establish realistic goals, and evaluate their child's rate of progress as compared to age-appropriate benchmarks. The ECIS can use the questionnaire in Figure 9.1 to help families document how they see their child's progress in EI. In addition, the documentation checklist in Figure 9.2 will help families keep track of the written and verbal communication related to their child's progress.

During intervention, families need ongoing support to implement the strategies proposed by the team. Strategies may include encouraging and facilitating the child's communicative initiations, appropriately using adaptive equipment, properly positioning the child to facilitate motor development, and decreasing challenging behaviors interfering with intervention. The ECIS is available to families receiving progress reports and other feedback on the efficacy of their child's EI experiences. The ECIS must inform

Documentation Checklist

It is essential to retain records of all written and verbal communication related to your child's early intervention services. This information may be used to maintain recommendations, measure progress, document results of discussions, and resolve disputes. Keeping all documentation in one place will help organize the information and make it easily accessible when it is needed. Examples of information to maintain in a child's record include:

_____ Letters and notes from doctors, therapists, etc.

_____ Results and reports from medical and educational evaluations

_____ Notes from meetings about the child's intervention

_____ Therapists' reports

_____ IFSP and IEP records

_____ Information regarding the child's developmental history

_____ Medical information including vaccinations, allergies, etc.

_____ Family medical histories

Parents and therapists may wish to design their own system of documentation that best meets their needs. A sample record-keeping worksheet for documentation of communication may include the following:

Problem/Topic: _____

Name of person or agency you talked to:_____

Name of contact person (may be same as above): _____

Date of contact: _____

Phone number: _____

Results of discussion: _____

Action taken: _____

_____

_____

Figure 9.2. Documentation checklist.

families of all available opportunities to revisit the appropriateness of goals based on their child's progress and changing priorities.

It is important to note that working with young children with disabilities and their families is often emotionally charged. As families struggle to determine who will assist them, they may seek support that goes beyond the scope of the ECIS role. It can be difficult to maintain clear boundaries when working so closely with someone's child, sometimes involving daily visits to their home and being intimately involved in many facets of their lives. The ECIS has a responsibility, however, to set and adhere to clear and unambiguous boundaries to maintain an appropriately objective and professional relationship with the family. The ECIS should not discuss personal matters with families. This involves paying attention to information shared on social networking websites and other social media. The ECIS is strongly encouraged to maintain strict privacy settings in online profiles to prevent blurring of professional and personal boundaries (Taylor, McMinn, Bufford, & Chang, 2010).

Grieving parents dealing with a recently diagnosed child may seek assurance that their child is fine. The ECIS has an obligation to be truthful and tactful with parents as she discusses the needs of the child and family. This supports the family in establishing realistic goals and timelines for success. As part of her service coordination role, the ECIS can recommend therapeutic services for families to cope with the challenges of having a child with a disability. To be clear about roles and boundaries, the ECIS should review roles, responsibilities, and schedules from the outset of service delivery. As family members may call therapists excessively during nontherapy times, the ECIS should be prepared to set and maintain a schedule outlining availability. This will assist the family in placing value in scheduled activities and empower the family to support their own child in the ECIS's absence (The College of Psychologists of Ontario, 1998).

Communicating With the Team

Because EI typically utilizes a transdisciplinary approach to service delivery, one of the most essential responsibilities for the ECIS involves facilitating communication among all service providers and family members. Depending on the child's specific needs, a number of specialists may be required to contribute their unique expertise in the areas of communication, motor development, and behavior.

The ECIS should follow several specific guidelines when communicating with parents and other team members, including:

1. *Utilize technology to increase availability*: The ECIS should have access to telephone, e-mail, and several methods for receiving and returning messages.

2. *Schedule time to respond to and coordinate team correspondence*: Technology such as web-based meeting participation, conference calling, and private message boards will help to facilitate regular communication among team members.

3. *Structure meetings to balance participation and encourage family participation*: This can be done by setting an agenda for group meetings and following a system for allotting all members a specified amount of time to present during meetings.

Communication with team members requires flexibility and accessibility. This means the ECIS has to be flexible in accommodating families' schedules. The ECIS should establish a system for disseminating information to all team members quickly and efficiently, such as creating a contact list for all team members. In some cases, the distribution of information may be time sensitive, and compliance with legally required time frames must be ensured. The ECIS should make every effort to make communication *pro*-active versus *re*active. Establishing a culture of regular communication and information sharing among team members can help increase comfort and familiarity with one another's professional roles and interaction styles, making communication more efficient during formal meetings and discussions.

With regard to participation in meetings, the ECIS may need to prepare the family members to support them in providing input for prioritizing their concerns in an objective, outcome-based manner. This preparation provides a focal point during the team meeting, potentially aiding in maintaining family members' emotional regulation in the face of difficult discussions. In addition, the ECIS may need to guide parents in using a record-keeping system to maintain progress documentation, discussion topics, meeting outcomes, and evaluation reports. The amount of information amassed during EI can be overwhelming, making it difficult for even the most experienced parents to recall what was said at crucial points throughout the process.

Finally, if disputes arise between parties with regard to the IFSP, IDEA outlines a sequence for resolution. Under the law, parents are provided the right to a due process hearing in which they pose arguments about a child's intervention services and a judge makes the final decision. In most cases, however, parents attempt to resolve differences with community agencies through a formal process of mediation or a resolution session prior to a due process hearing (IDEA, 2004). This can help the family members preserve a collaborative relationship with the agency as their child's care continues.

DIRECT SERVICES PROVIDED TO STUDENTS

Communicating with parents and team members is an essential role of the ECIS, although perhaps an even more critical role is providing direct services to children, parents, and teachers. With children, the ECIS conducts assessments and provides direct intervention.

ASSESSMENT

One of the first interactions the ECIS has with a child referred for services is conducting a screening of the child's developmental skills. A screening may involve observing the child engaged in naturally occurring activities or formally measuring the child's cognitive, language, motor, and social-emotional development. Common screening tools used in EI are the Denver II (Frankenburg & Dodds, 1990) and the Ages and Stages Questionnaire (Bricker & Squires, 1999). In cases where the results of the screening indicate the child is demonstrating potential developmental delays, the ECIS will recommend a more formal and comprehensive series of assessments. This may include administration of standardized assessments such as the Battelle Developmental Inventory (Newborg, 2006) and the Bayley Scales of Infant Development–III (Bayley, 2005).

Following the completion of assessments, the ECIS convenes a meeting with parents and other specialists whose input is required. At this time, the team develops the IFSP. Specific long-term goals and short-term objectives are created based on the results of the initial evaluations. In addition, the IFSP specifies the proposed amount of services required for the child to achieve her goals.

SERVICE DELIVERY

Initiating therapy to promote long-term success utilizing data-driven teaching requires the ECIS to be well versed in writing measurable objectives, generating data collection systems, and implementing prompt fading techniques. Once measurable objectives have been established, the ECIS creates data collection systems to track day-to-day demonstration of skills, demonstrate trends in performance, and determine appropriateness of intervention strategies. For example, if data show a child is not able to identify a specific color when provided with the prompt "Pass the green block," the ECIS is responsible for determining the level of prompting needed to promote more correct responses. For example, a pointing prompt would be considered more supportive than the previous step and would be monitored and faded as the child gains independence.

The ECIS carries a large part of the responsibility for the execution of individual and group therapy activities that have been recommended for the child. This requires knowledge of particular teaching strategies and experience in planning and carrying out activities integrating the goals and objectives from the IFSP. As specialists suggest particular methods of instruction, the ECIS must be adept in the use of relevant materials, equipment, and technology targeting the child's unique areas of need. In some cases, proficiency in the use of a particular method or therapy tool may be required. The ECIS serves as the liaison between specialists and parents, modeling and monitoring the recommended techniques.

Maximizing a child's active engagement in therapy sessions is also critical for the ECIS. This includes thorough preparation and ongoing maintenance of therapy equipment and materials, as well as balancing the use of familiar toys and materials with novel items and activities to maintain the child's interest and cooperation during therapy. Sessions should include both child-directed and adult-directed activities to facilitate participation and engagement while also ensuring ample opportunities for the child to practice target skills within sessions. In addition, activities should be designed to promote skill development within the child's natural routines to promote generalization of skills to activities outside the therapy session.

DIRECT SERVICES PROVIDED TO PARENTS AND TEACHERS

Due to the heavy emphasis on family centered services, the ECIS not only works directly with students, but also teaches parents how to meet the needs of their children. As children enter EI programs, the ECIS also provides support to teachers to ensure skill development.

DIRECT SERVICES TO PARENTS

To meet the diverse needs of their children, and because the ECIS often spends only 1–5 hours in the home each week, parents must learn to support the acquisition, mastery, and generalization of their children's skills. Modeling and coaching are two major tools the ECIS uses to facilitate this direct service. Modeling involves demonstrating teaching strategies and explaining to parents why they are used. For example, a child with a language delay may be learning to use sign language to ask for preferred items such as a well-loved book. The ECIS will demonstrate to the parent how to hold up a book, form the child's hands into the sign, and deliver the book when the child has made the sign. Learning a new communication system like sign language takes hundreds of repetitions of practice and parents must learn to provide that practice (Ingersoll & Dvortcsak, 2006; Peterson, Carta, & Greenwood, 2005).

Challenging behavior is a common concern for children in EI, and parents must learn to promote positive behavior (Gross et al., 2003; Kaiser & Hester, 1997; McIntyre, 2008). It is common for the ECIS to conduct a functional behavior assessment to identify the motivation for the challenging behavior, such as to gain attention. An intervention often involves withholding attention for challenging behavior, such as screaming, and providing attention when a child asks nicely, such as by saying, "Mommy." The ECIS must provide many examples of modeling the implementation of such an intervention and provide positive and corrective feedback to parents to ensure proper implementation. Consistency is critical in working to decrease challenging behavior.

DIRECT SERVICES TO TEACHERS

The ECIS provides a range of services to teachers in early childhood centers and preschool settings to ensure a child's growth and progress. In general, the ECIS supports teachers in providing instructional adaptations and modifications to the curriculum of the targeted students (Sandall, Schwartz, & Joseph, 2000). EI programs offer many engaging activities, such as centers, games, story time, and circle time. The ECIS often works with teachers to identify specific opportunities for children to practice communication, motor, and social skills. For example, if a circle time activity involves props, such as masks, a child with a social-emotional delay can be asked to pass out the masks, make eye contact with each child, and say each child's name as he hands her a mask. By embedding learning opportunities into ongoing activities, children have many chances to use their skills and receive feedback on them.

In addition to embedded instruction, the ECIS supports the EI teacher in setting up activity schedules for students. A teacher can use a general activity schedule for a whole day and smaller activity schedules for each activity. In EI classrooms, activity schedules are usually comprised of pictures depicting the activities such as circle, centers, and snack time. Picture schedules can help children with developmental delays learn the routines of the classroom and transition smoothly between activities. Teachers often use timers to indicate the beginning and end of activities during the day.

Applied behavior analysis (ABA) is a conceptual framework and a set of procedures used to teach the many skills young children need to learn (Cooper, Heron, & Heward, 2007). The major strategy in ABA is positive reinforcement—presenting preferred items and activities immediately after observing a desired skill and seeing that skill increase in the future. Positive reinforcement is critical in shaping new communicative skills and the ECIS, in conjunction with an SLP, can help teachers learn to use augmentative communication systems, such as sign language, picture exchange, communication boards, and voice output devices. ABA methods are prominent in the management of challenging behavior as the ECIS identifies the reinforcer for problem behavior and teaches students to ask appropriately for that reinforcer. In the area of social skills, the ECIS can teach teachers to program opportunities for children to interact. For example, in peer-mediated intervention, a teacher gives peers preferred items and prompts a target child to ask for them. Finally, the ABA methods of task analysis and chaining are useful in teaching adaptive skills, such as feeding, dressing, toileting, and hand washing. The ECIS with expertise in ABA methods can use modeling, prompting, coaching, and feedback to support teachers in using those strategies.

Solution to the Case Study

Jason's intervention began with three sessions per week of individual therapy with Susan in the family's home. Initially, Susan focused on developing a relationship with Jason while she worked on gradually increasing his willingness to engage in activities that she presented. Because Susan was aware that improving Jason's ability to eat solid foods was of highest priority to his parents, she wanted to begin working on this as soon as possible. This required a delicate balance of moving steadily toward introducing opportunities for food consumption while not placing too many demands on Jason too quickly. Susan began by observing as Jason's parents fed him a typical meal. She noted that Jason's positioning was a challenge, with his parents often changing his posture and readjusting him numerous times throughout the meal. She suggested that a consultation from an occupational therapist be initiated in order to explore specialized seats that may alleviate this problem during feedings. Once the appropriate seating was acquired, the next several weeks focused on coaching Jason's parents through short snack activities, targeting appropriate seating and gradual introduction of his favorite foods from a spoon.

After 3 months, a report of Jason's progress was due. Susan gathered documentation, including progress reports and therapists' data, and compiled the information into the appropriate segments of his IFSP. According to the data, Jason was consistently sitting in his specialized high chair for three brief snacks per day, and accepting at least five different types of foods from a spoon. At this point, Susan convened a meeting of all team members to review Jason's progress and update the goals and objectives in his plan. Jason's parents stated that they were very pleased with his progress thus far and wanted to maintain the gains that he had made, while shifting some of the focus of therapy sessions to interventions that would begin to improve his communication skills.

The next week, Susan scheduled a co-therapy session with the speech-language pathologist to work on strategies to facilitate language production. Together with Jason's parents, they decided to work on teaching Jason to make requests during the snack activities. Susan coached Jason's parents in strategies that would encourage him to request items that he wanted. The SLP provided the team with picture cards that Jason could point to as a way to indicate the foods he wanted to eat during snack times.

Because of the team's use of a transdisciplinary approach to Jason's therapy, he made steady progress in his communication skills and oral intake of solid foods during the initial months of therapy. At the 6-month review of his IFSP, Jason's parents reported that they were now consistently able to identify what Jason wanted to eat and they knew how to help him eat his favorite foods on a daily basis. New goal areas and next steps for therapy were established, including beginning to teach Jason how to feed himself during meal times and communicating when he wanted to be finished with the meal. Jason continued to make gains in his development with the team's consistent provision of therapy and close monitoring of his progress.

References

Bayley, N. (2005). *Bayley Scales of Infant Development* (3rd ed.). San Antonio, TX: Harcourt Assessment.

Bricker, D., & Squires, J. (1999). *Ages and Stages Questionnaires: A parent-completed child-monitoring system* (2nd ed.). Baltimore, MD: Brookes.

Brooks-Gunn, J., Berlin, L. J., & Fuligni, A. S. (2000). Early childhood intervention programs: What about the family? In J. Shonkoff & S. J. Meisels (Eds.), *Handbook of early childhood intervention* (2nd ed.). Cambridge, UK: Cambridge University Press.

Bruder, M. B. (1994). Working with members of other disciplines: Collaboration for success. In M. Wolery & J. S. Wilbers (Eds.), *Including children with special needs in early childhood programs* (pp. 45–70). Washington, DC: National Association for the Education of Young Children.

Bruder, M. B., & Dunst, C. J. (2005). Personnel preparation in recommended early intervention practices: Degree of emphasis across disciplines. *Topics in Early Childhood Special Education, 25,* 25–33.

The College of Psychologists of Ontario. (1998). *Professional boundaries in health-care relationships.* Retrieved from http://www.cpo.on.ca/assets/71EFBC74-EEDB-44FB-A3B0-8EFC342072E0.pdf

Cooper, J. O., Heron, T. E., & Heward, W. L. (2007). *Applied behavior analysis* (2nd ed.). Upper Saddle River, NJ: Merrill/Prentice Hall.

Dawson, G., & Osterling, J. (1997). Early intervention in autism: Effectiveness and common elements of current approaches. In M. J. Guralnick (Ed.), *The effectiveness of early intervention: Second generation research* (pp. 307–326). Baltimore, MD: Brookes.

Department of Education and Early Childhood Development, Victoria. (2005). *Early childhood intervention services (ECIS) program framework.* Retrieved from http://www.eduweb.vic.gov.au/edulibrary/public/earlychildhood/intervention/framework2005.pdf

Dunlap, L. L. (2009). *An introduction to early childhood special education: Birth to age five.* Upper Saddle River, NJ: Pearson.

Frankenburg, W. K., & Dodds, J. B. (1990). *The Denver II training manual.* Denver, CO: Denver Developmental Materials.

Groce, N. E. (1999). Disability in cross-cultural perspective: Rethinking disability. *The Lancet, 354,* 756–757.

Gross, D., Fogg, L., Webster-Stratton, C., Garvey, C., Julion, W., & Grady, J. (2003). Parent training of toddlers in day care in low-income urban communities. *Journal of Consulting and Clinical Psychology, 71,* 261–278.

Guralnick, M. J. (2000). An agenda for change in early childhood inclusion. *Journal of Early Intervention, 23,* 213–222.

Guralnick, M. J. (2005). Early intervention for children with intellectual disabilities: Current knowledge and future prospects. *Journal of Applied Research in Intellectual Disabilities, 18,* 313–324.

Heward, W. L. (2009). *Exceptional children: An introduction to special education* (9th ed.). Upper Saddle River, NJ: Pearson.

Individuals with Disabilities Education Improvement Act, Pub. Law 108-446 (December 3, 2004).

Ingersoll, B., & Dvortcsak, A. (2006). Including parent training in the early childhood special education curriculum for children with autism spectrum disorders. *Topics in Early Childhood Special Education, 26,* 179–187.

Kaiser, A. P., & Hester, P. P. (1997). Prevention of conduct disorder through early intervention: A social-communicative perspective. *Behavioral Disorders, 22,* 117–130.

McIntyre, L. L. (2008). Parent training for young children with developmental disabilities: Randomized control trial. *American Journal on Mental Retardation, 113,* 356–368.

Myers, S. M., & Johnson, C. P. (2007). Management of children with autism spectrum disorders. *Pediatrics, 120,* 1162–1181.

Newborg, J. (2006). *Battelle Developmental Inventory* (2nd ed.). Chicago, IL: Riverside.

Peterander, F. (2008). Preparing practitioners to work with families in early childhood intervention. *Educational and Child Psychology, 21,* 89–101.

Peterson, P., Carta, J. J., & Greenwood, C. (2005). Teaching enhanced milieu language teaching skills to parents in multiple risk families. *Journal of Early Intervention, 27,* 94–109.

Sandall, S., Schwartz, I., & Joseph, G. (2000). A building blocks model for effective instruction in inclusive early childhood settings. *Young Exceptional Children, 4*(3), 3–9.

Shonkoff, J. P., & Meisels, S. J. (2000). *Handbook of early childhood intervention* (2nd ed.). Cambridge, UK: Cambridge University Press.

Smith, B. J., Strain, P. S., Snyder, P., Sandall, S. R., McLean, M. E., Ramsey, A. B., & Sumi, W. C. (2002). DEC recommended practices: A review of 9 years of EI/ECSE research literature. *Journal of Early Intervention, 25,* 108–119.

Taylor, L., McMinn, M. R., Bufford, R. K., & Chang, K. B. T. (2010). Psychologists' attitudes and ethical concerns regarding the use of social networking web sites. *Professional Psychology: Research and Practice, 41,* 153–159.

Trawick-Smith, J. (2003). *Early childhood development: A multicultural perspective* (3rd ed.). Upper Saddle River, NJ: Pearson.

Withrow, R. L. (2008). Early intervention with Latino families: Implications for practice. *Journal of Multicultural Counseling and Development, 36,* 245–256.

Chapter 10

School Nurse

Mary Volle Cranston

CASE STUDY: SUSAN JOHNSON

In the summer of 2009, concerns were raised about the potential for a pandemic. A new flu, H1N1, had been identified and was beginning to impact the Southwestern portion of the United States. Being aware of the potential for an emergency situation, Susan Johnson, the school nurse of the local community's junior high began to prepare for this potential issue. Schools are a prime site for the propagation of illnesses in the community.

To prepare for this situation, Susan turned to national health resources to assist her in developing a plan for prevention of this illness. Her concern particularly focused on the special needs classes in the junior high school. Susan knew from the review of literature that H1N1 had its greatest impact on those under the age of 19 who had preexisting health conditions. Susan reviewed the recommendations of the Centers for Disease Prevention and Control (CDC) and assessed the resources she had readily available. She created a plan to implement in case of an H1N1 epidemic and discussed the situation with school administrators. Susan also let the faculty know of the possibility. To communicate her plan, Susan sent an e-mail to faculty and staff regarding the CDC's concerns over the risk of a pandemic event and addressed questions at the faculty development day prior to the first day of school.

In early September, Susan noted an increase in the number of students missing school due to fever, vomiting, and muscle pain. The students in the special needs classrooms represented a significantly larger portion of this population compared to the general school population. Susan notified the principal and implemented the

H1N1 plan, focusing on the special needs classroom where the issue began. Susan also notified the health department as well as other school nurses of the situation at the junior high.

Susan contacted and met with the teachers and staff of the special needs classrooms first. She carefully outlined what interventions staff could put in place to protect themselves and students from developing H1N1. She advocated for immunization among staff and students who could receive flu vaccinations. Susan wrote an article for the school's parent newsletter and made flyers that included information on identifying the symptoms of H1N1 and asking that parents keep children displaying these symptoms at home. Similar flyers were posted for the school at large, outlining for children simple interventions that could be put in place.

For the special needs classrooms, Susan sent a letter to all parents identifying the symptoms that could indicate their child had H1N1, identifying resources and actions to help prevent the illness, and asking for the parents' cooperation in protecting other children and faculty. She worked with faculty to make resources such as hand sanitizer and bacterial wipes for cleaning surfaces available to the classrooms. Tissue was purchased for the classrooms in addition to the supply donated by staff and families. Janitors were asked to empty the trash twice during the day to further diminish exposure to contaminated products. Hand sanitizers were also made available in the cafeteria to encourage hand washing before meals. Susan provided educational programs for the students and visited classrooms daily to reinforce teaching and observe students and support teachers.

Joe, a student with cerebral palsy, became quite ill and had to be hospitalized. During this hospitalization, Joe had to be placed on a ventilator and became more physically dependent due to increased fatigue and the restrictions using a ventilator created for him. Susan and Joe's teacher, Donna, kept in contact with Joe's parents. With Joe's parents' permission, the teacher kept his classmates informed of Joe's progress.

GENERAL ROLES AND RESPONSIBILITIES

School nurses play a highly varied and unique role in the health and wellness of children with disabilities in the school system. The primary focus of a school nurse is to ensure that all students within the system will be able to maximize their educational opportunities (National Association of School Nurses, 2002). What this means is that the school nurse is accountable for ensuring that all school children are well and able to take full advantage of the opportunities and learning provided to them in a school setting. Being healthy and having their physical and emotional needs met helps children to focus on the task at hand—learning. Children with disabilities, especially those who are medically fragile, who have complex medical issues, or who have trauma-related disabilities, can lose whole chunks of educational time because of medical issues. Moving to a school environment requires thoughtful assessment of these children's needs and removal of barriers that may interfere with or will need to be addressed during the provision of education (Wolfe, 2006). School nurses need to be a coordinator and communicator regarding the students' healthcare issues and environmental needs; a consultant to families, administrators, teachers, and staff regarding health; an advocate for the student as well as the staff; and an educator who assists the school system, family, and student in understanding the health challenges and health promotion choices they face.

NURSING PROCESS

To best understand the role of the school nurse, it helps to understand that nurses organize and deliver nursing care utilizing the nursing process. This process entails the following functions defined as assessment, identification of the nursing issues or nursing diagnosis, planning, intervention, and evaluation. This is why nurses are often adamant about participating in Individualized Education Program (IEP) meetings and Section 504 Plans. Nurses are taught to utilize information that they obtain from their own assessments along with the input from other disciplines, parents, and students to identify the student's needs and determine a plan of care with the best approaches for meeting these needs. Nurses may participate either actively as a team member or as a consultant in the assessment of a child's health status and the healthcare needs of a child with disabilities within the school system (American Academy of Pediatrics, 2000, 2008).

One of the most visible roles the school nurse carries out is that of urgent healthcare responder. When illness, injury, or health issues arise at school, it is the nurse's responsibility to stabilize the issue, return the child (able to learn) to the classroom as quickly as possible, or to refer the child to the parent for healthcare follow-up (Kruger, Radjenovic, Toker, & Comeaux, 2009; National Association of School Nurses [NASN], 2006). For the child with disabilities, this action requires careful assessment of changes in his health status. The nurse must have an active understanding of what is normal for each child to be able to safely and accurately evaluate the child's health state.

COMMUNICATION

School nurses are required to establish Individualized Health Plans (IHP) and Emergency Action Plans (EAP) for all students with special needs and disabilities (Raymond, 2009; Zimmerman, 2006). These plans address a child's health and urgent care needs in simple, easily understood language. The plans provide other nurses, faculty, staff, and the child's parents with a clear plan of how the child's needs and any emergency related to those needs will be addressed at school. Input from the student, his family, educators, healthcare providers, and related service personnel are needed in order to create a plan that will work best for that particular student while at school or while being transported to and from school by the district. Discussing the identified plan with the parents, staff, and student, and educating the teachers and other school personnel involved in the child's school day are essential roles of the school nurse. Communicating further with parents, students, and teachers assists the nurse in evaluating the impact of this plan, helping to ensure the health and safety of the child while he is at school.

Participating in the IEP or Section 504 Accommodation Plan assists the school nurse in assuring that the school system has the appropriate services available. Information from the IHP can then be incorporated into the IEP. These meetings provide the school nurse with an opportunity to communicate and explain clearly the student's health needs to all involved with that student in the school setting (Raymond, 2009). Questions from all parties can be answered. Furthermore, the nurse benefits from the opportunity to receive feedback regarding the IHP and the EAP from those who work in the classroom and know the student best. With this information, both plans can be corrected and evaluated for effectiveness.

Developing trusting relationships and clear communication with families as well as teachers is vital to ensuring that the ongoing needs of the student are met and clearly communicated to the school and its educators. The nurse often acts as a liaison between the school and the medical community. Her role is to assist healthcare providers and the family in understanding the needs of the school and the needs of the student. The nurse can be the one member of the student's team who can help translate the medical component of his needs for all parties (Selekman, 2006).

This same trust relationship must be developed between the school nurse and the educator as well. School nurses need to help teachers and faculty to feel comfortable in being able to express their fears and concerns regarding a child's health status. The teacher needs to feel that her questions about the child's healthcare condition are not unwelcome. Both the nurse and the teacher have a level of expertise and knowledge about the child that, when combined, can help facilitate positive outcomes.

Direct Services Provided to Children

The school nurse plays a variety of roles that are clearly defined (Selekman, 2006). First, school nurses must address the needs of the well student. This includes children with disabilities. Disability is not always an ill state. Even those with chronic illnesses and medical challenges are able to attain a level of wellness. This level of wellness is individual to the student, needs to be maintained, and if possible, enhanced for all students. Nurses must assess the immunization and TB status of all school-age children, assure that healthcare screenings are current (e.g., vision, hearing, dental, physicals), and refer students to community healthcare providers that can assist in addressing issues identified in the school system (American Academy of Pediatrics, 2008). School nurses also attempt to enhance awareness and educate students on positive health habits and the self-management of their health (American Academy of Pediatrics, 2008). Positive reinforcement of health practices among parents and students have been shown to impact lifelong health practices (NASN, 2004). Students with disabilities are not excluded from this group. These children and young adults face the same healthcare challenges and have the same need for the development of healthy life habits as any other child. This includes the need for an understanding of the role of exercise, diet, stress management, self-protection, and sexual education.

The management of children with chronic, ongoing health problems requires the school nurse to assist in coordination of this care between parents, providers, and the school. The nurse must come to understand the specific needs of the student, develop a management plan for these needs, and educate school personnel and students in regard to the child's medical needs and illness referred to as an Individualized Health Plan (IHP; NASN, 2008). School nurses must assess and evaluate the appropriateness of services provided by the school to the medically needy child. This involves the nurse gaining as much information as she can regarding the student's health status (Figure 10.1 can help nurses gather some of the information they need). Often nurses will develop or utilize an assessment format for diseases commonly encountered in the school setting. Parental permission is necessary for contact with healthcare professionals so nurses must also be good communicators and able to establish working relationships with parents and students. Interactions with families and involved healthcare providers allow the nurse to assess the student's health status, both the student's and the parents' understanding of the condition, and the impacts this condition has

---

Information Needed From Teachers

Information regarding the student:

Absence from school: Was it anticipated and why? _____

Plan for return to school: _____

Change in behaviors noted in the classroom (often this is an indicator of pain or discom-

fort): _____

Any new medical equipment, dressings, or requests regarding the child's health received

from the parents or noted on observation of the child? _____

Changes that the teacher is aware of in family dynamics: _____

Issues that the staff sees:_____

**Information regarding classroom activities or field trips (please provide at least 3 days
notice or more if possible):**

Date, time, and length of absence from school: _____

Who will be present with the student on this trip? _____

What is the environment like that the student will be in? _____

How long will the student be gone from school? _____

Is there any food-related activity planned? _____

What equipment might be necessary? _____

**If an event should happen in the classroom, the following information is most helpful to
the nurse (please check to see if your school district has a procedure in place for handling
events in the classroom):**

At what time did the event occur?_____

Who was with the student at the time? Who initially observed the event?_____

_____

What activity was being carried out?_____

What specifically did the staff member observe? Describe the behavior: _____

What did staff do to address the event? Make a step-by-step list of actions taken: ____

_____

What time did the event end? _____

How was the student immediately following the event? Describe the student's behavior

at that time. _____

Who was notified of the issue? _____

_____

Figure 10.1. Information needed from teachers regarding students' health.

had on the student's daily activities of life and ability to be independent in self-care (Raymond, 2009).

Once information is gathered, the nurse can identify and name the issue. A plan can be developed to address the key health-related issues and barriers in self-care and education that this condition might create for a student in a school setting. Goals are established in cooperation with the family and faculty to assure safety and facilitate the child's self-care. Clear interventions are identified to address the factors that create this child's needs for healthcare in the school setting and to facilitate the goals of safety and self-care in the school environment (Zimmerman, 2006).

If the student's medical condition could develop into a medical emergency, the nurse must also work to develop an Emergency Action Plan (EAP). This plan outlines actions that must be taken to respond to the situation in terms that are clear and easily understood by all school personnel. Clear, concise emergency contacts and procedures help staff and faculty assure safety for the affected student if the school nurse is not present at the time of the event (Zimmerman, 2006).

Evaluation of the interventions' effectiveness in meeting the established goals of the plan is not a task the nurse can delegate to others. As part of licensure responsibilities, a registered nurse must review and evaluate the effectiveness of each plan at least yearly. This includes plans for children within the school system who have health concerns but do not have special education needs. Any time an accommodation must be made in order to address the educational needs of the student related to healthcare, the nurse must have an IHP available for that student. This information must be kept private yet made available to the appropriate faculty and staff who may need to alter approaches or be aware of health precautions in the school setting.

For the medically fragile, nurses are often involved in providing ongoing, intensive management of the child's healthcare needs in the school system. Direct physical provision of care by the nurse or by an appropriately trained subordinate may be required. Collaboration with teachers, parents, and the child is essential to maintaining the child's ability to participate in the school setting. This involves not only nursing management of the medical issues of the child that requires direct care of the child but also consideration of the environment in which the child will spend his school day, the need for adaptation of that environment, and an understanding of the medical technology being utilized by the child to maintain his health and wellness or to compensate for the impact of the health issues (American Academy of Pediatrics, 2007; Zirkel, 2009).

One of the key issues that school nurses face is whether or not a procedure or treatment that is medically necessary for a child is educationally needed in the school system. This is a difficult decision and often requires research, contact with the pediatrician or specialist, evaluation of cost and who will pay for the services (e.g., school, insurance, or parent), and how safely the treatment or procedure can be carried out in a school environment (American Academy of Pediatrics, 2000). The nurse must be aware of when students are absent from school and how their healthcare status has changed prior to their return to school or admission. This allows the nurse to determine what kinds of resources and needs the school must have in place before the student can return to the classroom. To paraphrase Gregory (2006), school nurses share the responsibility with school administrators in fulfilling the obligation of caring for the complex student in the school setting.

Financial resources also create challenges for school nurses. Part of the nurse's role is to balance what is necessary for the child to be educated in the school setting and what is medically reasonable in the school environment. This is both an emotional and legally challenging issue. Schools as well as families may have limited resources. The challenge for the nurse is to find creative ways to provide the best level of care for the student and realistically adapt the environment (NASN, 2006; Wolfe, 2006).

Nurses are resource "navigators" (Gregory, 2006, p. 122). They can assist families in locating community resources and encourage the family to make use of these resources. The nurse may take on the role of assisting the family in addressing financial costs involved in the child's healthcare for such needs as medications or assistive technology. Nurses can help the family to understand how to work with both the healthcare and school system to achieve a good working relationship and to better communicate the student's needs. Families need to learn how to be an advocate for their child. The nurse can point the family to accurate, reliable information and resources to assist them in better understanding the child's health challenges.

Finally, the school nurse serves as an advocate. As an advocate, the nurse seeks to identify the needs of children and promote addressing those needs in the classroom and the community. At times, families have been overwhelmed by the challenges they have faced. Sometimes it is difficult for families emotionally or financially to address additional health or wellness issues even among students without disabilities. The nurse along with the staff advocates for the child. Helping parents and others to acknowledge the needs of the child is part of the nurse's role (Engelke, Guttu, Warren, & Swanson, 2008; NASN, 2006).

Direct Services Provided to Teachers

As noted above, dealing with healthcare issues can be overwhelming. The school nurse takes an active role in assisting teachers and faculty in understanding the healthcare issues of their students. How do these issues impact the student? What considerations need to be made in providing education for this child with this set of needs in the classroom? How can the school accommodate health issues as well as disabilities? The nurse is a resource on all healthcare issues. The nurse can assist educators in "educating themselves" on the conditions that affect their students. Although nurses may not be able to answer every healthcare question off the top of their heads, they know where to look for accurate and reliable healthcare information. Nurses often have a working knowledge of legitimate resources and websites that can provide information. The school nurse acts not only as an educator but also as a consultant for planning and creative problem solving for the health-challenged child.

Careful consideration of how to manage medical technology in the classroom must be made. Who needs training regarding the equipment, how to accommodate or make room for this equipment in the classroom, safety considerations for the equipment in the classroom, and how to address the needs of the student while minimizing disruption of the classroom all are part of the planning considerations that must be addressed. The nurse may need training and time to complete research on the technology to be utilized. She must be able to educate others involved in the student's care regarding the use of any new equipment. Often the nurse herself must use her core medical background and skills to investigate new healthcare needs or medical conditions. By law the nurse only has a set number days in order to gain this understanding, identify if it is possible to carry out this intervention or safely utilize this technology in the school setting, create a plan, and educate those involved in the care of the child. This varies from state to state (Gregory, 2006).

The school nurse must also address further accommodations for healthcare needs outside of the immediate school environment. Transportation staff must have an understanding of the student's healthcare needs and EAP in order to safely transport these children. Knowing when a field trip, special meal, or special event will occur for a classroom setting allows the nurse time to plan for the needs of the health challenged client. Teachers or aides may need training on how to manage the child's medical equipment when not in a school setting. Consideration may need to be given as to how the child's physical and healthcare needs can be addressed outside of the school setting. Setting up medications, providing clear written instructions, and assuring the child's safety while on field trips is part of the nurse's role. Does the person accountable for the child understand the child's healthcare condition and how that condition needs to be addressed?

Nurses are expected to carry out ongoing health counseling and follow-up on the psychosocial needs and wellness concerns for school students as well as school personnel. A classroom is a group of individuals who interact each day. Issues that impact one student often have a ripple effect throughout the class. Staff, faculty, and students come to care about one another. Changes in the health status of one student must be addressed with careful consideration of the student's and family's right to privacy (Freyer, 2004). The school nurse can work as a liaison between the family and the school to determine how best to communicate these changes with other students. The nurse can assist the student in returning to the classroom with new technology in place and help the student in diminishing the concern of his peers and teachers while dealing with his own sense of awkwardness regarding his absence and the change in his health status. Staff members sometimes need assistance in coping with the emotional challenges of working with children with disabilities. The school nurse may be a resource for them as well.

The classroom's health as a group is also of concern to the school nurse. Often school nurses act as epidemiologists. School nurses track health issues throughout the school system. The nurse looks for trends in illnesses and uses information on incidents and injuries to identify health and safety risks within all settings in the school. The nurse must report trends in infectious disease to local health departments and through these contacts can become aware of trends within the community. This awareness allows the nurse to proactively put interventions in place to maintain the health of children and staff.

The nurse must take into consideration the special needs of the student with disabilities. When addressing schoolwide preparations and policies, school nurses must consider what needs disabled students may have in the event of an emergency or natural disaster, prepare for these events, and put measures in place to ensure the safety of all students. The nurse must act as an advocate in the development of plans made by administrators and an advocate for inclusion of consideration of those who are disabled in the development of these plans. She must further advocate for the inclusion of the disabled in drills to ensure that the plan in place is realistic (Gregory, 2006).

The nurse is an advocate for change. Whether change needs to occur at the school, district, community, state, or national level, school nurses seek to find additional funding, motivate changes in policy or legislation or create programming and services that promote the health and wellness of children and families with disabilities. Acting as a health consultant, nurses can assist staff and administrators in creating an environment and situation that helps fulfill the needs of the complex student in the school setting and the community at large (Wolfe, 2006).

LEGAL RESPONSIBILITY AND CHALLENGES OF THE SCHOOL NURSE

The role of the nurse in schools is dictated by several different factors. First, the nurse must abide by the standards of the state's Nurse Practice Act. These regulations are set up by states individually and vary a great deal on issues such as delegation of tasks like tube feedings and medication administration or who can evaluate students' health and determine the effectiveness of treatments in school programs and standards of care. Abiding by these standards and regulations is vital to being able to maintain nursing licensure and preventing legal issues for the school district. The school district also plays a part in what a school nurse is allowed to do within the school system itself. District administrators often define the role of the nurse and parameters in which she or he can function within the school. The principal of each individual school further impacts the nurse's role. Nurses experience the same challenges that teachers do when they find themselves working in a hospital system or home teaching program. Teachers find themselves supervised by medical professionals who have limited understanding of the teacher's training and priorities just as the school nurse often finds him- or herself supervised by school administrators with the same level of preparation for supervising healthcare personnel (Engelke et al., 2008; Kruger et al., 2009).

Legally, the nurse must be careful to appropriately delegate any procedure that may be considered a nursing function to ensure that the staff who carries out this process is not only trained in how to do the task but that these individuals are capable of making decisions and knowing when not to carry out the task or recognize potentially harmful situations (Raymond, 2009; Spriggle, 2009). The nurse must follow up on any delegated tasks, even those delegated to Licensed Practical Nurses, and provide supervision to ensure the best care of the child (Gregory, 2006). Because of his or her licensure, a registered nurse cannot delegate the task of evaluating the impact of a procedure or medication to others. This is probably one of the greatest challenges for school nurses. Often the administration of medication is viewed as something anyone can do because it is a task individuals do for themselves at home. The challenge in schools is that the school holds legal accountability for what happens to the child in the school setting. The nurse, because of his or her licensure, holds even greater accountability.

The challenge that school nurses face is in meeting the needs of all. The role of the school nurse requires that the nurse fill multiple roles in the completion of his or her job. The American Academy of Pediatrics and the National Association of School Nurses have recommended that the ratio of school nurses to students should be 1 per every 750 students for general school populations and 1 for every 125 students for special needs schools (NASN, 2010). In reality, the average caseload for a nurse working in the school system is closer to 1 school nurse per 1,250 students. Often school nurses are challenged geographically as well because of responsibilities in multiple buildings not always located in the same town. This volume and distance challenges the nurse to be physically available for direct care as well as provides a challenge in quickly identifying and addressing healthcare issues in the general school population. Nurses must rely on family, faculty, and staff to assist in providing the best quality healthcare to the disabled student in the healthcare system.

SOLUTION TO THE CASE STUDY

When Joe was released to return to school, Susan contacted his parents to assess any changes in Joe's functional abilities, healthcare needs, and medications. Susan also contacted his healthcare provider to follow up on new medications and Joe's condition. Susan then worked with Donna to review Joe's health status and changes in his abilities and healthcare needs. Joe's weight had dropped from 90 pounds to 80 pounds. He had little physical reserve and increased limitations in his movements and speech. Joe was easily tired. He was taking inhalers to help open his airways, which caused him to experience an increase in spasticity. At the time of his return, Joe would need to use a wheelchair but his parents were hopeful that this would not be permanent.

Susan worked with Joe's parents. She helped them to locate a local loaner closet where they were able to obtain a pediatric wheelchair for temporary use at no cost to them. Forms were obtained from Joe's pediatrician to allow Joe to take his new medication and use an inhaler at school. Susan explained how Joe's parents could contact their insurance company to justify the purchase of an additional inhaler that could be left at school.

Susan and Donna let other staff know that Joe would be returning and helped prepare them for the changes in his appearance and ability. Susan talked to staff about the impact of bed rest and having been ventilated on Joe's health. Susan also talked to staff about how the medication to open Joe's airways had impacted his spasticity and what changes in his breathing should cause them to have him use his inhaler. Donna and Susan discussed with faculty and the family the changes that had been made to Joe's IEP and IHP and implemented an EAP for respiratory issues. This plan was then reviewed with faculty and staff prior to Joe's return to class. Referrals were made to both a physical therapist and to the speech therapist to assist Joe in regaining his mobility for transfers and movement as well as his ability to communicate in class. Rest periods were worked into Joe's schedule with a plan to slowly decrease the frequency and number of periods over time as Joe regained his activity tolerance. Susan would evaluate Joe twice daily for the first week and then every other day for 2 weeks to evaluate how well he was improving in tolerance.

Finally, plans were made to help his classmates welcome Joe back. Joe's parents expressed concerns that Joe was very upset about being unable to use his walker and were anxious about how his school day would go. With both Joe's and his parents' permission, Susan talked with Donna about how his classmates could help welcome Joe back to class. A banner was created to welcome Joe on his first day back. Peers were encouraged to tell Joe how much they had missed him and to be patient when he spoke with them. They were also told that he would come back in a wheelchair and be tired but that with their help they could make this better for Joe.

During the first week of class, Susan checked on Joe twice daily, then every other day and as needed. Donna and Susan both sent notes home to Joe's parents at the end of the day to let them know how Joe's day went. They asked that his parents use Joe's personal talker to send messages back to the school about how Joe was doing at home after being in school all day.

Although the above is an ideal scenario, students like Joe exist in every special needs classroom. Ultimately it is the goal of all involved to best meet the needs of any student. Although we cannot provide for their medical care, creating a safe environment and making accommodations for physical disabilities and health issues make it possible for children with special needs to be a part of the school system. Each child has the ability to achieve. By changing the environment and our approaches, we make it possible for all students to continue to develop in their independence and confidence in themselves as people. As a member of the team, school nurses can add to the success of both the student and the teacher in achieving education for all.

REFERENCES

American Academy of Pediatrics. (2000). Provision of educationally-related services for children and adolescents with chronic diseases and disabling conditions. *Pediatrics, 105*, 448–451.

American Academy of Pediatrics. (2007). Provision of educationally-related services for children and adolescents with chronic diseases and disabling conditions. *Pediatrics, 119*, 1218–1223.

American Academy of Pediatrics. (2008). Role of the school nurse in providing school health services. *Pediatrics, 121*, 1052–1056.

Engelke, M. K., Guttu, M., Warren, M. B., & Swanson, M. (2008). School nurse case management for children with chronic illness: Health, academic and quality of life outcomes. *The Journal of School Nursing, 24*, 205–214.

Freyer, D. R. (2004). Care of the dying adolescent: Special considerations. *Pediatrics, 113*, 381–388.

Gregory, E. K. (2006). Federal laws protecting children and youth with disabilities. In J. Selekman (Ed.), *School nursing: A comprehensive text* (pp. 301–321). Philadelphia, PA: F. A. Davis.

Kruger, B. J., Radjenovic, D., Toker, K. H., & Comeaux, J. M. (2009). School nurses who only care for children with special needs: Working in a teacher's world. *The Journal of School Nursing, 25*, 436–444.

National Association of School Nurses. (2002). *Issue brief: Role of the school nurse.* Retrieved from http://www.nasn.org/Default.aspx?tabid=279

National Association of School Nurses. (2004). *Issue brief: School health nursing services role in health care: Health promotion and disease prevention.* Retrieved from http://www.nasn.org/Default.aspx?tabid=271

National Association of School Nurses. (2006). *School nursing services role in health care: School nursing management of students with chronic health conditions.* Retrieved from http://www.nasn.org/Default.aspx?tabid=209

National Association of School Nurses. (2008). *Issue brief: Individuals with disabilities education act (IDEA): Management of children in the least restrictive environment.* Retrieved from http://www.nasn.org/Default.aspx?tabid=274

National Association of School Nurses. (2010). *Position statement: Caseload assignments.* Retrieved from http://www.nasn.org/Default.aspx?tabid=209

Raymond, J. A. (2009). The integration of children dependent on medical technology into public schools. *Journal of School Nursing, 25*, 186–194.

Selekman, J. (2006). *School nursing: A comprehensive text.* Philadelphia, PA: F. A. Davis.

Spriggle, M. (2009). Developing a policy for delegation of nursing care in the school setting. *The Journal of School Nursing, 25*, 98–104.

Wolfe, L. C. (2006). Roles of the school nurse. In J. Selekman (Ed.), *School nursing: A comprehensive text* (pp. 111–127). Philadelphia, PA: F. A. Davis.

Zimmerman, B. (2006). Student health and education plans. In J. Selekman (Ed.), *School nursing: A comprehensive text* (pp. 177–203). Philadelphia, PA: F. A. Davis.

Zirkel, P. A. (2009). History of expansion of Section 504 student eligibility: Implications for school nurses. *The Journal of School Nursing, 25*, 256–260.

Chapter 11

ABA Consultant

Barbara Metzger, Shelley M. Garza, and Edward M. Clouser, Jr.

CASE STUDY: HOUSTON

Houston is a 6-year-old boy diagnosed with moderate autism who has recently entered a first-grade classroom in the local, public elementary school. For the 3 previous years, Houston attended a private preschool and also received between 25–35 hours a week of Applied Behavior Analysis (ABA) from a private provider in his home. Although he made considerable progress in academic, play, social, and language skills as a result of the ABA program, Houston still has some delays and characteristics of autism. During the Individualized Education Program (IEP) meeting, Houston's parents requested that school personnel coordinate with the behavior analyst who will still be providing about 10–12 hours a week of ABA services in the home after school and on the weekends. The ABA consultant is a Board Certified Behavior Analyst (BCBA) and, according to the parents, is very knowledgeable about the education of children with autism. The school district personnel who will be providing services for Houston are wary of the parents' request: What is ABA and what will it be like working with a BCBA?

WHAT IS APPLIED BEHAVIOR ANALYSIS (ABA)?

Applied behavior analysis is an approach to changing behavior that employs procedures based on scientifically established principles of learning

(Cooper, Heron, & Heward, 2007). The field of ABA has almost become synonymous with autism treatment and education, although this is not an accurate portrayal of the field. For example, behavior analysts are interested in a wide variety of socially significant behaviors such as gun safety, obesity, and teaching reading. It is likely, however, that school district personnel will come into contact with an ABA provider through a student with behavior problems or autism.

School district personnel may be unfamiliar with the field of ABA and with the credentials of the field. Currently, there are three levels of certification for behavior analysts: (a) a Board Certified Behavior Analyst Doctorate level (BCBA-D), which requires a doctoral degree, coursework in behavior analysis, and supervised field experience; (b) a Board Certified Behavior Analyst (BCBA) which requires a master's degree, coursework in behavior analysis, and supervised field experience; and (c) a Board Certified Assistant Behavior Analyst (BCaBA) which requires a bachelor's degree, coursework in behavior analysis, and supervised field experience. The BCaBA is not to practice without supervision from a BCBA (Behavior Analysis Certification Board, n.d.). Although the number of BCBAs is comparatively small, that number is changing. Every year the total number of programs that prepare students for becoming a BCBA is increasing. Currently, more programs that prepare students for becoming a BCBA are housed in departments of education than in departments of psychology, suggesting that behavior analysts and educators are a good combination.

BENEFITS OF COLLABORATION

Because so many professionals can become involved in the education of one child, coordination and communication becomes imperative when planning and implementing an IEP. Consider that in addition to the classroom teacher, a speech therapist, occupational therapist, physical therapist, adaptive physical education teacher, job coach, educational psychologist, educational diagnostician, autism specialist, or behavior specialist may also provide services for one child. Services may also be provided outside the school setting, in the community, or at home by private or government procured service providers. There is not always collaboration among these services providers, especially when additional services are provided outside of the school setting. As with the case of Houston, the ABA provider is not an employee of the school district and thus it can be easy for school district personnel to view the behavior analyst as an outsider and a problem rather than as a valuable resource. There can be considerable benefit to the student as well as the professionals, however, when behavior analysts and school district employees work together.

What Does ABA Have to Offer to an Individual Student?

Students in both the regular education classroom and special education classroom can have behavior problems that interfere with learning, and behavior analysts are good at using reinforcement-based systems to improve behavior. Unfortunately, schools can be a very punishing place for students, especially those with disabilities (Latham, 2002). An ABA provider can assist school personnel in identifying strong and effective reinforcers for the individual student as well as strategies to maintain the effectiveness of reinforcers across time, thereby reducing the need for aversives. Everyone benefits when students behave well and there is less need for punishment. Yet sometimes a student has extreme behavior problems such as self-injury, aggression, or property destruction. A behavior analyst can assist school personnel in determining if the use of punishment is warranted, deciding what type of punishment would be the least intrusive but the most effective, as well as analyzing the data to determine if the punishment procedure is effective or if the intervention needs to be modified. If a teacher has tried everything he knows to address a student's behavior and is still not successful, a behavior analyst can be the perfect person to find a solution.

Teaching students with autism can be difficult, even for experienced school district personnel. An ABA provider with expertise in autism can be extremely helpful in meeting the many needs of the student with autism. For example, a student with autism may be nonverbal and not have the ability to communicate her basic wants and needs. The ABA provider can assist in strategies to teach nonvocal methods of communication such as sign language or a picture-exchange system as well as identify foundation skills that can lead to vocal communication. Additionally, the behavior analyst can assist in identifying missing prerequisite skills as well as developing curriculum to teach skills such as imitation and play skills. The field of ABA has a large number of teaching methodologies that have been experimentally validated as effective for teaching children with autism and severe disabilities. Behavior analysts are especially good at designing interventions that are specific to one child. For example, a child who refuses to leave the computer and join a circle time activity, who compulsively pushes every button and switch in the classroom, or who is very scared of buttons necessitates an individualized teaching strategy. When school staff members are unable to figure out a problem, the BCBA can often be the one person who can assist a child with highly challenging and distinctive learning and behavior problems.

WHAT DOES ABA HAVE TO OFFER TO SCHOOL DISTRICT PERSONNEL?

A BCBA has intensive and specific training that can be of tremendous benefit to school district personnel. For example, a competent behavior analyst can conduct a functional behavior assessment (FBA) and/or a functional analysis (FA) to identify the function of problem behavior and thereby construct an intervention that takes the function of the behavior into account. Although an FBA perhaps sounds like an easy assessment to perform, to do one correctly can be difficult and time consuming, especially if the student's problem behavior has more than one function and/or the student has multiple problem behaviors. An FA, which is an experimental analysis to determine the function of a behavior, requires specific training not available to most school personnel and can be difficult to conduct in an educational setting. Also, taking the information learned from the FBA and/or FA and then translating that information into a behavior intervention plan (BIP) can be difficult, especially for school district personnel who may not have had extensive training or practice. Once a behavior plan has been implemented, the ABA provider can also be helpful in assessing if it is effective as well as modifying that plan as the student's behavior changes over time. Regardless of if the student has a disability or not and the type of behavior problem, a BCBA should be able to design and assist in implementing a reinforcement-based behavior intervention that takes into account the function of the behavior.

An additional area of expertise of the BCBA that can be valuable for school district personnel is data collection and analysis. Behavior analysts are experts at developing data collection systems as well as presenting graphic displays of collected data. For example, it may be difficult for a teacher to determine which aspects of a student's performance need more intensive data collection and which need minimal documentation. The BCBA can save the teacher time and effort by constructing a simple data collection system that provides the needed information. Additionally, the ABA provider can assist in constructing graphic displays of data that in turn facilitate in interpreting the data and making data-based instructional decisions.

School district personnel may find it difficult to keep up with the research literature for a variety of reasons such as minimal preservice training in reading and interpreting research or just not enough time in the day. Part of the requirement for a behavior analyst to maintain his certification is to keep current with the research literature. Thus, the BCBA can be a resource by providing professionals in the general or special education setting with the most current research available on effective teaching strategies and procedures. Additionally, a good use of a behavior analyst is in developing and implementing training for school district personnel in current research-based practices. Providing school district personnel with instructional tools based on research will improve outcomes for students.

Collaboration, however, is not just to the benefit of the student. One of the best aspects of collaboration is that it expands the expertise of the professionals. An ABA provider working with an occupational therapist (OT), for example, can teach the OT how to use compressed practice and reinforcement to improve a student's fine motor skills. The OT can teach the BCBA the age-appropriate fine motor skills for a particular child or the necessary prerequisite skills for a specific skill. For example, the first author of this article, a behavior analyst, was teaching a student with autism how to tie his shoes. Despite her best efforts, the child was not progressing very rapidly. She asked the school district OT for assistance. The OT suggested that the student needed practice on tasks that involved the coordination of two hands, especially activities that required crossing his hands. The behavior analyst took the OT's advice and developed a teaching program for two-handed tasks on which the OT, classroom teacher, and behavior analyst all worked. The behavior analyst taught the classroom teacher and OT prompting and reinforcement procedures to make working on the tasks easier and more enjoyable for the student. After completion of the two-handed tasks program, the child easily learned to tie his shoes and all of the professionals learned something new. Collaboration with others offers many benefits, including a more effective use of individual talents and the transfer of knowledge and skills from one person to the other group members (Loan-Clarke & Preston, 2002). It is through collaboration that resources, expertise, and responsibility are shared among those working together (Pearson, 1999).

BARRIERS TO COLLABORATION

Although the collaboration of professionals in applied behavior analysis and education can be beneficial to all involved, sometimes working with professionals from other fields is challenging. The potential for disagreement is great in a setting in which people with different philosophical views, educational backgrounds, and areas of expertise work together on difficult issues, such as developing the most appropriate educational programming for a student. Professionals disagree. It does not necessarily mean that one person is right and another is wrong (although sometimes that is the case), but that intelligent, caring, dedicated, and knowledgeable professionals do not always see eye to eye. Learning about the sources of potential conflict between professionals can facilitate collaboration, thereby increasing the likelihood of optimal services for the student.

THEORETICAL DIFFERENCES: EMPIRICISM VERSUS CONSTRUCTIONISM AND POSTMODERNISM

Within a public school setting there are likely to be theoretical differences among service providers such as behavior analysts, occupational therapists, speech pathologists, and teachers. These differences can largely be attributed to the educational philosophy taught in undergraduate and graduate programs and the standards of the respective fields and should be taken into consideration when conflict arises.

ABA providers have a scientific philosophy that emphasizes empiricism as the primary means for gaining information about behavior, selecting the most appropriate interventions, and evaluating how a student is responding. Empiricism is the practice of objective observation and experimentation (Cooper et al., 2007). Although behavior analysts may have their own personal beliefs and biases based on more than just the available facts, they are required to remain objective in what they observe and the recommendations they make (Zuriff, 1985). For the behavior analyst, measuring behavior through data collection is essential in making conclusions regarding how well an intervention is working (Cooper et al., 2007). Behavior analysts utilize empirical, research-based practice to guide the interventions they recommend for students. Because these practices have been confirmed and supported over time through peer-reviewed research, these best practices are recommended for students. Thus, for the BCBA, information obtained through peer-reviewed, empirical research is considered superior to other sources of information. Also, behaviorism is a *modernist* philosophy that emphasizes a clear distinction between the teacher, who has the relevant facts and information, and the student, who must be taught what the teacher knows (Zuriff, 1985). The empirical approach that ABA providers rely upon often is in contrast to that of other providers in public schools who may have a *constructivist*, or *postmodern*, philosophy of education.

Postmodernism raises questions about the objectivity of observations and the truth of scientific knowledge, instead emphasizing the individual's mental representation of information (National Research Council, 1996). According to Macdonald (2003), postmodern curriculum emphasizes that students become producers of knowledge rather than consumers of knowledge. Constructivist teaching rejects the objectivity of knowledge in favor of a focus on the subjective understanding of the learner (Kim, 2005). That is, there is less of an emphasis on empirically supported approaches to teaching and transferring knowledge to students, and more of an emphasis toward a subjective, student-centered approach.

According to Kim (2005), there are three fundamental differences between constructivist teaching approaches and that which ABA providers support. First, Kim stated that "Learning is an active constructive process rather than the process of knowledge acquisition" (p. 9). ABA providers would disagree with this assumption, preferring that students acquire information in a particular way that is supported by research. A second tenant of the constructivist approach is that "Teaching is supporting the learner's constructive processing of understanding rather than delivering the information to the learner" (Kim, 2005, p. 9). ABA providers, however, believe that research has given us a particular means of determining what information is important as well as how it should be taught to the student. Finally, constructivism emphasizes putting teaching behind the importance of the learner, so that he or she is at the center. In contrast, ABA providers emphasize teaching and research-based procedures for doing so, then making modifications as necessary to address the individual needs of students. Service providers who have a constructivist philosophy of teaching are often in disagreement with ABA providers in a variety of other ways. For example, some school personnel may not view data collection to be as important as the behavior analyst, instead relying on more informal measures of knowledge. Also, school personnel may view multiple sources of knowledge as similar and equally valid, regardless of what the research literature states. There may be a reliance on information that is less empirical and rigorous than peer-reviewed research, such as case studies or surveys, to support why they choose a particular approach.

When one member of a team believes the empirical research is the only valid source of information for educating students and another member says something like "I just don't care what your research suggests," then it can result in no agreement on an IEP team and may escalate into opposing sides. Clearly, when the agenda of an IEP meeting shifts from deciding what is best for the student to proving who is right, no one wins. One problem with differing philosophical views on educating students is that they are often not discussed and not recognized—the person with a different belief system is just viewed as being difficult. When belief systems clash, compromise is the key to a successful collaboration. For example, consider the likely situation of an OT wanting to implement a sensory program when the behavior analyst objects because there is not empirical research to support that type of therapy. The behavior analyst can compromise by agreeing to the sensory intervention, but asking for data collection to inform the IEP team about the effectiveness of this intervention for this particular student. On the other hand, the OT can compromise by agreeing to take the data and also to agreeing to not implement the sensory activities immediately following the occurrence of undesired behaviors in case they function as a rewarding activity for the student. In this example, each side compromised, which hopefully resulted in a good decision for the individual student.

Models of Collaboration

Collaboration is a group of two or more people operating autonomously, whose aim is to achieve goals that no individual could achieve independently (Fishbough, 1997). In a school setting, collaboration among service providers and administrators is an essential part of developing a student's IEP. However, it may be the case that different service providers are accustomed to differing collaboration styles, thus creating the potential for conflict when they are required to work together in designing and prioritizing a student's programming.

According to Fishbough (1997), there are three primary models of collaboration: consulting, coaching, and teaming. During an IEP meeting, *teaming* is required by the individual members. In the teaming model, individual participants have a shared responsibility for the outcome of the meeting, and contribute equally to it. Those working in a public school setting are accustomed to such an approach, and may prefer it to other styles of collaboration with less equality among the participants. ABA providers, on the other hand, may differ in their approach to collaborating with others and thus school district personnel may view behavior analysts as noncollaborative.

Behavior analysts may be more used to functioning as a team leader and making recommendations rather than working as part of a collaborative team. In the private sector, behavior analysts usually operate independently, making most of the final decisions about programming as individuals instead of through a committee or group. This falls under the consulting model of collaboration that Fishbough (1997) described. In this model, information flows from the person with more knowledge about a particular topic to those with less knowledge. This is more of a one-way flow of information, versus the teaming model of shared responsibility and information transfer. The consulting model that ABA providers typically utilize can create conflict in an IEP meeting because school personnel may perceive the behavior analyst as not being respectful of their expertise. Thus, ABA providers must be capable of changing how they collaborate, which in turn will facilitate maintaining a positive working relationship with school district personnel and thereby allowing for IEP meetings to be successful. Also, it would be helpful for school personnel to recognize that many behavior analysts are highly skilled and that their expertise can greatly benefit services to students.

Broad Versus Specific Areas of Expertise

Behavior analysts do not limit their focus to problematic behaviors or work only with individuals with autism, as they are trained to view human behavior as everything people do (Cooper et al., 2007). Thus, it is not uncommon for an experienced behavior analyst to be a master teacher in that she has expertise in a wide range of areas such as the acquisition of language, play, social, self-help, and fine and gross motor skills. Most school personnel, however, have a more narrow professional focus. As the areas of expertise of most school personnel do not overlap, the potential for conflict is largely avoided. Because behavior analysts' areas of expertise do overlap with that of other providers, there is an increased potential for conflict. For example, it is common for speech pathologists and behavior analysts to address the same language deficit in a student, but may do so in differing ways and have opposing views as to teaching priorities. Thus, school district personnel may perceive that the BCBA is invading their territory and is challenging their expertise while the behavior analyst may view the school district personnel as not being willing to collaborate.

Behavior analysts must be willing to compromise when working with school district professionals for the benefit of the student, even if they disagree. ABA providers should take steps to learn how other professionals came to their decisions and assimilate this information into their own recommendations for a student. Likewise, other providers should be willing to consider the behavioral expertise of behavior analysts when addressing skill deficits or behavioral excesses.

Expectations for Student Performance

ABA providers have a goal to maximize the learning of a client, addressing socially significant behaviors in a way that is measurable and that others can replicate. Many behavior analysts working for school districts have previous experience in the private sector, where competition for clients/business is ongoing and maximum results are critical for continued employment. In contrast, public schools are not required to offer the best possible education to its students. Thus, it is likely that public school personnel and behavior analysts have extremely different definitions of the term *appropriate* regarding the services that a student should be provided and the expected results of those services.

In order to design educational programs and interventions that are feasible, ABA providers working in public schools must recognize the limiting circumstances in which teachers and other school district professionals work. As those limitations are typically absent in the private sector, it may be the case that the BCBA is not aware of them. First, school district personnel cannot just focus their attention on one or two students as can be done in a private setting such as a home or clinic. For example, it is not uncommon for teachers to have 20 or more students in a classroom, and for speech pathologists, occupational therapists, and school psychologists to have double (or triple) that number on their caseload. Because school district personnel must divide their time and attention among such a large group, they are limited in what they can implement. The interventions classroom teachers use to address their students' needs cannot be as specific and time-consuming as behavior analysts may be used to implementing. Data collection cannot be taken as frequently, and interventions cannot be as complex as those designed for children in private settings. Behavior analysts should realize that there is a limit as to what a teacher can realistically implement in her classroom, and interact with her accordingly. Additionally, it may be the case that a teacher is not trained to address the variety of needs her students have. They may not have not been exposed to many of the techniques that behavior analysts have been trained to use, and thus may find it difficult to implement the interventions ABA providers suggest without extensive training. Additionally, a teacher's training may not have included discriminating between research-based practices and those with less support in the research literature. Because of this, they may select interventions that are in disagreement with those ABA providers would recommend. Behavior analysts should recognize these facts and assist teachers in improving their knowledge and skills, focusing on the benefits to the students as well as their effectiveness as teachers. A BCBA working in a school setting must recognize the limitations of that environment and work to help school district professionals maximize what they can provide.

Tools for Collaboration

Collaboration with other professionals is difficult. The student's case manager has to ensure that each member of the team is: (a) providing the required number of hours agreed upon in the IEP, (b) supporting and complementing rather than inhibiting or voiding other services being provided, (c) implementing procedures consistently, (d) collecting data, and (e) sharing decisions and progress (or lack thereof) with others. In order to coordinate the many necessary services of a student, a high degree of organization is necessary. The checklist in Figure 11.1 incorporates suggestions for teachers organizing the services a student may receive in different settings. ABA providers who are aware of all other service providers and who work with

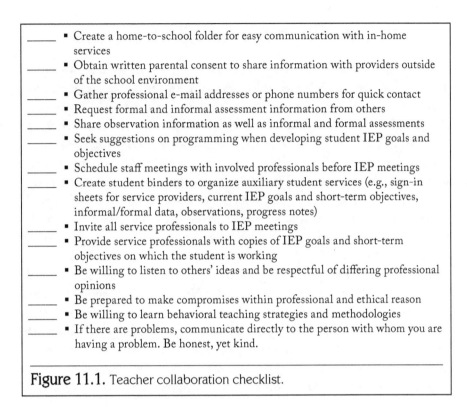

_____ ▪ Create a home-to-school folder for easy communication with in-home services
_____ ▪ Obtain written parental consent to share information with providers outside of the school environment
_____ ▪ Gather professional e-mail addresses or phone numbers for quick contact
_____ ▪ Request formal and informal assessment information from others
_____ ▪ Share observation information as well as informal and formal assessments
_____ ▪ Seek suggestions on programming when developing student IEP goals and objectives
_____ ▪ Schedule staff meetings with involved professionals before IEP meetings
_____ ▪ Create student binders to organize auxiliary student services (e.g., sign-in sheets for service providers, current IEP goals and short-term objectives, informal/formal data, observations, progress notes)
_____ ▪ Invite all service professionals to IEP meetings
_____ ▪ Provide service professionals with copies of IEP goals and short-term objectives on which the student is working
_____ ▪ Be willing to listen to others' ideas and be respectful of differing professional opinions
_____ ▪ Be prepared to make compromises within professional and ethical reason
_____ ▪ Be willing to learn behavioral teaching strategies and methodologies
_____ ▪ If there are problems, communicate directly to the person with whom you are having a problem. Be honest, yet kind.

Figure 11.1. Teacher collaboration checklist.

teachers and other educational providers will ensure a more streamlined approach to services.

School district staff can facilitate coordination with an ABA provider in several ways, but it is especially important that the behavior analyst is allowed access to what is going on in the school setting. Sometimes school district personnel get into a "circle the wagons" mode and are extremely reluctant to allow access to someone who is not a school district employee. Once the behavior analyst is able to observe the child in the school setting, it's essential that the school staff don't put on a show, but do their jobs as they normally would. It can be difficult for school district personnel to admit that they have a problem and need assistance, but ignoring a problem and refusing to ask for assistance benefits no one. It is likely that a BCBA will ask school district personnel to assist by collecting data. It is also likely that an ABA provider will ask school district personnel to change their behavior. For example, the BCBA may suggest that the teacher give the child compressed practice at a skill (i.e., several opportunities to practice a skill in a row) as opposed to one opportunity a day, or she may suggest that the speech therapist give the student a small reinforcer after every 3–5 correct responses. It is essential that if the behavior analyst makes a suggestion that school staff are not able or willing to implement, that she be told so and why.

SOLUTION TO THE CASE STUDY

*Houston's parents have made a reasonable request—they want the profession-
als to work together to help their child. They may not realize, however, that they
have asked the school district personnel as well as the ABA provider to do something that can be very difficult. There are several possible outcomes. Sometimes,
school districts will refuse the behavior analyst access to the classroom and thereby
eliminate any possibility for collaboration. The school district will implement its
services and the behavior analyst will implement her services without the benefit
of collaboration. This is not ideal for the student. Another possibility is that the
behavior analyst is allowed to observe at school, but is not given the opportunity to influence anything that is happening there. This may be sufficient if the
behavior analyst's only goal is to use the home-based services to assist Houston in
being successful in the school setting. However, it's a missed opportunity for the
professionals to learn from each other and for Houston to have optimal services.
The best outcome for Houston and his classmates, as well as the service providers,
is for the professionals to do exactly what Houston's parents requested, collaborate.
This will require patience, compromise, and not being defensive, as well as honest
and factual communication. Hopefully, in the future the behavior analyst will be
a standard and integral part of the IEP team, which would benefit students and
professionals.*

REFERENCES

Behavior Analysis Certification Board. (n.d.). *Experience standards—BCaBA.*
Retrieved from http://www.bacb.com/index.php?page=68

Cooper, J. O., Heron, T. E., & Heward, W. L. (2007). *Applied behavior analysis*
(2nd ed.). Upper Saddle River, NJ: Pearson.

Fishbough, M. (1997). *Models of collaboration.* Boston, MA: Allyn & Bacon.

Kim, J. S. (2005). The effects of constructivist teaching approaches on student academic achievement, self-concept, and learning strategies. *Asia Pacific Education
Review, 6*(1), 7–19.

Latham, G. I. (2002). *Behind the schoolhouse door: Managing chaos with science, skills
and strategies.* North Logan, UT: P & T ink.

Loan-Clarke, J., & Preston, D. (2002). Tensions and benefits in collaborative
research involving a university and another organization. *Studies in Higher
Education, 27,* 169–185.

Macdonald, D. (2003). Curriculum change and the post-modern world: Is the
school curriculum-reform movement an anachronism? *Journal of Curriculum
Studies, 35,* 139–149.

National Research Council. (1996). *National science education standards.* Washington,
DC: National Academy Press.

Pearson, J. (1999). Electronic networking in initial teacher education: Is a virtual faculty of education possible? *Computers and Education, 32,* 221–238.

Zuriff, G. E. (1985). *Behaviorism: A conceptual reconstruction.* New York, NY: Columbia University Press.

Chapter 12

Educational Diagnostician

Jessica A. Rueter and John N. Trice

CASE STUDY: RYAN

Ryan is a 9-year-old boy in the third grade. His father and his stepmother are concerned about his reading ability and have asked that a psychoeducational evaluation be conducted. His biological mother and father are divorced, but are in a custody battle over Ryan and his brother. Ryan currently lives in a rural area with his father and stepmother. His mother has standard expanded visitation rights and currently resides in the same rural community.

A previous evaluation that his mother had conducted determined that Ryan is a student with a reading disability (specifically dyslexia). The recommendations from this evaluation included a specialized school designed especially for students with dyslexia in a major metropolitan area. His father and stepmother have requested that updated testing be completed to determine the degree of severity of Ryan's dyslexia and what programming will be appropriate for Ryan.

Ryan is attending a private Christian school. In the event that the court does not allow his mother to move Ryan to the metropolitan area, she has petitioned the court that he and his brother attend the local public school. The three attorneys involved (one for the father and stepmother, one for the mother, and a court appointed attorney for Ryan and his brother) will use the results of the psychoeducational evaluation that has been requested by the father and stepmother and the previous evaluation as part of the court proceedings to determine custodial and educational rights of the parents.

Ryan is receiving evidence-based interventions in the general education classroom. In an interview with Ryan's current teacher, she revealed that she is a trained Reading First teacher and has implemented the following evidence-based interventions: Reading First Initiative techniques, graphic organizers, story analysis and mapping, sequencing tasks, vocabulary and prereading activities, and repeated readings. Ryan has had the same teacher since first grade. Because Ryan has had the same teacher for 2 years, the interventions have been implemented with progress monitoring data recorded over a long period of time. The educational diagnostician who conducted the evaluation collected all data used in the evaluation process.

INTRODUCTION

A multidisciplinary team is required to assess and make decisions about a student when considering special education services. Educational diagnosticians play a significant role in the multidisciplinary team. Parents are also an important member of the team and when appropriate and possible, the student will participate in the decision-making process as well. Defining and assuming clear roles and responsibilities for each team member is essential as decisions being made must be accurate and free of bias (Salvia, Ysseldyke, & Bolt, 2009).

The team may experience conflicts between what is best for a student in terms of educational need and the testing results (e.g., whether or not a disability is present). Regardless of the type of conflict that may exist between team members, roles and intentions must be clear, and decisions should be made carefully and based on each student's needs. It is also important for team decisions to stay with current research practices such as the growing trend to serve students in general education settings for most of their school day (Overton, 2009).

The Individuals with Disabilities Education Act Improvement (IDEA, 2004) dictates roles and responsibilities of the multidisciplinary team including the purposes and uses of assessment to make decisions. The law outlines explicit processes: early screening, initial evaluations, parental consent/participation, procedural safeguards, nondiscriminatory assessment, multidisciplinary team evaluations, Individualized Education Program (IEP) development, eligibility, placement, transition services and other special factors, and due process/hearing. However, when schools respond by using early intervention services to address the needs of students who are at risk for academic and behavior difficulties, fewer referrals for special education are needed and fewer students are labeled with a disability.

Cohen and Spenciner (2011) discuss the role of educational diagnosticians within the multidisciplinary team, the purposes and uses of assessment, and the Response to Intervention (RTI) model. As an early intervention process, the RTI model has changed the decision-making steps for the team and how to support students who are at risk for school failure. Implementing RTI involves a range of activities that include adjustments professional educators make within their classrooms to ensure high-quality and evidence-based instruction. Methods of data collection about a student's progress are critical and communication with parents and other teachers during the RTI model should be routine and ongoing.

RTI is a three-tiered model of intervention, better referred to as an early intervention strategy-based model designed to address bias in the referral process and prevent students from being unnecessarily tested for special education services. Steps within an RTI model should be outcome-driven and have clear focus of intervention. The tiers of the RTI model include: Tier I—universal interventions (all students); Tier II—target group interventions (some students); and Tier III—intensive and individualized interventions (individual students). Typically, a benefit to RTI is a reduction in referrals, evaluations, and eligibility placement meetings, which reduces the possibility of misdiagnosis, overidentification, and overrepresentation of students in special education (Cummings, Atkins, Allison, & Cole, 2008; Overton, 2009).

Although research provides information regarding the roles of the educational diagnostician, the literature is limited in scope; therefore, this chapter will include aspects related to assessment and contributions from experts.

General Roles and Responsibilities

Educational diagnosticians' roles vary from state to state and even the titles by which these professionals are known are often different. Regardless of their title, educational diagnosticians share an ability to diagnose the learning problems of students (Council for Exceptional Children [CEC], 2000). Only four states (Arkansas, Louisiana, New Mexico, and Texas) have state certification/licensure requirements for educational diagnosticians (Zweback & Mortenson, 2001). Responses to changes in federal and state mandates and ways to address demographic and legal data have resulted in the creation of positions such as the educational diagnostician. For example, Texas established this position in 1973 to help facilitate legislation involved in special education processes (Simpson, 2002).

Typical Duties of the Educational Diagnostician

The duties of the educational diagnostician include:

- serving as a member of a student's multidisciplinary evaluation team and when applicable, administering standardized assessment measures and providing input to the team regarding the student's strengths and weaknesses;
- working collaboratively with other evaluation personnel, such as speech-language therapists, occupational therapists, physical therapists, school psychologists, and counselors to determine eligibility for special education services;
- making recommendations about IEP accommodations and modifications within curricular content areas, including instructional approaches; and
- consulting with teachers, parents, and others regarding students' progress, educational needs, and other types of support (CEC, 2000).

Overall, responsibilities of the educational diagnostician are to conduct and interpret psychoeducational assessments, review students' educational and medical records, and maintain ongoing collaboration with other professionals, related service personnel, and parents. They also determine academic and behavioral strengths and weaknesses of the referred student and in some cases provide suggestions for learning strategies and interventions (Stephens, Kinnison, Naquin, & Rueter, 2007). Additionally, awareness of students' cultural and linguistic differences and ways to create and support responsive classrooms and teachers must be considered (Cartledge & Kourea, 2008).

General roles and responsibilities also involve scheduling and holding IEP meetings with teachers and parents to review assessment results and student progress and determine eligibility for special education services. Because the emphasis in most states has been on referral to placement for special education, not much time has been devoted to consultative and direct services related to early intervention services for students who are at risk for academic and behavioral disorders. Typically, educational diagnosticians have not included recommendations (of specific evidence-based strategies) when writing evaluations. Instead, the focus has been on whether the student is eligible for special education services (Mather & Wendling, 2005; Rueter, Stephens, & Kinnison, 2008).

In many cases, educational diagnosticians spend the majority of their time assessing students and writing reports, completing paperwork, and conducting IEP meetings. These activities have resulted in less time to focus on educational strategies or interventions (Stephens et al., 2007). Cook (1997) conducted a study about the role of the education diagnostician. The study results indicated that an educational diagnostician spends approximately 10 to 20 hours per week on testing, interpretation of testing, and report writing. The study also revealed that the two most important duties of the educational diagnostician were testing and coordinating and conducting IEP team meetings. However, there were disagreements as to which duty was the most important. For instance, half of the educational diagnosticians rated their primary role or first duty as testing while the other half rated coordinating and conducting IEP meetings as the number one priority.

EXPANDING ROLES OF THE EDUCATIONAL DIAGNOSTICIAN

Educational diagnosticians are typically not involved in the assessment of students until they have experienced failure within the general education classroom, however; that does not prevent these professionals from serving on early intervention teams. In contrast, with the implementation of RTI, educational diagnosticians will have the opportunity to expand or redefine their roles. With the use of curriculum-based measurements and progress monitoring, educational diagnosticians will be in a position to recommend individualized evidence-based interventions based on a student's profile. Consequently, educational diagnosticians are likely to be more involved in their local schools; specific roles would extend from the earliest execution of RTI foundational system design at the district level through the implementation stages (Stephens et al., 2007).

The roles Canter (2006) identified for system design in the field of school psychology can also be applied to educational diagnosticians' function in RTI implementation as depicted in Table 12.1. Through the execution of the RTI design and by providing services within each of the three tiers, educational diagnosticians will wear many hats (Stephens et al., 2007).

COMMUNICATION WITH TEACHERS AND FAMILY MEMBERS

Another role educational diagnosticians assume is that of a key stakeholder in terms of communication and collaboration with others. Communication with teachers and families is a critical component of successful implementation of school-based services for students (Sattler, 2008; St. James School District, n.d.). Raffaele and Knoff (1999) noted four core beliefs regarding effective home-school communication:

Table 12.1

Diagnostician Roles Within RTI System Design

1. Identify and analyze existing literature on RTI in an attempt to determine relevant and effective approaches for the local district (or state).
2. Assist administrators in the identification of important stakeholders and key leaders needed to facilitate system change.
3. Assist in the needs assessment techniques to identify potential concerns for RTI implementation.
4. Plan, design, and provide needed staff training to implement the RTI process (e.g., provide training in educational interventions and progress monitoring techniques).
5. Assist in designing an evidence-based model that best fits local needs and resources.
6. Maintain ongoing communication and consultation with educators, administrators, and parents.

Note. From "The Changing Roles for Educational Diagnosticians With a Response-to Intervention Framework in the Identification of Students With Learning Disabilities," by T. L. Stephens, L. Kinnison, G. Naquin, and J. A. Rueter, 2007, *The DiaLog, 36*(2), p. 18. Copyright 2007 by the Texas Educational Diagnostician Association. Reprinted with permission.

1. Effective home-school communication is proactive rather than reactive. This involves inviting all families to participate in the educational efforts and the communication process from the beginning instead of targeting only the families of children who are at risk for school failure.
2. Effective home-school communication includes sensitivity, respect, and understanding of the cultural and language differences of families. With the changing demographics of United States public schools, educators must acknowledge and appreciate the differences that families bring to the table and help the student and the family to do the same.
3. Effective home-school communication recognizes and values the contributions of parents and families irrespective of the formality or informality of these experiences. The message to the student is that both parents and educators have important knowledge and skills to share.
4. Effective home-school communication promotes parent and family involvement in the school process with meaningful two-way communication between home and school that is based upon mutual respect and trust.

The CEC (2000) stated that one of the qualities of an educational diagnostician is an ability to "resolve conflicts and defuse potentially adversarial

Table 12.2
Services Provided to Students by Educational Diagnosticians

Early Intervention Support	Special Education Support
Collect detailed direct and indirect observation about student performance.	Administer tests and conduct evaluations appropriate for the student.
Review permanent academic records.	Coordinate and schedule IEP team meetings.
Collect informal work samples in target settings.	Complete and monitor the IEP document.
Conduct informal assessments (e.g., reading, behavior).	Deliver informal support and services.
Hold interviews with the student to determine his perceptions and opinions about himself such as social, emotional, behavioral, and academic strengths and weaknesses.	Types of direct/indirect support: • tutor/teach • advocate/represent • counsel/advise/listen

relationships" (p. 2). Because educational diagnosticians are responsible for complying with IDEA (2004), it appears that coordinating individual team members' perceptions, personal agendas, and willingness or reluctance to collaborate is an added responsibility (Pratola, 2004). With these increased demands on the educational diagnostician, it is even more vital that multiple communications occur between parents and teachers, especially in cases such as implementation of an RTI model.

DIRECT SERVICES TO STUDENTS

There are two distinctive ways to provide direct services to students: (1) early intervention and (2) special education. Prior to special education services, levels of interventions are provided to students who are at risk for learning and behavioral issues. Once identified and placed in special education, services and supports increase in intensity. Table 12.2 illustrates ways in which educational diagnosticians provide services to students.

EARLY INTERVENTION SUPPORT SERVICES TO STUDENTS

IDEA 2004 stipulates that prior to identification and placement for special education, specific interventions and supports are required to be implemented for students who are at risk for being referred for special education services (Webber & Plotts, 2008). To begin providing support to students with academic or behavioral issues, educational diagnosticians facilitate instructional services with direct service providers such as teachers, administrators, and other educational support staff. However, educational diagnosticians are not likely to provide direct instructional services to students prior to placement in special education. Rather, they are more likely to provide indirect support services such as the following: collaboration of instructional methodologies with general education personnel, identifying evidence-based strategies, assisting teachers with informal classroom assessments and interpretation of data, conducting interviews, serving on early intervention teams, and gathering data from a variety of sources.

Support Provided to Students Who Receive Special Education Services

Addressing students' service needs is an important aspect of the educational diagnostician's job responsibilities. As such, educational diagnosticians provide an array of direct support to students once they are served in special education programs. Direct services include but are certainly not limited to: providing students a "safe place" for discussion of current issues or problems that the student is facing, informal counseling, tutoring in various content areas, and conducting transition interviews and assessments. Indirect services that educational diagnosticians provide include (but are not limited to): coordinating agency support services and monitoring students' IEPs by ensuring that accommodations and/or modifications are occurring. Educational diagnosticians are also required to organize and conduct IEP meetings in a timely manner, administer formal and informal assessments, and serve as advocates for students with disabilities at the campus, district, and state levels.

Direct Services to Teachers

Educational diagnosticians provide direct services to teachers as a means to support students who have disabilities. As professionals, their tasks may include acting as a liaison between general education staff and special education staff in order to facilitate effective outcomes for students with disabilities. Specifically, Lynch, Simpson, and Swicegood (2008) stated that, "The liaison and the builder of bridges between general and special education will likely fall to educational diagnosticians" (p. 11).

Educational Diagnosticians' Support to Teachers

The support that educational diagnosticians provide to teachers varies and takes on many forms. For example, educational diagnosticians are often asked to attend professional learning community meetings and faculty meetings to discuss changes in programming and policy decisions at the campus and district level. They also provide updates regarding special education legislation at the state and national levels. Moreover, educational diagnosticians provide support to teachers by being a resource to the general or special educator. When acting as a resource, this may be in the form of allowing an educator to vent about a particular situation without becoming defensive or reactive to what is being said. Rather, the educational diagnostician listens and provides a perspective that may have not been considered.

Other support services that educational diagnosticians provide to teachers range from observation of lessons to troubleshooting issues that are occurring in the classroom (e.g., behavioral, instructional sequencing). Furthermore, an educational diagnostician often acts as a liaison between special educators and site-based administrative staff who may not understand that special education classrooms and instructional techniques and strategies are different from a general education environment. Lesa Shocklee, an elementary educational diagnostician, noted the following about the services that educational diagnosticians provide to teachers:

"Kids come first" is the motto heard throughout the hallways of school. At every turn, a teacher is asking, "What can I do to help this student?" The role of an educational diagnostician is somewhat of a mystery to many educators. "What exactly do you do, they ask?" The simple answer is "Test, write reports and conduct IEP meetings." That, however, is only the tip of the iceberg!

The role of the educational diagnostician is taking on a new "look," if you will. With the attempt at implementing RTI, teachers are not sure where to turn to get training and gain understanding of what exactly RTI is, its purpose, and what we hope will be accomplished through implementation of this process. As a diagnostician I often sit back and think, "How could they not know this stuff?"

My role today is to guide them, help them, show them, and support them—the teachers. What seems second nature to a diagnostician becomes a stretch for many teachers who have never stepped foot into a special education classroom or attempted to remediate any type of learning difference within their classroom. I enjoy putting the pieces of the puzzle together, and helping determine what interventions to try, what accommodations may be put in place during the RTI process, and what strategies may assist with learning difficulties.

My participation with the RTI committee helps me to gain a clear understanding of the student's specific needs and difficulties, and the teacher's frustrations in not knowing how to help the student. My role in this situation is to provide recommendations for interventions, strategies, and remedial programs that assist both teachers and students. Other duties I have participated in include classroom observations, staff development related to all aspects of special education including IEP meetings, assessment, data collections, communication, modifications/accommodations, state assessment decisions, and any other aspect or issue that may arise.

Diagnosticians are a vital staff member at any campus. We provide direction and support for special education, and ensure the campus is functioning within the legal framework for the provision of services. So, while it seems that IEP meetings and testing are the only responsibilities for diagnosticians, this really is not the case.

EXPANDING SUPPORT SERVICES THROUGH AN INTEGRATED RTI FRAMEWORK

As RTI frameworks are beginning to be implemented across school districts in the United States, the services that educational diagnosticians provide to teachers, students, parents, and the schools that they serve will expand and unfold. The experience educational diagnosticians obtained through their work as educators and their expertise in issues of assessment will likely result in their being designated as a key stakeholder on RTI school teams (Hausman & Key, 2009; Stephens et al., 2007).

Rueter and colleagues (2008) suggested that as members of early intervention teams, educational diagnosticians will play critical roles in the implementation of Tiers I through III. Their roles will overlap within the tiered system; responsibilities may include: training and administration of universal screenings, curriculum-based measurement (CBM) implementation, interpretation of CBM data, progress monitoring of student performance, interpretation of academic data, and the selection and training of teachers on research-based interventions and programs. Additionally, educational diagnosticians will participate in the monitoring of intervention implementation techniques, using integrity checks to ensure interventions are being administered with fidelity. Finally, educational diagnosticians will continue to perform traditional duties such as administering norm-referenced assessments and scheduling, organizing, and conducting IEP meetings. Table 12.3 provides prevalent responsibilities of the educational diagnostician under an integrated RTI framework.

CONCLUSION

As service providers, educational diagnosticians play critical roles in assessment, communication, and providing services between general and special educators. Essentially, they are the professionals guiding their school's early intervention model to facilitate indirect and direct support to students who may be at risk for learning issues. Furthermore, educational diagnosticians continue to conduct assessments and make recommendations for eligibility and programming for students with disabilities as members of multidisciplinary teams.

SOLUTION TO THE CASE STUDY

The results of the assessment that was conducted revealed that Ryan continues to be a student with dyslexia. The diagnosis was based in part on cognitive, achievement, and specific reading assessments that were administered to Ryan in multiple testing sessions. Data collected from the teacher, cumulative records, parent interviews, and student interviews were considered. Furthermore, as a precaution, a dyslexia specialist was consulted in the final determination of the diagnosis. Finally, information from the previous assessment was also considered in the determination of the diagnosis.

Careful deliberation was made due to the legal nature of this case. Approximately 20 hours were documented in the assessment process and collection of informal data. Time spent writing the report was in excess of 20 hours. The decisions made by the court regarding parental and educational rights, placement, and programming are unknown to the educational diagnostician who conducted the assessment.

Table 12.3

Evaluation of Personnel Roles Within Tiers I, II, III

Roles	Tier I	Tier II	Tier III
Collaborate in the development of RTI team procedures.	X		
Provide CBM administration, scoring, and interpretation training.	X		
Provide Universal Screening Training.	X		
Assist, coordinate, and supervise classwide Universal Screenings.	X		
Observe students in the instructional environment in order to help identify appropriate intervention strategies, identify barriers to intervention, and assist in the collection of RTI data.	X		
Assist in identifying students who are nonresponsive to Tier I instruction.		X	
Assist in identifying students in need of Tier II evidence-based interventions.	X	X	
Assist in the identification and implementation of Tier II evidenced-based interventions.		X	
Provide integrity checks of Tier II interventions.		X	
Assist in identifying students who are nonresponsive to Tier II evidenced-based interventions.		X	
Collect observational data.		X	
Assist in identifying students in need of Tier III evidenced-based interventions.		X	X
Assist in the development of Tier III interventions.		X	X
Obtain parental consent for comprehensive evaluation.			X
Collect observational data.			X
Conduct norm-referenced cognitive and achievement testing.			X
Write multidisciplinary evaluation reports.			X
Conduct consistent and ongoing consultation regarding RTI implementation issues with regard to all students needs.	X	X	X
Collaborate and obtain input from parents regarding the RTI model.	X	X	X
Evaluate response data to use towards data-based decision making.	X	X	X
Assist Individual Education Program (IEP) committees in ensuring State Board of Education Rules and Regulations are followed.			X

Note. From "Consultants to Early Intervening Teams: The Changing Roles of Evaluation Personnel Within an Integrated Model Framework," by J. A. Rueter, T. L. Stephens, and L. Kinnison, 2008, *The DiaLog, 37*(3), 17. Copyright 2008 by Texas Educational Diagnosticians Association. Reprinted with permission.

References

Canter, A. (2006). Problem solving and RTI: New roles for school psychologists. *Communique, 34*(5). Retrieved from http://www.nasponline.org/publications/cq/cq345rti.aspx

Cartledge, G., & Kourea, L. (2008). Culturally responsive classrooms for culturally diverse students with and at risk for disabilities. *Exceptional Children, 74,* 351–371.

Cohen, L. G., & Spenciner, L. J. (2011). *Assessments of children with special needs* (4th ed.). Upper Saddle River, NJ: Pearson.

Cook, M. A. (1997). *The role of the educational diagnostician as perceived by special education directors, principals, and educational diagnosticians* (Master's thesis). Available from Dissertations & Theses: Full Text database. (Publication No. 1386381)

Council for Exceptional Children. (2000). *Educational diagnosticians—making a difference in the lives of students with special needs.* Retrieved from http://www.cec.sped.org/AM/Template.cfm?Section=Job_Profiles&Template=/CM/ContentDisplay.cfm&ContentID=1667

Cummings, K., Atkins, T., Allison, R., & Cole, C. (2008). Response to Intervention: Investigating the new role of special educators. *TEACHING Exceptional Children, 40*(4), 24–31.

Hausman, R. M., & Key, G. C. (2009). Changing of our professional roles: A historical perspective from personal experience. *The DiaLog, 38*(2), 3–12.

Individuals with Disabilities Education Improvement Act of 2004, P. L. No. 108-446, 20 U. S. C. §§ 1400 et seq.

Lynch, S. A., Simpson, C. G., & Swicegood, P. R. (2008). Ready or not, here it comes: Educational diagnosticians' perceptions of the Response to Intervention process. *The DiaLog, 37*(2), 4–11.

Mather, N., & Wendling, B. J. (2005). Linking cognitive assessment results to academic interventions for students with learning disabilities. In D. P. Flanagan & P. L. Harrison (Eds.), *Contemporary intellectual assessment* (pp. 269–294). New York, NY: Guilford Press.

Overton, T. (2009). *Assessing learners with special needs: An applied approach* (6th ed.). Upper Saddle River, NJ: Pearson.

Pratola, A. (2004). *An investigation of the perceptions of educational diagnosticians concerning their roles in the functional behavior assessment process in high schools in four districts in Delaware* (Doctoral dissertation, Wilmington College). Available from Dissertations & Theses: Full Text database. (Publication No. 3156274)

Raffaele, L. M., & Knoff, H. M. (1999). Improving home-school collaboration with disadvantaged families: Organizational principles, perspectives, and approaches. *School Psychology Review, 28,* 448–466.

Rueter, J. A., Stephens, T. L., & Kinnison, L. (2008). Consultants to early intervening teams: The changing roles of evaluation personnel within an integrated model framework. *The DiaLog, 37*(3), 14–20.

Salvia, J., Ysseldyke, J., & Bolt, S. (2009). *Assessment in special and inclusive settings* (11th ed.). Beverly, MA: Wadsworth.

Sattler, J. M. (2008). *Assessment of children: Cognitive applications* (5th ed.). San Diego, CA: Author.

Simpson, C. G. (2002). *Factors influencing the recruitment and retention of educational diagnosticians as perceived by special education directors in Texas* (Doctoral dissertation, Texas A&M University). Available from Dissertations & Theses: Full Text database. (Publication No. 3072535)

St. James School District. (n.d.). *Position title special education process coordinator/ educational diagnostician.* Retrieved from http://www.stjschools.org/forms/ district/job_desc/co/sped_coord_diag.pdf

Stephens, T. L., Kinnison, L., Naquin, G., & Rueter, J. A. (2007). The changing roles for educational diagnosticians with a Response-to-Intervention framework in the identification of students with learning disabilities. *The DiaLog, 36*(2), 16–20.

Webber, J., & Plotts, C. (2008). *Emotional and behavioral disorders: Theory and practice* (5th ed.). Upper Saddle River, NJ: Pearson.

Zweback, S., & Mortenson, B. P. (2001). State certification/licensure standards for educational diagnosticians: A national review. *Education, 123,* 370–379.

Chapter 13

Assistive Technology Specialist

Carrie Anna Courtad

CASE STUDY: JOHN

John is 11 years old and in the fifth grade. He has been diagnosed as having a learning disability along with ADHD. Overall, he is physically healthy and very athletic; however, he has some fine motor skills deficits. He is approximately a grade and half behind his peers in reading and has trouble producing written pieces longer than a few sentences. He has the support of special education teacher and occupational therapist, and the teachers at his school practice a team approach. He is in one teacher's class for language arts, another teacher's class for math, and a third teacher's class for social studies and science. He is included in the general education classroom with up to 45 minutes a day in the resource room for needed support. He also has 60 minutes a month of pull-out services to work with a physical therapist who works at increasing his hand strength and fine motor skills. His social studies teacher has concerns that Josh is failing to understand what he is reading and that when it comes to writing a report or answering questions Josh is unable to fully express what he knows. The language arts teacher reports that she is unable to read his papers and there is considerable conflict during journaling time, where students are meant to reflect on what they have previously read. John takes his book home and spends considerable hours doing homework; however, this is proving to be very stressful to home life. An upcoming IEP will discuss current goals and the transition to middle school.

INTRODUCTION

In today's schools we are very fortunate to have a large number of assistive technologies available for student use. Mandates requiring IEP committees to consider assistive technology (AT) for students with disabilities is fairly new in the field of special education. The Technology-Related Assistance for Individuals with Disabilities Act of 1988 (otherwise known as the Tech Act) was the first time a federal act defined assistive technology and services and promoted the use of AT for all people with disabilities. IDEA 1990, and then IDEA 1997, brought AT to students with disabilities by strengthening the definition of AT, outlining that districts were responsible for providing AT to students with disabilities as part of a free and appropriate education (FAPE), and considering how AT could improve the lives of students with disabilities beyond the classroom.

AT consideration is mandated as a part of the IEP process, yet there are no federal regulations as to how the IEP team is to implement it. AT consideration is one of five areas that the IEP team must discuss during the meeting (along with positive behavioral interventions, limited English proficiency, instruction in Braille, and communication needs). AT consideration includes both the devices and services and is defined with federal statutes as:

§300.5 Assistive Technology Device
    Assistive technology device means any item, piece of equipment, or product system, whether acquired commercially off the shelf, modified or customized, that is used to increase, maintain, or improve functional capabilities of a child with a disability. The term does not include a medical device that is surgically implanted, or the replacement of that device. (IDEA, 2004, Section 602(1)(A))

AT services include §300.6 Assistive Technology Service
    Assistive technology service means any service that directly assists an individual with a disability in the selection, acquisition, or use of an assistive technology device. Assistive technology service means any service that directly assists a child with a disability in the selection, acquisition, or use of an assistive technology device. The term includes—
    (a) The evaluation of the needs of a child with a disability, including a functional evaluation of the child in the child's customary environment;

(b) Purchasing, leasing, or otherwise providing for the acquisition of assistive technology devices by children with disabilities;

(c) Selecting, designing, fitting, customizing, adapting, applying, maintaining, repairing, or replacing assistive technology devices;

(d) Coordinating and using other therapies, interventions, or services with assistive technology devices, such as those associated with existing education and rehabilitation plans and programs;

(e) Training or technical assistance for a child with a disability or, if appropriate, that child's family; and

(f) Training or technical assistance for professionals (including individuals providing education or rehabilitation services), employers, or other individuals who provide services to, employ, or are otherwise substantially involved in the major life functions of that child. (IDEA, 2004, Section 602(2) (A–F))

GENERAL ROLES AND RESPONSIBILITIES OF THE ASSISTIVE TECHNOLOGY (AT) SPECIALIST

If your district or building has employed an AT specialist, then his job description looks very similar to the outlined service definition in IDEA. An AT specialist should be an active part of any training with, servicing for, obtainment of, or consideration of AT devices. When conducting the IEP, if teachers and other professionals are unable to make an informed decision when considering AT devices they will refer to the AT specialist. This person will conduct an evaluation of the student and the environment in which the student completes tasks (e.g., school classroom, cafeteria, restroom), and then suggest assistive technology devices that might aid in the student progressing in the curriculum according to FAPE. The AT specialist will obtain the device through grants or a lending library or purchase the equipment outright. The AT person will train teachers, students, and parents on how to use the device and will also perform general maintenance to keep the device in working order. The AT specialist will also periodically check back with the teachers, student, and family to make sure the AT device functions within the given environment and that it hasn't been abandoned (i.e., the student stops using the device). Generally speaking, after the initial evaluations, the AT specialist is responsible for maintaining, programming, and training for an assistive technology device.

What Happens if There Is
Not an AT Specialist?

If there is not a dedicated AT specialist in your area, then there are usually other professionals who have knowledge of assistive technology devices and services. If the IEP members do not feel like they have enough knowledge collectively about considerations for AT, then the IEP team should include someone who might have a specialized knowledge base in AT in the areas of consideration. Other people in the district or building who might have this knowledge could include speech language pathologists, occupational or physical therapists, and assistive technology suppliers. These professionals often have specialized knowledge of how to consider the AT needs of students with disabilities.

However, it is important that someone who also knows the child have some familiarity with assistive technology devices. It has been suggested that those who have knowledge of the student usually suggest possible devices that are more practical (Reed & Bowser, 2005) and less expensive (Behrmann & Schepis, 1994) than an outside team.

Zabala and colleagues (2000) developed the Quality Indicators for Assistive Technology services (QIAT). Later, professionals gathered together to create a consortium called QIAT. However, Zabala and colleagues were not the only group working to improve outcomes for students using AT. There are many different resources and websites that provide guidance to teachers, schools, and parents in the consideration, evaluation, and implementation of AT. Included in Table 13.1 is a list of websites that provide free guidance and resources that revolve around better practices of employing AT for students with disabilities.

Table 13.1
Websites With Free Resources on Assistive Technology

Name of website	URL	About the site
AT Training Online Project (ATTO)	http://atto.buffalo.edu/registered/ATBasics.php	This website is from the University of Buffalo, the State University of New York, and provides online training modules for elementary students using AT.
Georgia Project for Assistive Technology (GPAT)	http://www.gpat.org	This site is funded by the Georgia Department of Education.
Quality Indicators for Assistive Technology Services (QIAT)	http://natri.uky.edu/assoc_projects/qiat/index.html	Consortium of professionals providing resources for quality indicators and decision-making processes for schools, universities, parents, teachers, and policy makers.
Teaching AT	http://www.teachingat.info	Sponsored by Georgetown University Center for Child and Human Development and a consortium of other training centers, this site provides training modules and case studies for using, funding, and applying AT principles.
Texas Assistive Technology Network (TATN)	http://www.texasat.net	This website is a project through a council of Texas Educational Regional Service Centers and the Texas Education Agency. They have video training modules along with AT resources.
University of Kentucky Assistive Technology (UKAT) Project	http://edsrc.uky.edu/www/ukatii/toolkit/index.html	This is a University of Kentucky website that provides the tools need for AT considerations and evaluations.
Wisconsin Assistive Technology Initiative (WATI)	http://www.wati.org	This website is funded through Wisconsin Department of Public Instruction to ensure that students with disabilities have the thoughtful considerations and implementation of AT.

Communication With Teachers and Parents

The AT specialist should maintain contact with both the student's general education teacher and his or her parents. When the AT specialist communicates with the general education teacher, the technologist will be asking the general educator questions about the student's performance in the classroom and what the student is expected to do that he is able and unable to complete in a effective and efficient manner. The AT specialist will ask for information about the environment in which the student participates, such as how much technology other than assistive is currently being used in the classroom and the general cultural climate of the classroom. The AT specialist may also observe the student in the classroom and ask for samples of the work the student is trying to complete. The AT specialist is trying to recommend the most appropriate device for the student, one that will meet the student's academic, environmental, and emotional needs. If a student is terrified of being stigmatized and would be reluctant to carry conspicuous equipment, then it is wise to contemplate those feelings when considering AT.

The AT specialist would also provide training to the classroom teacher on the selected device so it may be integrated into the general education classroom. This could include how to operate the device(s), what type of tasks a student should be using the device for, and the benefits of the device. If any maintenance is needed on the device, then the AT specialist would provide that service as well. It is also important that the AT specialist check in with the teacher after the device has been implemented into the classroom to evaluate the progress and appropriateness of the device.

Parents of students with disabilities need to be included when services for AT are considered or delivered to their child. An important factor when considering the choice of device is how the student will use the AT device at home. Gathering information from the parents' perspective will foster better use of resources and less chance of abandonment of the device. The device or service has to work for all parties involved to ensure a greater chance of success. It is also important that parents know that there is a wide variety of AT devices available including less costly and more appropriate devices.

An AT specialist can help guide parents to view all options of AT, as parents might not understand how a device can help or possibly impede the student's education. An AT specialist can provide information and research about devices that are being considered, explain how the device might carry over into more than one environment, and train the parents on how to use the device. An AT specialist would also be able to explain why a particular device might not be beneficial to a student and discuss the results of trying to implement a device that would not allow the student to perform tasks more efficiently or effectively.

GENERAL ASSISTIVE TECHNOLOGY DEVICES AND SOFTWARE

Since 1990, technology devices, software, and support have multiplied. Prior to the laws defining assistive technology, it was traditionally viewed as appropriate only for individuals with severe multiple or physical disabilities. Many of the technology devices used today were originally developed for students with visual impairments; however, as technology became readily available, it was apparent that those with learning disabilities could benefit from the same technology. AT since has improved the capabilities of many students with disabilities. There are a wide variety of technology supports for students with disabilities, and a large number of these supports can be accessed for free and used with a regular computer, an MP3 player, and even smartphones. A computer and word processor has many features that can immediately improve learning and production for students with disabilities. Free assistive technology built into computers running either Mac OS X or Windows 7 operating systems include screen readers and text-to-speech accessibilities. These items allow digital text to be read aloud to the student, enabling her to access material that is above her reading grade level. There are a number of free programs along with some that are available for purchase. Word processors have standard features such as grammar and spell checkers, and these tools are helpful to students with disabilities who are in the editing phase of their writing. Digital text has made its way to the mainstream market, and with this access and a computer all students can be highly productive.

Text readers allow the text that appears on the computer screen to be read aloud using computer-generated voices that are already included in the operating system of most computers. Text reader software also can be downloaded for free or inexpensively. Text readers sometimes allow text to be imported into MP3 files, which can then be read aloud on players such as iPods. Some eBook readers (i.e., Kindle, Nook, Sony Reader) include text readers. These have become very popular and more textbook titles have become available in that format. Some text readers also have features that allow a student to speak what he would like to write and convert it to text, called voice recognition or speech-to-text capability.

Voice recognition frees up some of the executive functions associated with writing such as remembering how to form letters, spell words, and put thoughts into text on the page, allowing a student to concentrate on creating the writing as opposed to the mechanics involved in writing. However, there are drawbacks to voice recognition, as it takes a long time to train the computer to recognize the student's voice, it is not always accurate, and students have to have a certain level of cognitive ability to make the necessary corrections.

Figure 13.1 covers some typical technologies for three core academic subjects. It is not an exhaustive list, but a starting point for you to begin learning about potential AT. There are also technologies for personal management, daily living, recreation, and communication. The list provides an example of possible classroom assistive technologies that an AT specialist might consider for your student.

SOLUTION TO THE CASE STUDY

Mrs. Crawford is the AT specialist for John's school district. She was called in to complete an evaluation of John so that she may recommend potential AT services to meet John's needs. Mrs. Crawford interviewed all of John's general education teachers, his parents, his special education teacher, and the physical therapist. Mrs. Crawford also took note that each of the general education rooms had a set of student computers connected to printers. Mrs. Crawford recommended a portable word processor that John could bring with him to all of his classes. He would use this device when writing to increase his output, accuracy in spelling, and grammar and legibility. He could save files on the portable word processor and then print out the files on the classroom computers. Mrs. Crawford taught him how to hook up the portable word processor and how to save multiple files along with how to use the device's spell checker, grammar checker, and word prediction tools. Mrs. Crawford also brought a variety of graphic organizers to the social studies teacher and described how to guide John in finding the main and supporting details of the textbook. She accessed a digital form of the textbook and converted the textbook into multiple MP3 files and loaded it on to his personal MP3 player so he could listen to the chapters before they were covering them in class. Mrs. Crawford also did this for his language arts book. When John finds he does have to write in class, he has been provided with pencil grip to ease fatigue on his fine motor skills.

Academic Areas	a	b	c	d	e	f	g	h	i	j	k
Writing											
Handwriting			√			√	√			√	
Spelling				√		√					
Sentence Fluency			√	√		√					
Ideas					√						√
Organization					√	√					
Transcription			√	√		√	√			√	
Reading											
Comprehension					√			√			
Decoding								√	√		
Text Interaction					√	√		√	√		
Math											
Computing	√	√				√					
Organizing/Aligning		√			√	√				√	√
Problem Solving	√	√			√			√	√		√
Copying			√			√	√			√	√

Common Tools, Examples, and Approximate Prices

a. **Calculators:** These are devices to compute numbers or formulas and include talking or voiced calculators (reads the number out loud), large key calculators, and graphic calculators. Examples: Calc-U-Vue Talking Calculator from Learning Resources ($24.99–$33.99); Talk 'n Scan from RJ Cooper & Associates ($119.00).

b. **Computer Math Programs**: Math computer software contains a variety of features from correctly reading math problems to allowing on-screen input and translation to Braille. Examples: MathPad from IntelliTools ($79.95); MathTalk from Metroplex Voice Computing, Inc. ($300.00); MathType from Design Science ($57.00–$97.00).

c. **Voice Recognition Software:** Software that allows you to speak what you want to write and to input commands into the computer. Examples: Dragon NaturallySpeaking from Nuance ($99.99–$299.99); e-Speaking from e-speaking. com ($14.00).

d. **Word Prediction Software:** Software that makes word predictions as a person types. Examples: Co:Writer 6 from Don Johnson ($325.00); Aurora Systems from Aurora Systems Inc. ($149.00–$549.00).

e. **Templates or Graphic Organizers:** Aid in organizing ideas, figures, or numbers. Can be paper based or on a website. Example: Kidspiration from Inspiration Inc. ($69.00).

f. **Portable Word Processor**: Similar to computers or a word processing software. Examples: NEO from AlphaSmart ($169.00); Laser PC6 from Perfect Solutions ($150.00).

Figure 13.1. Possible classroom assistive technologies.

g. **Pencil Grips:** Devices that makes the grip of a writing utensil more comfortable no matter what subject the student is using them for. Found at teacher supply stores (prices vary).

h. **Text Readers:** Read text from Microsoft Word documents or from Internet browsers. Examples: WYNN Reader from Freedom Scientific Inc. ($375.00); Kurzweil 3000 from Kurzweil Educational Systems, Inc. ($395.00–$1495.00); ReadPlease from ReadPlease Corporation (Free–$49.95).

i. **Text Readers/Converters:** Read text and can convert text into MP3 files to play on MP3 players such as iPods. Examples: TextAloud from NextUp Technologies ($29.95); NaturalReader from AT&T (Free–$199.50).

j. **Raised lined paper:** Paper with larger or tactile lines to aid in staying on the line when writing or printing numbers. Found at teacher supply stores (prices vary).

k. **Graph paper:** Aids in lining up numbers in math problems or creating representations in geometry. Found at teacher supply stores (prices vary).

Figure 13.1. Possible classroom assistive technologies, continued.

REFERENCES

Berhmann, M. M., & Schepis, M. M. (1994). Assistive technology assessment: A multiple case study of three approaches with students with physical disabilities during the transition from school to work. *Journal of Vocational Rehabilitation, 4,* 202–210.

Individuals with Disabilities Education Improvement Act, Pub. Law 108-446 (December 3, 2004).

Technology-Related Assistance for Individuals with Disabilities Act, PL 100-407 (1988).

Reed, P., & Bowser, G. (2005). Assistive technology in the IEP. In D. L. Edyburn, K. Higgins, & R. Boone (Eds.), *The handbook of special education technology research and practice* (pp. 61–77). Whitefish Bay, WI: Knowledge by Design.

Zabala, J., Bowser, G., Blunt, M., Hartsell, K., Carl, D., Korsten, J., . . . & Reed, P. (2000). Quality indicators for assistive technology services in school settings. *Journal of Special Education Technology, 15*(4), 25–36.

Chapter 14

Itinerant Services

Christy Borders and Christine Clark-Bischke

CASE STUDY: MS. LOPEZ

Ms. Lopez has been teaching third grade for 5 years. She arrives in her classroom, as usual, a couple weeks before school starts to prepare for the new school year. Upon arrival, she is given her student list. She notices that Sara will be in her class this year. Ms. Lopez has seen Sara before; she is a student with a cochlear implant who uses an interpreter. Sara also has a visual impairment. Although Ms. Lopez feels comfortable with her instruction, she gets an anxious feeling in her stomach thinking about what this is going to mean for her classroom—there will be other adults in her classroom to support Sara. There are many questions running through Ms. Lopez's head: How will this impact my class schedule? What do I do with her equipment? How do I use the interpreter? What can Sara hear? What can Sara see? What do I need to change? How do I help my other students understand?

On Sara's Individualized Education Program (IEP), there are several services listed including a teacher of the hearing impaired for 30 minutes per week, a teacher of students with visual impairments for 30 minutes per week, an educational interpreter for 6 hours per day, and speech/language pathology for 30 minutes per week. Ms. Lopez wonders about the coordination of services and how this will impact her classroom.

Ms. Lopez is not alone in this scenario. Sara's itinerant teachers for students who are deaf and students who have visual impairments will help answer many of her questions and coordinate services. This chapter serves to provide an outline of what itinerant service delivery looks like in the classroom and gives some suggestions for working in collaboration with itinerant teachers.

ITINERANT SERVICES

DEFINITION

An itinerant is a person who travels from place to place, especially for duty or business. There is more specificity when thinking about special education service provision. An itinerant teacher is a teacher who travels from school to school in order to provide services and case management to students who often have low-incidence disabilities (i.e., hearing or vision impairment). This teacher's schedule is dependent on his or her current case-load needs.

RATIONALE

With the passage of educational policy (Individuals with Disabilities Education Improvement Act, 2004; No Child Left Behind Act, 2001) and an increase in audiological technology, education for children with hearing loss is shifting toward inclusive education. More than 59% of children with hearing loss and 90% of children with visual impairments in the United States were served in a general education classroom with typically developing peers during the 2007–2008 school year (Galludet Research Institute, 2008; National Center for Education Statistics, 2008). The consequence of this trend is that more than 15,000 children with hearing loss and more than 30,000 students who are visually impaired or blind nationwide are being served primarily by general education teachers and/or itinerant service providers (American Printing House for the Blind, 2009).

The need for itinerant teachers is based on the population served by these teachers. As mentioned above, itinerant teachers generally serve students falling into low-incidence disability categories (i.e., hearing or vision impairment). Because the number of these students is low and they are often spread out across multiple schools, the provision of itinerant service makes the most sense.

FREQUENCY OF HEARING IMPAIRMENT

Given the low numbers of children born with a hearing impairment, it is safe to assume that general education teachers may only have a student with a hearing impairment in their classroom every 5–10 years. Hearing impairment occurs in 2 to 3 out of every 1,000 children born in the United States (National Institute on Deafness and Other Communication Disorders [NIDCD], 2010). It is important to note that 9 out of every 10 children who are born with a hearing impairment are born to a parent who can hear (NIDCD, 2010).

FREQUENCY OF VISUAL IMPAIRMENT

Visual impairment occurs in 12.2 out of every 1,000 children under the age of 18 (National Dissemination Center for Children with Disabilities [NICHCY], 2004) including students with severe disabilities. Legal blindness (i.e., 20/200 or less vision in the best eye with correction) or total blindness (i.e., no light perception) occurs in .6 out of every 1,000 children. Visual impairments include genetic conditions passed on through the parents.

ESSENTIAL CHARACTERISTICS OF ITINERANT TEACHERS

Bullard (2003) described essential characteristics of itinerant teachers. She first explained that in order to be a successful itinerant teacher, one must be flexible. Due to the nontraditional schedule and role as a teacher and team support, an itinerant teacher cannot expect any one peg to fit in any given hole. Flexibility is very important when organizing a team of providers as well as switching the schedule "on the fly." Issues may (and will) arise at one school that the teacher may not have intended on visiting on a particular day and flexibility will allow the best service provision.

In conjunction with flexibility is patience as an itinerant teacher. Itinerant teachers may suggest changes to be made by a classroom teacher. Changing another person's system may require time and scaffolding. Patience allows the itinerant teacher to understand that changes in perceptions and strategies take time and allows for a healthy relationship with cooperating teachers.

In addition, Olmstead (2005) noted the importance of communication skills. Communication is essential as itinerant teachers serve as liaisons with the students, parents, and school personnel in accessing resources and creating an appropriate educational environment. Through this essential characteristic, itinerant teachers are able to build a rapport that can foster the relationships necessary for the success of their students. Communication also allows for networking among individuals who can assist in accessing community resources that could be beneficial in providing the generalization of skills outside of the school building.

Although Bullard (2003) suggested experience for itinerant teachers, this is sometimes not the reality of itinerant service provision. Unfortunately, many early career teachers are given an itinerant caseload because it meets the need of the district. Experience trying different strategies and life experience, in general, can help to increase an itinerant teacher's credibility when entering the classroom of another teacher. Although successful itinerant service provision is more probable with more experience, this is not always an option.

Lastly, Bullard (2003) suggested skill as a facilitator to be a successful itinerant teacher. One of the primary roles of an itinerant teacher (discussed in the next section) is team coordination. In order to bring numerous individuals together, facilitation rather than demand is required.

GENERAL ROLES AND RESPONSIBILITIES

WORKING WITH STUDENTS

One obvious responsibility of any teacher is to work with the students on his caseload. This can take on several different forms for an itinerant teacher. He may work one-on-one with his student or work with the student within the context of the general education classroom.

Pull-out. Itinerant teachers may take the child with the hearing or visual impairment out of the general education classroom for short periods of time to work on specific skills included within the student's IEP. For example, one student may be included in the general education classroom for all academic subjects, but have a service of aural habilitation or Braille instruction for 30 minutes a week designated in her IEP. Working on listening skills may be particularly difficult within the context of the general education classroom and may be best addressed in a smaller, quieter environment.

Push-in. Itinerant teachers may also work within the classroom to specifically address academic skills. The teacher of students with visual impairments or a supported instructional assistant/paraprofessional will often provide direct support during academic instruction to provide clarification or modification of materials typically presented in abstract or visual strategies. The itinerant teacher may reiterate the class content in a more concrete manner for the child with the use of concrete materials or manipulatives.

Working within the general education classroom. Oftentimes, itinerant teachers do not specifically address academic skills with their students, as those are adequately covered within the general education classroom. They may use content delivered in the general education classroom as a starting point for how to address deficits in self-advocacy, study skills, listening, repair strategies, and many other skill areas. While the child works within the general education classroom, the itinerant teacher may work with the child in another section of the room, highlighting strategies that could be incorporated to assist the student with the content.

Working With Teachers

Another responsibility of any itinerant teacher is to work with teachers who have his students in class. This can take on several different forms for an itinerant teacher. He may collaborate with these teachers, provide in-service, or help with curricular/material modification.

Collaboration. Although working directly with students is an option for itinerant teachers, in some situations (e.g., students with hearing impairments and students with severe disabilities) these teachers are more likely to function in a consultative role. The itinerant teacher provides services of brief duration and information to the general education classroom teacher that may assist the student and teacher in modifying the environment or curriculum to provide optimal access for the student with a hearing or vision impairment.

In-service. General education teachers often do not feel prepared to have a student with a hearing or visual impairment in their classroom (Luckner, 2006). One service that itinerant teachers conduct is in-service training. This allows the itinerant teacher to provide specific information that may assist the teacher in how to accommodate the student with a hearing or visual impairment. See the charts/checklist section for a sample outline of an in-service program for a general education teacher. In-service often contains information on hearing loss or visual impairment in general and specifically related to the student in the classroom, to the amplification device or assistive technology that the child may use, and to modification suggestions for the general education teacher.

Curricular/material modification. Students with even mild to moderate hearing loss (the least severe type) often experience language delays (Bess, Dodd-Murphy, & Parker, 1998; Briscoe, Bishop, & Norbury, 2001; Davis, Ellenbein, Schum, & Bentler, 1986; Moeller, 2000; Wake, Hughes, Poulakis, Collins, & Rickards, 2004; Yoshinago-Itano, 1999). Although this may seem obvious, it is often not understood just how delayed the student's language may be. In addition, students with mild to moderate vision loss may experience a delay in the development of reading skills. Any delay for a student would clearly impact every aspect of the school day. The itinerant teacher can work with the general education teacher to provide strategies for curricular or material modification so that the language and content is accessible to the student with hearing impairment and enlarged/appropriate materials are accessible to the student with visual impairments.

OTHER SERVICES

Team coordination. Students with hearing impairment are often seen by a variety of service providers including, but not limited to, itinerant teachers of the deaf, itinerant teachers of students with visual impairments, educational audiologists, interpreters, instructional assistants, speech/language pathologists, special education teachers, occupational therapists, physical therapists, and/or social workers. Students with visual impairments receive services from orientation and mobility specialists and many of the individuals listed previously. The construction of the educational team is dictated by individual student need but most often the team will consist of multiple members. If the student receives instruction primarily in the general education classroom, it is most likely that the itinerant teacher will be responsible for coordinating the service delivery team. This can be a very time consuming and stressful process if the essential characteristics mentioned previously in this chapter (i.e., flexibility, patience, experience, skill as a facilitator) are not present. The itinerant teacher, in this case, needs to organize all of the team members for meetings and/or any updates to programming.

Another important team the itinerant teacher works with is the general education staff at the school in which the student with hearing or vision impairment is placed. This goes beyond the general education classroom teacher and includes staff such as the general education instructional assistants/paraprofessionals, teachers of special classes (e.g., art, music, physical education), office staff, and school administration. Although it may seem like the general education classroom teacher is the only person with whom the itinerant teacher would work, one must consider that this child is part of the overall school community and equipment and language needs must be at least generally understood by any adult who may encounter the student.

Equipment support/troubleshooting. Luckner and Howell (2002) stated that only 42% of itinerant teacher time was spent providing direct instruction. In our opinion, this estimate may be high with less time spent on direct instruction and more time devoted to other forms of troubleshooting, materials preparation, and consultation. General education staff members have very limited experience, if any, with assistive technology or audiological equipment. Although the itinerant teacher should provide an in-service session on the equipment, there are times when the equipment needs to be repaired or evaluated by someone with more experience. Several studies have shown that on any given day, anywhere from 50% to 95% of hearing equipment is in disrepair (Elfenbein, Bentler, Davis, & Niebuhr, 1988; Gaeth & Lounsbury, 1966; Kemker, McConnell, Logan, & Green, 1979). Although this percentage is startling, it also illustrates the crucial role of an itinerant teacher in providing support for assistive technology and audiological equipment as needed. This also highlights the need for flexibility in an itinerant teacher. Often an itinerant teacher will feel that her schedule is set for the day when an unexpected phone call comes in regarding broken or nonfunctioning equipment. The importance of functioning equipment for student success requires that the schedule must be changed so that the itinerant can provide support in troubleshooting measures. Districts often employ educational audiologists who are not available for minor repairs or troubleshooting based on their large caseloads. This is evidenced by the American Speech-Language-Hearing Association's (2002) *Guidelines for Audiology Service Provision in and for Schools*, which suggests that there should be a minimum of one educational audiologist for every 10,000 students in a school district. Itinerant teachers of students with visual impairments are typically the only individuals within districts with advanced knowledge in troubleshooting assistive technology for their students. This additional responsibility is also impacted by large caseloads. A good article regarding troubleshooting can be found at http://www.audiologyawareness.com/ha_troubleshoot.asp.

Assessment. The itinerant teacher may assist with the annual and/or 3-year reevaluation of students who are deaf or hard of hearing and those who are visually impaired or blind. This assessment may take several different forms, including, but not limited to, standardized test administration, criterion-referenced assessment, direct classroom observation, and student/teacher interviews. In addition, itinerant teachers of students with visual impairments complete functional vision assessments, learning media assessments, and a review of ophthalmological reports for students who are visually impaired or blind. These assessments will help to inform the educational team regarding the current service provision.

COMMUNICATION WITH TEACHERS AND PARENTS

Given the amount of team coordination required, communication is essential. Not only will the itinerant teacher be communicating with teachers and other school team members, but with parents as well. Itinerant teachers get to see teachers face-to-face, but they may not have adequate time to share all of the information required. Communication is best delivered via e-mail and/or handouts. Itinerant teachers can provide communication notebooks for teachers and parents to write in notes and questions that can go back and forth between all of the individuals. In recent years, many itinerant teachers have engaged current technology to keep team members linked together in communication through the use of newsletters, websites, and wikis. Whatever the method, consistent communication is very important so that no one—the classroom teacher, parent, or other service provider—feels isolated in service delivery.

Questions to Ask

As a general education teacher, you may have many questions. Below is a list of questions to consider asking the itinerant teacher to help you feel prepared to best serve the students in your classroom.

General Questions

- What is your schedule? When can we expect to see you?
- How can I reach you if there is a change in our schedule?
- Who do I call if there is a problem with the equipment?
- What can my student hear? What does she understand?
- What can my student see? Does his vision fluctuate daily?
- Might his vision decrease over time?
- What do I do if the interpreter or paraprofessional is out?
- What role will the interpreter or paraprofessional have in classroom behavioral management?
- If the student with a hearing impairment is working independently, what will the interpreter or paraprofessional do in my classroom?

Instructional/Classroom Questions

- How can I prepare the other students for having a student with a hearing impairment or a visual impairment in the classroom?
- How does my student's hearing impairment impact her language and communication level?
- How can I make sure that my classroom is not too noisy?
- How does my student's visual impairment impact his academic and reading level?
- What are some strategies to make sure that my student has full access to the classroom instruction?
- How do I modify the language in my classroom without "talking down" to the students?

SOLUTION TO THE CASE STUDY

Ms. Lopez is contacted by the itinerant teacher of the deaf and itinerant teacher of students with visual impairments for an initial meeting. At this meeting, the itinerant teachers present many different pieces of information that assist Ms. Lopez in planning for Sara's year. The itinerant teachers present information verbally and through handouts (see the Appendix for this chapter) on exactly what Sara can hear with her cochlear implant, what Sara can see, what to do when the implant is not working, how to use/work with an educational interpreter, strategies for modifying the curriculum and materials, and strategies to make sure that Sara can access learning within the classroom. The itinerant teachers also explain how they each use the 30 minutes a week to work with Sara and that the time will be directed through conversations with Ms. Lopez and the other team members. Each week, the itinerant teachers will identify if any immediate needs have emerged (e.g., technology/amplification issue, materials modification, social/ emotional issue, specific academic difficulty) through the conversations via e-mail and/or Sara's communication notebook. First, immediate needs will be addressed and if none exist, the itinerant teacher will work with the educational interpreter and paraprofessional in the classroom to model strategies to help Sara access the classroom instruction. The itinerant teachers also gave Ms. Lopez their direct contact information in case anything arises in the classroom that demands immediate attention. Lastly, the itinerant teachers arrange a time during the first week of class to come into the classroom and talk with all of the students about hearing loss, vision loss, and interpreters.

After this conversation, Ms. Lopez's fears start to calm as she now realizes that she will have strong support from the itinerant teachers. Sara will have consistent service delivery through a team of individuals that will be coordinated through the itinerant teacher of the deaf.

REFERENCES

American Printing House for the Blind. (2009). *Annual report 2008*. Louisville, KY: Author.

American Speech-Language-Hearing Association. (2002). *Guidelines for audiology service provision in and for schools*. Retrieved from http://www.asha.org/docs/html/GL2002-00005.html

Bess, F. H., Dodd-Murphy, J., & Parker, R. A. (1998). Children with minimal sensorineural hearing loss: Prevalence, educational performance, and functional status. *Ear and Hearing, 19*, 339–354.

Briscoe, J., Bishop, D. V., & Norbury, C. F. (2001). Phonological processing, language, and literacy: A comparison of children with mild-to-moderate sensorineural hearing loss and those with specific language impairment. *Journal of Childhood Psychology and Psychiatry, 42,* 329–340.

Bullard, C. (2003). *The itinerant teacher's handbook.* Hillsboro, OR: Butte.

Davis, J., Ellenbein, J., Schum, R., & Bentler, R. (1986). Effects of mild and moderate hearing impairments on language, educational, and psychosocial behavior of children. *Journal of Speech and Hearing Disorders, 51,* 53–62.

Elfenbein, J., Bentler, R. A., Davis, J., & Niebuhr, D. (1988). Status of school children's hearing aids related to monitoring practices. *Ear and Hearing, 9,* 166–174.

Gaeth, J. H., & Lounsbury, E. (1966). Hearing aids and children in elementary schools. *Journal of Speech, Language and Hearing Research, 31,* 283–289.

Gallaudet Research Institute. (2008). *Regional and national summary report of data from the 2007–2008 Annual Survey of Deaf and Hard of Hearing Children and Youth.* Washington, DC: Gallaudet University.

Individuals with Disabilities Education Improvement Act, Pub. Law 108-446 (December 3, 2004).

Kemker, F. J., McConnell, F., Logan, S. A., & Green, B. W. (1979). A field study of children's hearing aids in a school environment. *Language, Speech and Hearing Services in Schools, 10,* 47–53.

Luckner, J. (2006). Providing itinerant services. In D. F. Moores & D. S. Martin (Eds.), *Deaf learners: Developments in curriculum and instruction* (pp. 93–111). Washington, DC: Gallaudet University Press.

Luckner, J., & Howell, J. (2002). Suggestions for preparing itinerant teachers: A qualitative analysis. *American Annals of the Deaf, 147*(3), 54–61.

Moeller, M. P. (2000). Early intervention and language development in children who are deaf and hard of hearing. *Pediatrics, 106.* Retrieved from http://www.pediatrics.org/cgi/content/full/106/3/e43

National Center for Education Statistics. (2008). *Table 51. Percentage distribution of students 6 to 21 years old served under Individuals with Disabilities Education Act, Part B, by educational environment and type of disability: Selected years, fall 1989 through fall 2006.* Retrieved from http://nces.ed.gov/programs/digest/d08/tables/dt08_051.asp

National Dissemination Center for Children with Disabilities. (2004). *Disability fact sheet, No. 13, Visual impairments.* Retrieved from http://www.nichcy.org/InformationResources/Documents/NICHCY%20PUBS/fs13.pdf

National Institute on Deafness and Other Communication Disorders. (2010). *Quick statistics.* Retrieved from http://www.nidcd.nih.gov/health/statistics/quick.htm

No Child Left Behind Act, 20 U.S.C. §6301 (2001).

Olmstead, J. E. (2005). *Itinerant teaching: Tricks of the trade for teachers of students with visual impairments.* New York, NY: AFB Press.

Wake, M., Hughes, E., Poulakis, Z., Collins, C., & Rickards, W. (2004). Outcomes of mild-profound hearing impairment at age 7–8 years: A population study. *Ear and Hearing, 25,* 1–8.

Yoshinago-Itano, C. (1999). Benefits of early intervention for children's hearing loss. *Otolaryngologic Clinics of North America, 32,* 1089–1102.

APPENDIX
Sample In-Service Outlines and Other Tools

In-Service on Hearing Loss Outline

I. Hearing
    a. How we hear

II. Degrees of Hearing Loss
    a. Hearing loss simulation

III. Types of Hearing Loss
    a. Conductive
    b. Sensorineural
    c. Mixed

IV. Speech Perception

V. Speech Discrimination/Word Recognition

VI. Assistive Listening Devices
    a. Hearing aids
      i. How they work
      ii. Components
      iii. Troubleshooting

    b. Cochlear implants
      i. How they work
      ii. Cochlear implant simulation
      iii. Components
      iv. Troubleshooting

    c. Sound field systems/FM systems
      i. How they work
      ii. Components
      iii. Troubleshooting

VII. Educational Considerations
    a. Teacher recommendations
    b. Classroom recommendations

In-Service on Vision Outline

I.   Vision
     a. How we see
     b. Parts of the eye

II. Degrees of Vision Loss
     a. Low vision
     b. Legal blindness

III. Types of Vision Loss
     a. Congenital vision loss
     b. Adventitious vision loss

IV. Visual Conditions/Diagnoses

V.   Assistive Technology
     a. Magnification
        i.   Closed circuit television (CCTV)
             1. How it works
             2. Components
             3. Troubleshooting

        ii. Handheld magnifiers
             1. How they work

     b. Braille translation software/Braille writers

     c. Screen reading software
        i.   How it works
        ii. Components
        iii. Troubleshooting

     d. Notetakers
        i.   How they work
        ii. Components
        iii. Troubleshooting

     e. Daily living aids

VI. Assessments
    a. Functional vision assessment
    b. Learning media assessment
    c. Ophthalmological exam
    d. Accommodations and adaptations

VII. Orientation and Mobility

VIII. Educational Considerations
    a. Teacher recommendations
    b. Classroom recommendations

Audiogram

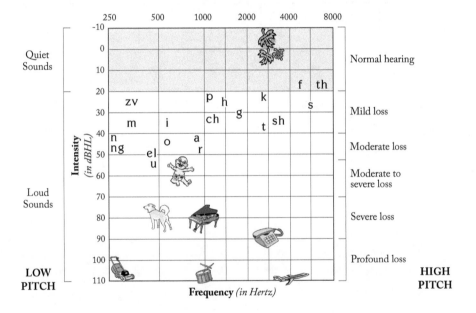

Daily Listening Check

Daily listening check

Day	"Ahh"	"Eee"	"Ooo"	"Mmm"	"Sss"	"Shh"	Name
Monday							
Tuesday							
Wednesday							
Thursday							
Friday							

Sample Communication Log

Day	Concern	Steps Taken	Questions
Monday			
Tuesday			
Wednesday			
Thursday			
Friday			

Accommodation Plan

Accommodations and Modifications for Individual Learner Plan Summary

Student name _____ School _____

Grade _____ Year _____

Services	Description	IEP requirement	Recommended
Assistive and instructional technology			
Content modifications			
Environmental modifications			
Modifications in materials			
Modifications of evaluations (testing/ homework)			
Instructional strategies			
Social/behavioral adaptations			
Cultural considerations			
Other			

Chapter 15

Audiologist

Cassandra M. Schmidt

CASE STUDY: NORMA

Norma is a third-grade student with a mild sensorineural hearing loss, bilaterally. She has been in a mainstream classroom since the middle of her first-grade school year. Her hearing loss was diagnosed when she was approximately 16 months old, and she has been utilizing hearing aids since that time. Because Norma's hearing loss was detected early on, she has been able to develop near-normal speech and language skills. She was placed in a kindergarten classroom for children with hearing loss and also completed most of first grade in that same setting. During Norma's annual review (in first grade) it was decided that she should be placed in the general education classroom provided that she continue to receive services. As mentioned previously, Norma has a mild hearing loss in both ears. Children with a mild hearing loss tend to fall "between the cracks" because they are not easily diagnosed and can often be misdiagnosed as having a learning disability. Currently she receives speech therapy for 90 minutes a week, one-on-one itinerant time for 30 minutes a week, and preferential seating in the classroom. Another service that she receives really benefits the entire classroom. The classroom that Norma spends the majority of her day in has a sound field amplification system. This system works by amplifying her teacher's voice so that everyone in the classroom can hear the teacher better. Recently, one of the members on the IEP team suggested that the services provided to Norma be reduced because "she appears to be doing just fine." Now, Norma and her family need to decide what is right for her and her education before they meet with the IEP team next month.

INTRODUCTION

Audiology is a healthcare profession that focuses on hearing. Most audiologists practice in either healthcare settings or the private sector. Some audiologists may choose to practice in education, rehabilitation settings, or industry (Stach, 1998). The focus of this chapter will be on the role of the educational audiologist and the services provided to students, parents, and teachers.

ROLES AND RESPONSIBILITIES OF THE AUDIOLOGIST

The main role of the audiologist, regardless of setting, is to identify hearing loss, prevent further hearing loss, and reduce the severity of communication disorders that may result from untreated hearing loss. The audiologist plays a crucial role in the early identification of hearing loss. This spans the entire population from infants to the geriatric population. The educational audiologist, however, specifically focuses on school-age children and the direct impact hearing loss has on learning. According to Stach (1998), one out of every 10 audiologists works in an educational setting. In most cases, this is usually in the public schools at the primary level. The educational audiologist will often wear a variety of hats. Her role is vastly different than that of the private practice audiologist. The educational audiologist may be responsible for diagnostics, schoolwide screening programs, and follow-ups through annual testing. Diagnostics is a broad term used to describe any type of audiological assessment. This can include testing for hearing loss in the sound-treated test booth, as well as middle ear assessment and functional listening abilities within the classroom. Another major role of the educational audiologist is the maintenance and assistance with amplification, including hearing aids and hearing assistive technology (HATs) for those students who need such services. In addition, the educational audiologist will usually conduct in-services for school personnel regarding:

- type and degree of the hearing loss,
- effects of the hearing loss on classroom ability and achievement,
- amplification and other HATs, and
- participation in Individualized Education Program (IEP) meetings.

Lastly, one of the most important roles that an educational audiologist has is to serve as an advocate for students with hearing loss. This includes working with parents, teachers, and other support staff to ensure that the hearing loss will have as minimal an educational impact as possible.

Communication With Teachers and Parents

The educational audiologist provides a very important role for the child with hearing loss. One of the most important roles, as briefly discussed earlier, is providing in-services to both classroom teachers and any other support staff that may work with the child with hearing loss. During the in-service, which should occur at least biannually, the following topics should be discussed:

- type, nature, and degree of hearing loss (can be brief, pertaining to those students on the current caseload);
- effects of untreated or poorly managed hearing loss, including:
  - delays in speech and language, and
  - delays in reading ability; and

- current amplification options such as:
  - hearing aids, cochlear implants, and hearing assistive technologies.

The goal of the in-service is to orient and remind staff of the basics of hearing loss and how that can affect the child in the classroom. It is important that all staff members working with a child with hearing loss are knowledgeable regarding the child's hearing loss and how it affects the child's ability to learn in the classroom.

The audiologist should develop a good line of communication with the parents of the child with hearing loss. A great tool to help with this is to utilize a communication notebook that the child can bring to and from school every day. This is a very effective way to communicate between the teacher, parent, audiologist, and other support staff.

Family Night

Family Night can be a monthly event where parents and siblings of children in the classroom can get together for a fun, yet educational evening. Having Family Night is another great way to incorporate parents into the classroom. This is an opportunity for parents of children with hearing loss to meet and get to know the parents of children without hearing loss. The goal of Family Night is to have some sort of topic to discuss with the parents for approximately 30 minutes, and then open the floor to parents for questions. After the discussion, parents can mingle with each other. Different topics should be used each month, so that parents have something new and exciting to look forward to. Some sample topics might include:

- the latest trends in reading strategies,
- a fun evening learning basic sign language, or
- tips for effective communication between parents and children.

During the discussion part, the children and siblings can be in an adjacent classroom participating in various activities that can mimic what the parents are learning about so they can discuss it later as a family.

How We Hear

In order for us to hear and perceive sounds and speech we need to have an intact auditory system. The ear consists of three main parts: the outer ear, the middle ear, and the inner ear. Each main part is responsible for the conduction of sound (see Figure 15.1). Sound passes through the system first through the outer ear (pinna), which collects the sound. The sound is then passed through the middle ear, which contains the three smallest bones in the human body. Sound then travels through to the inner ear, and lastly to the brain for final processing. If there is a problem in any of these parts, the sound may have difficulty traveling and/or reaching the brain.

The Audiogram

Hearing loss is plotted on a graph called an audiogram. The graph represents the individual's ability to detect tones presented to him via headphones in a sound-treated booth. Responses are plotted on the graph and inform us of the type and degree of hearing loss. Speech sounds can also be plotted on the audiogram, which illustrates the specific speech sounds the person may be missing depending on the degree of hearing loss. See Figure 15.2 for a closer look at the audiogram.

Type of Hearing Loss

There are three types of hearing loss:

- *Sensorineural*: This is the most common type of permanent hearing loss. This type of hearing loss occurs when there is a problem in either the inner ear or beyond. The degree (explained below) can be from mild to profound. See Figure 15.1 for depiction of the parts of the ear.

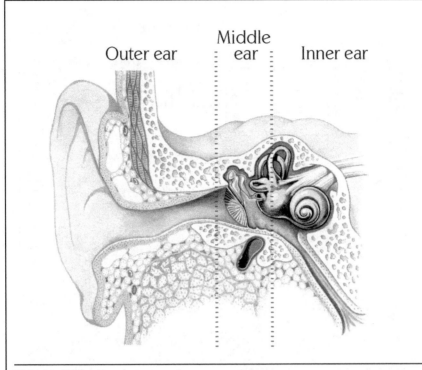

Figure 15.1. The human ear. Notice the three parts of the ear: *outer, middle,* and *inner ear.* The outer ear contains the pinna (ear lobe), external auditory canal, and the tympanic membrane (ear drum). The middle ear contains the three smallest bones in the human body (hammer, anvil, and stirrup), which help conduct the sound through to the inner ear and brain. The inner ear contains the semicircular canals (help with balance) and the cochlea (snail), and the auditory nerve, which sends the sound up to the brainstem.

- *Conductive*: This is the most common type of temporary hearing loss. This type of hearing loss can often be treated medically with either antibiotics or surgery. This type of hearing loss occurs when there is a problem in either the outer or middle part of the ear. This loss can be temporary, but if left untreated, or if treatment is unsuccessful, it can become permanent. The degree can be mild to moderate.
- *Mixed*: This type of hearing loss is basically a combination of sensorineural and conductive. The sound cannot pass through due to a problem in both the outer/middle and inner ear.

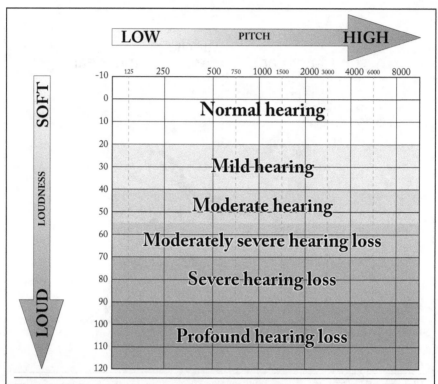

Figure 15.2. The audiogram. Notice the frequencies across the top, from left to right are low-pitched sounds to high-pitched sounds. The numbers on the left-hand side represent the level of loudness; 0 dB is a very soft sound, and 120 dB is a very loud sound.

The *type* of hearing loss (those mentioned above) can be classified by the following ways:

- *Unilateral hearing loss*: This is a hearing loss of any type and degree in one ear, and normal hearing in the other ear.
- *Bilateral hearing loss*: This is some type and degree of hearing loss in both ears. The loss may be the same type and degree in both ears or different.
- *Asymmetric hearing loss*: This is hearing loss that is different between the ears; in other words, both ears have hearing loss, but are not equal in their degree.

Degree of Hearing Loss

Hearing loss is classified according the decibel (dB) level at which the individual perceives the sound. Loudness is measured using decibels. The greater the decibel level needed, the greater (more severe) the hearing loss. Degree of hearing loss is directly related to the ability to understand speech. See Table 15.1 for a description of hearing loss classifications.

Table 15.1
Classification System of Hearing Loss Levels

Children

-10–15 dB	Normal
16–25 dB	Slight
25–30 dB	Mild
31–50 dB	Moderate
51–70 dB	Severe
71 dB +	Profound

Adults

-10–15 dB	Normal
16–25dB	Slight
26–40 dB	Mild
41–55 dB	Moderate
56–70 dB	Moderately-Severe
71–90 dB	Severe
91 dB +	Profound

Note. Notice that the classification system for children is more aggressive than that of adults. See Clark (1981).

DEGREE OF HEARING LOSS AND EFFECT ON COMMUNICATION

Hearing loss can have unfavorable effects on speech and language development. The earlier hearing loss occurs in a child's life, the more serious the effects on the child's development. Similarly, the earlier the problem is identified and intervention is begun, the less serious the ultimate impact. The following are four major ways in which hearing loss affects children (see http://www.asha.org for more information):

■ It causes delay in the development of receptive and expressive communication skills.

■ The language deficit causes learning problems that result in reduced academic achievement.

■ Communication difficulties often lead to social isolation and poor self-concept.

■ It may have an impact on vocational choices.

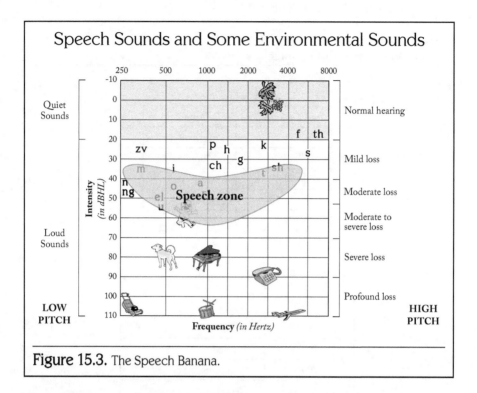

Figure 15.3. The Speech Banana.

A good way to visualize speech information is to look at Figure 15.3. The audiogram of familiar sounds is an excellent counseling tool. It illustrates everyday sounds that we are exposed to and the frequency and loudness level that they are. The Speech Banana is also illustrated. This depicts the speech sounds and where they fall in terms of their frequency information. If someone has a 30 dB hearing loss, he will have difficulty understanding any sounds that are *above* that line.

HEARING AIDS AND HEARING ASSISTIVE TECHNOLOGY (HAT)

The following is a brief overview of hearing aids and other HATs that are used by children with hearing loss.

Hearing aids are electronic devices that work by collecting acoustic sound via a microphone, converting that sound into an electronic signal for processing, and then reconverting it into an acoustic signal, which is then transmitted to the person via the receiver. Hearing aids come in a variety of styles including those that sit in the person's ear (in-the-ear [ITE]) and those that have components behind the ear (BTE), using an ear mold to connect to the person's ear. Most children utilize the BTE style. The electronic components (computer chip, microphone, and receiver) are housed within a casing that sits either in or behind the user's ear. The sound is transmitted to the users through a tube, which connects the hearing aid to the ear mold. The ear mold is a plastic piece that usually fills up the bowl of the ear and provides retention of the device. See http://www.phonak.com/us/b2c/en/products/hearing_instruments/versata_art/styles/sp.html for photos of earmolds.

Hearing Assistive Technology (HAT) is a broad term used to define any device that is used to aid in listening and communication. The most common type of HAT is an FM system. FM systems are frequently used because they help reduce the two main problems with effective listening: distance and noise. FM stands for *frequency modulation*, and the basic principle is that the sound is transmitted directly from one device to another using FM waves. This technology is often used in classrooms. The teacher will wear a microphone close to the mouth and the sound will be transmitted to the receiver. The receiver can be either a piece on the child's hearing aid or a speaker in the classroom. The latter of these is not only going to help the child with hearing loss, but will also help all of the children in the classroom, regardless of hearing loss. It will ensure that the teacher's voice can be heard clearly throughout the room.

Cochlear Implants

A cochlear implant is vastly different from a hearing aid. As discussed previously, a hearing aid converts acoustic signals, processes them, and then transmits them via a receiver into the wearer's ear. A cochlear implant is a device that is surgically implanted into the person's inner ear. The cochlear implant functions by sending electrical impulse signals into the inner ear, bypassing the outer and middle parts of the ear.

Direct Services Provided to Students

The educational audiologist's role in providing direct services to students will vary greatly from school to school. Mostly this is dependent on what other services the child is currently receiving. Oftentimes, the child with hearing loss will have a weekly or biweekly meeting with the audiologist to discuss problems relating to hearing loss and/or amplification issues (each school district follows different guidelines). During this time the audiologist will service the hearing aids and/or FM system and ensure that they are in working order. The audiologist and student may do an activity focusing on aural rehabilitation. These activities will help to strengthen the auditory system and continue to develop listening skills. See this chapter's Appendix for a list of aural rehabilitation activities that can be used to help strengthen the auditory system.

Another important task that the educational audiologist may undertake is implementing a schoolwide assembly. Topics can include general knowledge on hearing loss and how we hear, as well as information on noise-induced hearing loss. Noise-induced hearing loss affects people of all ages. U.S. government survey data revealed that 12.5% of children ages 6 to 19 (approximately 5.2 million children) have permanent damage to their ears' hair cells (inner ear) caused by exposure to loud noises (Niskar, 2001). In addition, 15.5% of children ages 12 to 19 had some hearing loss in one or both ears, highlighting the fact that noise-induced hearing loss grows more prevalent with age (Niskar, 2001). Noise-induced hearing loss is 100% preventable, thus making it a major discussion topic among school-age children. The educational audiologist can provide information to students in fun and interactive ways to help demonstrate the negative effects of excessive noise exposure.

For more information on noise-induced hearing loss and prevention, visit It's a Noisy Planet at http://www.noisyplanet.nidcd.nih.gov or Dangerous Decibels at http://www.dangerousdecibels.org, which has a great instructional kit for purchase that can be used with kids in kindergarten through fifth grade.

DIRECT SERVICES PROVIDED
TO TEACHERS

The educational audiologist's role in providing direct services to teachers likely consists of developing educational in-services and being the communication link for the child(ren) with hearing loss. As mentioned previously, in-services and other hands-on training will provide the teachers and other paraprofessionals with the necessary knowledge to successfully work with these children. It is important for the audiologist to work with the teacher in developing the appropriate skills needed to effectively work with a child with hearing loss. In addition to this, educational audiologists work directly with teachers and support staff when creating or updating IEPs. The audiologist will create appropriate modifications for the child with hearing loss. This can also include discussions relating to the impact the hearing loss may have educationally on the child and placement options.

Solution to the Case Study

Norma has her IEP meeting coming up next month and one of the members of the team wanted to discuss limiting the services that Norma currently receives. Even though Norma has a mild hearing loss, it is crucial that Norma continue to receive services as she continues her education in the mainstream. Research has shown that even children with mild or unilateral hearing losses can still fall behind academically to their hearing peers. She needs to continue receiving these services so that she can maintain her near-normal speech, language, and reading skills.

References

Clark, J. G. (1981). Uses and abuses of hearing loss classification. *ASHA, 23,* 493–500.

Niskar, A. S., Kieszak, S. M., Holmes, A. E., Esteban, E., Rubin, C., & Brody, D. J. (2001). Estimated prevalence of noise-induced hearing threshold shifts among children 6 to 19 years of age: The third national health and nutrition examination survey, 1988–1994, United States. *Pediatrics, 108,* 40–43.

Stach, B. G. (1998). *Clinical audiology: An introduction.* San Diego, CA: Singular.

Appendix

Charts and/or Checklists

Deaf and Hard of Hearing Students in the Mainstream

The handout titled Deaf and Hard of Hearing Students In The Mainstream is a great visual tool to be referenced daily. It contains useful tips for the general education teacher, paraprofessionals, and other support staff as well as visitors.

Deaf and Hard of Hearing Students in the Mainstream: Tips for Teachers

Auditory Considerations
- Use normal loudness and normal rate of speech.
- Seat student in the front of the classroom.
- Seat student away from any background noise.
- Wear FM system if used by student.

Visual Considerations
- Have student's attention before you start speaking.
- Keep your mouth clearly visible.
  - Avoid covering your face and mouth.
  - Stand still when speaking.

- Direct student's attention to the person speaking.
- Use visual aids as much as possible.
- Write key words, new vocabulary, and homework on the board.

Improving Communication
- Introduce the topic of discussion.
- Be cognizant of student's language and vocabulary level.
- If the student does not understand you:
  - Summarize the comments and questions of other students.
  - Assign a buddy or peer helper who can:
    - o Assist the student with classroom routines and procedures.
    - o Point to who is talking.
    - o Show the student the correct page.

Troubleshooting the Hearing Aid

If you are working with a hearing aid and are not able to receive any sound from it, try the following before contacting your audiologist.

- Replace the battery with a *fresh, new* battery.
- Look to see if there is any debris (ear wax) plugging the earmold, thus reducing the ability for sound to pass through. If there is wax or debris, try removing it with a cleaning tool.
- Check the integrity of the tubing (connecting the earmold to the hearing aid). Look for cracks where sound may be escaping. If there is a crack, then the hearing aid must be serviced by the audiologist.
- Check the integrity of the microphones. Look to see that they are not covered with dirt or debris. If they appear to be dirty, they will need to be replaced (most likely by the audiologist).
- If you are still having difficulty with the hearing aid, contact your audiologist to further assist you.

Activities

Many of the activities listed below can be done with or without visual cues, depending on the auditory abilities of the child. If you want to challenge the child and take away any visual information, you will need a speech hoop, which is used to block your face from the child. The hoop is made with acoustically transparent speaker material so that sound can pass through without being altered. Most electronic stores sell this type of material. The material is held taught by an embroidery loop. See Figure A15.4 for a picture of this type of hoop, created by the chapter author.

Ling 6-Sound Check

It is important to perform daily sound checks for younger children with hearing loss (as the child becomes older, he will become his own advocate). This is done to ensure that the child's amplification system is working properly. You will want to make sure that the child is wearing his hearing aids or using his HAT prior to doing the sound check. The Ling sound check is done by having the child sit in front of the teacher/paraprofessional, with the two parties facing each other. Using the speech hoop, the administrator will give one of the sounds to the child (Ling sounds: /ah/, /ee/, /oo/, /sh/, /mm/, /s/). The child then repeats the sound that he heard. If the child repeats the correct sound, the next sound is given. If the child repeats the incorrect sound, give it again. If he misses it a second time, give it once more *with* visual representation. This will show the child which sound was given

Figure A15.4. Photo of traditional speech hoop made with acoustic speaker material to allow speech to pass through without being altered. Using an embroidery hoop, the material is held tautly. The speech hoop is used to completely cover the speaker's mouth, cheekbones, or any other body part that can unintentionally give clues as to what the speaker is saying.

and help him produce it. It is helpful to use a tracking sheet to document which sounds the child is hearing and repeating correctly so that you can monitor his progress (see Figure A15.5). It is also helpful to vary the order of the speech sounds given so that the child cannot anticipate which sound is to occur next.

Auditory Training Activities

Activity: Play barrier games.

Materials: Visual barriers for all players; duplicate sets of materials (critical elements)

Objective: To increase auditory awareness and training while reducing the visual cues.

Procedures: Have the child sit across from you with the visual barriers in between yourselves. Depending on the level of difficulty, increase or decrease the number of critical elements. Give the child directions verbally and have her complete the task. For example, "Place the small red bear on the big yellow bench" (number of critical elements = up to 8 if there is more than one bear, more than one size, more than one bench, etc.). Remove

Name: _____

LING 6-Sound Daily Listening Check

Date	/ah/	/oo/	/s/	/ee/	/mm/	/sh/

Key:
✓ = correctly produced sound *without* visual cue
+ = correctly produced sound *with* visual cue
✗ = missed sound (insert sound that was substituted)

Figure A15.5. Tracking sheet for Ling 6-sound daily listening check.

the barrier to see if child completed the task successfully. If not, have her self-correct and tell you verbally.

Notes: Critical elements are any modifiers that will make it more or less difficult. They can be numbers of objects, varying colors, and varying sizes.

Activity: With the use of the speech hoop, play Go Fish!

Materials: Deck of cards or deck of Go Fish! cards for younger students; speech hoop

Objective: To increase auditory awareness and training while reducing visual cues.

Procedures: Sitting across from one another, have student play Go Fish! with the teacher using the speech hoop.

Activity: With the use of the speech hoop, play Simon Says.

Materials: Speech hoop

Objective: To increase auditory awareness and training while reducing visual cues.

Procedures: Have the student play Simon Says without having any visual cues. Use the speech hoop to reduce visual cues.

Notes: This activity would be great if there are two or more kids working toward the same goals, or who are at the same level.

Activity: Conditioned response with speech hoop (similar to barrier games)

Materials: Speech hoop, variety of objects (perhaps vocabulary words for the week)

Objective: To increase auditory awareness and training while reducing the visual cues.

Procedures: While using the speech hoop have the student listen to the directions and complete the required task. For example, the teacher says "Get the bear and put him in the tree."

Notes: Check for understanding by giving unusual directions such as "Put the ice cream in the oven."

Chapter 16

School Social Workers

Mary Jo Garcia Biggs and Sean A. Morales

CASE STUDY: EMMA

Emma is a 7-year-old girl in the first grade. Emma is often late to school and her parents have been contacted on several occasions regarding the early morning delays. Her parents report that she is disobedient and will not follow directions, including simple ones like getting dressed in the morning. They say that they have tried everything to discipline Emma but nothing works. They reported that they are at their wit's end and want to know what is wrong with Emma.

Ms. Bates, the general education teacher, reports that Emma is the sweetest little girl, very social, and that all of the children love her. Ms. Bates reported that Emma is learning to read, but is still functioning below the classroom norm. She also reports that during reading circle time she has Emma sit in a chair when the rest of the students sit on the floor. She stated that when Emma sits on the floor she tends to move about and invade the personal space of the other students near her. Sitting in the chair keeps Emma in one area of the room, but Emma fidgets and squirms the entire time. Ms. Bates states Emma tries hard but sitting still is extremely difficult for her.

The music teacher, Mr. Allan, reports that Emma will not follow directions; normally she will not stay seated and requires multiple prompts to complete a task. He states that the various items in the room often distract Emma. Ms. Healy, the physical education teacher, reports that Emma is great in class. She states that Emma is the first to volunteer to run the obstacle course and seems to enjoy run-

ning at the track and loves to participate in any of the outdoor sports. She reports no problems with Emma.

Emma consistently shares with her teachers that she tries "real hard" to be a "good girl" but sometimes she still gets in trouble. The teaching staff decided to contact a school social worker, in order to include a professional with experience in mental health, family, and cultural issues, to be involved in a planning team for Emma. The social worker was invited to contact and act as a liaison with the family; coordinate a team meeting with the family, student, and staff working closest with Emma; and work to incorporate an Individualized Education Program (IEP). More information describing this process and the individuals involved is discussed in the following sections.

INTRODUCTION

"Within the school setting, multiple individuals take part in designing intervention plans covering an array of issues. Understanding the roles that each individual plays, lays the foundation for successful communication" (Garcia Biggs, Simpson, & Gaus, 2009, p. 39). In the public school system, a social worker juggles multiple roles and skills. In the role of consultant, the social worker acts as an educator and provider of information to team members to develop a collaborative supportive plan. As a facilitator, the social worker assists in gathering groups of people for a specific purpose, such as creating dialogue to reduce student barriers that may interfere with the ability to maximize educational benefits for the student. As a broker, the social worker is involved in creating linkages and making referrals to needed resources. In the role of advocate, the social worker advocates for those who are unable to speak for themselves and to support the rights of others to work to obtain needed resources. Social workers also fill the role as educator by creating dialogue with parents, teaching parenting skills, preventing violence, or even explaining a medical diagnosis.

In the school setting, the social worker's "specialty in social work is oriented toward helping students make satisfactory adjustments and coordinating and influencing the effort of the school, the family and the community to achieve this goal" (National Association of Social Workers, 2002, p. 9). Using a multidisciplinary approach, a social worker can arrange a team meeting that includes the student and parents. Teachers play an important role in identifying children requiring specialized services who might not be identified otherwise and by referring those children to the social worker. The welfare of those children is critical if teachers don't recognize the behavioral and family problems or symptoms that may exist, including identifying situations of abuse and neglect that children are experiencing.

This chapter identifies the general roles and responsibilities of the social worker and discusses the need for communication between parents and teachers. Specific services to students, families, and teachers are identified, and the importance of those services and interventions to the student and team members are discussed.

GENERAL ROLES AND RESPONSIBILITIES

When considering the various roles of the social worker, it is important to recognize that the professional generally works within a multidisciplinary team on campus. Having school counselors and social workers in the schools tends to cause confusion over particular duties and services provided. The general roles and responsibilities of school social workers working with students with disabilities have become considerably more concrete and less ambiguous since the most current amendments of the Individuals with Disabilities Education Act (IDEA) in 2004. According IDEA, social work services in the schools include:

1. Preparing a social or developmental history on a child with a disability.
2. Group and individual counseling with the child and family.
3. Working with those problems in a child's living situation (home, school, and community) that affect the child's adjustment in school.
4. Mobilizing school and community resources to enable the child to learn as effectively as possible in his or her educational program. (34 C.F.R. Section 300.16)

However succinct this description may be, a more thorough explanation of the various roles that accompany these services is needed, as there are varying aspects to each. The following text will attempt to incorporate these descriptions and will discuss communication with teachers and parents, direct services provided to students, and direct services provided to teachers.

COMMUNICATION WITH TEACHERS AND PARENTS

Preparing a social/developmental history/psychosocial assessment form (see Figure 16.1) on a child with a disability is a prominent responsibility for the social worker and requires information and assistance from multiple parties. In order to provide the most thorough and culturally competent history, the social worker must not only know who to approach for the pertinent information needed to establish said report, but also to maintain a healthy and professional rapport with each contributing individual. The social worker generally contacts the parent/family/guardian first.

The major microsystems for the child continue to be the school and the home environments, and given that children spend most of their time in the home, a parent's participation becomes more crucial to support the student's emotional, social, and academic growth (Walberg & Lai, 1999). Research has concluded that children benefit both socially and academically when parents are involved with their education. Findings have shown that neither social status nor income predicted a student's achievement; more successful results were shown when an involved family created a supportive home environment for learning (Chavkin, 2006). The most efficacious results are found when both the school and family systems work in synergy; however, gaining a parental ally may not always be an effortless task for the social worker as barriers to participation can exist when other needs/concerns are present (e.g., transportation, work, and frustration with the school systems due to miscommunication; Franklin & Harris, 2007). This is one reason why the role of liaison for the social worker remains crucial to the child's development. Since the inception of IDEA, parents have been encouraged to be more involved in the planning and placements of their child, which then places the responsibility on the social worker to help empower families to share concerns with school officials and maintain open lines of communication between the home and school (Dupper, 2003).

The social worker also acts as an educator as she helps the family and/or teachers understand the student's disability (e.g., behaviors, medical and therapeutic interventions, and expected progress), needs, and how to navigate through community resources. Preparing and educating school staff on how to work with parents are invaluable strategies that help promote parental/guardian involvement. "Most school personnel have never received any training about parental involvement or, if they have, the training has been perfunctory" (Chavkin, 2006, p. 629).

The student's teacher should also be viewed as an integral source of information on the child's needs, behaviors, and aptitude in the classroom. The teacher observes the student not only in active environments such as the classroom, but also in noisier and more active settings such as the playground, allowing for a more cohesive perception of the student's idiosyncrasies, which is invaluable when completing a social history (Dupper, 2003). The daily interaction between the teacher and student allows teachers

Name of Agency or School
Psychosocial Assessment Format

Date of interview:_____

Name of social worker:_____

Date of report: _____

Name of client/student: _____

Address: _____

_____

Race/ethnicity: _____ Date of birth: _____ Age at time of PSA:_____

Next of kin/significant other(s):_____

Informants (origin and reliability of data): _____

Source of referral (Who made this referral?): _____

Statement regarding how confidentiality of the client is being maintained: _____

_____

_____

_____

Presenting Concerns: Describe the problem(s) affecting the client(s); when the diffi-culties began, who else in involved, when and where problem occurs, coping strategies used to date (including prior professional or nonprofessional help; i.e., social service age, indigenous workers); voluntary or involuntary client status:_____

_____

_____

_____

Personal Information: Client profile and current living situation; statement regarding client (e.g., age, gender, ethnicity, sexual orientation, differential ability, level of edu-cation, level of income); describe appearance and behavior; indicate initial impressions regarding functioning: _____

_____

_____

_____

Figure 16.1. Sample format of a psychosocial assessment. From *School of Social Work MSW Field Manual* by Texas State University, 2009, pp. 49–51. Copyright 2009 by Texas State University. Reprinted with permission.

Family: Indicate members of family of origin (i.e., names, relationship, ages, marital, significant other, parental status); prior and current status of relationship to family members; statement of client's overall impression of family functioning, family strengths and weaknesses; important situational crises (if any); history of abuse and/or neglect (if any); current and past marital or significant other(s), and family or family of; indicate persons in the household; members of extended family, family of procreation, foster family, and/or family of friends as appropriate: _____

_____

_____

_____

Health: Current and past illnesses, accidents, disabilities, symptoms, complaints, diagnosis; previous hospitalizations, treatments, procedures, medications; health behavior including diet, exercise, substance abuse, sexual practices, adaptations to past, current, and anticipated health status; include significant health history of family members or significant others: _____

_____

_____

_____

Psychological/Mental Health: Current and past cognitive, affective, social, and behavioral functioning; onset and duration of any current difficulties; critical events related to current status; current or past mental health diagnosis; previous hospitalizations, treatments, procedures, medications; attitudes, expectations of client, family, others in social environment. Include significant mental health history of family members. Client's and others' interpretation of current situation and of related events; knowledge, information, and beliefs regarding human behavior, social services, and so forth; current and recent efforts at problem solving; self-concept; insight; values; preferences regarding means and ends of service. Client's and others' emotional responses to current situation, critical events related to the situation; current level of anxiety, discomfort; motivation for change or action; commitment to services, attitudes toward the future, potential for improvement in current situation; self-esteem: _____

_____

_____

_____

Educational/Vocational/Rehabilitation/Employment: Formal or informal schooling or programs attended; level of performance or achievement; experiences, attitudes, expectations regarding abilities, achievements, and level of basic skills; include significant information on relevant family members; current and significant employment; current employer and position; critical incidents at work: _____

_____

_____

_____

Figure 16.1. Sample format of a psychosocial assessment, continued.

Peer Groups and Social Network: Description of informal peer relationships, including social, recreational, and self-help groups and networks; membership and participation in formal organizations and groups; leisure activities, hobbies, personal interests, recreational, volunteer, organizational activities: _____

_____

_____

_____

Finances: Current and recent sources and amount of income; financial responsibilities, debts, health insurance, public assistance, etc.:_____

_____

_____

_____

Legal Issues: Current or past incidents involving law enforcement, courts, incarceration, parole, or probation status; involvement as offender, victim, or witness to acts of violence or other antisocial events; immigration status; custody; guardianship; include significant history of family members:_____

_____

_____

_____

Ethnicity and Culture: Ethnic origins; client self-identification of ethnic identity; values, preferences, and expectations of behavior; issues of prejudice, discrimination, and oppression; opportunity, access, availability of resources; attitudes toward services, service providers; language and custom differences from community; descriptions of rituals, beliefs, and/or customs practiced; if first or second generation American, country of origin and year of entry into the United States; the socioeconomic and political conditions of the country left; reasons for coming to the U.S.; describe decision process of determining who came first, who was left behind and plan for reunification; other family/friends already in the U.S.; describe places stayed until finally settled: _____

_____

_____

_____

Religious/Spiritual Influences and Practice: Client's religious/spiritual influences and practices of all in household; client assessment of the role of spirituality/religion in life of client and client's family: _____

_____

_____

_____

Figure 16.1. Sample format of a psychosocial assessment, continued.

Relationships to Community Agencies: Relationships with community and other public organizations, employment and volunteer associations, religious groups, legal system, health and mental health organizations, support groups, or social welfare agencies:

_____

_____

_____

Assessment and Social Work Impressions: Provide a summary of the above, focusing on the current situation and precipitating event that brought the client to this social service setting; focus on possible psychosocial issues; also include strengths and weaknesses or obstacles for the client system:_____

_____

_____

_____

Intervention Plan: Identify the problems to be worked on and include specific short- and long-term goals for each in behavioral and measurable terms; objectives and interventions for accomplishing each of these goals, and specific time frames for goal accomplishment; must have an evaluation plan to measure effectiveness of the interventions; and include any arrangements for follow up (develop a systematic plan for evaluating the outcome of your intervention): _____

_____

_____

_____

Note: Important Considerations for the Psychosocial Assessment:
- The psychosocial assessment is a formal document, written in the third person using complete sentences including grammar and punctuation.
- Subheadings are used for better organization.
- The psychosocial assessment is primarily objective. Stick to factual information. Diagnostic impressions should be clearly identified as such, and should only appear at the conclusion of the factual information that comprises the bulk of the assessment.
- Maintain client confidentiality by altering all identifying information.
- Identify sources of information (i.e., "According to medical records . . .", "According to the client . . ."). Most PSAs have multiple informants and/or sources. Identify all that you use for your assessment.
- Include only information that is relevant to the client and identified problem(s). Do not repeat information across sections.

Figure 16.1. Sample format of a psychosocial assessment, continued.

to gather crucial information on the behavioral and family problems that may exist including identifying situations of abuse and neglect. It is the social worker's duty to gather the needed data from the teacher, educate the teacher on any interventions that may have to be implemented in the classroom, inform the teacher of the student's rights per IDEA, and collaborate with the teacher when designing and evaluating the aforementioned interventions or initiating child welfare referrals as appropriate.

DIRECT SERVICES PROVIDED
TO STUDENTS

With mental illness as one of the leading causes of disability for students and suicide still a growing concern among youth, competence in the areas of individual and family therapies, crisis intervention, and conflict resolution become paramount for the school social worker (Insel, 2005). According to Agresta (2004), most social workers spend a majority of their time counseling individuals and groups in schools. Where disabilities in the school system are concerned, however, the social worker should also be knowledgeable (e.g., have knowledge of screening/testing instruments, medications, and behaviors) of Attention Deficit/Hyperactivity Disorder (ADHD), various learning disabilities (LD), emotional and behavioral disturbances (EBD), and autism. Competence in these areas assists the social worker in being a more sound and ethical advocate, educator, and support for the student and family. Social workers also act as a liaison between the local mental health provider or mental health case manager for children with mental health issues to assist and coordinate services and ensure compliance with medications.

Social workers often work with children in groups. The size and types of groups are broad. There are groups for children with certain disabilities; groups for children having problems in their family or social environment; groups that provide social skills training and self-esteem building; groups for eating disorders like anorexia or bulimia; groups for self-mutilation (cutting); groups for children with substance abuse issues or for youth at risk of dropping out; prevention groups; groups for gay and lesbian youth; and groups for bullying, dating violence, and grief support. Social workers are also involved in crisis response teams for trauma, death of a student or teacher, or natural disasters (Knox & Roberts, 2006). Group treatment helps provide a support system for students who might feel ostracized or out of place, giving them an opportunity to share with others who have experienced similar issues or problems. There are some psychoeducational programs that have gained popularity in school systems such as those dealing with issues of dating violence or the Expect Respect program, developed by SafePlace (2008) in Austin, TX, to educate students on dealing with bullying, including what to do about bystanders who don't intervene or report bullying to administrators or teachers. Programs can also be developed and implemented around specific areas or needs of the community and school system.

DIRECT SERVICES PROVIDED TO TEACHERS

In order to meet the unique needs of the student body, families, and school, it is crucial for the success of each student that the social worker exhibits strong interpersonal skills when taking on the roles of consultant and collaborator. IDEA requires each student with a disability to have an IEP, which acts as a foundation that guides the development and delivery of services to each individual (Dupper, 2003). The plan requires the collaboration of a school administrator, psychologist/psychiatrist, teacher, social worker, and family to set goals, create tasks to attain said goals, and document provided services throughout the student's enrollment. Social workers can provide specific services to the teacher such as classroom and discipline management strategies, acting as a liaison between the teachers and the parents, and coordinating services with the school support services.

CONCLUSION

The case scenario was a good example of how identification of the problems that Emma was having were identified by the teacher. A social worker, whose foundation involves a strengths-based perspective, may be the missing link in creating a common thread among the various disciplines. In the school setting, there is a strong need to embrace expertise among those disciplines to improve the overall school climate, particularly for students with disabilities and special needs.

Collaboration with the teacher in this setting is critical, as identification of the concerns is the first step in problem resolution. Outside community members and professionals in other disciplines can play important roles in the assessment and treatment planning as each offers his or her unique expertise. The social worker and the multidisciplinary team approach includes students and parents in treatment design and planning, allowing for maximum benefit to the student and accountability for all involved. A social worker requires information from various sources in completing an assessment.

SOLUTION TO THE CASE STUDY

After hearing the reasons for the referrals, the social worker took the information from all of the sources about the primary problem but also referred the family to the pediatrician for a medical diagnosis screening possibly for ADD or ADHD. The parents, teachers, and social worker met as a team to create a behavioral intervention treatment plan to address disruptive behaviors and Emma's inabilities to complete her work and inattentiveness. Ms. Molina recognized knowledge and strengths of the various team members and utilized the various roles of those individuals. Ms. Molina was able to facilitate discussion between the team members that resulted in identifying a plan that will best meet the needs of Emma. Ms. Molina met with Emma to identify some of the weakness that she self-identified. Emma stated that she wanted to be a "good girl." When pressed for what that means, Emma stated that being a good girl means you do what your parents tell you to do.

Recommendations for children with ADHD are generally a combination of medications and cognitive behavior therapy that teaches students to think through potential consequences of their actions instead of reacting impulsively. These interventions also help to build skills that deal directly with the student's hyperactivity. A plan of this sort works only if everyone is on the same page, and if the teacher and parent are both doing the directive intervention for consistency across the treatment plan. For example, a positive reinforcement technique such as a token cost response may be implemented in such a case. This method rewards individuals for positive behavior changes like sitting still, not disrupting the class, and completing homework. The rewards are taken back if the individual continues to disrupt the class or has impulsive behavior. If teachers and parents are not on the same page, the child gets mixed messages—consistency must be maintained across the school and home settings.

Ms. Molina helped create a strength–based dialogue with Emma, her parents, and the other team members. Ms. Molina explained that while some behaviors at home were normal developmentally, the impact could be reduced. For example, every night before bed, Emma would work with her parents to decide on her attire for the next day. Each morning they would set a timer to see if Emma could be dressed before the buzzer went off. Beating the time would mean that Emma would gain a token for the day. Emma was excited to start this game. The team acknowledged that Emma was a "good girl" and explained the various strengths that Emma held, such as being a good friend, working hard to learn to read, and doing well in PE. Ms. Molina explained that the team was going to be working with Emma to help her in her school day and at home.

REFERENCES

Agresta, J. (2004). Professional role perceptions of school social workers, psychologists, and counselors. *Children & Schools, 26,* 151–163.

Chavkin, N. F. (2006). Best school-based practices for family intervention and parental involvement. In C. Franklin, M. B. Harris, & P. Allen-Meares (Eds.), *The school services sourcebook: A guide for school-based professionals* (pp. 629–640). New York, NY: Oxford University Press.

Dupper, D. R. (2003). *School social work: Skills and interventions for effective practice.* Hoboken, NJ: Wiley & Sons.

Franklin, C., & Harris, M. B. (2007). The delivery of school social work services. In P. Allen-Meares (Ed.), *Social work services in schools* (5th ed., pp. 317–360). Boston, MA: Allyn & Bacon.

Garcia Biggs, M. J., Simpson, C., & Gaus, M. D. (2009). Bringing together the disciplines. *Children & Schools, 31*(1), 39–42.

Individuals with Disabilities Education Improvement Act, Pub. Law 108-446 (December 3, 2004).

Insel, T. R. (2005). NIMH: Renewing priorities and organizational structure. *SRCD Developments, 48*(1), 1, 9–10.

Knox, K. S., & Roberts, A. R. (2006). Developing school-wide and district-wide crisis prevention/intervention protocols for natural disasters. In C. Franklin, M. B. Harris, & P. Allen-Meares (Eds.), *The school services sourcebook: A guide for school-based professionals* (pp. 549–558). New York, NY: Oxford University Press.

National Association of Social Workers. (2002). *NASW Standards for school social workers.* Retrieved from https://www.socialworkers.org/practice/standards/NASW_SSWS.pdf

SafePlace. (2008). *Expect respect program manual.* Retrieved from http://www.safeplace.org

Texas State University. (2009). *School of social work MSW field manual.* Retrieved from http://www.socialwork.txstate.edu/courses/field/fieldmanuals.html

Walberg, H., & Lai, J. (1999). Meta-analytic effects for policy. In G. J. Cizek (Ed.), *Handbook of educational policy* (pp. 418–454). San Diego, CA: Academic Press.

Chapter 17

Professional School Counselor

Sheryl A. Serres and Judith A. Nelson

Case Study: Matt

Matt Davis is a 13-year-old seventh grader who recently transferred to his current junior high school from another state. Records received from his previous school indicate that he had been tested and qualified for special education services in the areas of reading comprehension, math problem solving, and math calculations. Additionally, he was diagnosed by his physician as having Attention Deficit/ Hyperactivity Disorder (ADHD) when he was in the fourth grade. He takes no medication for the ADHD and has been placed in all regular classes with modifications in his current school setting. His parents are divorced, and his mother recently lost her job, prompting their move to be closer to her parents. Since coming to his present school, Matt has been sent to the assistant principal's office four times for inattentiveness in class and for disrupting the learning environment by answering out loud when not called upon. He appears lethargic and has not made any new friends. During lunch, he sits at a table with four other boys who do not engage him in conversation and who rarely speak among themselves. He has one younger sister who is a sixth grader at the same junior high. An Individualized Education Program (IEP) annual meeting will be scheduled within a month.

INTRODUCTION

The American School Counselor Association (ASCA, 2005) National Model maintained that professional school counselors are charged with serving the academic, career, and social/emotional needs of all students including students with disabilities. The school counselor is an advocate for students and families, particularly those whose voices may be minimized or devalued by the educational system. The ASCA National Model recommended that school counselors spend the majority of their time in direct services to all students so that every student receives the maximum benefits from the program. In addition, *The Professional School Counselor and Students With Special Needs* (ASCA, 2004) position statement suggested that professional school counselors provide direct services to students with disabilities, such as individual and group counseling, as well as indirect services, such as participating on multidisciplinary teams.

Removing systemic barriers for students with disabilities can provide opportunities in education and in maintaining healthy social relationships. In addition, the school counselor is the conduit between the school and the community for the purpose of connecting families of students with disabilities with resources they may not be able to access on their own. Rock and Leff (2010) described three categories of services provided by professional school counselors to support students with disabilities: (a) responsibilities to the multidisciplinary team in the RTI process; (b) responsibilities to the student regarding direct services such as counseling, vocational guidance, and transition programs; and (c) indirect responsibilities such as consultation, training, and referring students and families to community resources. Milsom (2006) visualized the counselor's role in serving students with disabilities as providing interventions that improve attitudes toward students who may learn or behave differently. She believed that these interventions include: (a) targeting school personnel utilizing staff development opportunities, (b) intervening with students by promoting acceptance and mutuality among students with and without disabilities, and (c) planning schoolwide programs and policies that recognize learning differences as normal in all children. Using the ASCA (2005) National Model as a template, the school counselor can effectively provide a variety of services to students with disabilities. See the Appendix for lists of services provided by professional school counselors.

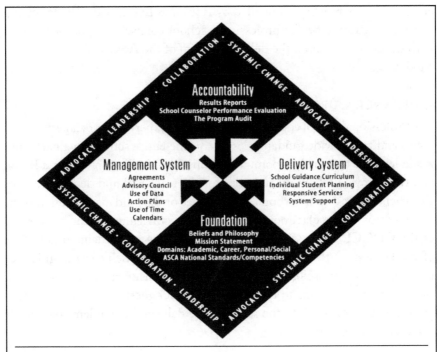

Figure 17.1. The American School Counselors Association National Model. Reprinted with permission of the American School Counselor Association.

GENERAL ROLES AND RESPONSIBILITIES OF THE PROFESSIONAL SCHOOL COUNSELOR

Professional school counselors implement comprehensive developmental guidance and counseling programs (CDGCP) based on a foundation (see Figure 17.1) that describes the learning processes and standards provided to all students including those with disabilities. Using a clearly defined management system, the counselor ensures that the program will be delivered to all students at the appointed times and that the stakeholders of the school approve of and support the guidance plan. The school counselor uses an accountability system to document with strong data how students are different as a result of the program. The professional school counselor uses the following delivery system to guide the program: guidance curriculum, individual student planning, responsive services, and system support. Students with disabilities benefit from the implementation of a CDGCP that is based on the ASCA (2005) National Model, and the delivery system of the program can include services to the multidisciplinary team, the student, parents, and teachers as recommended by Rock and Leff (2010). The following sections describe how the professional school counselor supports students with disabilities through the delivery system of the ASCA (2005) National Model.

GUIDANCE CURRICULUM

Professional school counselors have special expertise in social/emotional issues and can provide guidance lessons to the entire school, to a particular grade level, or to one classroom. The counselor initially can deliver a lesson and then provide follow-up activities for the teacher(s) and demonstrate for the teacher(s) how to incorporate the themes of the guidance lesson into the daily lessons of the classroom. The guidance curriculum is the stronghold of the CDGCP and is delivered systematically to all students in a variety of modalities: (a) the professional school counselor delivers the guidance lessons; (b) the counselor provides guidance lessons to the teachers who, in turn, deliver the lessons to their students; or (c) guest speakers and special programs are brought into the school to be delivered to students by outside resources and experts.

INDIVIDUAL STUDENT PLANNING

Professional school counselors have expertise in career and lifespan development, and, therefore, can be instrumental in postsecondary planning for students with disabilities. With training in career development and special knowledge of postsecondary opportunities, professional school counselors can provide information that is critical to a student's successful transition plan (Milsom, Goodnough, & Akos, 2007). As students mature, transition planning becomes a critical part of the IEP, and school counselors should be involved in that planning. As a member of the multidisciplinary team, the school counselor can also lend an added dimension to the student's classroom placements by being aware of the strengths and stressors that the student with disabilities might encounter in any particular setting. Often when students with disabilities are acting out in a certain class, the counselor can identify the underlying causes of the behavior, in which case the multidisciplinary team might decide that the student would be better served in another classroom. In addition, the team may revisit the IEP to see if the student's plan needs to be revised in any way.

RESPONSIVE SERVICES

Students with disabilities may need crisis counseling or counseling for developmentally typical challenges and transitions. Professional school counselors are mental health professionals who provide individual counseling and/or group counseling for students with disabilities, which might include the academic, career, or personal/social development domains of the ASCA (2005) National Model. Responsive services meet students' immediate needs including issues such as identifying feelings and expressing them appropriately, understanding the importance of self-control, recognizing the rights and responsibilities of others, and using effective communication, to name a few. According to Rock and Leff (2010), counselors can assist students with disabilities in acquiring self-determination skills including self-awareness, self-evaluation, problem solving, and self-advocacy.

SYSTEM SUPPORT

The professional school counselor can implement programming that enhances the understanding of the experiences of students with disabilities. Assessing the culture of a school is one way to take the temperature of the school climate and to determine attitudes toward students with disabilities. The school counselor is positioned to assist in the identification of the need for systemic changes that will benefit all students. Policies and programs should be assessed periodically to make certain that every student has an equal opportunity for learning and development. Schoolwide programs that promote respect for diversity will increase the likelihood that students with disabilities will be accepted as unique individuals with potential for success by both staff and students.

Acting as a consultant on behalf of students with disabilities provides indirect services to the students through parents, school personnel, and community resources. School counselors can consult with teachers regarding classroom management strategies that lend support to students who may be bullied because they are different. Ongoing staff development is crucial for teachers to have an understanding of the needs, challenges, and strengths of students with disabilities. Professional school counselors can be instrumental in planning, providing, and arranging for this type of professional development for teachers. Additionally, school counselors can provide training to parents of students with disabilities as to how they can best support and advocate for their child's needs.

Professional school counselors might be the only personnel on a school campus who have had specific training in group processes (Milsom et al., 2007). This expertise is essential to the continued healthy functioning of the multidisciplinary team through clear communication, management of conflict, and group reflection. The school counselor also can facilitate task groups such as IEP teams through their knowledge of related services and interventions, availability of resources, and their awareness of realistic timelines (Milsom et al., 2007). The ability of the school counselor to provide timely, honest, and open communication is essential in successful planning for students with disabilities.

COMMUNICATING WITH SCHOOL PERSONNEL AND PARENTS

Communication between school personnel and parents has long been perceived as important for children's education. Professional school counselors play a key role in bridging communication between the school and the home (Gibson, 2004). Counselors have special expertise in consultation and effective communication, and these skills can help lay a foundation of trust and collaboration that may prevent misunderstandings that fuel adversarial relationships between parents and school personnel. Far too often, meetings in which parents, teachers, administrations, and other service providers gather to report assessment findings, determine eligibility, and develop an IEP can produce tension between parties rather than the desired collaboration. Professional school counselors possess unique training that enables them to empathize with all team members, acknowledge each person's contributions, restate thoughts and feelings, summarize what has been said, link the contributions of various members, and promote better communication between parties in general.

COMMUNICATION WITH SCHOOL PERSONNEL

Professional school counselors are a vital link between various school personnel and special education service providers. Counselors often serve as leaders on multidisciplinary teams to coordinate the sharing of information about students with teachers and others who provide services to students with disabilities. Counselors protect confidentiality of students while working closely with others who instruct and serve the student. Counselors attend meetings that coordinate services for students with disabilities such as Admission, Review, and Dismissal (ARD) meetings; transition services meetings; and annual IEP meetings. Counselors share data from observations, assessment results, and interventions with teachers and service providers from a strengths-based format (Rock & Leff, 2010), focusing on what students *can* do, which skills they have acquired, and what unique abilities and skills students with disabilities possess. Additionally, counselors consult with other school personnel about child abuse and neglect issues on their school campuses and must act to enhance the communication between school personnel and child protective services (Bryant & Milsom, 2005). Counselors also serve as a liaison between the school and various community services that special needs students and their parents may want to access.

COMMUNICATION WITH PARENTS

Parents of students with disabilities experience many unique challenges and stressors (Baruth & Burggraf, 1983; Ray, 2003), and professional school counselors can help as they counsel and consult with parents and families (Milsom, 2002). Counselors are skilled in relationship building and should be proactive in contacting parents of students with disabilities. Early communication can prevent problems in the future by initially indicating that the counselor is caring and will act as an advocate for the student. The training of professional school counselors and their obligation to confidentiality position them as the appropriate professionals to which parents may express angry, frustrating, or confusing feelings. Counselors must also maintain cultural sensitivity, as the implications of having a child with disabilities can vary greatly between cultures (Rock & Leff, 2010).

Parents often lack the knowledge of resources and informational materials concerning the implications of their child's specific disability. This could be especially true with complex diagnoses such as various forms of autism, bipolar disorder, and anxiety and depression. If the child's disability is related to medical issues and diagnoses, parents may experience increased stress, fears, and financial burdens (Ray, 2003). Professional school counselors are knowledgeable about a variety of childhood diagnoses and disorders, have access to various workshops related to these disorders, and are well-informed about community resources to assist parents. It is vitally important that professional school counselors take the initiative to remain current in their understanding of various child and adolescent diagnoses. Increasingly, graduate programs are adding training and instruction in disabilities to their counselor education programs through additional coursework or through incorporating information into existing courses (Milsom & Akos, 2003).

Parents often perceive barriers to services they desire for their children (Ray, 2003). Professional school counselors must advocate for all children and maintain an understanding of the reasons behind parents' sometimes aggressive approaches at IEP meetings. Fearful that their children will not get needed services, feeling vulnerable due to lack of knowledge of special education law, and further threatened and baffled by the complex academic, emotional, and medical needs of their children; parents can appear resistant and defensive, and those feelings must be addressed in order for the child to benefit most from collaborative efforts. Professional school counselors have training in communication skills including active listening and reflection of content and feelings that helps parents manage their fears and contributes to building a greater foundation of trust in school personnel.

Additionally, professional school counselors have many resources that they can share with parents. They can offer information through printed materials, videos and DVDs, books, or other materials. Counselors can also support parents by offering parenting workshops during the school day or at other times convenient to parents.

DIRECT SERVICES PROVIDED TO THE STUDENT

The ASCA model requires that professional school counselors spend the majority of their time in direct services. The direct services professional school counselors provide to students with disabilities is determined by several factors including the nature of the disability, the age and development of the student, and the student's individual needs. Counselors can offer greatest benefit to students with disabilities when they are knowledgeable about the federal laws and procedures related to special education services (Leinbaugh, 2004). Common direct services professional school counselors provide to students with disabilities are discussed below.

INDIVIDUAL AND GROUP COUNSELING

Many needs and concerns experienced by students with disabilities are addressed by professional school counselors in individual and group counseling sessions. Professional school counselors employ a variety of counseling strategies including expressive arts, play therapy, bibliotherapy, stress reduction and relaxation, brief solution-focused counseling, and cognitive behavioral counseling techniques to assist students (McEachern, 2004). When an IEP directs that a student with disabilities receive counseling as a related service, this is often provided by the professional school counselor, although other mental health professionals such as a special education counselor or a school psychologist may also provide the service.

Many counselors have found group counseling to be an effective intervention in improving students' achievement as well as allowing students to experience a sense of support or connectedness to others who are experiencing similar difficulties (Steen & Bemak, 2008). Counselors engage younger students in groups using art activities to address issues such as self-esteem, social skills, and behavior management. For older students, group work is useful in preparing students with disabilities for transitions such as preparing and planning for college (Milsom, Akos, & Thompson, 2004) or for exploring job and career options (McEachern & Kenny, 2007).

Siblings of students with disabilities also have special needs and stressors. Counselors can include siblings in counseling sessions with special needs students. Siblings can also be included in groups with nondisabled students to increase greater understanding between students who deal with disabilities on a daily basis and those who are unfamiliar with the implications of disabilities. Families of children with disabilities often assert that their children are an enhancement to their lives and provide an opportunity for family development (Carnevale, Rehm, Kirk, & McKeever, 2008), and siblings of these children may have added social awareness from which more unaware students can benefit (Hames, 2005).

GUIDANCE LESSONS

Guidance lessons are conducted by professional school counselors in individual classrooms, allowing the counselor access to many students at one time. The lessons can address a variety of concerns relative to students with disabilities and their interactions with nondisabled students including study skills, social skills development, character development, positive behavior choices, and bullying prevention. Guidance lessons may also highlight the special contributions of famous persons with disabilities.

COLLEGE AND CAREER PLANNING

Professional school counselors may assess students' various career-related areas of functioning at appropriate developmental levels beginning in elementary school and continuing through high school. Some of these areas include career exploration behavior, interpersonal skills, self-perceptions, interests, values, decision making, and goal setting (Trusty & Niles, 2004). Counselors utilize many types of tools in career assessment and planning including inventories, portfolios, individual and group counseling, and computer-assisted programs such as DISCOVER and SIGI PLUS.

Counselors are aware of special services and accommodations provided to students with disabilities at postsecondary institutions, and they work with transition specialists to help ensure that students have options available to meet their specific interests and needs when transitioning from public school to postsecondary education or work-related experiences.

Assessment

Professional school counselors are trained in a variety of assessment techniques and can interpret many test results to students, parents, and school personnel. Counselors may conduct behavioral observations to determine the possible causes for students' behaviors, to determine the frequency with which various behaviors occur, and to assist in developing behavior modification plans when needed. Counselors may distribute and collect parent and teacher rating scales requested by multidisciplinary teams or other professionals such as a school psychologist or physician. Counselors emphasize assessing students' strengths (Rock & Leff, 2010), and counselors make other multidisciplinary team members aware of the specific strengths, competencies, and abilities of students with special needs.

Scheduling Classes

Professional school counselors are aware of the importance and influence a student's daily schedule has on his or her academic and social life. Counselors utilize test scores and assessment information in scheduling students into the appropriate level of academic instruction, and they use their professional judgment and student input to identify the specific elective courses that meet students' needs. In addition to the IEP requirements, counselors consider factors such as student personalities, teacher style, class size, and the time of day a class meets when scheduling students with disabilities.

Schoolwide Prevention Programs and Counselor-Initiated Assistance

Counselors can do much to normalize disabilities for nondisabled students and to cast students with disabilities in a positive light. Through developing and implementing various programs, counselors can increase interactions between students with disabilities and students who are not disabled. Some counselors coordinate peer-counseling programs in which peers assist students in challenging situations, and counselors may pair nondisabled students with students with disabilities in order to permit greater understanding and awareness. Professional school counselors can increase the status of these students in the eyes of their peers when they eat lunch at their table, solicit them for positions as student office assistants, or single them out to lead activities when appropriate. Inviting students with disabilities to present at various student groups and to educate others about their disabilities enhances the educational experience of both students with disabilities and their peers without disabilities.

DIRECT SERVICES PROVIDED TO TEACHERS

Teachers typically expect that professional school counselors will offer direct counseling services to students (Gilman & Medway, 2007), but counselors offer a variety of services to students with disabilities indirectly by providing direct services to teachers through consultation and instruction (Rock & Leff, 2010). The counselor is a resource for information on various topics concerning child and adolescent development and various disabilities and diagnoses that students may have. Professional school counselors can demonstrate to teachers how they might respond to students in ways that preclude defensiveness and elicit more cooperative behaviors from students. Counselors might also instruct teachers about how to reinforce positive behaviors in class.

Professional school counselors act to create and support a school climate that fosters acceptance of students with disabilities. One important activity counselors may utilize for accomplishing this goal is presenting guidance lessons in classrooms. Counselors can present classroom guidance lessons that focus on educating students about various disabilities and the contributions made by famous persons with disabilities. Discussions of this nature demystify disabilities to students and promote greater social awareness and acceptance. Counselors can then instruct teachers on how to incorporate guidance lesson content into regular curriculum instruction. Programmatically, counselors can initiate schoolwide programs that introduce regular education students to various disabilities and contribute to a school atmosphere of acceptance for all students, particularly those with special needs. Counselors can also provide materials to teachers at appropriate times. For example, during Disabilities Awareness Week, counselors might emphasize disabilities by offering copies of the Braille alphabet, pictorial demonstrations of the alphabet in American Sign Language, and special brochures or materials explaining various disabilities that can be shared in the classroom. Counselors can obtain these materials from special education service providers, thus serving as a liaison between classroom teachers and special education personnel. See the Appendix for additional ideas for Disability Awareness Week.

Counselors are cognizant of the toll it can take when overstressed teachers must manage several students with disabilities in regular classes. Counselors are trained in listening skills and can offer guidance and information while understanding the frustration teachers may feel when being held accountable for the achievement of challenging students. Counselors must maintain the confidentiality of both the information of students with disabilities and the teachers' frustrations.

Children with disabilities can be especially vulnerable to abuse or neglect. This may be due to increased stress and lack of support that parents of these children may feel. Additionally, a child with a disability may have communication difficulties that make it more unlikely the child would make his abuse known. Professional school counselors are knowledgeable about reporting abuse and neglect, and they can plan with administrators for in-service sessions to include information for teachers on this important issue (Bryant & Milsom, 2005). In this way, counselors help to protect all children.

SOLUTION TO THE CASE STUDY

Ms. Sanchez, the professional school counselor for seventh graders at Matt's school, made an appointment with two of Matt's academic teachers and his elective teacher to observe Matt in class and to conduct a behavioral assessment. She noted the precipitating events that solicited misbehavior and inappropriate responses from Matt. She found that Matt most frequently became disengaged when information was given verbally without the enhancement of visual or media materials. She also noted that other students appeared ambivalent toward Matt regardless of his contributions or lack of participation in class.

Ms. Sanchez obtained written permission from Matt's mother to include him in a group counseling setting to enhance development of appropriate interactions with his peers. Because she is aware that a transition plan will be developed for Matt when he turns 14 next year, she decided to include him in a career exploration group that would meet for 6 weeks during lunch. Students brought their lunch to the group, and Ms. Sanchez allowed them to take an interest inventory and share with the group their thoughts and feelings relative to the results. Additionally, each student in the group was assigned to explore one career of his or her choice and report back to the group at the last session. Ms. Sanchez met with Matt individually twice during the 6 weeks to ensure that he comprehended the career exploration assignment and to discuss his feelings about being in the group.

She also reviewed his schedule and found that by interchanging his math and science courses, she could place him in classes with two of the boys who sit at his lunch table, which would offer greater opportunity to develop friendships. She discussed this with Matt and his math and science teachers before making the change.

In preparing for the upcoming annual IEP meeting, Ms. Sanchez gathered all pertinent materials related to Matt's academic performance, as well as information concerning his social, emotional, and behavioral adjustments. She reviewed his most recent standardized test scores, consulted with the assistant principal concerning discipline records, solicited notes from all of his teachers concerning classroom participation and homework, and called Matt into her office to discuss his perceptions of his own progress. Ms. Sanchez reviewed data charts she created indicating an improvement in Matt's behaviors since his entry into the new school. In an effort to build a trusting relationship, Ms. Sanchez called Matt's mother to state that she would be at the IEP meeting and that she looked forward to meeting her. She also prepared a list of community resources including counseling agencies, medical facilities, boys clubs, churches, and other community supports to help Matt's mother obtain services in her new community.

Ms. Sanchez met with Matt's teachers to discuss the need for visual supports during class discussions and instruction. She further explained the specific needs and challenges faced by students with ADHD, giving them a handout listing various modifications and tips for use in instruction. Mrs. Sanchez made the principal aware of a growing need for in-service training for teachers concerning the special challenges faced by families with students who have disabilities. Finally, Ms. Sanchez visited individually with Matt's younger sister to determine her adjustment to the new school setting, to further assess the level of family adjustment to their new environment, and to offer support and encouragement.

REFERENCES

American School Counselor Association. (2004). *The professional school counselor and students with special needs.* Retrieved from http://asca2.timberlakepublishing.com//files/Special%20Needs.pdf

American School Counselor Association. (2005). *The ASCA National Model: A framework for school counseling programs* (2nd ed.). Alexandria, VA: Author.

Baruth, L. G., & Burggraf, M. Z. (1983). Marital counseling: Parents have special needs also. *Individual Psychology, 39,* 409–418.

Bryant, J., & Milsom, A. (2005). Child abuse reporting by school counselors. *Professional School Counseling, 9,* 63–71.

Carnevale, F. A., Rehm, R. S., Kirk, S., & McKeever, P. (2008). What we know (and do not know) about raising children with complex continuing care needs. *Journal of Child Health Care, 12,* 4–6.

Gibson, D. M. (2004). Consulting with parents and teachers: The role of the professional school counselor. In B. Erford (Ed.), *Professional school counseling: A handbook of theories, programs & practices* (pp. 349–355). Austin, TX: CAPS Press.

Gilman, R., & Medway, F. J. (2007). Teachers' perceptions of school psychology: A comparison of regular and special education teacher ratings. *School Psychology Quarterly, 22,* 145–161.

Hames, A. (2005). How younger siblings of children with learning disabilities understand the cognitive and social implications of learning disabilities. *European Journal of Special Needs Education, 20,* 3–19.

Leinbaugh, T. (2004). Understanding special education policies and procedures. In B. Erford (Ed.), *Professional school counseling: A handbook of theories, programs & practices* (pp. 647–654). Austin, TX: CAPS Press.

McEachern, A. G. (2004). Students with learning disabilities: Counseling issues and strategies. In B. Erford (Ed.), *Professional school counseling: A handbook of theories, programs & practices* (pp. 591–600). Austin, TX: CAPS Press.

McEachern, A. G., & Kenny, M. C. (2007). Transition groups for high school students with disabilities. *The Journal for Specialists in Group Work, 32,* 165–177.

Milsom, A. (2002). Students with disabilities: School counselor involvement and preparation. *Professional School Counseling, 5,* 331–338.

Milsom, A. (2006). Creating positive school experiences for students with disabilities. *Professional School Counseling, 10,* 66–72.

Milsom, A., & Akos, P. (2003). Counselor preparation: Preparing school counselors to work with students with disabilities. *Counselor Education and Supervision, 43,* 86–95.

Milsom, A., Akos, P., & Thompson, M. (2004). A psychoeducational group approach to postsecondary transition planning for students with learning disabilities. *The Journal for Specialists in Group Work, 29,* 395–411.

Milsom, A., Goodnough, G., & Akos, P. (2007). School counselor contributions to the Individualized Education Program (IEP) process. *Preventing School Failure, 52,* 19–24.

Ray, L. D. (2003). The social and political conditions that shape special-needs parenting. *Journal of Family Nursing, 9,* 281–304.

Rock, E., & Leff, E. H. (2010). The professional school counselor and students with disabilities. In B. Erford (Ed.), *Transforming the school counseling profession* (pp. 314–341). Upper Saddle River, NJ: Merrill/Prentice Hall.

Steen, S., & Bemak, F. (2008). Group work with high school students at risk of school failure: A pilot study. *The Journal for Specialists in Group Work, 33,* 335–350.

Trusty, J., & Niles, S. G. (2004). A practical approach to career assessment in schools. In B. Erford (Ed.), *Professional school counseling: A handbook of theories, programs & practices* (pp. 431–441). Austin, TX: CAPS Press.

Appendix

Direct Services Professional School Counselors Provide to Students With Special Needs

- Individual counseling
- Group counseling
- Play therapy
- Guidance lessons
- Career planning
- Postsecondary school preparation (e.g., college transitioning)
- Assessment (e.g., standardized, informal, rating scales, questionnaires)
- Scheduling
- Informal interactions with students (e.g., attending sports events, school events, eating lunch with students)

Indirect Services Professional School Counselors Provide for Students With Special Needs

- Providing parent training (e.g., workshops and media materials)
- Instructing and consulting with teachers
- Offering referral services and assisting parents in accessing these services (e.g., medical, dental, financial, social, legal, spiritual support systems)
- Reporting abuse/neglect to protective services
- Developing and engaging students in schoolwide prevention programs and counselor-initiated assistance programs to meet specific needs
- Consultation with administrators, teachers, and special education service providers

Direct Services Professional School Counselors Provide to Teachers

- Instructing and training concerning class management of students with disabilities
- Observing students in their classes
- Providing printed materials and other media resources
- Offering consultation to multidisciplinary team meetings

Direct Services Professional School Counselors Provide to Parents

- Parent training workshops
- Consultation
- Counseling
- Resources and materials (e.g., printed and media materials)
- Referral resources (e.g., agency counseling, medical, dental, social, legal, spiritual and community support systems)

Counselor-Initiated Activities for Celebrating Disabilities Awareness Week

- Feature pictures and brief stories of famous persons with disabilities on a prominent bulletin board or on multiple boards throughout the school building.
- Host a contest for all classrooms for the best bulletin board featuring a person with disabilities.
- Read brief bios of persons with disabilities who make significant contributions to their communities over the speaker during morning announcements.
- Invite persons with disabilities to be a guest speaker for classroom and schoolwide assemblies.
- Distribute copies of the alphabet in Braille to students and let them create their own names by drawing the appropriate dots.
- Have someone (e.g., deaf education teacher) teach the alphabet in American Sign Language to students.
- Showcase various tools and instruments used by persons with disabilities and let students touch and try them to demystify disabilities (e.g., wheelchair, cane, hearing devices).
- Host a contest for writing about or researching various disabilities.
- Invite students to share in their classes about family members or others in their lives who have disabilities or special needs.
- Check with the library to ensure that books and other media are ordered that address special needs and showcase these.
- Invite persons who have disabilities or special needs to career day to discuss their careers.
- Highlight veterans who have acquired disabilities through their protective service.
- Highlight college and university services for students with disabilities.

Chapter 18

Physical Educator

José A. Santiago and Emily A. Roper

Case Study: María

María is a 10-year-old Mexican American girl with Down syndrome. Raised by a single mother (Lydia), María and Lydia recently moved to an urban setting in Southeast Texas. María is attending Rodríguez Elementary School and is enrolled in a fourth-grade multiple impairment class. She has been placed in the general physical education setting. The general physical educator (Mr. Jackson) has received no preliminary information or documentation regarding María prior to her entrance into his class at the beginning of the school year. Upon entrance into his class, Mr. Jackson recognizes that María has Down syndrome. Although an IEP/multidisciplinary team has been organized for María, Mr. Jackson has not been approached regarding his potential involvement and has no knowledge that such a team exists for María. Skeptical about how to modify and adapt the physical education learning activities for María and aware that an IEP should be in place for María, Mr. Jackson approaches the special education teacher, Mr. Griffin. From his conversation with Mr. Griffin, Mr. Jackson is made aware that an IEP already exists and goals and objectives for physical education have been established without input from a professional with knowledge and/or experience in physical education or adapted physical education. He also learned that María is diagnosed with atlantoaxial instability. Mr. Jackson is then invited to the IEP meeting scheduled for next week.

INTRODUCTION

Physical education provides students an opportunity to learn motor skills; develop physical fitness, leadership, and cooperation skills; and acquire an appreciation and understanding of the importance of physical activity. The ultimate goal of a quality physical education program is to develop the student's knowledge, skills, and dispositions to live a healthy and physically active life. The general benefits of regular physical activity include increased health-related fitness (e.g., cardiovascular endurance, flexibility, and muscular strength), disease prevention, enhanced mental health and self-confidence, and decreased morbidity and premature mortality (U.S. Department of Health and Human Services, 1999).

The Individuals with Disabilities Education Improvement Act (IDEA) of 2004 mandates free appropriate education for all children with disabilities between the ages of 3 and 21 years (Block, 2007; U.S. Department of Education, 2010). By law, the general physical education teacher (GPE) is responsible for providing instruction to students with disabilities in the following areas: (a) health-related fitness (e.g., cardiovascular endurance, body composition, flexibility, muscular strength, muscular endurance), (b) skill-related fitness (e.g., agility, balance, coordination, power, speed, reaction time), (c) fundamental motor skills and patterns (e.g., volleying, kicking, throwing), (d) aquatics (e.g., water safety, swim strokes), (e) rhythm and dance (e.g., aerobics, traditional and modern dance), and (f) individual (e.g., archery, bowling, hiking) and team sports (e.g., soccer, volleyball; Block, 2007).

Lieberman and Houston-Wilson (2009) outlined the responsibilities of the GPE as follows:

> The GPE is responsible to prepare and implement units of instruction and lesson plans in line with the state and national standards; ensure the safety of all participants by minimizing foreseeable risks, checking on the integrity of the equipment, and maintaining a safe and secure physical environment; assess student performance and modify or enhance the curriculum based on students' needs; manage an array of student behaviors to ensure a successful and positive learning environment; engage in public relations to promote their physical education programs; and participate in professional development training. (p. 8)

The physical education services provided to students with disabilities must incorporate an Individualized Education Program (IEP) and are to occur within the general physical education setting. Those students who, upon a comprehensive assessment, require adapted physical education will be provided an IEP. The IEP is a process in which members of a multidisciplinary team collaborate to ensure that the student is able to obtain his or her designated goals (Auxter, Pyfer, Zittel, & Roth, 2010).

Adapted physical education includes adapting, modifying, and/or changing a physical activity so it is as appropriate for the person with a disability as it is for the person without a disability (Sherrill, 2004). For example, variation in the size or texture of a ball may be used to help a student more effectively learn to catch or throw a ball. The length of time required to complete a skill may be shortened or lengthened or an additional rest period may be implemented depending upon the ability of each student. A student with limited mobility may be instructed to walk rather than run while participating in soccer.

In addition to the knowledge and practical experience required of a GPE, the adapted physical educator (APE) has specialized training in motor assessment and evaluation, child development, the psychosocial aspects of disability, and extensive practical experience working with students with disabilities. Most often an APE has an undergraduate degree in general physical education with additional hours working with individuals with disabilities or a graduate degree in adapted physical education. Students interested in specializing in adapted physical education will take the Adapted Physical Education National Standards certification examination. The APE is most often placed within the special education department within the district office rather than a physical education department.

The GPE should be involved in all aspects of the IEP development as he is most often the individual responsible for implementing the physical education program, often with the assistance from the APE or other multidisciplinary team members. Horvat, Kalakian, Croce, and Dahlstrom (2011) indicated that 90%–95% of children with disabilities have been successfully integrated into the general physical education setting. As Sherrill (2004) stated, "this means the general physical educator, not specialists, have the major responsibility for accommodating individual differences" (p. 4). Therefore, within this chapter we will focus on the roles and responsibilities of the GPE, with particular attention directed toward the importance of the GPE in the IEP process, and the nature of communication between teachers, parents, and the GPE.

BENEFITS OF PHYSICAL EDUCATION FOR STUDENTS WITH DISABILITIES

In addition to the general health and wellness benefits of physical activity, students with disabilities have been found to benefit from physical education in a number of ways. Physical education provides an opportunity to develop locomotor (e.g., walking, running, hopping) and nonlocomotor (e.g., twisting, turning, curling) skills, object control skills (e.g., throwing, catching, kicking), physical fitness skills (e.g., cardiovascular endurance, muscular strength, agility, coordination), and the physical and motor needs associated with independent living (Auxter et al., 2010). Physical education has also been found to promote psychological empowerment, personal freedom, self-esteem, and self-control among students with disabilities (Block, 2007; Sherrill, 2004). Physical activity has been utilized to optimize body-mind functioning and reconstruct self-identity based on personal rather than societal standards, which is particularly important for students with disabilities.

Despite the benefits, many individuals within the field of education, and even parents of children with disabilities, hold stereotypical perceptions of what a child with a disability is physically capable of doing. Attitudinal barriers toward disabilities and physical activity often restrict not only what children with disabilities are encouraged to do, but also how they perceive their own physical abilities. Moreover, many parents and administrators fear bullying and teasing directed toward students with disabilities participating in the general physical education setting. Simpson, Gaus, Garcia Biggs, and Williams (2010) suggested that the physical educator "actively participate in programs for preventing bullying and must employ various strategies within the physical education setting" (p. 50). Mumford and Chandler (2009) discussed the use of cooperative learning groups in which students with disabilities interact with students without disabilities. It may also be beneficial to engage all students in disability awareness activities such as throwing and catching a ball while blindfolded. Such programs and activities provide an opportunity for students without disabilities to enhance their understanding of disabilities and challenge preconceived attitudes and negative stereotypes.

ROLES AND RESPONSIBILITIES

The GPE holds a number of roles and responsibilities when working with students with disabilities that will be addressed in the following sections.

Needs Assessment of Students

Assessment is defined as an information-gathering technique. Auxter et al. (2010) identified five purposes of educational assessment: (a) identifying students who might be experiencing developmental delays, (b) diagnosing the nature of a student's problem or delay, (c) supplying information that may assist with the IEP and appropriate student placement, (d) developing instruction specific to the student's needs, and (e) evaluating a student's progress. Once a GPE notices a frequent pattern of cognitive or motor delay, the GPE will begin an informal assessment by documenting observed behaviors of the student within the general physical education setting. If a disability is suspected, the GPE will then make a referral to the IEP/multidisciplinary team, where the formal special education process begins. It is important that the GPE include the following items when making the referral: (a) a description of the student's level of functioning, (b) the student's learning style and learning strengths, (c) social interactions with peers, (d) a description of the perceived problem, and (e) a description of any strategies employed and whether or not they worked.

Upon obtaining parental consent, a formal assessment of the student will begin. The GPE may utilize a variety of assessments including scales, checklists, and standardized tests to assess the student; the GPE may opt to consult with the APE in the initial assessment process. For example, the GPE could assess the student's physical fitness by measuring how well the student performs skills that require upper (e.g., pushups) or lower (e.g., hopping) body muscular strength and endurance. Gross motor skills can be assessed by how well the student performs dance (e.g., creativity, rhythm) or sport skills (e.g., throwing a baseball), or participates in organized games (e.g., dodging, chasing, tagging). The GPE will also assess behavior, cognitive abilities, and social skills by observing how the student enters and leaves the GPE setting, follows directions, lines up, accepts feedback, and interacts with other students; how motivated he or she is to learn; and how well he or she understands verbal and nonverbal instruction. There are a variety of standardized tests available to the GPE. One of the most popular, the Brockport Physical Fitness Test (BPFT), is a criterion-referenced health-related test of physical fitness used to assess students with disabilities. The BPFT provides 27 possible tests that incorporate traditional fitness tests and tests specifically modified for children with disabilities (Winnick & Short, 1999). Additional standardized tests to assess motor skills and skill-related fitness of students with disabilities include the Test of Gross Motor Development, Second Edition (TGMD-2; Ulrich, 2000) and Bruininks-Oseretsky Test of Motor Proficiency, Second Edition (BOT-2; Bruininks & Bruininks, 2005).

IEP/Multidisciplinary Team Member

Kowalski, Lieberman, Pucci, and Mulawka (2005) defined the IEP as educational goal setting—"a plan of action or guide for teachers and specialists to assist students with disabilities in education" (p. 33). The IEP involves a multidisciplinary team that consists of the following members: parents/guardians, special education teacher, classroom teacher, district representatives, school psychologist, related services personnel (e.g., speech-language therapist, vision specialist, social worker), adapted physical educator, general physical educator, and the student. The primary services of the IEP team include evaluating initial referrals of students, assessing students suspected of having a disability, developing an IEP with specific goals and objectives, deciding an appropriate placement, and serving as a support system for all professionals working with the student.

It is imperative that the GPE is involved in the IEP process. As Mumford and Chandler (2009) noted, "participation in the IEP process [provides] ongoing access to and communication with other professionals so that information and successful strategies can be shared across environments" (p. 11). Such information allows the GPE to acquire an in-depth understanding of how the student's disability may impede the learning process. Unfortunately, researchers have found that the GPE is often left out of the IEP (Kowalski, Lieberman, & Daggett, 2006; Kowalski et al., 2005; LaMaster, Gall, Kinchin, & Siedentop, 1998). LaMaster and colleagues (1998) found that the GPE was often unaware of which of his students had an IEP. Kowalski et al. (2006) suggested that when the GPE was aware of a student's IEP, the GPE was found not to be involved in the assessment and did not attend the IEP meetings. Some indicated not knowing when the IEP meetings occurred. Kowalski et al. (2006) discussed three problems associated with omission of the GPE in the IEP process. By not including the GPE in the IEP process, the GPE does not have the opportunity to share her own assessments of the student, thereby limiting the overall objectives and goals of the IEP. Also, ignoring physical education in the IEP process "further marginalizes physical education as an integral and important subject area necessary for appropriate educational development" (Kowalski et al., 2006, p. 36). Lastly, the involvement of physical education in the IEP process is a legal mandate of IDEA. Therefore, educational institutions not including the GPE are violating the law.

The GPE is in a unique position to assist in the IEP process as she sees the student every year, allowing for longitudinal assessment and evaluation. Physical education also provides a unique context in which students with disabilities can apply the cognitive, motor, and social skills they have developed.

It is also important that the IEP goals and objectives in physical education are developed by a GPE or APE (Kowalski et al., 2006). As Mumford and Chandler (2009) stated,

> the goals in the IEP should specifically state what the student needs to work on in physical education and how progress toward each goal will be measured and evaluated, where they will receive physical education, and the types of support that may be provided. (p. 13)

This type of information is best developed by professionals with knowledge and applied experience specific to adapted physical education. Based upon assessment of the student, a student's goal may be to perform three sit-ups without the assistance of a student aide by a specified date. Another student may work toward balancing on one foot with her eyes closed for 30 seconds. A student in a wheelchair may work toward pushing his wheelchair a distance of 20 meters within 30 seconds.

PLACEMENT AND INCLUSION IN GENERAL PHYSICAL EDUCATION

Inclusion in general physical education is about creating a learning environment in which students with disabilities have equal access to learning fitness, sport, and motor skills. The GPE must include students with disabilities to the maximum extent possible, referred to as the least restrictive environment (LRE), without compromising the learning or safety of other students in the general physical education setting. The LRE, a mandate of IDEA, is a continuum of environments where instruction takes place and services are provided as needed. LRE placement options range from inclusion to separate APE services (Lieberman & Houston-Wilson, 2009).

Conatser and Summar (2004) provided an outline of the continuum of placement options for physical education (see Figure 18.1). Students with disabilities should—by law—receive physical education instruction within the general physical education program; however, for many of these students the general physical education program may not be the LRE due to class size, noise level, lighting, or other environmental factors related to the gymnasium or outdoor space (Huettig, Simbeck, & Cravens, 2003). Under such circumstances, the APE (if available) can assist the GPE in developing the LRE within the general program or advise an alternative placement option. Before formal decisions are made regarding the placement of a student with a disability, it is critical that a thorough assessment of academic achievement and functional performance of the student is conducted (Columna, Davis, Lieberman, & Lytle, 2010). The data gathered from this comprehensive

Full-time regular PE
Peer assistant
Adapted PE consultant
Peer assistant with adapted PE consultant
Teacher assistant
Teacher assistant with adapted PE consultant
Part-time adapted PE (rotating)
Part-time adapted PE (fixed)
Full-time adapted PE
Full-time adapted PE with assistant

Figure 18.1. Sample of continuum of placement options for physical education. From Conatser and Summar (2004).

assessment must be considered by the IEP/multidisciplinary team to make decisions concerning the most appropriate learning environment for the student in physical education. Moreover, these data may be used to determine if the student needs adapted physical education services.

According to Auxter et al. (2010), factors such as physical education facilities and equipment, class size, administrative support, physical education curriculum, state- and districtwide assessments, support personnel, teaching style of the GPE, behavior management system of the GPE, and grading practices of the GPE must all be carefully examined before placing a student with disabilities in physical education. For example, members of the IEP team must consider if the gymnasium and/or activity area is architecturally accessible for a student who uses a wheelchair or crutches. The team members must also consider an alternate placement option for a student with disabilities if the class size in the general physical education setting is greater than 20 students.

Columna et al. (2010) developed a systematic eight-step process that may be useful to the IEP/multidisciplinary team when determining the appropriate physical education placement and services for a student with disabilities. This process involves: (a) informal screening; (b) referral process; (c) parental consent; (d) formal assessment; (e) data collection, data analysis, and written report; (f) determining eligibility for APE services; (g) placement decision for physical education; and (h) evaluation. It is important to note that every school district is required by law to have special education guidelines in place for determining eligibility of services; however, these guidelines may vary from district to district (Columna et al., 2010).

There are a variety of techniques and strategies employed to enhance inclusion within the general physical education setting. Mumford and Chandler (2009) discussed the use of peer tutors, or trained students in general physical education, who assist students with disabilities, providing them with one-on-one attention. Mumford and Chandler also recommended that the GPE establish a structure or routine during class that may assist a student who has a learning disability such as ADHD.

COLLABORATION WITH SPECIAL EDUCATION TEACHERS, ADAPTED PHYSICAL EDUCATORS, AND PARAEDUCATORS

In order to provide the most conducive and positive learning environment for a student with disabilities, the GPE must communicate and collaborate with the special education teachers (SE), adapted physical educators, and paraeducators. This may be a particularly challenging task due to philosophical differences among team members, lack of planning time, lack of training in the area of teamwork, and negative attitudes toward the concept of teamwork, hindering the process of collaboration and communication (Horton, Wilson, & Gagnon, 2003). Therefore, the GPE must develop and implement strategies to maximize collaboration and communication among these professionals.

A good working relationship is imperative between the GPE and the SE for a student with disabilities to be successfully included in the GPE setting. According to Horton and colleagues (2003), the SE is "familiar with the history and health of the student, behaviors, cognitive skills, learning styles, and teaching techniques to which the student responds" (p. 14). As a result, the SE can provide the GPE with information that is crucial for creating a conducive learning environment for the student. In general, the SE is in direct contact with the student's parents and therefore may be in a better position to facilitate communication between the GPE and the parents. Horton et al. (2003) further suggested that the GPE should involve the SE in the general physical education setting by informing the SE about the physical education curriculum, assessments, rules and expectations, and facilities and equipment used in physical education. For example, the GPE can invite the SE to participate and experience the dynamics of a physical education class.

If the IEP/multidisciplinary team decides that a student with a disability needs adapted physical education services, the GPE should collaborate and work closely with the APE. Huettig and Roth (2002) suggested that the GPE should provide the APE with screening and other performance-related information concerning the student with disabilities. In addition, it is important that the GPE share with the APE behavioral and instructional strategies presently employed, as well as the curriculum covered throughout the school year with the student (Huettig & Roth, 2002). The APE should also share with the GPE information gathered from formal and informal assessments and should assist the GPE with instructional strategies and modifications and adaptations for working with a student with disabilities in the general physical education setting. Table 18.1 outlines a number of website resources that the APE may share with the GPE teacher. Furthermore, the APE should provide the GPE with information regarding community leisure, recreation, sport, and fitness opportunities that may assist the student with transition into the community upon graduation (Auxter et al., 2010; Huettig & Roth, 2002).

Paraeducators often are assigned to assist a child with disabilities in the general physical education setting. In order to ensure the effectiveness of the paraeducator, the GPE should provide clear expectations, directions, and guidance (Lieberman & Houston-Wilson, 2009). The GPE should assist the paraeducator to understand the lessons planned, how the lessons will be delivered, and how the students will be assessed (Piletic, Davis, & Aschemeier, 2005). It is imperative that the GPE provide the paraeducator with a knowledge base of the physical education environment. The Adapted Physical Activity Council of the American Association for Physical Activity and Recreation developed a training manual that can be used to train paraeducators when working with students with disabilities in the general physical education setting. The training manual, *Paraeducators in Physical Education: A Training Guide to Roles and Responsibilities*, can be purchased from the American Alliance for Health, Physical Education, Recreation, and Dance (AAHPERD). According to Piletic et al. (2005),

> The paraeducator should work closely with the GPE in identifying and developing information with regard to the student's behavior management plan, providing learning cues and prompts to the student, modifying activities to match student's abilities, providing reinforcement to the student and assisting with assessment of the student. (p. 48)

The SE, APE, paraeducators, and GPE must collaborate and communicate to provide the most effective learning environment for the student with disabilities. This task may not be easy and may require a time commitment from all parties. As Horton et al. (2003) suggested, "time is the scarcest resource of all: Time is needed with a student for ongoing assessments, with

Table 18.1
Resources for Teaching Physical Education to Children With Disabilities

Name of organization/site	Website URL
Project Inspire	http://www.twu.edu/INSPIRE
PE Central	http://www.pecentral.org
pelinks4U	http://www.pelinks4u.org
Adaptive Aerobics	http://www.turnstep.com/Adaptive/index.html
Adapted Physical Education National Standards	http://www.apens.org
The National Center on Physical Activity and Disability	http://www.ncpad.org
American Association of Adapted Sports Programs	http://www.adaptedsports.org
Special Olympics	http://www.specialolympics.org

colleagues for reflection on intervention, and with the literature for evidence supporting best practices" (p. 16). Meetings among these professional members must occur on a regular basis if a successful learning environment is to be created for students with disabilities. In addition to formal meetings, ongoing discussions via e-mail, telephone calls, and observation notes may take place among these professionals (Block, 2007).

COMMUNICATION WITH PARENTS

The Individuals with Disabilities Education Improvement Act (IDEA) of 2004 requires that parents of children with disabilities be informed about their child's educational progress. Generally, the GPE is responsible for providing report cards to the students he teaches every 6, 9, or 12 weeks depending on the school level or as often as he provides reports to parents of children without disabilities.

Physical education teachers often struggle to identify effective ways to communicate with parents. Consequently, some parents are unfamiliar with the benefits and services available to their children through the school physical education program. The GPE involved in the education of a child with a disability must develop effective ways to enhance teacher-parent communications about both the physical education program and the child's progress within the program. Simple strategies can be implemented by the physical educator to share information with parents. According to Columna, Senne, and Lytle (2009), this communication can take several forms: (a) verbal

Montgomery Independent School District
Rodríguez Elementary School
Physical Education Department

Dear Ms. Lydia Martínez:

My name is Mark Jackson. I am the physical education teacher at Rodríguez Elementary School. I will be working with María three times a week for 45 minutes in the school physical education program. I would like to work in collaboration with you. In physical education, we will be working on activities to help María develop fitness, motor skills, and physical activity habits. Please let me know if there are any particular motor, recreational, or physical skills that you would like María to practice in class. Also, I would like to invite you to attend María's class to observe her participating in the physical education setting.

Please feel free to contact me if you have any questions regarding María's involvement in physical education. Thank you. I look forward to working with you.

Respectfully,

Mark Jackson
Physical Education Teacher
Rodríguez Elementary School
Work: (713) 242-XXXX
E-mail: mjackson@rodriguez.edu

Figure 18.2. Letter to parents in English.

communication (e.g., parent-teacher conference, phone call), (b) written communication (e.g., observation notes, checklists, rubrics), (c) use of technology (e.g., e-mails, computer-generated newsletters, social networking), and (d) community-action strategies. A community-action strategy may include informational sessions in the school for the parents of children with disabilities. Auxter et al. (2010) suggested that inviting parents of children with disabilities to visit the physical education setting may help lessen some of the fears that the parents may have with regard to their child's participation in the general physical education program. Huettig and colleagues (2003) suggested that at such sessions, the GPE ask parents for specific information about the child in order to better serve the child within the physical education setting. For example, the GPE may develop a checklist or questionnaire to ask the parents for information related to their child's communication skills, behaviors, interests, habits, special considerations, and equipment use (e.g., hearing aid, walker, braces). Figures 18.2 and 18.3 present examples of letters in English and Spanish that may be used by the GPE and sent home to parents.

Montgomery Independent School District
Rodríguez Elementary School
Departamento de Educación Física

Estimada Srta. Lydia Martínez:

Mi nombre es Mark Jackson. Soy el maestro de educación física de la escuela Rodríguez Elementary. María estará presente en mi clase de educación física tres veces en semana por 45 minutos. Me gustaría trabajar más de cerca con usted para ayudar a María. En nuestra clase estaremos trabajando en actividades dirigidas al desarrollo de aptitud física, destrezas motoras, y hábitos de actividad física. Agradecería me dejara saber si hay alguna actividad física, motora, o recreativa que a usted le interesaría que María practicara en la clase. Aprovecho la oportunidad para invitarla a que venga a la escuela para que pueda observar a María durante la clase.

Si tiene alguna pregunta con respecto a la participación de María en la clase de educación física, por favor déjeme saber. Muchas gracias por su atención y espero pueda trabajar con usted.

Respetuosamente,

Mark Jackson
Maestro de Educación Física
Rodríguez Elementary School
Trabajo: (713) 242-XXXX
E-mail: mjackson@rodriguez.edu

Figure 18.3. Letter to parents in Spanish.

Another common practice used by the GPE and APE is home visits. Home visits may be time consuming, but allow the GPE and APE to assess the level of support and assistance the child has or may need (Columna et al., 2009). Frequently, teachers communicate with parents only when there is a problem; therefore, it is strongly recommended that when communicating with parents of children with disabilities, teachers should start by praising or saying positive comments about the child (Auxter et al., 2010).

Physical education is considered a direct service. Unfortunately, students with disabilities continue to be excluded from physical education or receive poor quality physical education instruction because many parents are unfamiliar with the physical education requirements in the law (Block & Burke, 1999). The GPE must make every effort to communicate and welcome parents of children with disabilities in order to create a positive and safe learning environment for all children.

Solution to the Case Study

Upon learning that María has atlantoaxial instability, Mr. Jackson begins to gather research regarding this particular condition associated with Down's syndrome. From his research, he learns that atlantoaxial instability is a greater than normal mobility of the two upper cervical vertebrae (C1 and C2). Individuals with this condition are at greater risk for serious neck injury if they forcibly flex the neck. With this information, Mr. Jackson recognizes that there is a need for adapted physical education services for María. At the following week's IEP meeting, Mr. Jackson discusses the unique characteristics of atlantoaxial instability that will require modification and adaptation of physical education for María. Mr. Jackson requests that an adapted physical educator is made available for him to consult regarding the ways in which to assess María and design the best learning environment. He also recommends that a peer assistant is available in the general physical education setting to assist María. Upon consulting with the adapted physical educator (Ms. Miller), Mr. Jackson is recommended to avoid the following activities with María: head jarring or jerking activities, heading a soccer ball, or performing forward rolls, each of which places pressure on the neck. If such activities are being performed by other students in the GPE setting, María would be instructed to perform a log roll instead of a forward roll or catch the soccer ball rather than heading the ball. Further, Ms. Miller recommends that verbal directions be used at a minimum and manual guidance implemented to assist María. Other activities such as locomotor skills (e.g., walking, crawling), cardiovascular endurance activities (e.g., climbing stairs), and manipulative skills (e.g., kicking, striking) are recommended as important components to María's physical education program. Mr. Jackson also sends a letter home to Lydia, María's mother, inviting her to observe María in the general physical education setting. At her first visit, she expresses concern regarding María's involvement in the general physical education setting. Mr. Jackson then shares with Lydia the various goals and objectives established for María and the many benefits associated with her involvement in physical education. Lydia observes María's class on several occasions and receives monthly progress reports. Mr. Jackson also provides Lydia with information about community resources such as the Special Olympics that would allow María to participate in physical activities outside of school.

References

Auxter, D., Pyfer, J., Zittel, L., & Roth, K. (2010). *Principles and methods of adapted physical education* (11th ed.). New York, NY: McGraw Hill.

Block, M. E. (2007). *A teacher's guide to including students with disabilities in general physical education* (3rd ed.). Baltimore, MD: Brookes.

Block, M. E., & Burke, K. (1999). Are children with disabilities receiving appropriate physical education? *TEACHING Exceptional Children, 31*(3), 18–23.

Bruininks, R., & Bruininks, B. (2005). *Bruininks-Oseretsky test of motor proficiency* (2nd ed.). Minneapolis, MN: NCS Pearson.

Columna, L., Davis, T., Lieberman, L., & Lytle, R. (2010). Determining the most appropriate physical education placement for students with disabilities. *Journal of Physical Education, Recreation and Dance, 81*(7), 30–37.

Columna, L., Senne, T. A., & Lytle, R. (2009). Communicating with Hispanic parents of children with and without disabilities. *Journal of Physical Education, Recreation and Dance, 80*(4), 48–54.

Conatser, P., & Summar, C. (2004). Individual education programs for adapted physical education. *Strategies, 18*(1), 35–38.

Horton, M. L., Wilson, S., & Gagnon, D. (2003). Collaboration: A key component for successful inclusion in general physical education. *Teaching Elementary Physical Education, 14*(3), 13–17.

Horvat, M., Kalakian, L., Croce, R., & Dahlstrom, V. (2011). *Developmental/adapted physical education: Making ability count* (5th ed.). San Francisco, CA: Benjamin Cummings.

Huettig, C., Simbeck, C., & Cravens, S. (2003). Addressing fears associated with teaching all of our children. *Teaching Elementary Physical Education, 14*(3), 7–12.

Huettig, C., & Roth, K. (2002). Maximizing the use of APE consultants: What the general physical educator has the right to expect. *Journal of Physical Education, Recreation and Dance, 73*(1), 32–35.

Individuals with Disabilities Education Improvement Act, Pub. Law 108-446 (December 3, 2004).

Kowalski, E., Lieberman, L., & Daggett, S. (2006). Getting involved in the IEP process. *Journal of Physical Education, Recreation and Dance, 77*(7), 35–39.

Kowalski, E., Lieberman, L., Pucci, G., & Mulawka, C. (2005). Implementing IEP or 504 goals and objectives into general physical education. *Journal of Physical Education, Recreation and Dance, 76*(7), 33–37.

LaMaster, K., Gall, K., Kinchin, G., & Siedentop, D. (1998). Inclusion practices of effective elementary specialists. *Adapted Physical Education Quarterly, 15*(1), 64–81.

Lieberman, L. J., & Houston-Wilson, C. (2009). *Strategies for inclusion: A handbook for physical educators.* Champaign, IL: Human Kinetics.

Mumford, V. E., & Chandler, J. P. (2009). Strategies for supporting inclusive education for students with disabilities. *Strategies, 22*(5), 10–15.

Piletic, C., Davis, R., & Aschemeier, A. (2005). Paraeducators in physical education. *Journal of Physical Education, Recreation and Dance, 76*(5), 47–55.

Sherrill, C. (2004). *Adapted physical activity, recreation, and sport: Crossdisciplinary and lifespan* (6th ed.). New York, NY: McGraw Hill.

Simpson, C. G., Gaus, M. D., Biggs, M. J., & Williams, J. (2010). Physical education and implications for students with Asperger's syndrome. *TEACHING Exceptional Children, 42*(6), 48–56.

Ulrich, D. A. (2000). *The test of gross motor development* (2nd ed.). Austin, TX: PRO-ED.

U.S. Department of Health and Human Services. (1999). *Physical activity and health: A report of the Surgeon General executive summary.* Retrieved from http://www.cdc.gov/nccdphp/sgr/pdf/execsumm.pdf

U.S. Department of Education. (2010). *Building the legacy: IDEA 2004.* Retrieved from http://idea.ed.gov/explore/home

Winnick, F., & Short, F. (1999). *The Brockport physical fitness test manual.* Champaign, IL: Human Kinetics.

Chapter 19

Orientation and Mobility

Christine Clark–Bischke and Stacy M. Kelly

CASE STUDY

Scott is 12 years old and in the process of transitioning from elementary to middle school. He is totally blind due to retinoblastoma (cancer of the eye) in both eyes at the age of 5. He has been receiving services from a teacher of students with visual impairments and an orientation and mobility specialist. Scott's family moved into a new school district over the summer.

Mrs. Boyington is a school counselor at Bluffdale Middle School. She has just received notification that Scott will be attending Bluffdale in the fall. Scott will need assistance orienting to the new school, especially with the middle school being twice the size of his elementary school. Bluffdale Middle School has never served a student with visual impairments before Scott. Mrs. Boyington has contacted the district's special education department for guidance and has been given the name of the orientation and mobility specialist. Mrs. Boyington is concerned as she doesn't know how Scott will ever independently travel throughout such a large school. She has contacted the classroom teachers and, during their conversations, the teachers mentioned concerns with Scott maneuvering throughout their busy classrooms. Mrs. Boyington has many questions: How can we support Scott? Will he need a peer to help him travel from classroom to classroom? Do the classroom teachers need to change their classroom layout? How do I help the other students understand Scott's needs?

Introduction

Mrs. Boyington is not the first school counselor to experience this situation. The orientation and mobility (O&M) specialist will help answer many of the questions asked by Mrs. Boyington and other classroom teachers while providing services for Scott. This chapter serves to provide an outline of what orientation and mobility service delivery may look like within the classroom, school, and community settings. In addition, the chapter gives some suggestions for working in collaboration with orientation and mobility specialists.

General Roles and Responsibilities

Definition

Orientation is having the capability to use the remaining senses (e.g., auditory and tactile) in order to understand one's location within an environment at every given moment in time, while mobility is having facility, capacity, or capability of movement (Jacobson, 1993). Therefore, orientation and mobility can be defined by combining the two terms. Hill and Ponder (1976) established that O&M is the instruction of techniques, skills, and concepts necessary for individuals who are visually impaired (those who are blind or have low vision) to travel safely, efficiently, and gracefully in any environment as well as under any environmental situation or condition.

Mobility aids (i.e., methods or devices to aid in mobility) used by students with visual impairments include the human guide technique (also known as the sighted guide technique), a long cane, a precane or adapted mobility device, electronic travel aids (ETAs), and electronic orientation aids (EOAs). Dog guides are another type of mobility aid used by individuals with visual impairments. However, dog guide candidates must be at least 16 years of age. Therefore, dog guides primarily are used by adult-aged individuals with visual impairments. The purpose of mobility aids is to enable the traveler to preview his travel path before he encounters it.

Rationale

Orientation and mobility encompasses all areas of life including independent travel, safety, confidence, basic needs, and general health and well-being. In addition to many other things, orientation and mobility has a very important social component that enables individuals who are visually impaired to experience life as travelers within homes, schools, and communities.

Educational policies such as the No Child Left Behind Act of 2001 (NCLB) and the Individuals with Disabilities Education Improvement Act of 2004 (IDEA) sustained the concept that services for students with disabilities must be determined on a case-by-case basis. For this reason, the need for services from an O&M specialist is determined on an individual basis for the more than 58,388 U.S. students who are receiving special education services for their visual impairments (American Printing House [APH] for the Blind, 2009). Students who have a visual impairment that is severe enough to affect their ability to get around receive instruction to learn to travel safely and efficiently from an O&M specialist.

Federal legislation has established O&M as a related service. The O&M specialist develops and implements Individualized Education Programs (IEPs) for children with visual impairments as a member of the multidisciplinary team (Joffee & Ehresman, 1997). The need for children with visual impairments to receive orientation and mobility training provided by qualified personnel was documented in the 1997 amendments to the Individuals with Disabilities Education Act (IDEA) and the Individuals with Disabilities Education Improvement Act of 2004.

Essential Characteristics of Orientation and Mobility Specialists

O&M specialists are professionals who have been specifically instructed to work with individuals who are visually impaired in any and all aspects of orientation and mobility. They are not therapists. They are specialists instructed to provide services to people from birth through adulthood with uncorrectable vision pathologies and/or to those who function as blind or visually impaired, including students with multiple disabilities. O&M specialists are formally educated to assist students who are visually impaired in attaining the goals they have in the area of O&M. Many O&M specialists hold certification in orientation and mobility in addition to either a bachelor's and/or master's degree.

The role of the orientation and mobility specialist crosses many disciplines. O&M specialists are knowledgeable about medical conditions and the eye diseases related to certain medical conditions. O&M specialists understand how visual impairments may impact functional travel skills and functional travel vision. They are familiar with various types of magnification devices for long distance use as well as trained in the use of mobility aids (i.e., methods or devices to aid in mobility) for students with visual impairment and other assistive technology used by students with visual impairments.

O&M specialists are specially instructed to work with students who have other disabilities in addition to their visual impairment. O&M specialists can adapt the equipment (e.g., adapted mobility aids) and curriculum they use to meet the particular needs of each learner. For example, students with visual impairments who use wheelchairs, walkers, crutches, or support canes to address their additional disabilities experience an O&M program tailored to their unique characteristics.

These specialists are also familiar with state and federal laws regarding the education of their students and are knowledgeable about local agencies and resources for this population of students. The O&M specialist provides O&M instruction to students with visual impairments and information to teachers and other service providers to assist educators in supporting students who are visually impaired throughout the school experience and within their communities.

In addition, these specialists need to be prepared and flexible. The schedules of O&M specialists are consistently changing due to student schedules, caseloads, and weather conditions. Only on rare occasions will their schedules remain consistent. O&M specialists also need to be self-directed, as they typically work in isolation with a student.

COMMUNICATION WITH TEACHERS AND PARENTS

For successful implementation of a student's IEP or Individualized Family Service Plan (IFSP; for younger children), it is necessary for all teachers, specialists, and parents to communicate regularly. Given the limited amount of time that O&M specialists are available to work directly with a student, communication is essential. Communication can occur as face-to-face discussions before, during, or after instruction with a student, phone calls, or through e-mail. In addition, the O&M specialist can provide handouts with information related to the services provided to the student. Through communication, all of the individuals supporting the student can gain a greater understanding of the student and his individual needs. Without this communication, important information related to student needs or skills may not be available to the O&M specialist (or individuals) causing services to be impacted (Olmstead, 2005). Communication with the O&M specialist often occurs through the teacher of students with visual impairments as the classroom teacher typically has more interaction with this teacher than the O&M specialist. Regardless of how or when the communication happens, it is imperative that communication between the

Table 19.1

Potential Questions for Orientation and Mobility Specialists

General questions	Instructional/classroom questions
■ What is your role as the orientation and mobility specialist? ■ How does the student travel (e.g., use of long cane, use of vision)? ■ What is your schedule? When can we expect to see you? ■ How can I reach you if there is a change in our schedule?	■ How can I prepare the other students for having a student with a visual impairment in the classroom? ■ How does a student's visual impairment impact his ability to maneuver within the classroom and school environments? ■ How can I make sure that my classroom is accessible for a student who is visually impaired? ■ What special types of devices does the student use in the classroom and other school environments and when is the student expected to use the special devices? For example, the student may use mobility aids such as the long cane for regular travel throughout the school day and/or the human guide technique (also known as the sighted guide technique) in some circumstances. The student may use magnification devices for long-distance viewing.

general education teacher, student, parents, other service providers, and the O&M specialist occur often during the school year.

Questions to Ask

General education teachers, school counselors, or other educational specialists may have many questions related to orientation and mobility. Table 19.1 includes a list of questions to consider asking the orientation and mobility specialist to help in supporting students with visual impairments within classrooms, schools, and communities.

Direct Services Provided to Students

Working Within the General Education Classroom

Although the majority of direct services provided to a student with a visual impairment will be provided outside of the general education classroom, there are services and skills that can be incorporated within the classroom. Many of the skills necessary for independent travel within the general education classroom include: use of self-protective and trailing techniques, turns (i.e., 90 degree, 180 degree, 360 degree), spatial awareness, laterality, directionality, route shapes, and landmarks and clues. Table 19.2 provides a definition of many commonly used orientation and mobility concepts.

These skills allow the student to identify his location within the classroom, physical positioning to travel safely within classrooms, routes to get to his desired location, and potential obstacles within the route. In addition, the O&M specialist can provide guidance to the general education teacher for supporting the student when the arrangement of the classroom changes during activities or to provide a different learning environment for the student.

Working Within the School Environment

The O&M specialist will spend a large amount of time with the student prior to the beginning of a new school year and during the first few weeks assisting in the creation of routes to necessary destinations within the school environment, allowing the student to travel safely and independently throughout the school. In addition, the O&M specialist will provide instruction to the student for independent travel from an automobile (or bus) or designated area near the school building to the school building. Within this instruction, the O&M specialist may teach the student any of the following skills: body awareness, turns (i.e., 90 degree, 180 degree, 360 degree), spatial awareness, laterality, directionality, route shapes, landmarks and clues, street crossings, indoor travel, use of self-protective techniques indoors, use of trailing techniques indoors or outdoors, outdoor travel, travel in adverse weather conditions (i.e., snow, ice, rain, hail, heat, cold), travel in familiar environments, regularly traveled routes, travel in unfamiliar environments, use of mobility aids for O&M, and soliciting assistance or aid from others.

Table 19.2
Examples of Orientation and Mobility Concepts

Concept	Definition
90-degree turn	Turning one quarter of a full 360-degree turn in either direction
180-degree turn	Turning one half of a full 360-degree turn in either direction
360-degree turn	Turning an entire full 360-turn in either direction
Address system	The numbering system commonly used to identify room numbers indoors or specific points of interest outdoors
Body awareness	Awareness of one's body
Directionality	Concept of position or location that involves points or lines toward something or someone
Indoor travel	Travel that takes place in indoor locations or areas
Landmarks and clues	Available sensory information that can help in becoming oriented to an environment
Laterality	Concept of position or location that involves understanding of left and right sides
Outdoor travel	Travel that takes place in outdoor locations or areas
Parking lot travel	Practice of safe travel skills that takes place in open parking lots with and without automobiles present
Public transportation	The use of passenger transportation services available for use by the general public
Residential travel	Travel in locations where housing is the predominant use of land space
Route shapes	A strategy used to envision or describe a route prior to, during, or after traveling
Rural travel	Travel in locations that are less-populated and nonurban
Self-protective and trailing techniques	Basic travel and safety techniques used to navigate
Semi-business and business travel	Travel in a commercial area of a town or city
Shopping and dining	Experience navigating and accessing shopping and dining experiences
Soliciting assistance or aid from others	A skill that involves being willing and able to safely and effectively ask for assistance from others during indoor or outdoor travel experiences
Spatial awareness	The distance two or more objects are apart from each other

Table 19.2. Examples of Orientation and Mobility Concepts continued

Concept	Definition
Street crossings in each type of environment (i.e., residential, semi-business, business, rural)	Street crossings in a variety of different circumstances
Systematic searching	Searching in an organized way using available sensory information
Travel in adverse weather conditions (i.e., snow, ice, rain, hail, heat, cold)	Adverse weather conditions can change the way the traveler perceives the environment. Skills are developed to cope with and understand new demands that arise during adverse weather conditions.
Travel in familiar environments	Travel in environments encountered often
Travel in unfamiliar environments	Travel in environments rarely encountered or not encountered before at all
Vehicle familiarization	Exploring parked vehicles of all kinds (e.g., automobiles, school buses) using a variety of senses to understand the vehicles while building upon prior knowledge and experience

WORKING WITHIN THE COMMUNITY

With the ultimate goal of a maximum degree of independent travel in familiar and/or unfamiliar settings, the O&M specialist will also spend time working with the student within the home and local community. Many of the skills necessary for independent travel in any setting include: vehicle familiarization, address system, route shapes, landmarks and clues, residential environments, semi-business and business environments, rural travel, shopping and dining, street crossings in each type of environment (i.e., residential, semi-business, business, rural), parking lot travel, public transportation, indoor travel, outdoor travel, travel in adverse weather conditions (i.e., snow, ice, rain, hail, heat, cold), night travel, travel in familiar environments, regularly traveled routes, travel in unfamiliar environments, traveling unfamiliar routes, use of mobility aids for O&M, and soliciting assistance from others. O&M specialists often include the student with visual impairments in the planning of community outings to encourage the development of other important independence skills (i.e., communicating with others, organization, and planning in advance). Many O&M specialists will work with their students in community settings during the evening to avoid impacting their academics. Additional instruction can be provided to students with visual impairments after they graduate from high school through schools for the blind or rehabilitative service.

ASSESSMENT

Students who are visually impaired with or without additional disabilities may be eligible for O&M services. The need for orientation and mobility services is determined on an individual basis through interviews, observations, and assessments of students who are visually impaired. Regular evaluations of student progress in the area of O&M are also part of the ongoing assessment process.

It must be determined through the assessment process if a student who is visually impaired is eligible to receive O&M services. Not all students who are visually impaired have the need for O&M services. The assessment process provides the documentation of the particular need for each individual student.

The O&M assessment is conducted by an O&M specialist to determine eligibility for orientation and mobility services. The O&M specialist identifies the current level of functioning in all areas of orientation and mobility to determine student needs for programming. The O&M assessment takes into account background information provided by other evaluations, including the interpretation of functional vision assessment as the data relate to O&M.

The O&M assessment evaluates the impact of the visual impairment on the ability to (a) learn body, spatial, and environmental concepts; (b) use senses for orientation and travel; (c) move around safely and purposefully; and (d) remain oriented in familiar and unfamiliar environments. Students may qualify for O&M services when their visual impairment interferes with any or all of the assessment areas. For those students who are eligible to receive O&M services, an O&M specialist should oversee the provision of instruction and/or provide direct instruction.

DIRECT SERVICES PROVIDED TO TEACHERS

CONSULTATION SERVICES

Itinerant O&M specialists are only present in one location for a limited amount of time before they travel to other schools to provide services for other students. The role of the O&M specialist with direct services provided

---

Suggested Discussion Items

- The role of the orientation and mobility specialist
- The human guide technique (also known as the sighted guide technique)
- How the student travels (e.g., use of long cane, use of vision)
- Specialized equipment the student uses for travel (e.g., the long cane, precane or adapted mobility device, telescope or other magnification device)
- Safe travel skills for the student with visual impairment
- How to handle emergency evacuations and nonemergency practice evacuations such as fires, fire drills, and so on with a student who is visually impaired
- Recommendations for classroom and school environment setup
- Methods of effective communication with students who are visually impaired including direction giving, when to offer assistance, and how to offer assistance

---

Figure 19.1. Topics for orientation and mobility in-service.

---

to teachers (e.g., consultation, in-service) maximizes the impact of O&M services for students with visual impairments. With the special guidance provided by the O&M specialist through direct service provided to teachers, the educational team can address areas of O&M development whether the O&M specialist is present or not.

Consultation is a method by which an expert uses her expertise to "evaluate a problem and provide recommendations to the consultee" (Cook, Klein, & Tessier, 2008, p. 346). Consultation services provided by the O&M specialist may include: vision simulations to assist the teacher in better understanding the visual condition/function of the student with visual impairments, suggestions for classroom arrangement, presentations to peers on the devices used by the student with visual impairments for traveling throughout his environment, support when mobility devices are not functioning correctly, and strategies for supporting the student with visual impairment.

In-Service

Additionally, the O&M specialist provides in-service education to school staff. In-services are intended to contribute toward the development of students' O&M skills and overall independence throughout school environments as well as answer many of the questions educators commonly have about working with students who are visually impaired. Figure 19.1 presents activities that may be included within an orientation and mobility in-service.

- Teacher contact information
- Daily classroom schedules (e.g., specify how the schedule changes daily, weekly, monthly)
- Contact with physical education teacher and instructors of other special activities
- Schedule for physical education class and other special activities
- Dates and locations of planned field trips (preplanning on behalf of the O&M specialist can make all the difference)
- Dates and locations of community outings
- Dates and locations of other notable special events
- Variation in classroom setup (e.g., are student desks rearranged weekly to vary the learning environment?)
- Lunchroom, playground, and outdoor recess routines
- If familiar with the student who is visually impaired, teaching strategies that have been tried with the particular student and what works well or does not work well with the particular student

Figure 19.2. Information provided by general education teachers to support orientation and mobility specialists.

Charts and/or Checklists of Information Needed from the Teacher

Information provided by the general education teacher regarding scheduling changes and variation in classroom setup or specific routines will be very beneficial for the orientation and mobility specialist. Figure 19.2 outlines many of the informational items that can be beneficial. This information may be updated on a regular basis throughout the school year as major events approach or schedules change (e.g., quarterly or every semester).

Solution to the Case Study

Ms. Woodside, the district's orientation and mobility specialist, scheduled a meeting with Mrs. Boyington and Scott's teachers. During this meeting, Ms. Woodside provided them with information on O&M, tools that Scott will be using within the school, and strategies for supporting Scott while encouraging his independence. She provided them with a copy of the dates she will be working with Scott and encouraged them to touch base with her on those dates if they have any questions or concerns. In addition, Ms. Woodside spent several days working with Scott to orient him to the school and identify routes to areas within the school. After the completion of this meeting and observing Ms. Woodside working with Scott,

Mrs. Boyington feels confident that Bluffdale Middle School can successfully meet the needs of the students attending in the fall, including Scott.

REFERENCES

American Printing House for the Blind. (2009). *Annual report 2008*. Louisville, KY: Author.

Cook, R. E., Klein, M. D., & Tessier, A. (2008). *Adapting early childhood curricula for children with special needs*. Columbus, OH: Pearson Prentice Hall.

Hill, E., & Ponder, P. (1976). *Orientation and mobility techniques*. New York, NY: AFB Press.

Individuals with Disabilities Education Improvement Act, Pub. Law 108-446 (December 3, 2004).

Jacobson, W. H. (1993). *The art and science of teaching orientation and mobility to persons with visual impairments*. New York, NY: AFB Press.

Joffee, E., & Ehresman, P. (1997). Learners with visual and cognitive impairments. In B. B. Blasch, W. R. Wiener, & R. L. Welsh (Eds.), *Foundations of orientation and mobility* (2nd ed., pp. 483–499). New York, NY: AFB Press.

No Child Left Behind Act, 20 U.S.C. §6301 (2001).

Olmstead, J. E. (2005). *Itinerant teaching: Tricks of the trade for teachers of students with visual impairments*. New York, NY: AFB Press.

Chapter 20

Physical and Occupational Therapists

Annette R. Parnell

Case Study: Dan

Dan is a 16-year-old sophomore in high school. Recently his behavior in class has been distant and less focused on class material. He also exerts more fidgety behavior, as if he does not want to sit for the entire class session. It has even gotten to the point where Dan has asked every day over the past week for a bathroom pass during the same class. A teacher notices the change in behavior and slight drop in quality of his in-class and out of class assignments, and therefore addresses the situation and concern with Dan.

Dan tells his teacher that his back has been bothering him over the past 2 weeks, and certain positions such as sitting, especially in the hard classroom desks, hurt him the most. He also states that his parents just took him to the doctor yesterday, who recommended physical therapy to help with his pain. The first appointment is that evening after school.

Introduction

A physical therapist is a healthcare provider who works as part of a healthcare team to promote optimal function. Since the 1970s, physical therapists in the United States have assumed greater responsibilities that typically had been performed by general medical practitioners and orthopedic surgeons. The United States military started by using their physical therapists as primary neuromusculoskeletal evaluators. Over time, evaluation and treatment by physical therapists became more proficient on identifying their patient's etiologies (Seidel, Ball, Dains, & Benedict, 2006).

As a skilled clinician, physical therapists are specialists of the human body's movement mechanics. It is a dynamic profession with an established theoretical and scientific base and widespread clinical application in the restoration, maintenance, and as mentioned before, promotion of optimal function for any human being (American Physical Therapy Association [APTA], 2001). Physical therapists provide daily care to more than 750,000 people by doing the following:

- diagnosing and managing movement dysfunction and enhancing physical and functional abilities;
- restoring, maintaining, and promoting not only optimal physical function but optimal wellness and fitness and optimal quality of life as it relates to movement and health; and
- preventing the onset, symptoms, and progression of impairments, functional limitation, and disabilities that may result from diseases, disorders, conditions, or injuries.

GENERAL ROLES AND RESPONSIBILITIES

A patient may come to a physical therapist through a medical referral or, by self-referral to seek advice and/or guidance. Licensed physical therapists can work in many different healthcare fields. Specifically, as practicing clinicians, physical therapists work in different institutions, each of which differs in setting, patient characteristics, required tasks as a physical therapist, and range in performed activities. The main classifications of institutions include: outpatient, inpatient, rehabilitation or skilled nursing facility, home healthcare, and school physical therapy. See Table 20.1 for a description of each facility's differences from a physical therapist's point of view.

Depending on the facility, different forms of payment, coverage, appointment scheduling, and flow of treatment may occur. However, all physical therapists, in any setting, have general goals to work toward and are specialists in providing care in their setting. In these situations physical therapy sessions may include the educational team (e.g., one-on-one aides, classroom aides, teachers, other related services) to optimize a child's ability to access, explore, and participate within his educational environment. Physical therapists also provide education to parents. Education would not only include information on obstacles in the classroom, but may also focus on things such as the lunchroom, stairs, curbs, transportation on level and not level ground

Table 20.1

Various Physical Therapy Facility Classifications

Various physical therapy facility classifications	
Outpatient office or group practice	Medically stable patients, who usually have independent transportation, who are limited in their activities of daily living (ADL) due to decreased mobility and/or increased pain.
Inpatient acute care hospital	Admitted hospital patients under medical supervision. Physical therapists work to help maximize functional independence during the stay and to prepare for a safe discharge.
Rehabilitation hospital, skilled nursing facility	Under supervision of a physician, 24 hours of skilled nursing care is available. Physical therapy is available on site during scheduled hours to work on regaining maximal function and independence.
Home healthcare	A physical therapist travels to individual homes to provide care as needed and as able depending on the environment. The goal is to maximize independence for patients to transfer to an outpatient physical therapy setting.
School physical therapy	A PT works with students with disabilities to gain optimal function within the educational environment; there is a focus on gross motor skills and mobility. PTs may travel between different schools, which are where sessions usually occur, serving the best interests of children both within the school setting and in overall quality of life (APTA, 2001).

Note. See APTA (2001) for more information.

around the campus, navigating around peers, playing on the playground, and interacting with peers.

As teachers may know, for certain students a team of professionals may be involved in their education program. A physical therapist (PT) can examine and evaluate a variety of motor or sensory disabilities; however, a different specialist such as an occupational therapist (OT) may take over evaluating and treating sensory or fine motor deficits. An occupational therapist is a health professional who helps individuals improve their ability to perform tasks and engage in specific activities that make up daily life. Occupation refers to activities that may support the health, well-being, and development of an individual (American Occupational Therapy Association [AOTA], 2008). For children and youth, occupations are activities that enable them to learn and develop life skills (e.g., school activities), be creative and/or derive enjoyment (e.g., play), and thrive (e.g., self-care, care for others) as both a means and an end (see http://www.AOTA.org for more information). When necessary, a physical or occupational therapy program can be implemented to help children maintain optimal educational potential. The type of service provided will be decided by the interdisciplinary educational team evaluating the student and will depend on the available staff. A PT and an OT may work together in a school setting on forming goals and some variables of treatment may overlap depending on the spectrum of services. In other words, fine motor skills, gross motor training, and even working on correct speech during a therapy session can occasionally be combined; however, goals between different professions stay specific. Collaboration between the different healthcare professionals, specifically a PT and an OT, is very important. For example, if a student is being fitted for a new wheelchair, a PT may do the work of fitting the student, positioning him correctly and then work on mobility training. An OT may work on getting the adaptive equipment needed for the student for different activities such as feeding or writing.

As noted above, the primary goal of a school physical therapist is to work with his students on improving their gross motor skills and mobility within the educational environment. A school physical and occupational therapist also assumes a role in the development of an Individualized Education Program (IEP) or an Individual Family Service Plan (IFSP). Recommendations are usually made to help increase a child's ability to participate in educational activities (APTA, 2001). General roles and responsibilities of a physical and occupational therapist working in any type of setting are consistent. See Table 20.2 for a description of general roles and responsibilities of a physical and occupational therapist.

COMMUNICATION WITH TEACHERS AND FAMILY MEMBERS

Communication is an essential part of healthcare. A physical therapist and occupational therapist regularly keep in contact with other healthcare team members, such as nurses, doctors, or even insurance companies. Also, proper communication with the patient and/or guardians (if the patient is underage or if mental impairments are noted) ensures a wholesome delivery of care, progress, and work toward an achievement of personal, as well as the physical therapist's, goals. For a physical therapist to stay organized with each case and patient, documentation is required and set up in a consistent format. As many other healthcare providers, physical therapists are educated to use a SOAP format: Subjective, Objective, Assessment, and Plan.

Table 20.2
General Roles and Responsibilities of a Physical and Occupational Therapist

Diagnose	Through the use of specific tests and measures, physical therapists name the apparent dysfunction or impairment that they have discovered at the time of evaluation. In schools, occupational therapists evaluate children's capabilities, recommend and provide therapy, modify classroom equipment, and help children participate in school activities. Some therapists provide early intervention therapy to infants and toddlers who have, or are at risk of having, developmental delays.
Movement impairment restoration	As specialists in the mechanics of the body's movement, physical therapists are skilled to help restore and maintain maximal movement to enhance physical and functional activities. Occupational therapists use treatments to develop, recover, or maintain the daily living and work skills of their patients. The therapist helps clients not only to improve their basic motor functions and reasoning abilities, but also to compensate for permanent loss of function.
General wellness	As a healthcare provider, physical therapists attempt for optimal wellness through fitness, wellness, and quality of life as it relates to movement and health. It is important that occupational therapy practitioners promote a healthy lifestyle for all individuals and their families, including people with physical, mental, or cognitive impairments.
Prevention	A physical therapist's duty is to prevent the onset, symptoms, and progression of impairments, functional limitation, and disabilities that may result from diseases, disorders, condition, or injuries. The occupational therapist's duty is to apply medical, behavioral, social, and occupational science to prevent physiological, psychological, social, and occupational illness, accidents, and disability, and to prolong the quality of life for all people through advocacy and mediation and through occupation-focused programs.
Team member	As part of a healthcare team, physical and occupational therapists are responsible for proper communication with other involved parties or healthcare providers.
Continued education	To uphold a physical or occupational therapy license to practice in the United States, each state has requirements per law that are to be met for continued learning and updated information through educational courses.

TEACHERS

A teacher may come across some of these notes written by a physical therapist, depending on the type of setting she is working in; usually the teacher has direct access to a student's IEP, which would include a physical or occupational therapist's goals for the year. Conferring with members of other disciplines about the physical and/or occupational therapy plan of care may be part of the coordination of care. In the school system, a meeting may be set up for a discussion of concerns regarding motor or sensory impairments. It helps to know how other providers' system works and what each member is bringing to the table. Outlines of physical therapy documentation notes are provided in the Appendix. More specifically, the subjective section is patient-centered, with his report of the current situation. Functional statements and restrictions in his activities of daily living are specified. In the objective section, physical therapists provide documentation of the examination, evaluation, and intervention, which will lead to a conclusive diagnosis. The assessment has the description of the diagnosis, explanation of benefits from physical therapy intervention, necessity, and prognosis after a plan of care is put into practice. The plan discusses the recommendations for interventions from the physical therapist per findings from the first visit (O'Sullivan & Siegelman, 2005).

From the initial examination note, data can be reviewed from the very first day of physical therapy. Through an interview with the patient, it is essential to gather specifics on all aspects of health, including past and current information from medical records. A complete review of systems includes addressing any impairments of the cardiovascular system, pulmonary system, integumentary system, musculoskeletal system, and neuromuscular system. A patient's initial onset of symptoms, detailed history, review of systems, and current description of symptoms, followed by objective measurements, are important to have documented in the initial examination (IE). Following the first visit, daily notes will be kept by the physical therapist, written in a SOAP format. Each visit may differ in either exercises performed or manual techniques used, but by having documentation of this and the patient's response to the treatment as noted in the assessment, a physical therapist can refer back to the notes for future treatment planning. A progress note (PN) is used to either update the findings in a patient's chart, or to send a doctor or insurance company demonstration of progress or no progress if that is the case. With the PN, a reevaluation of the subjective report and objective measurements compared to the IE can directly be seen. The plan of care and further communication between healthcare providers is then kept up to date. A discharge note (DC) contains the final status of a patient and recommendations from a physical therapist. The measurements, again, can be compared to previous IE or PN data. A teacher may look for information on a patient's subjective status or motor recommendations (e.g., sitting tolerance, preferred posture, the exercises that would help continue to benefit him).

Usually, occupational or physical therapists working in a school setting use daily notes and reevaluate a student's progress or status quarterly using a progress note. Currently there are no specific formatted note requirements in the school system for the healthcare professionals to follow, as long as the documentation includes specific individual goals. Appendix A shows a sample note-taking form.

Conferring with the patient and family regarding the plan of care, interventions, and their outcomes is one part of education. The multiple layers of communication lie within the understanding and comprehension of the material being addressed. Depending on the type of physical therapy being provided, different communication setups are available. In general, a teacher would be able to advise a physical therapist on different teaching strategies and techniques that have worked for a specific student to achieve desired goals. Physical therapists may reach out to a teacher for recommendations on learning styles, communication deficits, and cultural differences that may have already been addressed in the classroom (O'Sullivan & Siegelman, 2005).

Specifically, in a school setting, physical and occupational therapists have a determined number of minutes per quarter that they need to spend with a student, as noted in the IEP. Through collaboration with the educational team, including the parents, the number of minutes required per student is based off of his disability. Most often, physical and occupational therapists have more contact with teachers than parents because they are servicing students in the school building. Thus, teachers play a vital role in a student's physical health when able to share concerns and improvement within the educational environment with other healthcare providers. When a student participates in physical therapy outside the school, the teacher may either receive letters of communication with classroom recommendations, plans of care, and limitations for the student, or have regular discussions with the parents.

Family Members

Depending on the type of facility in which physical therapy is being provided, direct communication may not be offered between a teacher and a physical therapist. Family members may be the middlemen. A teacher may be the first to notice the unusual behavior or decrease in quality of work of a student or even the inability of the student to keep up with his peers. She may be the first to address the current situation with a student's parents. If the child ends up needing services, whether special education or related services, meetings for eligibility will be held and then if the child is eligible an IEP will be created. It is important that the PT is in attendance at the IEP meeting to discuss the assessment and to help to develop the IEP goals. In an outpatient or other setting, once the family members proceed with the proper medical procedure for care, the teacher may or may not become involved.

For a minor, a guardian must consent to physical therapy, and therefore communication usually begins between the physical therapist and a family member at the initial examination. By the end of any physical therapy session the patient will receive recommendations to improve the area of concern (or the area with pain). For Dan, who is a minor, he and his parents would leave the initial examination with ideas on how to sit differently in his chair or it will be recommended that he take frequent breaks, which hopefully would help decrease his back pain. A home exercise program (HEP) usually is assigned and students may be advised to perform the HEP in the middle of the day while at school. A school nurse may need to be involved if the recommendation is coming from a source outside of the school. Some students with severe disabilities may also have physical therapy time implemented into their class schedule.

Teachers and family members can help a student by providing accessibility for the student to perform such recommendations. Take Dan's example from the case study; his outpatient physical therapist recommends for him to be able to switch positions every 20 minutes or when the back pain increases. As a result of this recommendation, the teacher changes Dan's seating location to the back of the classroom so that he can stand and listen to a lecture when he is uncomfortable, versus having to ask to leave the room. In another example, if laying on his stomach was found to be good for Dan, his teacher could allow him to complete writing assignments while lying flat on the floor.

At home, family members can either assist the student or help him remember to complete the home exercise program that was provided. Regular participation in the HEP will benefit the outcome of physical therapy sessions, as well as improve student understanding of the importance of partaking in his rehabilitation.

Direct Services to Students

A physical therapist can help a student advocate for himself through instruction on ways to complete activities of daily living without discomfort. Depending on the area of treatment, not only are stretches and exercises a part of a HEP, but often ways to not reinjure the area. Many tricks such as shifting position to relieve pain, sitting on a sweatshirt, or using a pillow to support the back can be actions that people can apply as individual benefits. These options are usually discussed as part of a regular physical therapy session.

Ethically, it is a physical therapist's role to help provide services for the student to be able to carry over wellness and prevent future injury. The ability of a student to understand the reason he is in pain is essential for him to understand why physical therapy and exercises outside of a clinic are important. This is where the importance of proper education and a certain level of comprehension are essential. A student can advocate for herself not only by going through the motions but by understanding why having good posture, body mechanics, and regular performance of exercises will benefit her. If cognition is limited due to a student's disability, motor memory through repetition is optimal. In a school setting, the aides and teachers are educated on how to be a student's advocate if the student is unable to be one for him- or herself. Through follow-up visits, a physical therapist will continuously make corrections or progressions to the program, and will be available to answer questions or concerns to help the student accept a new lifestyle.

Different tools, such as handouts with pictures, demonstrations, and repetition in the clinic, will benefit the student. Usually a comparison of initial status either by a pre- and posttest, or by comparing numbers on progress notes will help a student understand the benefits and be able to assess the change herself. It is the hope of a physical therapist that a student can accept a lifestyle change and be his or her own advocate. In doing so, the greatest achievement of wellness and prevention of further injury has been gained.

Direct Services to Teachers and Parents

A phone conference is an easy way to provide the teacher with either an update or recommendation of what the student needs at any particular time. All physical therapists in any facility will provide direct services to members who are a part of a specific case, as long as release of records has been approved. As mentioned above, a minor will need guardian approval for physical therapy, and therefore direct services are initiated between a physical therapist and parents or guardians from the beginning. Parents can be the middlemen or provide the teacher with the contact information for the physical therapist, if he is from a facility outside of the school. In some cases, a meeting can be set up in the school for teachers and the parents to meet with the physical therapist if an update on goals or the IEP is made.

Beyond direct communication between the physical therapist and teacher, there are services provided for teachers and parents to educate themselves on impairments, dysfunctions, or specifics of what a physical therapist is skilled in. Teachers can access websites such as those for the American Physical Therapy Association (http://www.apta.org;) or American Occupational Therapy Association (http://www.aota.org), both of which provide support for any questions related to complaints of pain or discomfort of students. The APTA mission statement, which supports the public as well as the physical therapy profession, is as follows:

> The mission statement of the APTA, the principal membership organization representing and promoting the profession of physical therapy, is to further the profession's role in the prevention, diagnosis, and treatment of movement dysfunctions and the enhancement of the physical health and functional abilities of members of the public. (APTA, n.d., para. 1)

APTA employees are available to the public over the phone to guide concerns or answer questions related to physical therapy. As a school physical or occupational therapist, relationships with state education departments, local school districts, and other agencies may be available.

Any physical therapist or physical therapy assistant (PTA) accredited school has counseling and guidance available. Accredited clinics or programs can be found online through general searches. Again, the APTA website is a resourceful tool for services or even evidence-based published articles about physical therapy. Physical therapy is becoming a strong evidence-based profession that gains information and services provided by accredited schools or institutions. Therefore, if teachers or parents are looking for services related to physical therapy beyond communication with a physical therapist, they are guided toward the most recent, peer-reviewed, published evidence.

Services in a school may be more specific from a specialized school physical or occupational therapist. A physical or occupational therapist plans and implements a program (after examination and evaluation) to help children maintain optimal educational potential and benefit from special education (APTA, 2001). Direct services should be available upon request for the teacher either working on positioning, transferring a student from one chair to another, or even with direct management of a student. With the proper legal approval, distribution of a student's medical records and history of physical impairments and treatments are available and may be translated from a healthcare perspective for a teacher.

INFORMATION NEEDED FROM THE TEACHER

A teacher's involvement in improving the health and status of a student's pain or mobility function can be directly reflected on the status of the student in the classroom. A teacher would usually be able to be in contact with a student daily throughout a school week and can notice if less discomfort and more focused behavior is presented. An update of the student's performance in the classroom, with assignments, or with peer interaction, would provide information on his ability to communicate, concentrate, and be more interactive.

SOLUTION TO THE CASE STUDY

Dan's mother brought him to his first outpatient physical therapy examination. The physical therapist sat down with Dan and his mother for a thorough personal subjective and objective assessment of his current situation. Dan was able to describe how he has never had any problems with his back before, but about 2 weeks ago started to experience soreness across his lower back that has only continuously become worse. No specific injury or activity was performed to his knowledge to cause his pain. His mother added that his medical doctor took radiographs of his spine, and other tests and measures as a routine check-up and did not find any fractures or medical concerns about his pain. From the paperwork and medical screening questionnaires, answered by Dan and his mother prior to the appointment, a complete review of systems was completed and the results were negative.

Dan's initial pain level at worst was rated 8 out of 10, and aggravating symptoms included sitting, standing for longer than 30 minutes, bending over to pick anything up off the floor, and pain with sneezing when in a sitting position. He has not tried any pain medication, ice, or heat to try and relieve the pain, only moving around from different positions that have helped decrease the intensity of discomfort across his lower back.

The physical therapist was able to take notes on Dan's initial posture when sitting and standing, spinal range of motion, core strength, and back and lower extremity strength and flexibility. All other systems testing for the neurologic, cardiovascular, gastrointestinal, genitourinary, pulmonary, integumentary, and endocrine systems were negative. Dan's physical therapist was able to make a clinical physical therapy diagnosis of a movement impairment in his lumbar (lower) spine and felt that she could help with his subjective complaints of pain by intervening with a specific plan of care.

Dan and his mother were educated on the mechanical dysfunction of his spine and why he was experiencing discomfort with specific tasks such as those mentioned above. Immediately, Dan was given an HEP specific to the impairments found by the physical therapist and educated on how to properly complete all of the exercises as well as improve his posture. The physical therapist was able to show Dan the proper way to sit while in school and when at home doing his homework. It was recommended that for now, if his pain increased throughout the school day, Dan should change positions, such as standing up in the back of class during instruction that consists of sitting for longer than 20 minutes at a time. The physical therapist answered any questions Dan or his mother had, and gave her phone number to his mother in case any questions, situations, or concerns came up in between physical therapy sessions. It was recommended for Dan or his mother to communicate to his teachers the plan of care, and they were told that if any of his teachers had questions they could call. Communication was offered over the phone or in writing if any specific instructions or recommendations in the classroom were needed.

Over the next 4 weeks, Dan had physical therapy twice a week for an hour each session. On each visit, a SOAP note was completed by the physical therapist to assess any change, and Dan was able to report less discomfort and improved concentration during class on a regular basis. Initially he was able to work out a plan with his teachers to sit in the back of the room so that he could stand if needed versus asking to leave the room and miss instruction. He even reported noticing an increase in his grades and quality of work. The physical therapist was able to note improvements in his posture, and other objective measurements such as flexibility, strength, and spinal range of motion.

By the end of 4 weeks, the physical therapist, Dan, and Dan's mother sat down for a reevaluation and compared his current status to his initial measurements and subjective report. His mother was very pleased that Dan was feeling better, and she had a good report from his teachers at the parent-teacher conference that he was able to focus better and sit through an entire class without unusual behavior. Due to Dan having a good understanding of his HEP, no difficulty with any activities of daily living or functional tasks, and good objective measurements, he was discharged from physical therapy with instruction to continue his HEP.

References

American Occupational Therapy Association. (2008). AOTA's societal statement on play. *American Journal of Occupational Therapy, 62,* 707–708.

American Physical Therapy Association. (2001). *Guide to physical therapist practice* (2nd ed.). Alexandria, VA: Author.

American Physical Therapy Association. (n.d.). *APTA mission statement.* Retrieved from http://www.apta.org/AM/Template.cfm?Section=Home&CONTENT ID=43124&TEMPLATE=/CM/ContentDisplay.cfm

O'Sullivan, S. B., & Siegelman, R. P. (2005). *National physical therapy examination review & study guide.* Evanston, IL: International Educational Resources,.

Seidel, H. M., Ball, J. W., Dains, J. E., & Benedict, G. W. (2006). *Mosby's guide to physical examination* (6th ed.). St. Louis, MO: Mosby.

APPENDIX

Data Collected on the First Day
of Physical Therapy

Initial Examination

Patient name: _____

Date seen: _____

Referring physician: _____

Patient ID: _____

Diagnosis: _____

Date of birth: _____

Subjective

Current Condition
Details:

Chief complaint: Patient states _____,

and complains of _____.

Date of surgery/type of injury (if appropriate): _____

Pain History

Pain Area (Analog Pain Scale Rates From 0–10):

Area	Best	Worst

Functional Status

Functional Activity	Status	Level

Medical History

Medical Conditions: _____

Surgeries

Type	Date

Medications:

Objective

Observation

Blood Pressure, Heart Rate, Respiratory Rate, Integumentary, Gait, Posture, Vestibular: _____

Lumbar Spine (or other body part)

Active Range of Motion (ROM) or Passive ROM

Motion	Range of Motion
Flexion	
Extension	
Sidebending Right	
Sidebending Left	
Rotation Right	
Rotation Left	

Muscle Testing

Measurement	Right Strength	Right Flexibility	Left Strength	Left Flexibility

Special Tests

Special Test	Right	Left

Joint Mobility

Joint	Force Direction	Grade	End-Feel

Dermatomes

Dermatomes	Right	Left

Palpation _____

Assessment

Description

Patient presents to PT with signs and symptoms consistent with _____

_____ . He or she will/will not benefit from PT

_____ . PT would consist of

_____ .

Potential to reach goals: Excellent/Good/Fair/Poor

Plan

Goals

Length	Status	Goal
Short term	Not met	
Short term	Not met	
Short term	Not met	
Long term	Not met	
Long term	Not met	
Long term	Not met	

Treatment Plan

Recommend physical therapy for _____time(s) a week for _____week(s), with treatment to consist of: _____

_____

Initial treatment consisted of: _____

Physical therapist's signature, title, and license number (if required by state law): _____

Physician's recommendations or comments:

Prognosis:

_____ Excellent _____ Good _____ Fair _____ Poor

_____ I have no revisions to this plan of care

_____ Revise plan of care as follows _____

_____ Discharge patient

Continue _____ times per _____ for _____ weeks/months

Physician Signature: _____ Date: _____

In signing this document, physician certifies that prescribed rehabilitation is a medical necessity.

Sample of a Daily Physical Therapy Session Note, Written in a SOAP Format (Subjective, Objective, Assessment, and Plan)

Patient name: _____

Date seen: _____

Referring physician: _____

Patient ID: _____

Diagnosis: _____

Date of birth: _____

Goals

Length	Status	Goal
Short term		
Short term		
Short term		
Long term		
Long term		
Long term		

Subjective

Patient reports _____

Objective

The session consisted of _____

Assessment

Physical therapist's review of improvements, impairments, new dysfunctions found, and overall treatment appraisal: _____

_____

_____

_____

Plan

Continue with PT, add, or discharge any tasks for the next visit?

Billing

List of charges:

_____

Physical therapist's signature, title, and license number (if required by state

law): _____

Sample of a Progress Note

Note. The progress note is completed per the therapist discretion, or upon medical necessity; however, it is usually performed every 1–3 months of treatment.

Patient name: _____

Date seen: _____

Referring physician: _____

Patient ID: _____

Diagnosis: _____

Date of birth: _____

Subjective

Subjective Findings

Patient states _____

Pain History

Initial examination (IE) date:

Pain Area	Current	Best	Worst

Progress note (PN) date:

Pain Area	Current	Best	Worst

Pain Description: _____

Functional Status

Functional Activity	IE Date		PN Date	
	Status	Level	Status	Level

Objective

Hip

Active Range of Motion

Motion	IE Date		PN Date	
	Right	Left	Right	Left
Flexion				
Extension				
Abduction				
Adduction				
Internal Rotation				
External Rotation				

Passive Range of Motion

Motion	IE Date		PN Date	
	Right	Left	Right	Left
Flexion				
Extension				
Abduction				
Adduction				
Internal Rotation				
External Rotation				

Muscle Testing

	IE Date		PN Date	
Measurement	**Right**	**Left**	**Right**	**Left**

Palpation _____

Assessment

Description: _____

Patient has been _____

Plan

Goals

Length	**Status**	**Goal**
Short term		
Long term		
Long term		

Treatment Plan

Recommend continuing/holding PT for _____ time(s) a week for _____

week(s), with treatment to consist of: _____

_____

Physical therapist's signature, title, and license number (if required by state

law): _____

Physician's recommendations or comments:

Prognosis:

_____ Excellent _____ Good _____ Fair _____ Poor

_____ I have no revisions to this plan of care

_____ Revise plan of care as follows _____

_____ Discharge patient

Continue _____ times per _____ for _____ weeks/months

Physician Signature: _____ Date: _____

In signing this document, physician certifies that prescribed rehabilitation is a medical necessity.

Sample Discharge Note

Note. The measurements can be compared to previous IE or PN data. The discharge note (DC) contains the final status of a patient and recommendations from a physical therapist.

Patient name: _____

Date seen: _____

Referring physician: _____

Patient ID: _____

Diagnosis: _____

Date of birth: _____

Subjective

Subjective Findings

Patient states _____

Pain History

IE/PN date:

Pain Area	Current	Best	Worst

Discharge date:

Pain Area	Current	Best	Worst

Pain Description: _____

...

Functional Status

Functional Activity	IE/PN Date		DC Date	
	Status	Level	Status	Level

Objective

Observation _____

Shoulder

Active Range of Motion

Range of Motion

	IE/PN	DC
Motion	Right	Right

Gross Strength

	IE/PN	DC
Motion	Right/Left	Right/Left

Passive Range of Motion

Measurement	IE/PN Date		DC Date	
	Right	Left	Right	Left

Special Tests

	IE/PN	DC
Special Test	Right	Right

Joint Mobility

IE/PN Date

Joint	Force Direction	Grade	End-Feel	Symptoms

DC Date

Joint	Force Direction	Grade	End-Feel	Symptoms

Palpation _____

Assessment

Description: _____

Patient has been _____

Plan

Goals

Length	Status	Goal
Short term	Met	
Short term	Met	
Short term	Met	
Long term	Met	
Long term	Met	
Long term	Met	

Treatment Plan

Recommend discharge with home exercise program or _____

_____

_____

Physical therapist's signature, title, and license number (if required by state law): _____

Physician's recommendations or comments:

Prognosis:

_____ Excellent _____ Good _____ Fair _____ Poor

_____ I have no revisions to this plan of care

_____ Revise plan of care as follows _____

_____ Discharge patient

Continue _____ times per _____ for _____ weeks/months

Physician Signature: _____ Date: _____

In signing this document, physician certifies that prescribed rehabilitation is a medical necessity.

Chapter 21

Principal

Mary Kay Scharf

Research tells us that principals are the linchpins in the enormously complex workings, both physical and human, of a school. The job calls for a staggering range of roles: psychologist, teacher, facilities manager, philosopher, police officer, diplomat, social worker, mentor, PR director, coach, and cheerleader. The principalship is both lowly and lofty. In one morning, you might deal with a broken window and a broken home. A bruised knee and a bruised ego. A rusty pipe and a rusty teacher. (Sherman, 2000, p. 2)

CASE STUDY: ALEX

Alex is a 9-year-old boy with autism spectrum disorder. He has above-average intelligence; however, problems with work completion have resulted in below-grade-level achievement. Even small changes in the classroom routine agitate Alex, causing an inability to focus on the task at hand, and he is often sent to the principal's office for disruptive behaviors. It's early in the school year, but the classroom teacher believes all students in the classroom should meet the same expectations and recently told his parents that if Alex could not do the work of the other third graders and behave like a third grader, he would not be able to stay in her classroom. The special education teacher provides in-class support 30 minutes a day. As a result, she has observed the issues and provided strategy recommendations and materials to the teacher, but has been met with resistance. The parents, who have previously advocated for an inclusive setting, are wearing down and recently told the special education teacher they may "write this year off" and request he be placed back in full-time special classes until next year, when he is assigned a new teacher. The parents called the principal and requested the change in placement.

THE PRINCIPAL

In high achieving, inclusive schools and districts, leaders believe in their core that students learn best when they are educated in heterogeneous educational settings, period. (Capper & Frattura, 2009, p. 42)

The role of the school principal has evolved and grown dramatically over time, with the greatest emphasis being the principal's impact on student achievement. A review of literature in 2004 conducted by the Wallace Foundation (Leithwood, Seashore-Louis, Anderson, & Wahlstrom, 2004) reviewed factors contributing to achievement and concluded that the contribution of the educational leader is second only to classroom instruction. It is generally recognized that effective principals are the agents of change in improving educational opportunities for all students.

Ironically, the principal's role in the facilitation of *inclusive* education for children with special needs is often *excluded* from research, textbooks, and professional publications (DiPaola & Walther-Thomas, 2003). Hundreds of resources regarding the roles of other team members are easily located on the Internet, in the libraries of universities, and even in the public library. Although the role of the principal in this process is often omitted, it has been defined most simplistically as "encourager," and as extensively as crediting principals for laying the foundation upon which inclusive environments can be successful (Kennedy & Fisher, 2001). Raymond (2010) indicated that "a principal's pro-active, committed attitude is vital to overcoming difficulties that may arise during the inclusion process" (p. 35).

Despite the fact that principals are not expected to be experts in special education (DiPaola & Walther-Thomas, 2003; Seyfarth, 1999), as instructional leaders they have fundamental responsibilities to support teachers, develop personal connections with students, develop schoolwide plans, and help develop and maintain a supportive, caring community (Solomon, Schaps, Watson, & Battistich, 1992; Stainback & Stainback, 1996). A more extensive list of attributes, skills, and knowledge in the literature is displayed in Table 21.1. Four practical categories of responsibility include building a culture for inclusion, supporting and developing teachers, supporting and developing parents, and managing the details.

BUILDING A CULTURE FOR INCLUSION

The most important role the principal plays in facilitating successful inclusion experiences is generally symbolic. This is described by many simple actions that are often unnoticed as a significant contribution. Examples include visiting the special education classroom, getting to know the students, and becoming involved with the educational concerns of all students (Sage & Burrello, 1994). These behaviors model a culture of acceptance for staff and students in which student learning is the top priority (Sigford, 2006).

In his book, *Inclusion Strategies That Work for Adolescent Learners* (2009), Toby Karten outlined administrative actions that further cultivate a schoolwide culture of acceptance:

- Value educators who support students in inclusive settings.
- Listen to educators' concerns to proactively address and promote positive inclusive experiences that honor everyone's efforts and prevent frustrations from escalating.
- Advocate a school environment with a proactive support system that specifies what standards students must understand.
- Hold continuous high expectations for inclusive progress to send out a clear message to staff, students, and families with a mission statement that the purpose of an inclusive education is to prepare students for a life beyond school.
- Connect with communities to maximize everyone's potential. (p. 17)

The actions of an effective leader communicate a powerful message to the school community. Shaping the culture in this way is accomplished through the intentional application of these strategies and actions. "Given principals' roles and responsibilities, they are uniquely positioned to mobilize human and material resources that will provide supportive and challenging learning environments for all students" (DiPaola & Walther-Thomas, 2003, p. 21). The positive impact of the administrator on the success of inclusion is reiterated by Florida teacher Erin Scott-Weddington. Now in her seventh year of teaching, students with mild to moderate disabilities have been included

Table 21.1
Leadership for Facilitating Inclusion

Attributes	Skills	Knowledge
The principal must be a working member of the team (Tiegerman-Farber & Radziewicz, 1998).	Monitor the evaluation and placement process (Seyfarth, 1999).	Gain basic knowledge of various disabling conditions (Sage & Burrello, 1994; Seyfarth, 1999; Sigford, 2006).
The beliefs and attitudes of the principal toward inclusion is a key factor in influencing others (Sage & Burrello, 1994).	Provide information to parents and teachers about special education programs (Sage & Burrello, 1994; Seyfarth, 1999).	Be well informed about programs and accommodations that enhance learning (Seyfarth, 1999).
Principals of inclusive schools go the extra mile to work with staff, parents, and community members (Salisbury & McGregor, 2005).	Provide support for teachers and students and provide support to teachers to meet the educational needs of students with disabilities (Sage & Burrello, 1994; Seyfarth, 1999).	Understand fully the evaluation/identification/ implementation process (Seyfarth, 1999) and the legal requirements (Huefner, 1994).
Principals who lead inclusive schools tend to be risk takers who seek innovative solutions (Salisbury & McGregor, 2005).	Assure full compliance of educational law (Seyfarth, 1999).	Understand the importance of school culture as a key variable in successful school change. (Deal & Peterson, 1999).
	Assure the identification process is consistently and fairly used (Seyfarth, 1999).	
	Arrange for common planning time for collaborating teachers. (Tiegerman-Farber & Radziewicz, 1998).	
	Identify the needs of staff and provide for ongoing staff development (Capper & Frattura, 2009; Karten, 2009).	
	Provide time to meet parents early in the year, understanding the value of the parent relationship (Raymond, 2010).	

in her general education classroom every year. She cites the knowledge and active involvement of her principal as one reason the experiences have all been positive. The principal must be committed to the success of the children in these placements; the expectations for full participation of teachers and staff members in shared responsibility should be clearly communicated and modeled and not waiver.

Supporting and Developing Teachers

In nearly every publication reviewed, the emphasis on continuous professional development in the inclusion process was emphasized. Providing opportunities to increase skills and knowledge further demonstrates administrative support and reiteration of the priority. In the culture of acceptance with unified direction, the presence of highly qualified, precisely trained professionals is necessary to ensure the achievement of diverse learners (Capper & Frattura, 2009). Training must be provided based on identified needs (Bateman & Bateman, 2002; Karten, 2009), resulting in differentiated opportunities across grade levels and areas of expertise. General and special educators, as well as paraprofessionals and special area teachers, may share targets for improvement or be varied. Assessment data, surveys, interviews/discussions, and observations are all useful for identification of improvement targets.

An often-overlooked aspect of professional development is the opportunity for team members to develop and explore their collaborative roles and to plan for student instruction. Typical practice in schools involves assigning teachers to work together to deliver instruction in the general education setting, but rarely is sufficient time for planning and professional dialogue provided. Planning occurs in small chunks of time outside of the school day or in the highly desired common planning time. A less desirable scenario involves planning in passing or no collaborative planning at all. An effective administrator provides support for teachers as they develop new competencies and professional relationships. Structuring the master schedule to accommodate common planning time for partner teachers is essential. Opportunities for sustained planning can only be accomplished during longer blocks of time, perhaps during in-service days or specially scheduled work sessions. Although each of these results in cost, the least expensive and potentially most meaningful strategy is the administrator's encouragement of the collaborative team process. When teachers are recognized for their effort and outcomes, motivation to pursue continuous improvement is heightened.

Finally, the value of mentoring as professional development should be highly regarded for the potential to develop skilled educators. Professional development is typically structured in brief workshops or training sessions. Teachers who participated in even simplistic monthly dialogues "found meaningful ways to build support and collegiality enabling continuous professional growth and development" (Hicks, Glasgow, & McNary, 2005, pp. 8–9). Formal mentoring programs, informal mentoring relationships, and structured guidance by the principal should be intentionally planned and included in the professional development component of the school improvement plan. See Table 21.2 for potential targets for professional development.

Supporting Parents

The role of parents in facilitating inclusive educational placements is unquestionably critical to successful outcomes. When schools embrace families, accountability further expands to the home (Karten, 2009). Because of this, developing the relationship between home and school personnel is quite valuable. Initially, parents must be communicated with to establish the relationship and demonstrate the value the school places on their participation (Raymond, 2010). Sigford (2006) specified that communication must include more than the typical conference to convey the attitude of partnership most valued by parents. This includes seeking information and suggestions from parents in the early stages of building the connection and continues with creating varying opportunities to exchange information throughout the school year.

In a 2003 study, parents identified the attitude of the principal as the second most important variable in successful inclusive placements, surpassed only by the attitude of the teacher (Elkins, van Kraayenoord, & Jobling, 2003). To demonstrate this highly desired collaborative attitude, principals should model communication with parents and also require teachers and other service providers to communicate effectively. These communications may include:

- technology-based general communications such as an updated website and posted newsletters and personal communications through e-mail;
- traditional communication such as notes, journals, and phone calls;
- collaboration in scheduling meetings followed by timely notifications;
- invitations to observe, participate, or volunteer; and
- typical avenues of communication such as conferences, curricular nights, and open houses.

Table 21.2
Potential Targets for Professional Development

Foundational	Structural	Instructional
Special education procedures	Collaboration skills	Differentiated instruction
Disability awareness	Co-teaching strategies	Modifications/supports
Inclusion overview	Scheduling	Curriculum
	Communication planning	Material development
	Program effectiveness	Student data analysis
	Working with paraprofessionals	Assistive technology
	Classroom arrangement	

As principals model and monitor respectful communication with parents, they must expand this responsibility to be sure teachers develop effective conferencing strategies. Although ongoing communication with families is most important, the responsibility to appropriately and thoroughly prepare for conferences is sometimes overlooked. Furthermore, there are conditions and situations that sometimes occur during these meetings for which pre-planned responses are necessary. These strategies help keep the meeting on track for time and content. Children deserve and parents expect teachers to be prepared with meaningful information. For students in inclusive settings, parents rightfully expect both the general education and special education teachers to be present. In addition to the following considerations, principals should include training topics that result in positive and meaningful experiences for parents and positive outcomes for students such as:

- preparation and scheduling to include all appropriate teachers and assistants;
- starting the conference on time with positive personal and educational information;
- responding to nonstudent issues such as divorces, personal health issues, and complaints about other teachers (this should include strategies for refocusing the discussion);
- providing time for questions and listening to parents; and
- using a preconference questionnaire to help parents and teachers prepare for the meeting, hopefully increasing the efficient use of time.

The principal's role in facilitating home-school relationships includes providing opportunities for parents to increase skills and knowledge. The need for training and development should incorporate all stakeholders, including the parents (National Education Association [NEA], 1994). Specifically, school districts should provide training programs to facilitate parent participation in the educational planning for their child with special needs. Beyond the explanation of educational jargon, parent rights, and navigating the special education process, communication training designed to assist parents to interact more effectively with school personnel will increase the quality of participation (Scharf, 1990). Following training of this nature, parents reported increased confidence and quality of interactions. Additional training topics designed to support and develop the skills of parents include supporting social skills development, at-home strategies for behavioral and educational intervention, and planning for transition to work and life.

Managing the Details

It is no surprise that reams of paper and stacks of books could be used to address the details associated with the management of special education; inclusion-related topics range from supplying specialized materials to assuring procedural compliance. Tiegerman-Farber and Radziewicz (1998) identified seven variables that occur outside the classroom, yet are necessary for successful inclusion to occur. Although these items do not all relate directly to serving students with special needs in the general education classroom, each contributes to the appropriate operation of the school community. The inclusion process is better grounded in schools in which day-to-day operations are routinely stable and are designed to promote the mission of inclusion. These responsibilities include:

- architectural plans (e.g., school and room accessibility, sufficient space for required equipment and support personnel);
- building requirements (e.g., room assignments to address class sizes/space allocation and proximity for efficient transitions, making sure the conditions of the classroom and school are conducive to learning);
- health and safety requirements (e.g., consistent adherence to codes and good practice resulting in a safe school setting for children of all ages and abilities);

- discipline and security (e.g., promoting success experiences by clearly communicating a schoolwide discipline system resulting in consistent expectations and responses across all school settings);
- financial resources (e.g., timely provision of materials, staffing, and training through adequate budgeting and efficient purchasing procedures);
- scheduling (e.g., enhancing collaborative opportunities by scheduling common planning time for teachers and block scheduling of special area classes to facilitate age-appropriate inclusion); and
- staff development (e.g., developing the supportive culture, knowledge, and skills of the school community through the prioritization of professional improvement activities such as guided discussions, data analysis, planning sessions, and specialized training).

Laura Bass is a special education teacher who has facilitated inclusion in Bloomington, IL, for 10 years. In her experience, delivering instruction in the general education classroom is much more successful when teachers can be fully focused on the child and collaborative planning. When teacher time is lost to managing details unrelated to direct instruction, such as resolving logistical problems, conflicts, and material needs, the teaching and learning process suffers.

Karten (2009) included other categories such as developing interdisciplinary teams, ongoing data analysis for instructional effectiveness, and increased technology. Additional administrative details are included on the following website: http://www.ualberta.ca/~jpdasddc/incl/a4.htm. This teacher-friendly resource provides extensive information about support, organization, and instructional planning. The site describes the principal as someone who can help overcome difficulties that arise ("The Principal," n.d.). Here, teachers and parents are provided with more detail and significance in expectations of the principal's role. Initial items are related to building the culture and developing teachers. See Figure 21.1 for a list of details on what the principal can do in inclusive settings.

By assuring details such as these are appropriately addressed in a timely manner, the principal facilitates successful inclusion and further demonstrates the value placed on this service to children. The call to lead by example is familiar and is a common attribute of effective leaders.

- Assure every parent that his or her child is welcome in the school.
- Ensure that all children get a quality education.
- Ensure that all teachers have the opportunity to attend workshops and conferences so that they continue to grow and gain the necessary skills and knowledge.
- Ensure that supports and resources are available to all children in the school.
- Be an active participant on the collaborative planning team.
- Divide and coordinate responsibility.
- Provide continuity from year to year.
- Provide lesson preparation time.
- Provide relief time for meetings.
- Help teachers and assistants from different schools meet to share experiences and find solutions to mutual challenges.

Figure 21.1. What principals can do for inclusive schools ("The Principal," n.d.).

CONCLUSION

The role of the principal in education has evolved significantly over the years. A positive outcome is the accountability for the achievement of every child, including those with special needs. It is clear that the role of the principal in special education continues to evolve, but is generally viewed as critical to the success of an inclusive school community. Building the culture for inclusion involves embracing the initiative by modeling the acceptance of differences and communicating the expectation for shared responsibility. Developing the skills and knowledge of the serving professionals and the parents is accomplished by facilitating the planning, communication, and training needs necessary for successful partnerships. Finally, the timely management of administrative "details" outside the classroom such as assuring procedural correctness, acquisition of materials and equipment, and maintaining a safe and accessible facility must be consistently completed for teachers to successfully meet the instructional needs of students.

SOLUTION TO THE CASE STUDY

Although the principal, Mr. Newby, visited the classroom daily and Alex had been sent to the office somewhat frequently, he was unaware of the seriousness of the transition problems. As in any school, the behavior of teachers sometimes changes in the presence of the principal. When the parents called, Mr. Newby listened to their concerns and suggested a meeting for early in the next week. By putting off the meeting for a few days, there was an opportunity to gather more information and observe Alex more closely. When the principal started at the school a year earlier, his support of inclusive education was evident; he communicated his beliefs about this service delivery model and facilitated dialogues and activities to further develop the attitudes and skills of all school personnel. Although he was surprised with the attitude of Alex's teacher, he realized it was rare for her to have a student with this degree of disability. (He wondered what came first—was she inexperienced and therefore had not had an opportunity to develop in this area or was she not assigned students because previous grade level teachers were aware of her treatment of students with special needs?)

He set up separate meetings with each of the teachers and also met with the P.E. teacher regarding how Alex was doing in a different type of class. Asking open-ended questions, the principal listened to understand the teachers' concerns and hear solutions. Not surprisingly, from the classroom teacher, he heard concerns and complaints and no suggestions. The principal identified several challenges including reestablishing a trusting relationship with the parents, increasing the strategies of the classroom teacher without alienating or embarrassing her, and establishing a routine for ongoing review of all placements to prevent escalating problems such as this one.

When the principal called the parents to confirm the appointment, he was intentional with his words in order to communicate his strong belief in the inclusive placement, his shared concern for the problems they described, and his optimism and commitment to an improved experience for Alex. His goal was to renew the optimism of the parents and shape positive participants for the upcoming meeting.

He was delicate in private with the classroom teacher, but clearly communicated the expectation for shared responsibility and problem solving. Essentially, he asked probing questions that required reflective thinking and evidence of differentiated instruction. This inquiry, paired with "suggestions" provided clear direction to the teacher relating to her responsibility for this student. Furthermore, to address the comment regarding the student's "not being allowed to stay," a more direct approach was used to inform the teacher of the inappropriateness of such a comment and she was given alternatives to communicating concerns with parents.

The team meeting opened with a statement of renewed mission to work together to help Alex be more successful in third grade. His parents seemed relieved to be approached with such a collaborative attitude and the tone of the meeting was quite positive. As the classroom teacher identified her concerns, she was more prepared with what she had tried, would try, or needed help with. The previously ignored strategies and materials of the special education teacher were more eagerly reviewed and more positively accepted. Through open, collaborative dialogue, a new plan was developed to facilitate a successful placement for Alex.

The principal learned multiple valuable lessons from the situation. First, he realized important issues such as this one should not be casually reviewed, such as in a "no news is good news" approach to supervision. The success of students in

*inclusive settings should be viewed more intentionally and repeatedly during the
opening weeks of school. Building in a formal review date at the end of the meeting, he demonstrated a commitment to improvement and good faith to the parents.
He learned that sharing one's vision a single time for information purposes does
not result in a shared mission or vision. Repetitive opportunity to discuss and/or
model his expectations for interactions with students with special needs and taking responsibility for the achievement of each and every child is the foundation for
positive change. To model this last belief, Mr. Newby planned to make frequent
follow-up contacts with Alex, his teachers, and his parents.*

REFERENCES

Bateman, D., & Bateman, C. F. (2001). *A principal's guide to special education.*
Arlington, VA: Council for Exceptional Children.

Capper, C., & Frattura, E., (2009). *Meeting the needs of students of all abilities.*
Thousand Oaks, CA: Corwin Press.

Deal, T., & Peterson, K. (1999). *Shaping school culture: The heart of leadership.* San
Francisco, CA: Jossey-Bass.

DiPaola, M. F., & Walther-Thomas, C. (2003). *Principals and special education:
The critical role of school leaders* (COPPSE Document No. 1B-7). Gainesville:
University of Florida, Center on Personnel Studies in Special Education.

Elkins, J., van Kraayenoord, C., & Jobling, A. (2003). Parents' attitudes to inclusion
of their children with special needs. *Journal of Research in Special Educational
Needs, 3,* 122–129.

Hicks, C., Glasgow, N., & McNary, S. (2005). *What successful mentors do.* Thousand
Oaks, CA: Corwin Press.

Huefner, D. S. (1994). The mainstreaming cases: Tensions and trends for school
administrators. *Educational Administration Quarterly, 30,* 27–55.

Karten, T. (2009). *Inclusion strategies that work for adolescent learners.* Thousand
Oaks, CA: Corwin Press.

Kennedy, C., & Fisher, D. (2001). *Inclusive middle schools.* Baltimore, MD: Brookes.

Leithwood, K., Seashore-Louis, K., Anderson, S., & Wahlstrom, K. (2004). *How
leadership influences student learning.* New York, NY: Wallace Foundation.

National Education Association. (1994). *NEA policy statement on inclusion.*
Washington, DC: Author.

The principal. (n.d.) Retrieved from http://www.ualberta.ca/~jpdasddc/incl/a4.htm

Raymond, H. (2010). *Inclusive education stories and strategies for success.* Retrieved from
http://www.ualberta.ca/~jpdasddc/inclusion/raymond/ch2.html#Administrators

Sage, D., & Burrello, L. (1994). *Leadership in educational reform.* Baltimore, MD:
Brookes.

Salisbury, C., & McGregor, G. (2005). *Principals of inclusive schools.* Retrieved from
http://www.urbanschools.org/pdf/principals.inclusive.LETTER.pdf

Scharf, M. K. (1990). *The effects of communication training on parent participation in
school programs for children with disabilities* (Unpublished doctoral dissertation).
Illinois State University, Normal, IL.

Seyfarth, J. (1999). *The principal: New leadership for new challenges*. Upper Saddle River, NJ: Prentice Hall.

Sherman, L. (2000). The new principal. *NW Education Magazine, 5*(3), 2.

Sigford, J. (2006). *The effective school leader's guide to management*. Thousand Oaks, CA: Corwin Press.

Solomon, D., Schaps, E., Watson, M., & Battistich, V. (1992). Creating caring school and classroom communities for all students. In R. Villa, J. Thousand, W. Stainback, & S. Stainback (Eds.), *Restructuring for caring & effective education: An administrative guide to creating heterogeneous schools* (pp. 41–60). Baltimore, MD: Brookes.

Stainback, S., & Stainback, W. (1996). *Inclusion: A guide for educators*. Baltimore, MD: Brookes.

Tiegerman-Farber, E., & Radziewicz, C. (1998). *Collaborative decision making: The pathway to inclusion*. Upper Saddle River, NJ: Prentice-Hall.

Section 5

High School Years and Beyond

This section addresses the role that professionals in high school and postsecondary settings take and the knowledge and expertise they bring to the conversation. Each chapter begins with a case study that has a problem. The next sections address the general roles and responsibilities of the professionals, how and what they communicate to teachers and parents, direct services they provide to students, direct services they provide to teachers, charts and/or checklists of information needed, and finally a solution to the case study. After reading all of the chapters in this section, the reader will have a better understanding of all of the different professionals they may work with, how to better collaborate with them, and what to expect regarding information they will provide.

Chapter 22

Transition Specialists

Debra L. Shelden and Nicole M. Uphold

CASE STUDY: THOMAS

Thomas is a 17-year-old junior in high school. He has a learning disability in reading comprehension; however, he has worked hard and has developed compensation strategies for himself such as previewing, highlighting, and borrowing a friend's reading notes. He receives his academic instruction in the general education class. He attends a resource class for one period a day for assistance on classwork and instruction on study habits such as note taking, goal planning, and organization. He recently had his IEP meeting, which focused on his life after high school. He attended his meeting along with his English teacher, special education teacher, mom, and assistant principal. This was the third transition-focused IEP meeting Thomas has had. Each year, he and his team review the transition plan from the prior year and make revisions. His special education teacher, Mrs. Derring, asked him what he would like to do after leaving school. Thomas stated that he wants to be a helicopter pilot. He has thought about joining the Army to get training but does not want to make the commitment. He would have to enlist for 6 years due to the specialized training a helicopter pilot receives. Also, he is not sure the Army would be a good fit for him. Instead, Thomas said he will go to college to get a degree but is not sure what his major would be. The IEP team had a discussion about engineering and mechanics. Thomas said that either sounds fine, but that neither sounds as good as being a helicopter pilot. Thomas agreed that he needs to learn more about college majors and possible careers.

INTRODUCTION

The transition specialist is an emerging position in the special education field. Transition services were first mandated in the 1990 reauthorization of the Individuals with Disabilities Education Act (IDEA). Transition services are defined as "a coordinated set of activities for a child with a disability . . . designed within a results-oriented process . . . to facilitate movement from school to post-school activities" (IDEA, 2004, Section 602). As a result of IDEA, transition programs were developed throughout the country (Kohler & Hood, 2000), focused on teaching students the specific skills required to be successful adults. They also linked students with adult service providers before the students left their high schools. A variety of personnel assisted in the development and implementation of these programs, including secondary special education teachers and vocational education teachers. Additionally, some program development and implementation responsibilities were assumed by individuals in the new position, called a *transition specialist.*

The Division on Career Development and Transition of the Council for Exceptional Children (DCDT, 2000a) has defined a transition specialist as "an individual who plans, coordinates, delivers, and evaluates transition education and services at the school or system level, in conjunction with other educators, families, students, and representatives of community organizations" (p. 1). Along with defining the role, DCDT developed competencies needed for transition specialists. These competencies are based on best practices in transition and include knowledge and performance standards. The standards are organized around the Taxonomy for Transition Programming, a widely accepted conceptual framework for providing transition services (Kohler, 1996), and the Council for Exceptional Children's (CEC) professional standards.

Transition specialists work with students, families, teachers, and adult service providers to ensure successful postschool outcomes for students. The roles and responsibilities for individual transition specialists vary based on differences between administrative and direct service responsibilities. Many transition specialists have an administrator role, rather than a role of primarily providing direct services to students with disabilities. These transition specialists are likely to be district-level positions. They assist teachers with providing effective transition services and activities to students with disabilities. Other transition specialists function more as case managers for secondary students in special education, providing planning, assessment, and instructional services directly to students. These transition specialists are likely to be building-level positions. Other transition specialists have a blend of these two roles.

General Role and Responsibilities

The primary role of the transition specialist is to develop and implement transition services. How the specialist does this depends on who he serves. Transition specialists who are employed at the school level provide more direct services to students, while transition specialists employed at the district level are more likely to coordinate transition services (Blanchett, 2001; Zhang, Ivester, & Katsiyannis, 2005). The responsibilities of the specialist will vary in response to the needs of the school or district in which he works. However, all transition specialists have responsibilities related to the five areas of the Taxonomy for Transition Programming: (a) program structure and attributes, (b) interagency collaboration, (c) student development, (d) student-focused planning, and (e) family involvement (see Table 22.1).

Program Structure and Attributes

Transition specialists help develop and administer transition programs. They conduct program-wide evaluations of students' needs and develop programs to help them receive the services they need to become successful adults. Transition specialists need to have a thorough understanding of services available in the community.

Transition specialists should have knowledge of federal, state, and local legislation related to transition, and they need to know the current transition regulations and assist teachers with following the law. For example, federal law mandates that students have a transition plan completed when the student turns 16 years old. A transition specialist would make sure that each teacher has a transition plan for the student once the student has turned 16 years old. Transition specialists also assist administrators with determining resources to support students as they transition from school to adult life.

An important responsibility of transition specialists is program evaluation. Program evaluation consists of collecting data from those involved in the transition program (e.g., teachers, administrators, adult service providers, families, and students). They may accomplish this through interviewing stakeholders or collecting data through short surveys (see Figure 22.1 for a sample parent letter and survey). Transition specialists are also responsible for the analysis of data (e.g., postschool outcome data, parent and student satisfaction surveys). District-level transition specialists might use their evaluations to create or amend policies related to transition planning.

Table 22.1
Transition Specialists' Roles and Responsibilities

Transition taxonomy component	Services to students	Services to family	Services to teachers and other school personnel	Other responsibilities
Program structure and attributes	▪ N/A	▪ N/A	▪ Provide trainings regarding transition regulations. ▪ Collaborate with administrators to develop transition-related policies.	▪ Evaluate transition programs.
Interagency collaboration	▪ Provide students with information on adult service providers. ▪ Make referrals.	▪ Provide families with information on adult service providers. ▪ Make referrals.	▪ Connect teachers with adult service providers.	▪ Attend interagency collaboration meetings. ▪ Sit on interagency councils. ▪ Develop interagency agreements.
Student development	▪ Conduct transition-related assessments to identify postschool goals and transition activities. ▪ Offer life skills instruction. ▪ Offer self-determination instruction.	▪ Assist family in identifying opportunities and strategies to promote life and self-determination skills at home.	▪ Assist teachers in infusing transition activities into existing academic and life skills curricula. ▪ Assist teachers in providing instruction on self-determination skills.	▪ Develop community-based instruction sites. ▪ Collaborate with business partners.

Table 22.1. Transition Specialists' Roles and Responsibilities, continued

Transition taxonomy component	Services to students	Services to family	Services to teachers and other school personnel	Other responsibilities
Student-focused planning	▪ Prepare students to participate in or lead transition-related IEP meetings. ▪ Identify accommodations that will support student involvement. ▪ Assist students in identifying postschool goals and transition activities.	▪ Educate families on student-led IEPs.	▪ Educate teachers on the transition process, including postschool goals, transition activities, and relationship to the rest of the IEP. ▪ Educate teachers on student-led IEPs. ▪ Assist in identifying team members' roles in implementing the IEP.	▪ Develop partnerships and agreements with adult service providers and other community organizations.
Family involvement	▪ N/A	▪ Conduct transition-related assessments with family members. ▪ Provide families with training and resources on the transition planning process. ▪ Assist families in taking an active role in transition planning.	▪ Assist teachers with gaining family involvement.	▪ Plan transition fairs.

Dear Parents,

I'm conducting an evaluation of our transition program for Somewhere School District. We would like to get parent input about services your child is receiving or you would like your child to receive. Please fill out the following form and return to school.

Thank you for your help. If you have any questions, please feel free to contact me at 123-456-7891.

Sincerely,
Transition Specialist

What services is your child receiving?	
Community-based vocational instruction	Career assessment
Goal setting instruction	Life skills instruction
Study skills instruction	Instruction related to getting a job
Instruction related to getting into college	Instruction related to finding a place to live

Other:

Are you satisfied with the transition services your child is receiving?	Y N

If no, why not?

Any additional comments:

Figure 22.1. Sample parent letter for program evaluation.

School-level transition specialists might use their evaluations to change the transition services and activities being provided to students with disabilities.

INTERAGENCY COLLABORATION

Collaborating with adult service agency representatives is another important role for transition specialists. School-level transition specialists focus on collaboration so students can receive transition services. They might make referrals to an agency, help arrange a meeting between an agency and a student, and/or provide information to teachers about available services from agencies.

District-level transition specialists focus on collaborating with agencies to implement policy or make program changes. Transition specialists focus on getting adult service providers to offer services to students while they are still in high school. This sometimes involves working with service providers to change their policies or resource allocation. Transition specialists sit on interagency councils to help make decisions regarding local transition services. They also assist in creating interagency agreements that outline which transition services adult agencies might offer to students.

STUDENT DEVELOPMENT AND STUDENT-FOCUSED PLANNING

Many of the services provided by transition specialists in these areas will be discussed later in the chapter. District-level transition specialists usually do not provide direct services to students. However, they might be involved with setting policy related to student involvement in Individualized Education Program (IEP) planning, community-based instruction, and assessment. In addition, transition specialists would assist with developing community-based instruction sites and making recommendations on aligning transition activities to general education and life skills curricula.

FAMILY INVOLVEMENT

Transition specialists have varied amounts and types of direct family contact. Transition specialists often hold transition fairs to provide families with information about services available in the community. Adult service providers set up booths at the fair to answer questions from families about their services. The transition specialist would coordinate all aspects of the fair, including setting up a meeting place and time, inviting agencies and families, and dealing with any issues that arise. Further information regarding communication between transition specialists and families will be discussed later in the chapter.

COMMUNICATION WITH TEACHERS AND FAMILY MEMBERS

Facilitating communication is central to the role of a transition special-ist. For district-level transition specialists, that role includes developing rela-tionships and agreements with a variety of community-based organizations, in addition to developing relationships with school personnel, students, and families. Much of this communication will center around program structure and interagency collaboration responsibilities. For building-level transition specialists, facilitating communication among team members is critical. The transition specialist will communicate directly with the students and family members regarding transition assessments and transition plans. He or she will need to be able to communicate the results of those assessments in a clear manner. He or she will also need to communicate with family mem-bers about their responsibilities for implementing transition activities in a respectful and culturally sensitive manner. The transition specialist is often the first person to communicate with the family about possible adult service organizations. The purposes, eligibility criteria, and application processes for these agencies can be extremely complicated, and the transition special-ist will need to be able to present information on those organizations in a way that does not overwhelm family members.

The building-level transition specialist also has primary responsibility for monitoring progress on the transition plan. The transition specialist may convene quarterly meetings for students with extensive and complicated transition plans to monitor progress. In other cases, he or she may request written updates. This can be done using communication tools similar to those that a case manager might use to document progress on the annual goals and objectives of an IEP (see Chapter 4 on the general education teacher for sample communication charts). He or she may circulate progress checks to individual team members (see Table 22.2) or one comprehensive list to all members of the student's team. This monitoring would include monitoring progress on both transition activities and the IEP goals, which should relate to the student's transition activities and postschool goals.

DIRECT SERVICES TO STUDENTS

As we discussed in the section on roles and responsibilities, the nature of the transition specialist position can vary substantially, depending on whether that person holds a building-level or district-level position. Building-level transition specialists will typically have more responsibility for provid-

Table 22.2
Sample Transition Activities Progress Check

Student Name _____ Sophomore student _____ Date _Jan. 26, 2010_
Team Member's Name _General Education Teacher_

These are the transition activities from [student name]'s current transition plan. I will be meeting with [student's name] for a quarterly update on February 28. Please return your progress report by February 21 so that I can discuss it with the student and plan necessary adjustments.

Transition Activity	Person Responsible	Progress			Comments
Request accommodations in general education classes	General education teacher with support from transition specialist	None	(In Progress)	Met	Consistently requests his own accommodations for tests but needs help in identifying possible accommodations for projects
Explore job characteristics for four possible career choices	General education teacher	None	In Progress	(Met)	Completed this activity as one of the paper assignments in class

Student Name _____ Sophomore student _____ Date _Jan. 26, 2010_
Team Member's Name _____ Social Worker _____

These are the transition activities from [student name]'s current transition plan. I will be meeting with [student's name] for a quarterly update on February 28. Please return your progress report by February 21 so that I can discuss it with the student and plan necessary adjustments.

Transition Activity	Person Responsible	Progress			Comments
Social skills training	Social worker	None	(In Progress)	Met	Has made great progress on accepting feedback; we continue to work on asking questions and initiating conversations

ing direct services to students than will district-level transition specialists. Those direct services to students will be focused on the student development and student-focused planning components of transition programs.

STUDENT DEVELOPMENT

Student development includes life skills instruction, career and vocational curricula, structured work experience, assessment, and support services (Kohler, 1996). Transition specialists are actively involved in many of these program activities. Planning, conducting, and interpreting transition-related assessments are key responsibilities for transition specialists. Effective transition assessment includes both comprehensive transition assessments, which provide brief overviews of goals and needs in all major adult outcome areas, and more targeted assessments of particular areas of need (Clark, 2007). The transition specialist will often be the person responsible for conducting the comprehensive transition assessments with the student, and in many cases will conduct the more targeted assessments as well. He or she will also be responsible for interpreting the assessments, reviewing the assessments with the student and family, and assisting them in understanding the implications of those assessment results for both post-school goals and transition services received while still in secondary school. The transition specialist will also assist the student and family in identifying needed support services, either from school professionals or community organizations and agencies, based on the assessments.

In some cases, transition specialists will also provide direct services related to life skills instruction. For students who are substantively engaged in a functional life skills curriculum, their special education teachers will likely have primary responsibility in this area. Students who are fully accessing the general education curriculum, however, may receive limited life skills instruction through their school programs. A transition specialist working with these students may use assessment data to identify areas of need and then assist the student and family in identifying strategies for addressing those skill areas outside of the student's school program.

Another critical area of student development is self-determination. Self-determination includes several components, including choice making, decision making, problem solving, goal setting and attainment, self-management, self-advocacy, and self-awareness (Wehmeyer, 1996). Promoting self-determination is critical to facilitating positive postschool outcomes for individuals with disabilities (Wehmeyer & Palmer, 2003, Wehmeyer & Schwartz, 1997). Transition specialists may provide direct services related to self-determination by conducting self-determination assessments and identifying self-determination skill priorities based on those assessments. They may also provide instruction on key areas of self-determination related to transition planning, particularly in the areas of self-advocacy and self-awareness.

Student-Focused Planning

The student-focused planning component of transition programs includes IEP development, student participation, and planning strategies. Building-level transition specialists will typically work closely with students to facilitate their involvement in the transition planning process. IDEA calls for active student involvement in the development of transition-focused IEPs. The transition specialist can facilitate that in many ways, including providing direct service to students. He or she may meet with the student to discuss the purpose of the transition-focused IEP meeting and to identify possible team members beyond the typical school personnel. She may help prepare the student to lead his or her own IEP meeting and direct the development of the transition plan within the IEP using formal curricula (Martin, Marshall, Maxson, & Jerman, 1996) or conducting less structured instruction to prepare students for active involvement. He or she may also take responsibility for identifying accommodations that will support the student's active involvement in the transition-focused IEP meeting.

Building-level transition specialists may also be involved in pre-IEP activities that facilitate having a transition-focused IEP. Using the results of the transition assessments that have been conducted, he or she may meet with students to identify postschool goals and discuss possible transition activities that can promote progress toward those goals.

Direct Services to Teachers

Both district-level and building-level transition specialists will provide direct services to teachers. District-level transition specialists may focus their efforts with teachers on increasing their capacity to be actively involved in planning for and providing transition services, while building-level transition specialists may actively collaborate with teachers on aspects of transition planning and implementation. Although there may be some responsibilities related to program structure, interagency collaboration, and family involvement, most direct services to teachers will likely focus on student development and student-focused planning. DCDT (2000b) has identified responsibilities of secondary special educators in providing transition services; the transition specialist provides support to teachers in meeting those responsibilities.

One of the general roles of transition specialists is to have an understanding of how secondary education can support positive postschool outcomes for individuals with disabilities. They should have an understanding of how to align existing curricula with transition activities to promote student development. In that vein, transition specialists can provide direct support to both general and special education teachers, making recommendations on how to infuse content and activities into the existing academic and life skills curricula with real-life examples and connections to adult life. The transition specialist may also work with teachers to identify opportunities and strategies for teaching self-determination skills to students, including teaching both general and special education teachers how to incorporate instruction on self-management and problem solving into daily instructional activities. She may also collaborate with classroom teachers to ensure that students have natural opportunities to practice requesting their own reasonable accommodations and to receive feedback on their skills in that area.

Transition specialists, whether building- or district-level, will likely have primary responsibility for training teachers on the general student-focused transition planning process. Many special education teachers have limited transition-related training (Benitez, Morningstar, & Frey, 2009), and general education teachers are likely to have even less. The transition specialist will provide training on the general transition-planning process and the student-centeredness of the process, including the components of a transition plan, the relationship of the transition plan to the rest of the IEP, and team members' responsibilities for implementing transition plans.

A transition specialist might work with other school personnel to get them involved in the transition planning process. Because the role of the transition specialist is to help facilitate movement to all aspects of adult life, the specialist will work with school personnel to provide transition services. For example, a student who has a mental illness may have counseling identified as a transition activity. The transition specialist may be responsible for identifying both school-based and community-based counseling services while the student is in school, assisting the student and family in accessing community-based services, and recommending postschool counseling services. The specialist might also work with the assistive technology specialist to assist the student in obtaining a piece of equipment that will help the student be independent in her postschool life.

Solution to the Case Study

Mrs. Derring talked with the transition specialist, Mr. Davis, to help with Thomas's career plans. Mrs. Derring briefly explained Thomas's situation. Mr. Davis gave Mrs. Derring some suggestions. First, Mrs. Derring should refer Thomas to Vocational Rehabilitation for comprehensive career planning. Second, Mr. Davis explained that Thomas needs to research careers and avenues to becoming a helicopter pilot. Mr. Davis stated he could meet with Thomas's English teacher to discuss class assignments related to career research. Finally, Mr. Davis stated that Thomas's mother needs information to help her son transition from school.

Mr. Davis gave Mrs. Derring the referral forms for Vocational Rehabilitation and explained the documentation that needs to be sent to the agency along with the forms. When the forms were complete, Mrs. Derring and Mr. Davis met to go over the forms.

Mr. Davis met with Ms. Sarkat, Thomas's English teacher, to discuss a class assignment related to careers. Mr. Davis explained that she could have the class research several careers and put together a presentation for the rest of the class. The students would be able to practice their research and presentation skills, while also learning about a variety of skills. Ms. Sarkat said she was interested and the two developed a rubric.

Finally, Mr. Davis sent information to Thomas's mother about the upcoming transition fair. Mr. Davis followed up with a phone call to personally invite her and give an overview of what she would find at the fair.

As a result of the transition specialist's involvements, Thomas learned that a college in his state provided a bachelor's degree in Flight Technology, which prepares students to become commercial helicopter pilots. In addition, Vocational Rehabilitation provided vocational assessment that showed that the career of helicopter pilot is a good match for Thomas's interests and skills. Vocational Rehabilitation agreed to pay for part of Thomas's tuition at the college. Thomas went to college and is now a helicopter pilot.

References

Benitez, D. T., Morningstar, M. E., & Frey, B. B. (2009). A multistate survey of special education teachers' perceptions of their transition competencies. *Career Development for Exceptional Individuals, 32,* 6–16. doi: 10.1177/0885728808323945

Blanchett, W. J. (2001). Importance of teacher transition competencies as rated by special educators. *Teacher Education and Special Education, 24*(1), 3–12.

Clark, G. M. (2007). *Assessment for transition planning* (2nd ed.). Austin, TX: PRO-ED.

Division on Career Development and Transition, Council for Exceptional Children. (2000a). *Transition specialist competencies: Fact sheet.* Reston, VA: Author.

Division on Career Development and Transition, Council for Exceptional Children. (2000b). *Transition related planning, instruction, and service responsibilities for secondary special educators: Fact sheet.* Reston, VA: Author.

Individuals with Disabilities Education Act, 20 U.S.C. §1401 et seq. (1990).

Individuals with Disabilities Education Improvement Act, Pub. Law 108-446 (December 3, 2004).

Kohler, P. D. (1996). *Taxonomy for transition programming.* Champaign: University of Illinois, Transition Research Institute.

Kohler, P. D., & Hood, L. (2000). *Improving student outcomes: Promising practices and programs for 1999–2000.* Champaign: University of Illinois, National Transition Alliance.

Martin, J. E., Marshall, L. H., Maxson, L., & Jerman, P. (1996). *Self-directed IEP.* Longmont, CO: Sopris West.

Wehmeyer, M. L. (1996). A self-report measure of self-determination for adolescents with cognitive disabilities. *Education and Training in Mental Retardation and Developmental Disabilities, 31,* 282–293.

Wehmeyer, M. L., & Palmer, S. B. (2003). Adult outcomes for students with cognitive disabilities three years after high school: The impact of self-determination. *Education and Training in Developmental Disabilities, 38,* 131–144.

Wehmeyer, M. L., & Schwartz, M. (1997). Self-determination and positive adult outcomes: A follow-up study with mental retardation or learning disabilities. *Exceptional Children, 63,* 245–255.

Zhang, D., Ivester, J., & Katsiyannis, A. (2005). Teachers' view of transition services: Results from a statewide survey in South Carolina. *Education and Training in Developmental Disabilities, 40,* 360–367.

Chapter 23

Employment Support Facilitator (Job Coach)

Anthony J. Plotner and Kathleen Marie Oertle

CASE STUDY: LINCOLN

Lincoln is a 19-year-old just beginning his senior year in high school. Lincoln has a moderate intellectual disability and has trouble developing social relationships. Lincoln enjoys going to school because he likes to learn new things. He also enjoys swimming and spending time at the pool. He also has difficulty learning larger pieces of information at one time. Lincoln spends half of his mornings in the resource class where he works on increasing his study skills and his self-determination skills such as goal setting and self-advocacy. He spends the other half of his mornings in general education classes such as health, work and family studies, and English. Three afternoons a week Lincoln has been working in the community. With the assistance of the local Community Rehabilitation Provider (CRP), the transition team was able to get Lincoln a job in one of his areas of interest. For 3 months, Lincoln has worked 20–25 hours a week at the local YMCA where he checks members into the swim club and gym and loans out YMCA lockers, towels, and other equipment with the assistance of a job coach. Lincoln also has the duties of ensuring the gym, pool, and locker areas are clean and to make sure the observation deck is ready for the evening events.

Lincoln recently had his IEP meeting that focused on his senior year and life after high school. This was the first time he has discussed his YMCA job with his transition team. The transition team consisted of Lincoln, his mother, his special education teacher, Lincoln's vocational education teacher, a transition specialist, a Vocational Rehabilitation (VR) counselor, and the CRP job developer. While they discussed his current employment situation, an issue was raised by Lincoln's mother. First, Lincoln's mother (Kara) was concerned because Lincoln could not adequately explain the full scope of his job—he was only focusing on the cleaning aspects. Also, Lincoln expressed disappointment that he hasn't made any friends besides his boss at work and that "[the job] wasn't what I expected."

INTRODUCTION

Many people define themselves through their job or career. Jobs provide a sense of security, a social network of associates and friends, and, potentially, a comfortable lifestyle. Unfortunately, acquiring and maintaining a job is especially difficult for persons with disabilities (Leung, 1999, Plotner & Trach, 2010). Misconceptions by employers about the nature of disabilities can have detrimental effects on employment. Interestingly, there was a time when it was considered implausible that a person with a developmental disability could work in competitive employment. Within the past two decades, however, that perception has changed significantly, much to the credit of supported employment (Wehman & Kregel, 1992). A critical component of quality supported employment services is that of the job coach. This chapter will provide an overview of supported employment and will discuss the evolving role of the job coach in facilitating successful employment outcomes for transition-age youth with disabilities.

Supported employment is a term used to describe a system of integrated employment support for people with disabilities. Supported employment utilizes ongoing, person-centered practices that are specialized and evolve to meet the support needs of the individual as they change. Support needs are anticipated and inquiries regarding customer satisfaction are routine. Supported employment practices are centered on evidence-based principles (Bond, 2004; Brooks-Lane, Hutcheson, & Revell, 2005; Cimera, 2010; DiLeo & Langton, 1996; Lavin, 2000; Luecking, Fabian, & Tilson, 2004). See Table 23.1 for the principles of supported employment.

Prior to the 1980s, all employment services for people with disabilities were delivered in facilities (e.g., institutions, sheltered workshops) that were separate from the community. Despite some agencies continuing to offer these types of segregated services, a value shift from special, separate programs to community-based, inclusive services has occurred. Changes in employment services from segregated to integrated reflect society's value shift from institutionalization to de-institutionalization, which grew out of the Civil Rights movement of the 1960s (Nirje, 1969). Growth of the knowledge base in the fields of education and rehabilitation and supported

Table 23.1
Supported Employment Principles and Principle Statements

Supported Employment Principle	Principle Statement
Workforce inclusion	Community-based, competitive employment is a realistic goal that can be made possible through supported employment strategies.
Autonomy	Promoting consumer choice, preferences, and self-determination is primary in assisting people with disabilities in meeting their employment goals.
Employment first	Prevocational readiness training does not improve community employment outcomes but rather impedes these outcomes.
Support continuum	Time unlimited and ongoing employment supports may be necessary for some individuals.
Person-centered	Support services need to be individualized for optimal results.
Financially sound practice	Supported employment practices are cost-effective.
Facilitation of support	Job coaches facilitate employment supports but are not *the* support.

employment success provided the means for inclusion in community-based, integrated employment (Rubin & Roessler, 1995). Nevertheless, many individuals continue to experience situations that mirror both values (i.e., segregated, facility-based, and inclusive, community-based services). However, it is clear that research supports employment practices that are community based and inclusive (Boeltzig, Gilmore, & Butterworth, 2006; Brooks-Lane et al., 2005; Cimera, 2010; Oertle, Plotner, & Trach, 2009).

Moving toward a more evidence-based practice philosophy, the Rehabilitation Services Administration (RSA) leadership and resulting policy no longer consider nonintegrated employment settings (i.e., sheltered workshops) as a positive outcome for people with disabilities accessing Vocational Rehabilitation (VR) services (U.S. Department of Education, 2006). Entire states, such as Alaska, the District of Columbia, Hawaii, Maine, Minnesota, New Hampshire, New Mexico, Rhode Island, Vermont, and West Virginia, have followed the federal government's lead and closed all of their institutions for persons with intellectual disabilities

(DiLeo, 2007a). In addition, the Employment First initiative challenges special education providers and community service agencies, among others, to stop using segregated services and practices (e.g., day training programs, sheltered workshops, and enclaves), employing marketing strategies that focus on helping the "unfortunate," and practicing fundraising techniques that devalue people with disabilities, especially people who have intellectual, developmental, psychiatric, and significant disabilities (DiLeo, 2007b) to truly make integrated employment the priority. Research findings indicate that integrated employment strategies such as supported employment lead to better employment outcomes (e.g., stable employment, viable wages, community inclusion), are economically sound practices (Cimera, 2010), and assist individuals to improve their quality of life (Beyer, Brown, Akand, & Rapley, 2010). The position of job coach emerged with the Supported Employment movement and continues to evolve as the field is studied and grows.

Job Coach Support

Supported or customized employment consists of many aspects of matching employees to employers/jobs based on their strengths and interests. Job coaching is just one aspect included in supported and customized employment. A job coach is an individual who provides individualized, on-the-job training to employees (often with disabilities). The job coach analyzes the job to be performed and then systematically instructs employees by collecting data at the work site to teach the required job and related skills to an employee. Initially, the job coach remains on the site full time with the worker, but as job tasks are mastered, the job coach begins to fade his support. Traditionally, job coaching has been viewed quite narrowly and is often misunderstood in transition services (Plotner & Oertle, 2011). It should be mentioned here that many entities (i.e., schools, community rehabilitation providers [CRP], Vocational Rehabilitation) may have different job descriptions/responsibilities and even varying titles for these individuals. For example, CRP job developers and school-based vocational coordinators and transition specialists sometime perform job coaching duties, but are also responsible for approaching and developing relationships with employers to be considered as an employment agency.

Job coach responsibilities that encompass a much wider scope of support and services are needed to achieve successful transition outcomes. The dated model or philosophy of a "do for" attitude of many job coaches still exists today. This traditional, outdated role of the job coach is one that solely provides instruction on various job tasks that are not mastered by the supported employee. The job coach should be viewed as more of an employment supports facilitator because he should have a larger role than simply providing task instruction. A number of noninstructional interventions that are also part of the job coach function include establishing rapport with supervisors and coworkers; explaining training techniques and involving supervisors and coworkers in training; potentially explaining the worker's learning styles, background, and behavioral characteristics to coworkers; and facilitating employee/coworkers' socialization (Moon, Goodall, Barcus, & Brooke, 1985; O'Brien, 2004). The job coach may also be responsible for communication with residential support staff, arranging transportation, and other tasks that occur away from the job site (Nisbet & Hagner, 1988). Four core job coach dimensions include: (1) providing individualized support, (2) teaching and learning, (3) facilitating natural supports, and (4) collaborating and connecting with stakeholders.

Providing Individualized Support

It is the role of the job coach to provide individualized support, as needed, in the following areas: advocacy and self-determination, identification of individuals' interests and skills, understanding and use of accommodations, model employment behaviors and actual job training, and ongoing job follow-up and retention services. Job coaches may provide various types of supports based on the individual's needs. Generally speaking, job coaches provide individualized training, support, and supervision for the instructional phase of the job.

Job coaches use various assessments to uncover information to develop individualized employment strategies. Although interest inventories and career development tools can provide information as to the employment interests and skills of individual job seekers, job and task analyses are two types of assessments that job coaches utilize to learn more about the inherent (natural) characteristics and demands of a given job. This will allow job coaches to understand what is required to be successful on the job as a whole and within each job task. Information generated through job analysis provides a foundation for matching job seekers' interests with the job duties. Job coaches use task analysis to identify and develop individualized supports and reinforcers to assist in teaching the various aspects of the job. Analysis is completed for specific jobs and does not take into account the abilities or limitations of the student (i.e., supported employee). Once the assessment information is collected and analyzed, job coaches use what they have learned to:

- establish a daily work routine and schedule,
- provide systematic training of specific job duties,
- model appropriate work-related behaviors,
- assist the students in social integration and self-advocacy skills, and
- gradually decrease job coach support.

The concept of fading is a critical component of the job coach and should be individualized and planned from the beginning of the work experience. Fading includes the general decrease of duration and intensity of artificial prompts and reinforcement to more natural types of support. Fading is often the most difficult adjustment and doesn't mean that supports cease; rather, ongoing supports are provided, but gradually decrease. Once fading has been completed, follow-along procedures will be implemented (Wehman, Sale, & Parent, 1992). Job coaches gradually increase the time off the job site as the individual continues to be independent with the naturally occurring supports of the workplace. It is important to remember that fading cannot be done too quickly or too slowly. Fading too slowly can often leave coworkers with the wrong conclusion that the supported employee cannot or will not be able to complete the job. Also, a consequence of fading too quickly is not connecting the employee with natural supports. On the other hand, fading too slowly will often leave employees too dependent on the job coach.

TEACHING AND LEARNING

LEARNING STYLES

Styles of learning relate to how individuals process, integrate, and understand information. A commonly used classification of learning styles is auditory, visual, tactile, and kinesthetic (Kolb & Fry, 1975). Job coaches take into consideration the various learning preferences of the individuals they are supporting as well as their own learning style when presenting and teaching information. For example, some individuals learn better through listening. In this case, a job coach would identify and use sound cues as prompts to support learning the tasks of the job. In other cases, individuals prefer learning through reading or watching. In these situations, a job coach would encourage the individual to use observation, pictures, color coding, visualization, and written cues to learn and remember the various aspects of the job. In addition, some individuals learn through touch, movement, and experiences. Job coaches working with someone who prefers touch and movement can use demonstration or model how to do the task. Although it is true that learning styles can be categorized by one's senses, most learning preferences are a combination of more than one sensory operation. In order to support all learning styles, job coaches must use a variety of teaching strategies, verbal discussion, visuals, demonstration, and active experiences.

TYPES OF LEARNING

Domains of learning include cognitive, psychomotor, and affective. In the cognitive domain, skills include knowledge, comprehension, application, analysis, and synthesis of information. Learning may also be viewed within the categories of knowledge and skill. Types of intelligence can be classified as logical-mathematical, linguistic, spatial, musical, kinesthetic, interpersonal, and intrapersonal (Gardner, 1983). Because different teaching techniques are best used for different types of learning, job coaches analyze the learning they want to occur and select an appropriate strategy to engage the individual. Job coaches consider the individual's existing attitudes, knowledge, and skills, and how they can best acquire the knowledge and skills to do their job more effectively. Job coaches then vary their teaching methods and individualize strategies to meet a variety of learning needs.

UNIVERSAL DESIGN FOR LEARNING

Job coaches consider the wide variety of characteristics of individuals to maximize their learning, respect diversity, and ensure physical access. When job coaches use universal design for learning (UDL), they use a variety of delivery methods; provide full access to information by using captioned videos, printed materials in electronic format, and accessible online information; offer effective and prompt feedback; and allow multiple means for individuals to demonstrate competency. Modeling UDL approaches as a job coach conducts training will encourage employers to incorporate these approaches in their own training.

UDL maximizes the learning of all and reduces the need for individual accommodations (Scott, McGuire, & Foley, 2003). Taking into consideration learning styles, multiple types of learning processes, different modes of presentation, and universal design for learning, job coaches maximize their teaching efforts by supporting individuals' learning preferences and needs.

Facilitating Natural Supports

As previously mentioned throughout this chapter, job coaches have evolved. One notable role has been the utilization of natural supports. The role of job coaches has been challenged, suggesting that their presence might interfere with social interaction of coworkers (Chadsey, Linneman, Rusch, & Cimera, 1997; Mank, Cioffi, & Yovanoff, 1999; Murphy & Rogan, 1994). The issue is how training efforts affect social integration. Traditionally, a job coach provided by the supported employment agency or CRP is utilized to train the worker with disabilities and provide extended support to the worker (Lee, Storey, Anderson, Goetz, & Zivolich, 1997). Although the use of the job coach model sometimes may appear to be an effective way of training specific job skills, concerns about whether or not this is the best way to facilitate social integration for supported employees remain (Butterworth, Hagner, Kiernan, & Schalock, 1996; Hagner, Butterworth, & Keith, 1995; Lee et al., 1997; Storey & Certo, 1996). However, successful job coaches can be effective at promoting social inclusion by having awareness and attempting to take on more of a behind the scenes role.

Natural supports are defined as the assistance, relationships, and interactions that allow a person to maintain a community job of their choosing; correspond to the typical work routines and social actions of other employees; and enhance the individual's work and nonwork social life among her coworkers and other members of the community (Murphy & Rogan, 1994). A real-life example of using natural support during training would be to have the manager or a coworker provide the training. In recent years, the job coach has become more of a facilitator than coach. For example, conducting a job or task analysis over a period of a few days hardly gives someone a broader understanding of a job than someone who actually works in the job (i.e., coworker). The concept of natural supports is based on the understanding that relying on typical people and environments enhances the potential for inclusion more effectively than relying on specialized services and personnel.

Collaborating and Connecting With Stakeholders

Quality collaboration and coordination are critical aspects of supporting individuals with disabilities in employment. Job coaches are in a position to make or break the relationships necessary for successful collaboration and coordination. Learning how to support collaboration requires job coaches to reflect on what they do that works and what gets in the way of achieving collaboration. Job coaches who utilize practices that maximize the use of social resources available to workers with disabilities are promoting actions that lead to job success and increase interdependence. The reality is that all of depend on others to do our jobs successfully. This is true for people with and without disabilities. When job coaches do not facilitate collaboration and coordination among the social resources available, this leads to overdependence on the job coach and isolation in the workplace (O'Brien, 2004).

As facilitators, a primary responsibility of job coaches is to assist with communication among those involved in supporting the employment of the individual. Examples of who may be social resources and involved in the collaboration and coordination of supported employment are the supported employee (person with disability), employer, coworkers, family members, school personnel, rehabilitation-related service providers (e.g., vocational rehabilitation counselor, community rehabilitation providers, centers for independent living personnel), and other funding sources. Communication among collaborators may focus on day-to-day activities but also includes exchanges regarding how job duties are completed, use of natural supports, and any necessary accommodations. Job coaches discover and organize the capability of the social resources (i.e., people in and around the job situation). Depending on the job and the supported employee, collaboration and coordination may include (O'Brien, 2004):

- identifying ways the workplace or the job needs to be adapted,
- providing necessary assistance with adaptations and accommodations,
- conducting training the person may need to addition to that usually available to new hires,
- addressing problems when they cannot be worked out without outside assistance,
- managing crises, and
- facilitating orientation to the job and workplace.

Remember, the purpose of the job coach's position is to provide any necessary assistance to the supported employee, employer, supervisor, coworkers, or others involved to support the person with a disability as a valued member of the workplace. Quality collaboration and coordination means that job coaches must learn about the job and about the workplace culture and assist in teaching about the job responsibilities as well as the workplace's expectations, routines, and rituals (e.g., interactions with coworkers, breaks, lunch, celebrations, after work activities) while not getting in the way, but promoting the connections among the supported employee and his coworkers and supervisor. Job coaches facilitate coworkers, supervisors, people with disabilities, and others involved in supported employment to connect and collaborate as human beings with similarities, differences, likes, dislikes, interests, fears, goals, hopes, and dreams. In this role, job coaches are principal to collaboration that helps the supported employee engage in the workplace and with his social resources.

CONCLUSION

The job coach takes on many roles and has proven to be effective if approached correctly. Coaching transition-age youth on the job continues to be a critical component of supported employment; however, the role and responsibilities of job coaches have expanded beyond systematic task instruction to an employment support facilitator. Employment support facilitators must act as the liaison between employment and school. The dimensions discussed throughout this chapter emphasize key components when working with students to ensure successful outcomes.

SOLUTION TO THE CASE STUDY

At Lincoln's IEP meeting, it was discovered that Lincoln could not articulate his job duties beyond cleaning and stated that his work was not what he expected. Following the IEP meeting, the special education teacher and transition specialist arranged to observe Lincoln at the YMCA and discuss these issues further with both Lincoln and the job coach. Upon further discussion, Lincoln stated that this job was not what he expected because he thought he would develop friendships with his colleagues. Additionally, he was not getting to interact with YMCA members as much as he thought. While at the YMCA, the transition specialist and special educator observed the job coach and Lincoln sharing the job and working as a team to complete the various job duties.

It was also observed that the job coach would complete the tasks that would appear to be more challenging for Lincoln (e.g., interacting with YMCA members). During conversations and observations, the transition specialist and special education teacher found that the job coach and Lincoln did not completely understand the role of the job coach. It was also apparent that, throughout this work sharing, the job coach was not aware of or did not attempt to facilitate any social interaction for Lincoln with his coworkers or YMCA members. It was the intrusiveness of the job coach's presence that did not provide the opportunities for Lincoln to interact with colleagues. While Lincoln was attempting to check in YMCA members, the job coach took this responsibility upon himself and did not allow for Lincoln to interact with the members. The primary role of the job coach was not to facilitate independence and social integration, but rather to make sure the job got done by any means necessary.

As a result of these observations and discussions, the job coach unintentionally interfered with Lincoln's access to training typically offered to employees of the YMCA. Therefore, the transition team and the job coach developed a fade plan that would support Lincoln utilizing a seasoned coworker as a trainer. This plan leads to mastery of each of his job responsibilities and to his social integration. In addition, Lincoln's plan included strategies that ensured that he had substantial time and support to reach independence on the job as well as a foundation to develop meaningful relationships with colleagues. Specifically, job coach strategies included working with the coworker trainer to discuss Lincoln's learning preferences to maximize his success. Also, the job coach will evaluate a fading timeline based on supervisor evaluations and other data as available. As a result of the changes of the job coach's role, Lincoln has become more satisfied with his job. Lincoln continues to work at the YMCA where he completes all aspects of his job and job coach support services have faded over time; however, the job coach continues to follow along with progress checks every 2 weeks. Lincoln is now participating fully in work and nonwork functions with his coworkers.

REFERENCES

Beyer, S., Brown, T., Akand, R., & Rapley, M. (2010). A comparison of quality of life outcomes for people with intellectual disabilities in supported employment, day services and employment enterprises. *Journal of Applied Research in Intellectual Disabilities, 23*, 290–295.

Boeltzig, D., Gilmore, D., & Butterworth, J. (2006, July). The national survey of community rehabilitation providers, FY 2004–2005. Report I: Employment outcomes of people with developmental disabilities in employment. *Research to Practice, 44*, 1–6.

Bond, G. R. (2004). Supported employment: Evidence for an evidence-based practice. *Psychiatric Rehabilitation Journal, 27*, 345–359.

Brooks-Lane, N., Hutcheson, S., & Revell, G. (2005). Supporting consumer directed employment outcomes. *Journal of Vocational Rehabilitation, 23*, 123–134.

Butterworth, J., Hagner, D., Kiernan, W., & Schalock, R. (1996). Natural supports in the workplace: Defining an agenda for research and practice. *Journal of the Association for Persons With Severe Handicaps, 21*, 103–113.

Chadsey, J. G., Linneman, D., Rusch, F. R., & Cimera, R. E. (1997). The impact of social integration interventions and job coaches in work settings. *Education and Training in Mental Retardation and Developmental Disabilities, 32*, 281–292.

Cimera, R. E. (2010). National cost efficiency of supported employees with intellectual disabilities: 2002 to 2007. *American Journal of Intellectual and Developmental Disabilities, 115,* 19–29.

DiLeo, D. (2007a, August 9). *On the road in Iowa and Kansas* [Web log post]. Retrieved from http://raymondsroom.blogspot.com

DiLeo, D. (2007b). *Raymond's room: Ending the segregation of people with disabilities.* St. Augustine, FL: Training Resource Network.

DiLeo, D., & Langton, D. (1996). *Facing the future: Best practices in supported employment.* St. Augustine, FL: Training Resource Network.

Gardner, H. (1983). *Frames of mind: The theory of multiple intelligences.* New York, NY: Basic Books.

Hagner, D., Butterworth, J., & Keith, G. (1995). Strategies and barriers in facilitating natural supports for employment of adults with severe disabilities. *Journal of the Association for Persons With Severe Handicaps, 20,* 110–120.

Kolb, D. A., & Fry, R. (1975). Toward an applied theory of experiential learning. In C. Cooper (Ed.), *Theories of group process.* London, England: Wiley & Sons.

Lavin, D. (2000). *Reach for the stars: Achieving high performance as a community rehabilitation professional.* Spring Lake Park, MN: Rise.

Lee, M., Storey, K., Anderson, J. L., Goetz, L., & Zivolich, S. (1997). The effect of mentoring versus job coach instruction on integration in supported employment settings. *The Journal of the Association for Persons with Severe Handicaps, 22,* 151–158.

Leung, P. (1999). Job development and placement: New directions. *Journal of Job Placement and Development, 15,* 1–4.

Luecking, R. G., Fabian, E. S., & Tilson, G. P. (2004). *Working relationships: Creating career opportunities for job seekers with disabilities through employer partnerships.* Baltimore, MD: Brookes.

Mank, D., Cioffi, A., & Yovanoff, P. (1999). Impact of coworker involvement with supported employees on wage and integration outcomes. *Mental Retardation, 37,* 383–394.

Moon, S., Goodall, P., Barcus, M., & Brooke, V. (Eds.). (1985). *The supported work model of competitive employment for citizens with severe handicaps: A guide for job trainers.* Richmond: Virginia Commonwealth University, Rehabilitation and Training Center.

Murphy, S., & Rogan, P. (1994). Natural workplace supports quality checklist. In S. Murphy & P. Rogan (Eds.), *Developing natural supports in the workplace: A practitioner's guide* (pp. 99–104). St. Augustine, FL: Training Resource Network.

Nirje, B. (1969). The normalization principle and its human management implications. In R. B. Krugel & W. Wolfensberger (Eds.), *Changing patterns in residential services for the mentally retarded* (pp. 179–195). Washington, DC: U.S. Government Printing Office.

Nisbet, J., & Hagner, D. (1988). Natural supports in the workplace: A reexamination of supported employment. *Journal of the Association for Persons with Severe Handicaps, 13,* 260–267.

O'Brien, J. (2004). *Getting the job done: Learning to expand the social resources available to people with severe disabilities at work.* Retrieved from http://thechp.syr.edu/obrien1.htm

Oertle, K. M., Plotner, A., & Trach, J. S., (2009). *Supported employment program evaluation: Evaluation report.* Champaign, IL: Transition Research Institute.

Plotner, A. J., & Oertle, K. M. (2011). *Community rehabilitation provider success: Where we are at and how we can improve.* Manuscript in preparation.

Plotner, A. J., & Trach, J. S. (2010). Leadership development perspectives from community rehabilitation program directors, managers, and direct-service personnel. *Journal of Rehabilitation, 76*(2), 3–9.

Rubin, S. E., & Roessler, R. T. (1995). *Foundations of the vocational rehabilitation process* (4th ed.). Austin, TX: PRO-ED.

Scott, S. S., McGuire, J. M., & Foley, T. E. (2003). Universal design for instruction: A framework for anticipation and responding to disability and other diverse learning needs in the college classroom. *Equity and Excellence in Education, 36,* 40–49.

Storey, K., & Certo, N. J. (1996). Natural supports for increasing integration in the workplace for people with disabilities: A review of the literature and guidelines for implementation. *Rehabilitation Counseling Bulletin, 40,* 62–76.

U.S. Department of Education, Office of Special Education and Rehabilitative Services. (2006). *Rehabilitation Services Administration annual report, fiscal year 2002, report of federal activities under the Rehabilitation Act.* Washington, DC: Author.

Wehman, P., & Kregel, J. (1992). Supported employment: Growth and impact. In P. Wehman, P. Sale, & W. Parent (Ed.), *Supported employment strategies for integration of workers with disabilities* (pp. 4–5). Stoneham, MA: Butterworth-Heinemann.

Wehman, P., Sale, P., & Parent, W. (1992). *Supported employment strategies for integration of workers with disabilities.* Stoneham, MA: Butterworth-Heinemann.

Chapter 24

College Mentoring Programs

Kelli S. Appel

CASE STUDY: MICHAEL

Michael is a student with a learning disability who just graduated from high school. He worked really hard to keep his grades up and was thrilled to be accepted to a large university about 150 miles from his hometown. Michael plans to major in graphic design. After a summer of working and spending time with friends and family, Michael is excited to move into the dorm. His parents help him move in and wish him well. He meets his roommate, but they don't have much in common. Within the first few weeks of class, Michael and his roommate are barely speaking because they argue about the type of music and TV in the room and when to have people in the room. Michael decides to go to the local mall for something to do . . . only he takes the wrong bus and never gets there. He then decides he can manage without leaving campus—it will be much easier. Michael enjoys his psychology class, but he is really struggling with his English 101 class. He failed his first paper. He isn't sure what to do on the next paper, but he decided he will just hope for the best. Michael finds himself thinking about how much easier it would be if he just moved back home and worked at his uncle's restaurant.

INTRODUCTION

College mentoring programs, which have varying levels of support and guidance, have become prevalent on many college campuses to provide students with much-needed opportunities for support. A mentoring program is even more crucial for students with disabilities. Although in recent years more students with disabilities are gaining access to higher education (both community colleges and universities), students with disabilities in college have a low retention and graduation rate. Students with disabilities may be more overwhelmed by the transition to college than other students, may be hesitant to seek help or unaware of their options, and may have difficulty seeking peer support independently. Mentoring programs have had a positive impact on retention and graduation rates, and have also influenced student characteristics such as perseverance and achievement in higher education (Budge, 2006). Students who feel connected to their college (including people, programs, the campus, and the community) are more likely to graduate from that college (Chen, 2008). College mentoring programs provide a coordinated approach to pull together various supports.

Mentoring programs have been used successfully within the business sector, community services, and K–12 schools. Some colleges have a mentoring program available for all new students; others only have mentoring programs for certain populations, such as minorities, nontraditional students, or students with disabilities. This chapter will introduce mentoring programs, clarify components of effective mentoring programs, and give general education teachers suggestions related to specific skills that should be included in the high school curricula.

GENERAL ROLES AND RESPONSIBILITIES

Some college mentoring programs are informal; the opportunity to connect is provided, but little other structure is in place. For example, students may be invited to attend social events where peer mentors are available to answer questions. Students and mentors aren't formally matched, and there are no expectations as to next steps in the mentoring relationship. A formal college mentoring program uses a variety of strategies to support mentors and mentees with a clear structure and is more effective. In a formal college mentoring program, support will be geared to both academic and personal challenges.

A formal college mentoring program should be one of several support options available to students with disabilities. In addition to a specific office that monitors accommodations for students with disabilities, many community colleges and 4-year universities have special courses to teach students (both with and without disabilities) skills that impact their transition to college such as financial management or study skills. There may also be workshops on organization, note taking, and technology available to students. Some community colleges and universities offer a short bridge course prior to the formal start of the freshman year. These bridge courses often enhance academic skills by preteaching some of the content from the traditional English, math, and science courses. This enables students to gain confidence and experience with the college atmosphere. Bridge courses can be the start of the formal mentoring program. Ideally, mentoring programs should be purposefully connected with other support options such as tutoring centers.

Advisors or admissions counselors typically work proactively to inform high school guidance counselors of the unique supports, such as mentoring programs, that their institutions offer. They often send information for guidance counselors to share with teachers and prospective students and families. Colleges and universities also often display materials about support options and activities for high school seniors. Students and parents should be taught to proactively seek out and evaluate support options as a part of the process of choosing a higher education program.

COMMUNICATION

Communication with representatives from college mentoring programs will primarily be initiated by teachers, transition specialists, or students and their families. It is important for schools to provide any helpful information about mentoring programs to students and families by the junior year, so they can consider this information when choosing their path into higher education. It is helpful if students and families have this information prior to making a college visit so they can ask questions and follow up with specific ideas or concerns on their visit. Figure 24.1 presents a checklist of indicators that can be used to evaluate potential college mentoring programs. Students and families may find it useful to have a brochure or informational sheet including this information.

Figure 24.2 lists specific skills that teachers should address to help prepare students with disabilities for an effective mentoring experience. Teachers should augment the standard curriculum to ensure students have had instruction and feedback in self-determination skills, with an emphasis on self-advocacy. These skills will be crucial to gaining the maximum benefit of the mentoring relationship. In addition, self-advocacy skills will positively impact all areas and phases of students' lives. Second, teachers should incorporate knowledge competencies necessary for students to understand and evaluate mentoring programs. General education teachers and special

---

Does the College Mentoring Program:

Clearly communicate goals and principles?

Yes   No

Match mentees with a faculty member from major/interest area?

Yes   No

Match mentees with a peer mentor?

Yes   No

Consider shared background and experiences in the matching process?

Yes   No

Provide training for mentors?

Yes   No

Encourage volunteer service opportunities?

Yes   No

Schedule frequent, convenient meeting times/places?

Yes   No

Encourage mentors/mentees to communicate through methods preferred by the mentee, such as texting and social networking?

Yes   No

Fit within a system of supports with multiple options for students with disabilities?

Yes   No

Figure 24.1. Quality indicators of college mentoring programs.

education teachers will need to work together to plan lessons that address these knowledge and skill competencies.

Students may also find experience with high school mentoring programs helpful when transitioning to college mentoring programs. For high schools that do not have formal mentoring programs, teachers can consider connecting students with electronic mentoring options. These programs are available through online searches and connect students with a peer or adult mentor. Communication is limited to e-mail, but the program can begin to build interest in mentoring and skills that will transfer to a college mentoring program.

Self-Advocacy
1. Ask clarifying questions
2. Ask for help when needed
3. Identify strengths and weaknesses

Knowledge
1. Aware of benefits of college mentoring programs
2. Aware of types of college mentoring programs
3. Aware of specific programs for each higher education option

Figure 24.2. Important skills for mentees.

TYPES OF SERVICES PROVIDED TO STUDENTS

Mentoring programs are often available at both community colleges and 4-year universities. Mentoring programs provide services intended to assist freshmen with their transition to college, including coursework and the extended campus community. Typically, mentoring programs focus on first-year students, though frequently the mentor and mentee continue their relationship beyond the freshman year. Mentoring programs that are designed specifically for specific groups, such as students with disabilities or nontraditional students, are more likely to provide support for the entire college experience. Although increasing retention and graduation rates is a common goal, mentoring programs in community colleges also assist students to become accepted into 4-year universities (Hayes, 2008). An important outcome of effective mentoring programs is increased access to information and resources available on campus. Many colleges have specially designed opportunities for students, but freshmen may not make the connection or may be hesitant to access the resources without a mentor's support. Examples of activities that mentors provide include: advice regarding schedule of courses, campus and community tours, tutoring, final examination preparation, goal setting, and using campus and community transportation systems.

There are several variations of college mentoring programs: peer mentoring, faculty mentoring, group mentoring, e-mentoring, or a combined approach. Peer mentors are most often experienced college students who have demonstrated success in the college program. Peer mentors may have been mentees previously. Students often feel a strong connection with a mentor close to their age who they feel understands their challenges. If the program includes peer mentors who also have a disability, students can benefit from having a strong role model who has similar challenges. Peer mentors also provide an opportunity for a social companion at a time when the student may know very few people on campus. Relationships with peer mentors are likely to last beyond the freshman year. Another benefit to participation in a peer mentoring program is the opportunity to become a mentor at a later time. Students with disabilities may gain valuable leadership skills through becoming a peer mentor after having success as a mentee. Faculty mentoring is not used as often, but when the faculty mentor is from the department of the mentees' chosen major, the mentee can gain a connection to his department and learn of resources related to the major. A faculty mentor also has extensive knowledge of campus resources and what skills are needed throughout the entire program. Students may feel reluctant to approach faculty mentors, so the mentoring program needs to make sure structures are in place to connect the mentor and mentee. Mentees should be encouraged to ask questions of the faculty mentor and to follow through with opportunities to spend time with the mentor. Scheduled meetings and activities make the faculty mentor/mentee a positive option. Group mentoring involves one peer/faculty mentor assigned to a small group of freshmen. Meetings and activities usually occur with the whole group. This type of mentoring often includes more social events, such as going out to lunch or to movies, and can help students to develop social networks with others who have common interests and backgrounds. Group mentoring can be desirable for students who are hesitant to meet with someone new or are anxious about a new relationship. This type of mentoring also allows students to get to know other students in the group and may promote friendships and other support relationships. One drawback to group mentoring is the possibility that students may have questions or concerns that they don't want to address in front of other group members, and they may not have developed a close enough relationship with the mentor to initiate individual assistance. An effective mentoring relationship may take longer to develop in a group situation. The final type, e-mentoring, may appeal to students who prefer to communicate through technology. Electronic mentoring often focuses on mentoring relationships for freshmen in certain majors, such as engineering or business, and matches them with successful graduates working in the designated fields. This type of mentoring allows mentors with specific skills and experiences to be involved regardless of geographical distance.

A combined approach is ideal for students. Having a peer mentor allows students to benefit from the insights of a peer who has experienced a similar transition, while having a faculty mentor allows students to benefit from a mature perspective with deeper ties to the college program and community. Electronic mentoring is an option that can enhance the structured program. Students may find that they can get campus-level tips, resources, and companionship from a peer or faculty mentor, but an e-mentor who is working in their chosen field may be able to provide support related to their career and give them motivation to continue in the major. Students may find that they have a valuable connection within their career that they will still utilize after graduation. In a combined approach, if any one of the mentoring relationships is not effective, the student can still access support through another component of the mentoring program. The more support a student can receive, the higher the likelihood of success.

According to the Mentoring Resource Center Fact Sheet (U.S. Department of Education, 2008), research has confirmed that quality volunteer opportunities lead to a feeling of empowerment and connection with the community. College mentoring programs are beginning to incorporate this component in both peer and faculty mentoring programs. Completing a service project together allows mentors/mentees to feel they belong to their new community and provides a structured way to get to know each other. When mentors and mentees spend time together focused on a shared experience, the relationship becomes stronger. Service projects often relate to participants' major area of interest. For example, education majors may create and implement activities at a community-based program for children or engineering majors may work on construction through Habitat for Humanity. Mentors can learn a great deal about mentees' strengths and challenges through service learning.

DIRECT SERVICES PROVIDED TO TEACHERS

College mentoring programs will not provide direct services to high school teachers, but will provide information, as discussed earlier in the chapter. General education teachers may be involved in planning and providing instruction (see Figure 24.2) related to skills that will enable students to succeed in higher education, including being in an effective mentoring program. For example, students may need to learn how to search online to see what resources are offered at various programs and what vocabulary is used for supports in different programs. For example, programs in higher education use many different titles and descriptions for tutoring centers and offices that verify and manage accommodations for students with disabilities. Students will need to learn the components of effective mentoring programs and what questions they could ask to seek out this information. In addition, students need to realize that being open to different types of assistance is a life skill that they will need in higher education and beyond. If students have the skills addressed in this chapter, they will gain the maximum benefit from a college mentoring program. These examples of instruction and activities may be a part of a student's transition plan, so the general education teacher will collaborate with the transition specialist and special education teacher.

Solution to the Case Study

Michael's rough start, which led to poor performance, a feeling of helplessness, and consideration of dropping out of college, could have been avoided by the proactive support of a college mentoring program.

While at the summer freshman orientation, Michael remembers that he learned though his teachers and guidance counselor that his university had a mentoring program, so he signs up to be a mentee. He met another freshman signing up at the same time and they exchanged e-mail addresses. Before classes start, Michael meets both his assigned peer mentor and faculty mentor at a kick-off picnic. He's excited to find his faculty mentor is from his interest area, graphic design.

When Michael has difficulty getting along with his roommate, he shares this issue with his peer mentor and his mentor reassures him that this is a common issue and makes some suggestions. Michael has started spending some time with the freshman he met through the mentoring program at summer orientation. Early in the semester, Michael's peer mentor invites him to go to the local mall with a small group of mentors/mentees. He shows him how the bus system works.

When working on his first paper, Michael told his faculty mentor that he wasn't sure if he was on the right track. His mentor reminded him of the services provided by the University Writing Lab and also suggested he make an appointment to talk to an advisor at the Disability Concerns office for other support options. Michael tried his suggestions, and did fairly well on the assignment. Because he still had some questions about how to do better, both mentors urge him to make an appointment to meet with the English 101 professor. He now feels he is prepared to do even better on the next paper. Michael knows he has lots of hard work ahead, but he enjoys the relationships he has made with people on campus and believes he can continue to learn and improve. He knows he has mentors who care about his success and will be there for any questions or concerns.

References

Budge, S. (2006). Peer mentoring in post-secondary education: Implications for research and practice. *Journal of College Reading and Learning, 37,* 73–87.

Chen, G. (2008). *The value of community college mentoring programs.* Retrieved from http://www.communitycollegereview.com/articles/64

Hayes, D. (2008). *Community college mentoring programs help students stay engaged.* Retrieved from http://diverseeducation.com/artman/publish/printer_11467. shtml

U.S. Department of Education, Office of Safe and Drug-Free Schools. (2008). *Mentoring resource center fact sheet* [Fact sheet]. Retrieved from http://www. edmentoring.org/pubs/factsheet19.pdf

Chapter 25

Resident Assistant

Jeffrey P. Bakken and Lisa Devereux

CASE STUDY: CLAIRE

Claire is a freshman undergraduate student at Illinois State University. She has minimal hearing in both ears and uses a hearing aid. She mainly relies on American Sign Language to communicate. Her major is deaf education. In her classes, she has an interpreter; however, she insists on taking notes herself. This has led Claire to miss valuable portions of the lecture because she is constantly looking down.

Claire lives in a residence hall on a floor for speech pathology and special education majors. Two other residents know sign language because they are deaf education majors as well. They attend Deaf Redbirds meetings with Claire once a week. Deaf Redbirds is a student organization that provides opportunities for socialization for people who are deaf or hard of hearing and people who desire contact with the deaf community. The organization wishes to create deaf awareness in service, social, and athletic events. Claire enjoys going to sporting events and dinners with these students. She is a very social girl and wants to develop friendships with the other residents on the floor. Unfortunately, she has difficulty communicating with these residents, which prevents her from expanding these friendships.

A lack of communication with other students has also led Claire to have difficulty in school. She is unable to ask for help from her peers and she feels disconnected in the classroom. After the first semester, Claire has obtained a failing grade in three classes. These grades were sent home, and her parents wanted to know why this happened. Claire did not explain to them why this occurred, so they persisted to ask anyone who they thought would have an answer. They called school faculty and even her resident assistant, but none of these people were able to talk to them without the student's permission.

Claire is continuing her second semester with the same services that she had first semester. She recently expressed her school concerns to her resident assistant.

INTRODUCTION

A resident assistant can help a student who has a disability in a variety of ways. A resident assistant's main role is to provide a safe and supportive environment for all residents. Resident assistants have a wide variety of knowledge about campus resources and they are thoroughly trained in understanding different situations in which students need to be referred to other campus resources. If a resident assistant is unaware of the specific campus resource that a student may need, then the resident assistant is required to find the resource so that the student receives necessary support. A resident assistant can help a student who has a disability by referring her to the Office of Disability Concerns (or a similar office on campus that works with students who have disabilities). If a student has an issue that may not specifically require this office, then the resident assistant can refer the student to whatever office is appropriate or provide advice for the student based on what has worked for past residents. Much of the information in this chapter is based on services available at Illinois State University; however, many campuses have similar services and accommodations—they may just be listed under different names.

GENERAL ROLES AND RESPONSIBILITIES

The resident assistant has many responsibilities for each resident in the floor community. It is important for the resident assistant to facilitate the personal development of residents in a variety of ways, including meeting their social, physical, and emotional needs and by being sensitive to their individual concerns. They must also organize floor and hall events to encourage active participation and involvement on a one-on-one, small-group, and large-group basis. It is also important for them to develop and maintain a community atmosphere within the residence halls. Finally, the resident assistant plays an important role in the academic development of the residents. The resident assistant must create a variety of educational programs. These educational programs may involve education about the specific requirements within each major, development of study groups, and referral to tutoring resources. An important area of education is information about the university and what it has to offer. Resident assistants are encouraged to take their residents on tours of the university the first week of school. On the tour, the resident assistant is encouraged to locate the different academic buildings, libraries, health services, student union, and any other resources that may be valuable to the student population. Many of the residents may have heard of these places, but do not know what resources they have to offer, so it is important to review what services each facility provides for the students. Although the resident assistant has an important responsibility to communicate with the residents on the floor, no communication is allowed with the residents' parents. The resident assistant can file communication reports if a resident is having a problem, but parents cannot be contacted without the permission of the resident. It is important for parents to understand this. Even though they may be paying the bills, unless the student actually gives permission, parents cannot access information about the student or find out or discuss student grades.

In the student's case, it is the resident assistant's responsibility to create programs so that the student can be involved with the other residents. If the student discloses that she has a disability, then the student may request a special accommodation to participate in a program. The resident assistant or the student must contact the Office of Disability Concerns or a similar office that provides services to students who have disabilities on campus within 5 business days of the event to request an accommodation. Accommodations for events may include: an interpreter, preferential seating, closed captioned video, and accessible parking spaces. As a general rule, resident assistants are encouraged to be available as often as possible. They can use a variety of listening approaches and allow residents to drop them a note, if contact is necessary. Depending on what the student says, the resident assistant can refer her to a variety of campus resources. These resources can be the Office of Disability Concerns, the tutoring center, or even counselors in Student Health Services. Finally, the resident assistant completes a communication report. The residence hall coordinator can then follow up with the student. The report process is different for each university; however, there is usually some sort of written documentation required for each interaction between a University Housing Services employee and a student. The key is that the student with a disability is aware that the resident assistant has a wealth of information that can benefit the student and that the resident assistant is there for help or guidance when the need arises.

Communication With Teachers and Parents

As previously stated, resident assistants are not allowed to communicate with the parents. This is valuable, because it allows the resident to feel comfortable knowing that information discussed with a resident assistant will be kept confidential. The resident assistant can only assist the resident to make the best choice for herself.

If a student is having problems in a class or classes then she should communicate with her resident assistant. Together they can then brainstorm possible solutions to solve the problem. In addition, the resident assistant should probably suggest that the student talk to someone at the Office of Disability Concerns. It is the student's responsibility to be proactive and to ask for more assistance.

The resident assistant should also encourage the student to speak to her teachers (see the Appendix for helpful suggestions). The student should communicate her classroom concerns and needs to her current teachers, so that they can provide extra support when it is necessary. It is important for this communication to happen so instructors are aware of the student's needs and what they might need to do to make instruction more meaningful to that student. Instructors can provide accommodations for the student such as study guides and printed notes. It is important for the student to advocate for herself by communicating with the instructor. Unlike high school, there are no Individualized Education Programs (IEPs) in college (see Table 25.1). In college courses for credit, modifications are not allowed. If the student does not notify the instructor that she is having difficulties in the course, the instructor may not even be aware of the student's disability or ways to help the student. Also, according to the Office of Disability Concerns, it is the student's responsibility to speak with her professors about delivery information regarding exams taken at the Office of Disability Concerns. The professor must also sign an exam permission form, which allows the student to either take the exam at a different time from the rest of the class or to use notes, a book, a calculator, or any other resource other than paper and pencil. If the student wants these accommodations, then she must communicate with the professor often and well in advance of any exams. When there is a problem and parents would like to be involved, they can also communicate their concerns to the Office of Disability Concerns. The teachers, student, and Office of Disability Concerns can collaborate to find the best accommodations for the student.

Table 25.1
K–12 Versus Postsecondary Institutions

K–12	Postsecondary
The student is identified with a disability through an assessment.	The student self-identifies his or her disability to the Office of Disability Concerns.
Assessment is provided by school personnel.	The student must provide documentation of disability.
Parents are involved in determining the appropriate program.	A case coordinator determines accommodations and no planned program is written for the student.
An Individualized Education Program (IEP) is written for the student to determine goals.	No yearly meeting is held to assess student progress. The student is responsible for his or her success or failure.
A multidisciplinary conference (MDC) is held to assess the student's progress.	The student has responsibilities to manage his or her educational progress.
The student has the right to a free appropriate public education.	The student has right to equal access in the university.

DIRECT SERVICES PROVIDED TO STUDENTS

A variety of services can be provided for a student (depending on her disability) through the Office of Disability Concerns. All students who require these special services must contact this office and provide proof of their disability (see Table 25.2). For example, Claire would need to provide an audiogram or documentation from an audiologist or doctor to prove she has a hearing impairment. Then, she submits a request form that is sent to a committee for review to be either approved or denied. If a student does not have proof of her disability, then she needs to go through an evaluation process to document her disability (see Table 25.3).

Within a classroom, there are a variety of accommodations for students who have disabilities. FM systems (an amplification system including an instructor who has a microphone) are often used in classrooms. Closed-captioned videos and transcripts are also a popular support. Most frequently, a student who is deaf or hard of hearing will have an interpreter and a note-taker. The Office of Disability Concerns also provides students with a variety of other classroom accommodations, such as a typist, Braille materials, or accessible seating. Note-takers regularly meet with the student to make copies of the notes. A typist provides assistance to the student by typing

Table 25.2
How to Become a Client of the Office of Disability Concerns

1. The student must self-identify the disability to the Office of Disability Concerns to begin the process of requesting and receiving accommodations.

2. The student will be asked to provide documentation of his or her disability and complete a Request for Disability Services form. Services cannot be provided without appropriate documentation.

3. The Documentation Review Committee reviews the documentation submitted and the Request for Disability Services form to determine eligibility for services and accommodations.

4. After the Documentation Review Committee has reviewed the documentation, the student is contacted if additional documentation is needed. If the documentation is sufficient for the student to be eligible for services, then the student is contacted to schedule an initial appointment with a coordinator.

5. At the initial appointment, the student and the coordinator will complete an intake form and discuss approved accommodations specific to the student's individual needs. The student will learn the procedures for requesting accommodations and once the student becomes a full client, a Disability Concerns ID card (verifies a documented disability and lists approved accommodations) will be created. The student will read and sign a Contract of Client Responsibilities for Disability Concerns.

papers. If the student requires accessible seating, she may need a seating adaptation. These adaptations may include a specific type of chair, table, or writing surface. Testing accommodations consist of testing in a separate room, extended time, a reader, or a scribe. Another accommodation is alternative format for instruction, which consists of electronic text, Braille, and alternative text. If converted text is an approved accommodation for the student, the student must request this service through the Text Conversion Lab. If a student needs a textbook in an alternative format, then the student must submit a list of books that need to be converted. Assistive technology is also used as an accommodation. Some examples of assistive technology include: zoomtext, scanners, telecommunication devices for the deaf, closed-circuit TV to enlarge text, and screen reader programs.

Within the residence halls, there are often a variety of supports for students who have disabilities. For a student who is deaf or hard of hearing, a doorbell may be located outside of the door that makes the lights in the room flash when the button is pressed. Also, students may use a videophone to see visitors. Students can receive emergency alert texts, or if there is an emergency within the residence hall, then the student's room phone could be called by a resident assistant, which again causes a light to flash near the phone. Offices of Disability Concerns often provide residents with a source

Table 25.3
Documentation Requirements

Note: All reports must include: comprehensive background information, diagnosis, prognosis, limitations, and impact of disability.

Learning Disability	The student must provide a complete psychoeducational evaluation and a report that includes the following adult assessment measurements:
	▪ Complete adult aptitude assessment (Wechsler Adult Intelligence Scale; WAIS IV) including all subtest and standard scores
	▪ Individual achievement test (Wechsler Individual Achievement Test, Second Edition; WIAT-II) including standard scores for all subjects assessed
	▪ Information processing should assess areas such as: short and long-term memory, sequential memory, auditory and visual perception, and processing speed
Attention Deficit/Hyperactivity Disorder	The student must provide a complete psychoeducational evaluation and a report that includes the following adult assessment measurements:
	▪ Complete adult aptitude assessment (Wechsler Adult Intelligence Scale; WAIS IV) including all subtest and standard scores
	▪ Individual achievement test (Wechsler Individual Achievement Test, Second Edition; WIAT-II) including standard scores for all subject areas assessed
	▪ Information processing should assess areas such as: short- and long-term memory, sequential memory, auditory and visual perception, and processing speed
	▪ Attention and distractibility
	Report should also include:
	▪ Medications
	▪ Diagnosis with the American Psychiatric Association's *Diagnostic and Statistical Manual of Mental Disorders, Fourth Edition (DSM-IV)* criteria
	▪ Impact the disability has on academic performance
	▪ Recommended accommodations pertinent to the testing results
	Information relating to prescribed medication, including information on side effects and the impact of medication changes

Table 25.3. Documentation Requirements, continued

Deaf and Hard of Hearing	The student must provide recent audiological documentation from a certified audiologist that includes: • Diagnosis • Prognosis • Limitations (if any) • Impact of hearing loss
Visual, Physical, or Medical Disabilities	The student must provide a copy of the following information as it applies to the disability on the letterhead of the individual's healthcare provider with that provider's signature on the report: • Diagnosis and original diagnosis date • Etiology/cause (not applicable in congenital disabilities) • Impact/limitations • Medications and side effects as well as their impact on cognitive ability • Suggestions/recommendations for accommodations. • Any additional information that helps the Office of Disability Concerns to assist the student in a postsecondary educational setting
Psychiatric Disabilities	The student must provide the following components on letterhead of the individual's mental healthcare provider with that provider's signature on the report: • A specific, current psychiatric diagnosis from the *DSM-IV* indicating nature, frequency, and severity of symptoms for the individual (documentation must describe how the student's disability functionally impacts the ability to participate in a postsecondary educational setting) • Information related to side effects of prescribed medication and suggestions for accommodations • Suggestions relating to the specific impacts of the disability and how the individual might be accommodated in the educational setting

to obtain alarms that they can place under their pillows, which vibrate to wake them. Students who have physical disabilities often are given accessible rooms and facilities. Also, students who have medical needs are given special rooms according to those needs. Environmental accommodations consist of accessible parking permits, a library assistant, and even accommodations with campus dining to meet dietary restrictions.

DIRECT SERVICES PROVIDED TO TEACHERS

The resident assistant can first ask the student if she is asking for help from the Office of Disability Concerns. If the student has not yet communicated that she is struggling due to a lack of necessary accommodations, then the student should be encouraged to talk to the office. The student may not be aware of the extra supports that it provides. Also, the resident assistant can ask the student if she has communicated her concerns to teachers. The teachers cannot provide a specific support unless the student requests it.

The Office of Disability Concerns can provide support to the teacher in a number of ways (see Table 25.4). First, it notifies the teachers well in advance that they will have a student who has a disability in their classes. Teachers are usually notified as soon as the student registers for the class. These teachers are given tips for working with students and their interpreters (if applicable). Also, any videos that the teachers may use can undergo text conversion or closed captioning to facilitate learning for the student. The teacher is then able to meet the student before the first day of class. Teachers can work closely with the student before class to find the best way to support her. Also, teachers can work with the student during their office hours, as well as before and after class, to explain new concepts and to provide a syllabus for instruction for the next class. Teachers can provide study guides and outlines to provide extra support for the student.

SOLUTION TO THE CASE STUDY

The student spoke with her resident assistant and explained that she felt disconnected in her classes and on the floor. She also explained that she is distraught about her poor grades in her course work. Her resident assistant asked the student for ideas about how to make her feel more connected with the other residents on the floor. The student suggested teaching sign language to the floor and educating the floor about the deaf culture. Now, the student leads this program once a week with

Table 25.4
Rights and Responsibilities

Rights	Responsibilities
- Access to all university offerings, including courses, programs, services, activities, and facilities. - Receive reasonable accommodations, which may include academic adjustments or auxiliary aids and services. - Information available in accessible formats. - An equal opportunity to learn. - Privacy of all information regarding his or her disability.	- Meet qualifications and maintain necessary standards for courses, programs, services, activities, and facilities. - Self-identify as an individual with a disability to the Office of Disability Concerns when accommodations are needed. - Document the impact of the disability in the university setting. - Follow published procedures for obtaining reasonable accommodations.

the support of two other residents from the floor. Also, a majority of the residents now attend the Deaf Redbird meetings, because they now know basic sign language to communicate at club meetings and events.

The student's resident assistant also suggested that the student talk to the Office of Disability Concerns, as well as her teachers about her grades and feelings of being disconnected. The Office of Disability Concerns suggested that the student have a note-taker to supplement the notes that she is already taking. The student agreed to having a note-taker, because it will also allow her to ask the note-taker questions when she has them. This has allowed the student to pay closer attention to the lecture, while also allowing her to form a connection with a classmate. The student still takes notes of her own as well, which allows her to continue to feel independent. The student will continue to take tests in the classroom with the rest of the students; however, she will be given extra time to complete the assessment if it is necessary.

The student's grades have improved with these supports, and she has become a more active member in her school community. She has joined other clubs with residents on her floor, because she now feels comfortable requesting an interpreter and support from other students. She enjoys school and no longer has a feeling of being disconnected.

APPENDIX
Charts and Checklists of Information Needed

Checklist for an Incoming Postsecondary Student

Questions:	✓
Do I have all proper documentation of my disability as listed according to the Office of Disability Concerns?	
Have I self-identified my disability to the Office of Disability Concerns?	
If I already have my Disability Concerns ID card, have I presented the card to my professor and notified him or her of necessary accommodations?	
Do I understand the process and time restrictions that I must abide by for me to request an event or testing accommodation?	
Are all of my needs being met?	

Steps to Asking a Professor for Help

1. Present Disability Concerns ID card to the professor.
2. Set up a specific time to meet with the professor on a weekly basis either during his or her office hours or by appointment.
3. Communicate what accommodations are going well and what needs to be changed.
4. Advocate for yourself. If there is a slight change or accommodation that you may need, ask the professor for help.
5. Be thoughtful and respectful of the professor. If you need extra help or a specific testing accommodation, let him or her know well in advance.

Section 6

Bringing It Together: The Full Circle

This section will establish the importance of collaboration and consultation and explain the importance of the Full Circle process. The focus of this last section will be to describe this specific approach to working with all of the aforementioned providers and bringing it all together. A graphic representation of the Full Circle approach will be presented and will show how all providers can work collaboratively with the family and each other. This graphic will depict the important relationships that should be established to more effectively plan and implement successful best practices in the general education classroom. After reading this section the reader should understand the importance of total collaboration and consultation and how all professionals involved can effectively work together to achieve success for students with disabilities.

Chapter 26

Bringing It Together: The Full Circle

Jeffrey P. Bakken & Cynthia G. Simpson

In order for students with disabilities to be successful in school, it will take effective communication and collaboration between many different professionals. Given that most professionals who work in the education field specialize in their own unique discipline, yet are required to work with many other professionals regarding the instruction of students with disabilities, it is important that collaboration is outlined and explained, as is the process of how individuals can work together to help students with disabilities achieve success in the general education classroom. Collaboration is a process, and it is important for all individuals who are involved with a student with a disability to understand what each individual brings to the conversation. Collaboration needs to be a back-and-forth process with the many individuals involved working together to meet the needs of the students they serve. Figure 26.1 depicts this process.

Knowledge of the situation, the needs of the student, and the part each professional plays is key to the development of a successful inclusion plan. We believe it is essential for all professionals who are involved in the education of a student with a disability to understand the specific knowledge and expertise that each professional adds to the programming of a child with special needs.

In addition, it is vital to understand the importance of working together, communicating effectively, and collaborating. Understanding these key aspects will help all participants in this process achieve success and be more efficient and effective. In addition, the student, who is the key benefactor,

Figure 26.1. A visual representation of the back-and-forth process of collaboration.

will receive the most appropriate services to be successful in the inclusive environment. After all, that is the focus—the student's success.

In order for professionals to work together they must understand what roles each performs and how as a team they can help students with disabilities. What are their general roles and responsibilities regarding their profession? How do they typically communicate with teachers and parents and what do they communicate (what information)? What are the direct services they provide to students with disabilities? Finally, what direct services do they provide to teachers to aid them in working with students with disabilities? A major portion of this book focused on this information because of its importance in helping professionals to understand one another's duties and how they can work together to benefit students with disabilities in the inclusive classroom. Therefore, knowledgeable professionals shared their expertise in each chapter, emphasizing a multidisciplinary team approach to educating students with special needs.

For students with disabilities to have successful experiences in the inclusive classroom, professionals must work together, value what each person does, share responsibilities, and effectively communicate and collaborate. Professionals should work together to provide insight, suggestions, and services that will directly benefit students, helping them be successful and strive toward their fullest potential.

Glossary of Terms

Abandoned: term for when a student or teacher is no longer using a suggested technology device.

Accommodations: changes in materials, instruction, or assessment that allow students to participate and access general education without significantly altering the nature of the activity (e.g., more time to complete assignments, a seat in the front of the class, or tests given orally instead of on paper); it is not a change to what the student is required to learn.

Accredited school: nationally recognized and qualified institution for education.

Activities of daily living (ADL): tasks that are included to function in a regular day (e.g., walking, dressing, sitting, standing); can be used for measurement of functional status of a person.

Activity schedule: a sequence of objects, pictures, or words illustrating activities for children to complete in a therapeutic or educational setting.

Adapted physical education (APE): a program that has the same objectives as the general physical education program, but in which adjustments are made in the regular offerings to meet the needs and abilities of students with disabilities.

Adaptive skills: the ability of an individual to meet the expectations of changing environments.

Adult service providers: various community organizations that provide support, training, or case management services to individuals with disabilities.

Advocate: one who works with/on behalf of individuals in order to attain services/resources for those in need that would not otherwise be provided.

Agility: ability to rapidly and accurately change the position of the body in space.

Amplification device: a device that increases the volume and/or the clarity of sounds in the environment.

Antecedent-behavior-consequence log: a form used to log instances of behavior that are observed in order to systematically identify the variables that may precede/trigger or follow/maintain target behavior.

Applied behavior analysis (ABA): discipline of science based on behavioral principles systematically applied to improve socially significant behaviors of the consumer and those interacting with the consumer.

Assessment: structured and unstructured methods (e.g., standardized tests, behavioral observations, inventories, rating scales, interviews) of determining a student's interests and academic, social, emotional, or behavioral functioning.

Assistive technology device: includes any item, piece of equipment, or product system that is used to increase, maintain, or improve the functioning of individuals with disabilities; it may be purchased commercially off the shelf, modified, or customized; it does not include a medical device that is surgically implanted or the replacement of such a device.

Assistive technology service: is any service that directly relates to the selection, acquisition, or use of an assistive technology device for a student with a disability.

Assistive technology specialist: person who has knowledge of assistive technology, maintains technology devices, evaluates devices, and trains people how to use devices.

Asymmetric hearing loss: hearing loss that is different between the ears; in other words, both ears have hearing loss, but are not equal in their degree.

Attention Deficit/Hyperactivity Disorder (ADHD): a disorder manifested by extreme levels of inattention, impulsivity, disorganization, and excessive body motion.

Audiology: the study of hearing and balance; includes assessment of the auditory system including the outer, middle, and inner parts of the ear, as well as the pathway from the ear to the brain.

Audiological technology: devices such as hearing aids, cochlear implants, or FM systems that increase access to sounds in the environment.

Augmentative and alternative communication (AAC): all forms of communication (other than oral speech) that are used to express thoughts, needs, wants, and ideas; includes anything from low-tech paper-and-pencil writing or drawing to high-tech electronic communication devices.

Aural habilitation: services and procedures for facilitating adequate receptive and expressive communication in individuals with a hearing impairment.

Balance: ability to maintain equilibrium in a held or moving position.

Behavior Analyst Certification Board (BACB): nonprofit corporation formed in 1998 to establish professional credentialing standards in the field of Applied Behavior Analysis.

Behavioral disorder (BD): a disability that manifests in severe difficulties in establishing and maintaining social relationships as well as learning problems that cannot be explained with other health or intellectual factors.

Behavior intervention plan (BIP): plan of action developed to work on specific target behaviors based on a functional behavior assessment or functional analysis. Ideally, the BIP specifies antecedent and consequence manipulations as well as the teaching of functionally equivalent responses that address the functions of the targeted behaviors.

Behind-the-ear hearing aid (BTE): a type of hearing aid that sits behind the user's ear and uses an earmold to funnel the sound from the hearing aid into the ear canal; the style that is most commonly used by children.

Bibliotherapy: counseling sessions centered on the themes presented in books to help children resolve emotional or behavioral difficulties.

Bilateral hearing loss: is some type and degree of hearing loss in both ears; may be the same type and degree in both ears or different in each.

Board Certified Behavior Analyst (BCBA): independent practitioner who has been certified by the Behavior Analyst Certification Board to practice in the field of Applied Behavior Analysis.

Body composition: muscle, bone, fat, and other elements in the body.

Brief solution-focused counseling: a theoretical model of counseling that is less lengthy and focuses on finding solutions rather than exploring problems and feelings.

Broker: intermediary position that assists in connecting individuals with resources.

Cardiovascular endurance: ability of the heart and vessels to process and transport oxygen from the lungs to the muscle cells.

Case manager: the special education teacher who develops the IEP and coordinates services for the student with a disability.

Closed captioned: a system that displays text on a television or video screen; a transcription of the audio portion of a program is displayed as it occurs either verbatim or in edited form, sometimes including nonspeech elements.

Closed-circuit television (CCTV): magnification system capable of higher levels of magnification that can manipulate the brightness and contrast of the image.

Cochlear implant: a device that bypasses the damaged portions of the ear and directly stimulates the auditory nerve.

Cognitive behavioral counseling techniques: counseling techniques that focus on helping students develop healthy thought patterns and take concrete steps to accomplish their goals and overcome unproductive thoughts and actions.

Collaboration: a school philosophy and teacher practice involving at least two people with mutual respect and interest working together in an interactive process to solve problems and work toward common goals.

Collaborative planning: partnership of stakeholders working, learning, and preparing together for the meaningful delivery of instruction for all students.

Collaborative teaching: partnership of teachers sharing the delivery of instruction to broaden the meaningful participation of all students.

Collaborative team: refers to a group of educators that may include a parent, a general education teacher, a special education teacher, and related-service professionals such as a school psychologist, a speech language pathologist, an occupational therapist, and an administrator.

Conductive hearing loss: this is the most common type of temporary hearing loss, which can oftentimes be treated medically with either antibiotics or surgery; occurs when there is a problem in either the outer or middle part of the ear; can be temporary, but if left untreated, or if treatment is unsuccessful, it can become permanent; can be mild to moderate in degree.

Conflict resolution: process that utilizes various methods in order to assist individuals in resolving conflict.

Consultation: a term reflective of an expert-driven model in which someone with extensive knowledge in a certain content area is paired with a teacher or other professional to provide training and technical assistance.

Consultative coaching: involves a team of two or more professional colleagues working together to reflect on current practices; expand, refine, and build new skills; share ideas; teach one another; conduct classroom research; or solve problems in the workplace.

Consultation services: educational support provided to classroom teachers for students with disabilities by itinerant teachers when direct services are not required.

Coordination: ability to integrate separate motor systems with varying sensory modalities into efficient patterns of movement.

Co-teaching: a general education teacher and a special education teacher working together to instruct students with and without disabilities in the general education classroom.

Craniofacial anomalies: congenital malformations of the skull and face such as cleft palate.

Crisis intervention: time-limited intervention oriented to the present that addresses urgent situations caused from stressful or traumatic events.

Culture for inclusion: when the pattern of actions of the school community broadly embraces and promotes the successful participation of all of its members, despite individual differences.

Curriculum-based assessment: a method of assessment that is used to determine where a student's performance is relative to a curriculum.

Curriculum-based evaluation: a method of evaluation that is used to determine where a student's performance is relative to a curriculum through a hypothesis testing approach with results being used to inform instructional decision making.

Curriculum-based measurement: a method of progress monitoring that uses a student's respective curriculum; formative assessment; short, timed assessments tied to the curriculum.

Differentiation: sometimes referred to as differentiated learning, this involves providing students with different avenues to acquiring content (e.g., processing, constructing, making sense of ideas) and developing teaching materials so that all students within a classroom can learn effectively, regardless of differences in ability.

Discharge (DC): written note compiled by a physical therapist that contains the final status of a patient, and recommendations from a physical therapist; its measurements can be compared to previous data.

Dysphagia: a swallowing impairment or disorder.

E-mentoring: using electronic methods, such as e-mail and social networking, to mentor.

Early intervention: any form of therapy, treatment, educational program, nutritional intervention, or family support for children from birth to age 5 designed to reduce the effects of disabilities or prevent the occurrence of learning and developmental problems for children at risk for such problems.

Early intervention team: individuals who collaborate to determine support for students.

Earmold: a custom piece that is used to connect to a behind-the-ear hearing aid and helps deliver the sound into the user's ear; also provides retention of the hearing aid into the ear.

Education for All Handicapped Children Act: also known as P.L. 94-142, this 1975 federal legislation required the public school system to provide certain kinds of services to learners with disabilities.

Educational audiologist: professional trained to identify, diagnose, measure, and rehabilitate hearing impairments.

Educational diagnostician: the person connecting pre- and postassessment, services, and communication between teachers, parents, and students.

Educator: provides essential information to individuals/clients/institutions in order to attain/maintain services.

Electronic text: text that is in a form that a computer can store and display on a computer screen.

Embedded instruction: teaching skills in the context of ongoing, naturally occurring activities and routines to promote child engagement, learning, and independence.

Emergency action plan (EAP): a plan of care established to address emergency response to a potential healthcare crisis specific to a child within that school setting; gives a specific sequence of steps to follow that could guide staff to best address the child's emergency even when the school nurse is not present; created by nursing staff either originally or as a prepackaged plan that is individualized.

Facilitator: one who plans and implements methods of enhancing service delivery.

Fading: the process of gradually and systematically reducing and removing direct job coach or trainer support or instruction; done to promote maximum workplace inclusion as well as independence.

Flexibility: range of motion possible at any given joint.

FM system: a communication system for improving speech comprehension in difficult listening situations; a radio microphone is worn by the speaker that transmits wireless signals via frequency modulation to a receiver that is worn by the listener or to speakers in the room.

Free appropriate public education (FAPE): the term used in IDEA that states that school systems must provide children with disabilities with special education services and accommodations (including AT) at no cost to the parents.

Functional analysis (FA): an analysis of specific functions of behavior in which antecedents and consequences are arranged in an experimental design to simulate the environmental conditions found in the consumer's natural setting, so that they may be observed and measured.

Functional behavior assessment (FBA): nonexperimental method of assessment to obtain information on the function(s) of behavior, which is then used to develop a behavior intervention plan.

Group counseling: counseling conducted with groups of students in which the dynamics between students help resolve emotional issues.

Health-related fitness: the components of physical fitness that help promote health; includes cardiovascular endurance, muscular strength, muscular endurance, flexibility, and body composition.

Hearing aid: an electronic device worn in or behind the ear that amplifies sound; uses microphones to collect the sound, a computer chip to analyze and process the sound, and then a receiver to send the signal to the user's ear.

Hearing assistive technology (HAT): any type of device that helps an individual to hear and communicate more effectively; an example of this would be a Frequency Modulation (FM) system, which helps decrease the background noise and distance for better listening.

Hearing impairment: an impairment in hearing that adversely affects a child's educational performance.

Home exercise program (HEP): a specific routine of stretches or strengthening exercises put together by a physical therapist for individual impairments.

In-the-ear hearing aid (ITE): this style of hearing aid sits in the user's ear.

Inclusion: describes the goal of integrating learners with disabilities into regular education classroom environments where all accommodations and services to learners with disabilities are provided; means no longer segregating learners with disabilities into separate classrooms, schools, transportation, and living arrangements.

Individualized health plan (IHP): a plan to address the healthcare needs of a student in the school setting.

Individual student planning: focuses on the individual student's plan for academic, career, and social/emotional success.

Individualized Education Program (IEP): federal education policy that requires schools to develop and implement a written plan for instruction of learners with a disability that keeps the individuals' unique needs in mind; each public school child who receives special education and related services must have an IEP, which must be designed for one student and must be a truly individualized document.

Individualized Family Services Plan (IFSP): a legal document required by the Individuals with Disabilities Education Act (IDEA) specifying the coordination of early intervention services for infants and toddlers with disabilities from birth to age 3.

Individuals with Disabilities Education Act (IDEA): is a modification and revision of the Education for All Handicapped Children Act of 1975 created in 1990; outlines federal guidelines for services to learners with disabilities.

Individuals with Disabilities Education Improvement Act (IDEA): reauthorized the Individuals with Disabilities Education Act (IDEA) in 2004 to help children learn better by promoting accountability for results, enhancing parent involvement, and using research-based practices and materials.

Initial examination (IE): data collected on the first day of physical therapy.

Instructional assistants/paraprofessionals: individuals who assist in a student's education by providing additional assistance to the student and teachers.

Integrated RTI frameworks: model of outcomes-driven intervention that includes standardized testing to identify students with specific learning disabilities.

Interagency collaboration: coordination of services among school-based professionals and programs as well as community-based organizations and adult services.

Interagency councils: committees comprised of representatives of school and adult agencies that engage in identification of needs and program improvement at the local or state level.

Interpreters: individuals who mediate between speakers of different languages.

Interventions: methods used to instruct students in specific content or behavioral areas to improve their learning or behavior.

Itinerant: a professional or teacher who travels to a student's school to provide direct services.

Job analysis: a process of gathering information to gain knowledge of the job description, responsibilities, specifications, and tasks, which is used to match the job seeker's interests with the workforce needs of an employer.

Job coaching: the systematic training and support of employees that occurs on and off the worksite.

Kinesthetic: a teaching and learning style in which learning takes place by the student carrying out a physical activity, rather than listening to a lecture or watching a demonstration; also referred to as tactile learning.

Learned helplessness: a term referring to a condition where a person believes that no matter what the effort he or she puts forth, failure will result.

Learning disability (LD): a learning disorder resulting in significant problems using and understanding the processes of language such as listening, speaking, writing, and/or spelling.

Least restrictive environment (LRE): a requirement under IDEA that states that students with disabilities, to the maximum extent possible, must be educated within the general education classroom.

Locomotor skills: rolling, crawling, walking, running, jumping, sliding, galloping, and skipping.

Manipulative skills: kicking, catching, throwing, striking, and bouncing.

Mentoring: helping someone succeed; guiding and advising.

Mixed hearing loss: this type of hearing loss is basically a combination of sensorineural and conductive; sound cannot pass through due to a problem in both the outer/middle and inner ear.

Mobility: the facility, capacity, or capability of movement.

Mobility aides for orientation and mobility: methods or devices to aid in mobility that are specific to orientation and mobility training, including the human guide technique (also commonly known as the sighted guide technique), long cane, precane or adapted mobility device, electronic travel aids, and electronic orientation aids.

Modification: an actual change to the curriculum (e.g., the student will work in a lower level book instead of the one at grade level or the student will be given different questions on assessments and homework).

Motor skills: movement abilities that improve with practice and relate to one's ability to perform specific sports and other motor tasks such as walking, running, striking, and throwing.

Multidisciplinary: of or pertaining to several different disciplines of study.

Multidisciplinary teams: a group of professionals, related service specialists, and parents who convene to develop students' IEPs, monitor progress, and problem solve.

Muscular endurance: ability to maintain contraction of a muscle against resistance.

Muscular strength: ability to contract a muscle against resistance.

Natural supports: the assistance, relationships, and interactions that are typically present on a worksite; correspond to the typical work routines and social actions of other employees; and enhance the individual's work and nonwork social life among his or her coworkers and other members of the community.

No Child Left Behind: legislation from 2002 that encompasses numerous initiatives designed to ensure that all learners gain the maximum benefits from their experiences in school; requires states to have rigorous curriculum standards, to develop plans to assess learners' performance on tests related to these standards, and to intervene to help learners whose achievement falls below certain levels; holds schools accountable for the annual progress of all learners receiving a free and appropriate education.

Occupational therapist (OT): a health professional who helps individuals to do and engage in the specific activities that make up daily life.

Orientation: the capability to use one's remaining senses in order to understand location in an environment at every given moment in time.

Orientation and mobility: instruction of techniques, skills, and concepts necessary for people who are visually impaired to travel safely, efficiently, and gracefully in any environment as well as under any environmental situation or condition.

Orientation and mobility specialist: a professional who instructs a student who is visually impaired or blind in orientation (the process of using sensory information to establish and maintain one's position in the environment) and mobility (the process of moving safely, efficiently, and gracefully within one's environment).

Pervasive developmental disorder (PDD): a disorder that results in significant deficits in communication, behavior, and socialization that manifests in a child's early years (i.e., birth to age 3).

Physical activity: bodily movement that is produced by the contraction of skeletal muscle and that substantially increases energy expenditure.

Physical education: education through movement; an instructional program that gives attention to the psychomotor, cognitive, and affective learning domains.

Physical therapist (PT): a professional who provides service to individuals and populations to develop, maintain, and restore maximum functional ability throughout the lifespan.

Physical therapy assistant (PTA): a licensed PTA is part of the healthcare team that works under the supervision of a physical therapist; works with similar tools toward the same goals as a PT.

Play therapy: counseling conducted in a specially designed playroom that utilizes the natural play activities of children to resolve emotional or behavioral difficulties.

Positive behavior supports (PBS): an approach to school management that allows school personnel to define effective routines and procedures, maintain a positive school climate, and provide a safe and orderly learning environment.

Positive behavior intervention and support (PBIS): a systematic, prevention-focused framework for addressing social behavior in a positive manner in schools.

Positive reinforcement: presenting an item or event immediately after the occurrence of a behavior and observing a future increase in the rate of that behavior.

Postschool outcomes: outcomes achieved by young adults with disabilities after exiting secondary school, including employment, independent living, and postsecondary education and training.

Power: ability to rapidly contract and coordinate muscles to perform to maximum effort.

Program structure: practices related to human resource development, program evaluation, program philosophy, program policy, resource allocation, and strategic planning.

Progress monitoring: a scientifically based practice that is used to assess students' academic performance and evaluate the effectiveness of instruction; can be implemented with individual students or an entire class.

Progress note (PN): a review of the measurements taken on the initial examination day completed per the therapist's discretion or upon medical necessity; however, usually performed every 1–3 months of treatment.

Progress reports: updates on the progress of IEP goals and objectives; frequency of the reports is decided while developing the IEP, but are usually sent once a quarter.

Pull-out services: educational services, provided by an itinerant teacher or instructional assistant, to a student outside of the classroom to support IEP goals.

Push-in services: educational services provided by an itinerant teacher or instructional assistant to a student within the classroom to support instruction.

Reaction time: difference between the stimulation and the response to the stimulation.

Recommendations: suggestions that will best support student learning and progress.

Regular education initiative (REI): formally introduced in 1986 by former Assistant Secretary of Education, Madeleine C. Will, and advocated that the general education system become more responsible for the education of learners with disabilities within the general education environment.

Related services: developmental, corrective, and other supportive services as may be required to assist a child with a disability to benefit from special education (e.g., transportation, physical therapy, speech-language pathology, counseling services).

Response to Intervention (RTI): integrates assessment and intervention within a multilevel prevention system to maximize student achievement and to reduce behavior problems; schools identify students at risk for poor learning outcomes, monitor student progress, provide evidence-based interventions, and adjust the intensity and nature of those interventions depending on a student's responsiveness.

Responsive services: when the professional school counselor meets the immediate social and emotional needs of students.

RIOT: an acronym that stands for Record review, Interview, Observation, and Test—the four activities that are completed during an evaluation.

School culture: shared beliefs and priorities that drive the pattern of actions within the school community.

School guidance curriculum: a plan for the systematic delivery of guidance lessons to all students.

Screen reader: a software application that interprets what is displayed on the computer screen and re-presents it to the user with text-to-speech, sound icons, or a Braille output device.

Self-advocacy: the ability to support oneself by communicating one's strengths, needs, preferences, aspirations, and values.

Self-determination: when a person engages in goal-directed, self-regulated, autonomous behavior.

Self-esteem: confidence and satisfaction in oneself.

Sensorineural hearing loss: the most common type of permanent hearing loss, which occurs when there is a problem in either the inner ear or beyond; can be from mild to profound.

Severe disabilities: people with severe or multiple disabilities may exhibit a wide range of characteristics, depending on the combination and severity of disabilities, and the person's age; often includes the following traits: (a) limited speech or communication, (b) difficulty in basic physical mobility, (c) tendency to forget skills through disuse, (d) trouble generalizing skills from one situation to another and (e) a need for support in major life activities.

Skill-related fitness: includes agility, balance, coordination, power, reaction time, and speed.

Special education: specially designed instruction, at no cost to the parents, to meet the unique needs of students with disabilities.

Speech-language pathologist: a professional who treats speech, language, and swallowing disorders.

Speed: ability to move quickly in a short period of time.

Sport skills: include dribbling, shooting, rebounding, spiking, volleying, serving, trapping, pitching, tumbling, punting, diving, skiing, and batting.

Students at-risk: individuals who exhibit academic and/or behavioral concerns that could result in school failure.

Support services: types of indirect/direct ways to guide interventions and resources to support student progress.

Supported employment: a term used to describe a system of integrated employment support for people with disabilities; utilizes ongoing, person-centered practices that are specialized and evolve to meet the support needs of the individual as they change.

System support: when the counselor's activities support the school system such as consultation, leadership, and professional development.

Task analysis: a process of gathering information to gain knowledge of what an employee is required to do in terms of the step-by-step processes to achieve a task, including a detailed description of what needs to be done and how to do it; can be used for many purposes such as to design training and develop supports as needed.

Tiers of intervention: levels or stages that increase in intensity based on student need for support.

Transdisciplinary collaboration: a framework in which members of an educational team share roles and systematically cross discipline boundaries to contribute knowledge and skills, collaborate with other members, and collectively determine the services that would most benefit a child.

Transition plans: components of the IEP that relate to postschool life, including multiyear course of study, identification of postschool outcomes, identification of transition-related assessments and results of those assessments, multiyear transition activities and services that will facilitate the desired postschool outcomes, and related annual goals and objectives.

Transition services: coordinated set of activities designed to facilitate movement from school to postschool activities.

Transition specialist: an individual who plans, coordinates, delivers, and evaluates transition education and services at the school or system level.

Treatment integrity checklist: a form used to assess the degree to which specific components of an intervention/treatment plan are being implemented as intended.

Treatment integrity/fidelity: the extent to which an intervention or treatment is implemented as intended.

Unilateral hearing loss: a hearing loss of any type and degree in one ear and normal hearing in the other ear.

Visual impairment: a term that refers to individuals who are blind and individuals with low vision; even with correction the impairment adversely affects educational performance.

Voice recognition: allows the user to speak to the computer, instead of using a keyboard or mouse, to input data or control computer functions.

Word prediction programs: allow the user to select a desired word from an on-screen list located in the prediction window.

About the Editors

Cynthia G. Simpson, Ph.D., is an associate professor of special education at Sam Houston State University. She received her doctoral degree from Texas A&M University and did her undergraduate studies at Texas State University-San Marcos. Dr. Simpson has more than 17 years of experience in the public and private sector as a preschool teacher, special education teacher, elementary teacher, educational diagnostician, and administrator. She maintains an active role in the field of special education as an educational consultant in the areas of assessment, family advocacy, and inclusive practices. Her professional responsibilities include serving on the National Council for Accreditation of Teacher Education (NCATE)/National Association for the Education of Young Children (NAEYC) Review Panel, as well as holding the position of state advisor to the Texas Educational Diagnostician Association (TEDA). She also represents college teachers as the Vice President of Legislative Affairs for Texas Association of College Teachers. Dr. Simpson has many publications to her credit and is a featured speaker at the international, national, and state levels. She was the recipient of the 2008 Susan Phillips Gorin Award, the highest honor that can be bestowed on a professional member of the Council for Exceptional Children by its student membership, the 2007 Texas Trainer of the Year (awarded by the Texas Association for the Education of Young Children), the 2007 Katheryn Varner Award (awarded by the Texas Council for Exceptional Children), the 2009 Wilma Jo Bush Award (awarded by the Texas Educational Diagnostician Association), the 2010 Teacher Educator

Award (awarded by the Texas Council for Exceptional Children), and the Sam Houston State University College of Education Service Award. Dr. Simpson serves on multiple review boards and is an editor for *Early Years* and *The Dialog*. Through her work, she has committed herself toward improving the lives of children with exceptionalities and their families.

Jeffrey P. Bakken, Ph.D., is a professor and chair of the Department of Special Education at Illinois State University. He has a bachelor's degree in elementary education from the University of Wisconsin-LaCrosse, and graduate degrees in the area of special education-learning disabilities from Purdue University. Dr. Bakken is a teacher, consultant, and scholar. His specific areas of interest include transition, collaboration, teacher effectiveness, assessment, learning strategies, and technology. He has written more than 100 academic publications, including books, journal articles, chapters, monographs, reports, and proceedings; and he has made more than 200 presentations at the local, state, regional, national, and international levels. Dr. Bakken has received the College of Education and the University Research Initiative Award, the College of Education Outstanding College Researcher Award, the College of Education Outstanding College Teacher Award, and the Outstanding University Teacher Award from Illinois State University. Additionally, he is on the editorial boards of many scholarly publications, including *Multicultural Learning and Teaching*, *Remedial and Special Education*, and *Exceptional Children*. Through his work, he has committed himself toward improving teachers' knowledge and techniques as well as services for students with exceptionalities and their families.

About the Authors

Kelli S. Appel is currently the undergraduate program coordinator for the Department of Special Education at Illinois State University (ISU). Ms. Appel also serves as a faculty mentor to new students and organizes a service program for ISU students and adults with Down syndrome. Previously Ms. Appel taught courses and supervised field experiences for ISU; she was also a classroom teacher for high school students with cognitive disabilities. She holds a master's degree in special education.

Judah B. Axe, Ph.D., is an assistant professor of special education and behavior analysis at Simmons College and a Board Certified Behavior Analyst. His research on teaching language and social skills to children with autism has been recognized by the California Association for Behavior Analysis and the Berkshire Association for Behavior Analysis and Therapy (BABAT). Dr. Axe is an associate editor for the *Journal of Behavior Assessment and Intervention for Children* and on the board of editors of *Behavior Analysis in Practice* and *The Analysis of Verbal Behavior.* In addition, Dr. Axe serves on the boards of the Verbal Behavior Special Interest Group of the Association for Behavior Analysis International, the Cambridge Center for Behavioral Studies, and BABAT.

Rita L. Bailey, Ed. D., is a speech-language pathologist and Board Recognized Specialist in Swallowing and Swallowing Disorders. She is an associate professor in the Department of Communication Sciences and Disorders at Illinois State University. Dually certified in both speech-language pathology and special education administration, she also serves as a special education administrative consultant for a large special education cooperative. Her primary clinical and research interests include the management of feeding and swallowing problems in school-age children, working with families and school-based teams, implementation of augmentative/alternative communication options, and communication and swallowing issues associated with tracheotomy.

Mary Jo Garcia Biggs, Ph.D., is an associate professor and distance education coordinator at Texas State University-San Marcos, School of Social Work. She holds her doctoral degree from Texas A&M University and is a licensed clinical social worker. Her research interests include diverse and vulnerable populations, at-risk groups, distance education and technology, and gerontology.

Stacey Jones Bock, Ph.D., is an associate professor at Illinois State University and co-director of the Autism Spectrum Institute. She is the principal investigator of the Illinois Autism/PDD Training and Technical Assistance Project at Illinois State University, which provides technical assistance to schools and families. Her experiences as a paraprofessional, classroom teacher, and consultant have provided her with many opportunities to team with families and schools.

Nicole E. Boivin received her bachelor's degree in speech pathology from the University of Maine at Farmington and her master's degree in communication disorders from the University of New Hampshire. She holds the American Speech-Language-Hearing Association's Certificate of Clinical Competence and holds a Board Certified Behavior Analyst credential. Currently, she is a Ph.D. candidate in Applied Behavior Analysis at Simmons College in Boston, MA. Her professional experience includes working with individuals who have developmental disabilities, autism spectrum disorder, traumatic brain injury, and augmentative communication needs. Ms. Boivin is currently the senior program director for education with Spurwink Services.

Christy Borders, Ph.D., is an assistant professor at Illinois State University in the special education, deaf/hard of hearing program. She has taught deaf/hard of hearing students in a variety of education settings including public, private, and clinical environments. Dr. Borders' research interests include developing and implementing interventions for students who are deaf and hard of hearing with additional disabilities as well as those served in general education settings.

Shana Brownlee was a special education teacher for 13 years. During this time she collaborated with special and general educators as well as parents and support staff to meet the needs of children. She has her master's degree in education and is now an educational facilitator for the Illinois Autism/PDD Training and Technical Assistance Project at Illinois State University.

Laura Casey received her bachelor's degree in elementary education from the University of Maine at Orono and her master's degree in special education from Lesley University. She has worked as a teacher and administrator in the field of early intervention for more than 10 years. She is currently the program director for early childhood services at Woodfords Family Services of Portland, ME, a nonprofit agency offering a wide variety of family supports and educational services in Southern, Central, and Midcoast Maine.

Gary Cates, Ph.D., is associate professor of psychology at Illinois State University. He is part of the core faculty in school psychology and teaches and conducts research in the area of academic assessment and intervention. In addition, he consults and provides trainings in Response to Intervention and data-based decision making in schools.

Christine Clark-Bischke, Ph.D., is an assistant professor at Illinois State University in the Low Vision and Blindness Program. Her areas of expertise include visual impairments, early childhood special education, and working with families. She is a certified Teacher of Students with Visual Impairments and Developmental Therapist/Vision Specialist. Her research interests include families of children with disabilities, children with visual impairments (including children with multiple disabilities), and early intervention.

Edward M. Clouser, Jr., received a bachelor's degree in psychology from Southwestern University, followed by master's degrees in clinical psychology and special education from Sam Houston State University. He began to focus on autism and behavior analysis in 2001, and has since worked in clinic, home-based, and both public and private school settings. Additionally, he has developed several video-based products used by educators to teach specific skills to children with autism.

Carrie Anna Courtad, Ph.D., is an assistant professor in the Department of Special Education at Illinois State University. She received her Ph.D. from

Michigan State University, where she was a Special Education Technology Scholar. Dr. Courtad's research interests include topics revolving around assistive technology, reading, and preservice teachers' self-efficacy and knowledge of assistive technology. Previously, she taught in public school systems for more than 10 years.

Mary Volle Cranston is an instructional assistant professor of nursing at Mennonite College of Nursing at Illinois State University. She graduated from the University of Iowa and Northern Illinois University. Ms. Cranston would like to thank Laura Baue, RN, Cathy Troyer, RN, and Susan Schwingle, RN, all certified school nurses who assisted her in the completion of her chapter.

Lisa Devereux is a senior studying special education at Illinois State University. Currently, she is a resident assistant in a special education themed living and learning community at ISU. She looks forward to a teaching career at the secondary level.

Barbara M. Fulk, Ph.D., is a professor in the Department of Special Education at Illinois State University. She teaches courses related to methods for teaching diverse learners, consultation and collaboration, and assessment. Dr. Fulk has published on the topics of cognitive strategies for students with mild disabilities, motivation, and transition planning.

Shelley M. Garza received a bachelor's degree in psychology from Brigham Young University, became a Certified Therapeutic Recreation Specialist, and began working in early childhood education. She received a master's degree in special education from Sam Houston State University and currently works as a special education teacher of students with autism.

Jennifer Gibson has 22 years of experience as a general educator in grades 3–8. She has co-taught in inclusion classrooms and worked with a variety of students with special needs during this time. She recently received her master's degree in special education from Illinois State University.

Stacy M. Kelly, Ed.D., COMS, is a faculty member in the Low Vision and Blindness Program at Illinois State University. Prior to joining the faculty at Illinois State University, Dr. Kelly was a National Center for Leadership in Visual Impairment (NCLVI) Doctoral Fellow. Dr. Kelly has taught students who were blind or visually impaired as a teacher of the visually impaired. She is also a Certified Orientation and Mobility Specialist (COMS) and a certified school administrator. Dr. Kelly's areas of interest include blindness and low-vision-specific assistive technology, education of children with visual impairments, orientation and mobility, and quantitative research.

Carrie Kreissl is an advanced graduate student in the School Psychology Program at Illinois State University. Her research and professional interests lie in the area of academic intervention and Response to Intervention. In addition, she focuses on determining and implementing effective interventions for preschool children with autism.

Jacob V. Linnell is an advanced doctoral student in the school psychology program at Illinois State University. Part of his graduate-level training has focused on Response to Intervention and data-based decision making. His research interests currently focus on military families, specifically child functioning in the school setting.

Barbara Metzger, Ph.D., received her master's degree and doctoral degree in behavioral psychology from West Virginia University. She has worked as a consultant for applied behavior analysis programs for children with autism and as a program manager in the public schools. Currently she serves as the coordinator for the Low Incidence Disabilities and Autism Program at Sam Houston State University.

Nichelle Michalak is an educational facilitator and external coach for the Illinois Autism/PDD Training and Technical Assistance Project at Illinois State University. She has provided ongoing support to families and schools supporting children on the spectrum. Ms. Michalak also teaches online courses at the undergraduate and master's levels that focus on educating children and youth with autism spectrum disorders.

Sean A. Morales is currently a graduate student at Texas State University-San Marcos, School of Social Work. He holds a bachelor's degree in social work and plans to pursue his doctoral degree in social work.

Diana Nabors, Ed.D., is an associate professor at Sam Houston State University in the Department of Language, Literacy and Special Education. She currently teaches classes in the field of early childhood. Her research interests include family collaboration and early childhood curriculum.

Judith A. Nelson, Ph.D., is an assistant professor at Sam Houston State University in the Educational Leadership and Counseling Department.

Kathleen Marie Oertle, Ph.D., earned her doctoral degree in special education, master's degree in rehabilitation counseling, and bachelor's degree in animal science from the University of Illinois at Urbana-Champaign. Dr. Oertle also earned her A.A.S. in veterinary technology at Parkland College. She has previously worked as a job coach and developer, program evaluator and researcher, Perkins Grant project coordinator, certified rehabilitation counselor, and certified veterinary technician. Dr. Oertle's research interests include access, equity, and opportunity for underrepresented groups especially for people with disabilities. More specifically, her work focuses on improving transition outcomes, collaborating across systems, and promoting inclusion. Dr. Oertle currently works as a visiting research scientist in the Graduate College at the University of Illinois.

Annette R. Parnell, DPT, is a certified physical therapist who is currently practicing in the state of Illinois. She received her master's degree in physical therapy from Northern Illinois University in 2007 and her doctoral degree in physical therapy at Northeastern University 2010. Her primary independent clinical experience includes working in the orthopedic field at outpatient facilities.

Anthony J. Plotner, Ph.D., received his doctoral degree from the Department of Special Education at the University of Illinois. Dr. Plotner is currently an assistant professor in the Department of Educational Studies at the University of South Carolina and the Director of the CarolinaLife program. He has also worked as a research fellow on an OSEP grant (Secondary Curriculum Outcomes and Research). His primary research interests include the community inclusion of individuals with significant disabilities: specifically, transition to adulthood, postsecondary education opportunities, supported employment, and the collaboration across systems to promote positive student outcomes. He has provided staff development to high school vocational coordinators, state vocational rehabilitation professionals and their community partners in evidence-based practices regarding career development, person-centered planning, and transition planning.

Jessica A. Rueter, Ph.D., is an assistant professor at Sam Houston State University in the Department of Language, Literacy and Special Populations. She currently teaches graduate courses in the educational diagnosticians' program and undergraduate preservice teacher preparation courses. As a veteran educator, Dr. Rueter has more than 15 years of service working in public schools. She continues to be active in the assessment field by providing consultation and testing services for public schools and through private referrals.

Emily A. Roper, Ph.D., is an assistant professor at Sam Houston State University in the Department of Health and Kinesiology. She specializes in the psychosocial aspects of sport and physical activity.

José A. Santiago, Ed.D., is an assistant professor at Sam Houston State University in the Department of Health and Kinesiology. He specializes in curriculum and instruction in physical education.

Mary Kay Scharf, Ed.D., is currently the principal of Oakland Elementary School in Bloomington, IL. In her 29th year of service, she has experienced teaching within a state-operated institution, was principal of a segregated school for children with severe disabilities, initiated inclusion as Director of Special Services in an elementary district, and now works with others to create and maintain a culture of inclusion in her current school.

Cassandra M. Schmidt, Au.D., completed her doctorate degree in audiology in 2010 from Illinois State University where she also earned a bachelor's degree in deaf education. She has a strong clinical interest in the pediatric population with an emphasis on aural/oral rehabilitation. She also enjoys educating individuals on the damaging effects of loud noise exposure and promoting healthy listening habits in both the pediatric and adult populations.

Sheryl A. Serres, Ph.D., is an assistant professor at Sam Houston State University in the Educational Leadership and Counseling Department.

Debra L. Shelden, Ph.D., is an associate professor of special education at Illinois State University. She coordinates master's degree and advanced certificate programs, including advanced study in secondary transition services. She teaches courses related to secondary transition, curriculum development, life skills instruction, and research methods. Dr. Shelden's research interests include secondary transition services, family and school collaboration, and teacher preparation and professional development. Prior to working in higher education, she worked with individuals with intellectual disabilities in supported living and employment programs.

Tammy L. Stephens, Ph.D., is an assistant professor of special education at Texas Woman's University. Dr. Stephens has experience working as a public school special education teacher and an educational diagnostician.

John N. Trice, Ph.D., is an assistant professor at the University of Central Arkansas in the Department of Early Childhood and Special Education. He currently teaches graduate courses in assessment and emotional/behavioral disorders and undergraduate courses in cultural diversity and special education. Dr. Trice has more than 10 years of public school teaching experience, working directly with students with EBD, autism, learning disabilities, and other disorders.

Nicole M. Uphold, Ph.D., is an assistant professor of special education at Illinois State University. She teaches courses in secondary transition services and curriculum development. Dr. Uphold's research interests include student involvement in educational planning, self-determination, and secondary transition services. Prior to working in higher education, she worked as a vocational rehabilitation counselor in a high school and was a classroom teacher for students with intellectual disabilities.

Christine Woodbury is a doctoral candidate at Texas Woman's University. Christine has experience working as an educational diagnostician within public and private school settings.

CPSIA information can be obtained
at www.ICGtesting.com
Printed in the USA
LVHW101936240119
605132LV00012B/202/P